The Second Line of Defense

The Second Line of Defense

American Women and World War I

LYNN DUMENIL

THE UNIVERSITY OF NORTH CAROLINA PRESS

Chapel Hill

This book was published with the assistance of the Greensboro Women's Fund of the University of North Carolina Press.
Founding Contributors: Linda Arnold Carlisle, Sally Schindel Cone, Anne Faircloth, Bonnie McElveen Hunter, Linda Bullard Jennings, Janice J. Kerley (in honor of Margaret Supplee Smith), Nancy Rouzer May, and Betty Hughes Nichols.

Manufactured in the United States of America

Designed by Jamison Cockerham
Set in Arno by Tseng Information Systems, Inc.
Cover illustration: Red Cross worker, 1917. Harris and Ewing Collection, Library of Congress.

The University of North Carolina Press has been a member of the Green Press Initiative since 2003.

LIBRARY OF CONGRESS CATALOGING-IN-PUBLICATION DATA
Names: Dumenil, Lynn, 1950– author.
Title: The second line of defense : American women and World War I / Lynn Dumenil.
Other titles: American women and World War I
Description: Chapel Hill : The University of North Carolina Press, [2017] | Includes bibliographical references and index.
Identifiers: LCCN 2016027779| ISBN 9781469631219 (cloth : alk. paper) | ISBN 9781469631226 (ebook)
Subjects: LCSH: World War, 1914–1918—Women—United States. | World War, 1914–1918—Social aspects—United States. | Women—United States—Social conditions—20th century.
Classification: LCC D639.W7 D86 2017 | DDC 940.3082/0973—dc23
LC record available at https://lccn.loc.gov/2016027779

FOR

NORMAN

Contents

Figures

Acknowledgments

One of the many pleasures of the final stages of publishing a book is the opportunity to thank the people and institutions who have facilitated the process of turning ideas, reading, and research into a finished project. I am grateful for the funding provided by the Office of the Dean of the Faculty at Occidental College, the National Endowment for the Humanities, and the Haynes Foundation. The staff at the National Archives, College Park, the Library of Congress, the Huntington Library, the Schlesinger Library, the Sophia Smith Special Collections at Smith College, the Museum of Modern Art, the Margaret Herrick Library of the Academy of Motion Pictures Arts and Sciences, California State University, Northridge, Special Collections, the Seaver Center for Western History Research, and the University of Minnesota Libraries have been unfailingly helpful. A number of people helped in the sometimes daunting task of tracking down images. I appreciate the efforts of Joan Cohen, Rob Brooks, Sloan DeForest at the Mary Pickford Foundation, Alice Mott at the Victor Herbert Archives, John Powell at the Newberry Library, Lynsey Sczechowicz at the Hagley Museum, and Eric Stedman at Serial Squadron. I particularly want to thank librarians at Occidental College—Ryan Brubacher, Dale Stieber, Hoda Abdelghani, and John De La Fontaine—for their great patience and efficiency in helping me get the materials I needed.

Other individuals have made significant contributions. Sharon Park and John Ulrich offered timely and excellent research assistance. It has been a pleasure working with my editor at the University of North Carolina Press, Mark Simpson-Vos, whose insights improved the book significantly. I also appreciate the efficiency and skill of the staff at the press—Dorothea Anderson, Mary Carley Caviness, Lucas Church, Jessica Newman—who have managed the process of converting manuscript to book so beautifully. Jamison Cockerham provided an excellent design. Finally, I'm grateful to Jim O'Brien for his fine work in creating the index.

I am immensely appreciative of the insights provided by friends and colleagues. Ellen Carol DuBois, Nina R. Gelbart, Susan A. Glenn, Michael Kazin, Amy Lyford, Elaine Tyler May, Lary May, and Lisa Sousa read portions of the manuscript and offered keen assessments. Elinor Accampo found time in a busy schedule to read the entire book, and she gave me superb suggestions informed by her expertise in early twentieth-century French history. Elliott J. Gorn identified ideas that needed more development with surgical precision and offered encouragement at every step of the project. Daniel Horowitz read much of the manuscript more than once. Besides his uniformly excellent comments, he, as well as Helen Lefkowitz Horowitz, have been warmly supportive for the many—I won't admit just how many—years this book was in preparation. Two anonymous reviewers made valuable suggestions that substantially strengthened the book. My debt to all these generous readers is simply enormous.

I was also fortunate to have a large contingent of cheerleaders—friends and family—who listened to me talk about women and World War I patiently and enthusiastically. Special thanks to Michael Cohen, Emily Cohen Meth, Jason Meth, Margaret Dumenil Kelly, David and Lyssa Axeen, Gretchen Goette, Marcia Homiak, Deborah Smith, Sharla Fett, Karen McLeod, and Libby Sayre. And what to say about my husband and fellow historian, Norman S. Cohen? His insightful comments on multiple drafts were invaluable, but his generous spirit, political passion, infectious humor, and unfailing commitment are the reasons why the book is dedicated to him, as always, with love.

Abbreviations

AEF	American Expeditionary Force
AFFW	American Fund for French Wounded
AFL	American Federation of Labor
APL	American Protective League
ASPL	American School Peace League
AUAM	American Union Against Militarism
AWH	American Women's Hospitals
AWM	American War Mothers
BLA	Bureau of Legal Advice
CLB	Civil Liberties Bureau
CO	conscientious objector
CPI	Committee on Public Information
CTCA	Commission on Training Camp Activities
CU	Congressional Union
DAR	Daughters of the American Revolution
IWW	Industrial Workers of the World
NAACP	National Association for the Advancement of Colored People
NACGN	National Association of Colored Graduate Nurses

NACW	National Association of Colored Women
NAWSA	National American Woman Suffrage Association
NWLB	National War Labor Board
NWP	National Woman's Party
UNIA	Universal Negro Improvement Association
WAAC	Women's Auxiliary Army Corps
WAAL	Woman's Auxiliary of the American Legion
WCCS	War Camp Community Service
WCND	Woman's Committee of the Council of National Defense
WCTU	Woman's Christian Temperance Union
WILPF	Women's International League for Peace and Freedom
WLA	Woman's Land Army
WOH	Women's Overseas Hospitals
WOSL	Women's Overseas Service League
WP	Woman's Party
WPP	Woman's Peace Party
WSNL	Woman's Section of the Navy League
WSS	Women's Service Section of the U.S. Railway Administration
WTUL	Women's Trade Union League
YMCA	Young Men's Christian Association
YWCA	Young Women's Christian Association

The Second Line of Defense

Introduction

> What a good time the women are having in the war! And, in a way, they really are. For into that somewhat drab thing called every-day life has come the call of duty that makes every one, man, woman, and child, who has red blood, get up and do whatever duty bids.
>
> *Cleveland Plain Dealer*, October 28, 1917

In a 1918 address on the Young Women's Christian Association's Industrial Program for working women, YWCA staffer Henrietta Roelofs recounted the story of a young women receiving a poem, "To the Girl I Have Left at Home Behind Me," from a soldier that described her as "sitting patiently, suffering, sorrowing, waiting for the time when he should win the war and come home to her." But in reality, Roelofs noted, the woman was "probably working in a munitions factory and the queer part of the thing is that the boy knew it but so little had the real military value of her work entered into his mind that he still was holding in his imagination the same idea which men held a hundred years ago." Roelofs, invoking both defense industry workers and the 30,000 U.S. women who served in various capacities near the fighting front in Europe, asked, "Can we not get into our minds the actual status of women from a military point of view—not only from a humanitarian point of view but the actual value of women in winning the war."[1]

In her comment, Roelofs fused women's paid defense-industry labor with patriotism and independence, qualities that legitimated their claim to full citizenship. During World War I, observers routinely described women workers, especially those who were breaking down barriers that had limited their work opportunities, as the "second line of defense," whose service in the nation's interest paralleled that of male soldiers. Black and white working-class women were vital to war mobilization. The same was true across the class and racial divide: elite and middle-class women through their existing organizations, like the Young Women's Christian Association (YWCA) and the wartime government-sponsored Women's Committee of the Council of National Defense (WCND), ardently engaged in what was generally termed "war work." Mostly as volunteers, they raised funds for the American Red Cross and Liberty Loan defense funds, conducted registration drives to identify women willing to participate in war mobilization, conserved food, promoted a "children's year" to conserve the health of the nation's future citizens, organized recreational "hostess houses" on military bases, and knitted socks for soldiers. While traditional notions of women's role in the home and family frequently surfaced in the wartime rhetoric and images of these women, these volunteers generally presented themselves as competent individuals who contributed significantly to the winning of the war. They insisted that they had thus earned equal citizenship, a claim that became an important part of the final drive for woman suffrage and the ratification of the Nineteenth Amendment in 1920. Above all, they rejected the notion of the passive woman dependent upon the male soldier to save her, insisting instead upon women's agency in their own lives and in the face of war.[2]

This book explores women's wartime experiences in the context of politics and protest, home-front mobilization, service abroad, blue-collar and white-collar work, and popular culture representations. It frames them in the broader context of the social, cultural, and political history of the era. Challenging the notion that war brought transformative changes, I nonetheless emphasize the way in which diverse women used the war for their own agendas of expanding their opportunities, sometimes economic ones, sometimes political, sometimes personal. Examples abound and capture the voices of such women as Josephine Lehman, the small-town Michigan woman who passed her civil service exam and journeyed alone to take up a clerical war job in Washington, D.C.; Pearl Jones, an African American woman thrilled to find work as a manual railroad laborer, much preferring it to the poorly paid and demeaning work of a servant; pacifist Fanny Witherspoon, who before the United States entered the war joined with other antiwar women to challenge conventional diplomacy and during the war cofounded a civil rights agency to protect the rights of conscientious objectors; Nannie Burroughs, an African American activist who mounted a petition campaign to call for racial justice after a brutal race riot in East St. Louis, Illinois; Mrs. Shelley Tolhurst, a Los Angeles woman active in that city's Woman's Committee for National Defense, who felt that the committee's war contributions allowed women for the first time to be legitimated as "citizens in the government"; Marian Baldwin, employed by the Young Men's Christian Association as a canteen worker serving refreshments and building morale for the troops near the front in France, who loved the excitement and sense of service that her work gave her so much that she doubted she would ever be so happy again; Rose Winslow, a member of the National Woman's Party and among those suffragists arrested for picketing the White House to demand for women the democracy the nation was presumably fighting for abroad.

In the face of the brutality of World War I, the optimism expressed by American women who engaged in war work—either paid or voluntary—seems surprising. In part it can be explained by the exciting sense of purpose activist women enjoyed as they contributed to war mobilization. Equally important, most Americans experienced World War I as a terrible but remote event thousands of miles and an ocean away. Begun in August 1914, the war pitted the Triple Entente (or the Allies) of Great Britain, France, and Russia, plus Italy, which joined the Allies in 1915, against the Central Powers of the German and Austro-Hungarian Empires. Brutal trench warfare dragged on for four years and cost over 8.5 million combatant lives on both sides. Almost as many civilians died. Devastating much of the continent, the war profoundly disrupted the European political, physical, and economic landscape. When the United States abandoned its neutral position and joined the war on the side of the Allies in April 1917, American women ardently hoped for an American victory. But the chaos and pain of war barely touched the United States. Distance allowed Americans to view the promise of war more positively than their European counterparts. Of the more than 4 million American men mobilized, only 116,516 soldiers died (or less than 3 percent). By contrast, almost 16 percent of British soldiers died. Americans were required to conserve food, but there was no food rationing, and little personal sacrifice was demanded except for those who served in the military and their families. For many, if not most, the conflict that raged abroad was an abstraction.

Perhaps the greatest disruption on the home front stemmed from the pervasive hypernationalist patriotism that caused the suppression of dissent, especially among immigrants and radicals, including many women. Some prewar women pacifists changed their position once the United States entered the war and willingly engaged in volunteer war work that they hoped would lead to U.S. victory and, by extension, a more democratic world. Others remained aloof from the enthusiasm for serving as the "second line of defense" and hardly saw the war as an opportunity for progress of any sort. But the demand for conformity meant their voices were rarely heard. African American civil rights activists similarly needed to be discreet. And while many black women hoped that war service would earn them respect and further the struggle for civil rights, by war's end the persistence of racial violence and segregation in the military and at home led to much disillusionment, even as it fostered a new militancy in the 1920s. Despite these exceptions, the dominant tone was one of optimism, an optimism fueled in part because women viewed the war as a vehicle for agendas that often related only indirectly to the war itself.[3]

The obvious question, then, is, did the experience of women in the Great War meet their expectations? More broadly, what was war's impact on American women's lives? It undoubtedly accelerated the success of the suffrage movement and intensified the Great Migration of African Americans, two long-lasting developments that shaped American history and American women's lives. The war years marked significant developments, as many women challenged barriers to their political and economic independence and to their personal freedom. The perception of a liberated woman who ignored Victorian strictures about proper behavior during the war was ubiquitous. The media routinely offered striking evidence of women crossing barriers—photographs of uniformed telephone operators at switchboards near the front, of enormous parades featuring uniformed Red Cross nurses and volunteers, of munitions workers in overalls, and of movie heroines facing danger and outwitting spies. These images help to explain why Americans thought the war was so transformative for women. Some writers bemoaned the trend, but others could hardly contain their enthusiasm. As Anne Emerson reported in a 1918 *Forum* article, "Today SHE is everywhere; a Salvation lassie, serving coffee and doughnuts on the firing line; in the Red Cross Emergency Hospital at the front; in the munitions factory at home; filling the gaps in man-made industry everywhere. . . . She is omnipresent."[4]

But despite these perceptions of dramatic transformation, few of the changes women experienced during the war—the breakdown in sex-segregated labor patterns, most notably—were permanent. Undoubtedly, many of those deeply engaged in the war effort found their own lives significantly affected by their newfound opportunities, but structural or ideological changes that affected women's status as a whole were less dramatic. In particular, conventional assumptions about women, especially those that featured women's role in the home, coexisted uneasily with more modern expressions. Male employers and employees mightily resisted the incursion of women into jobs thought to be the exclusive purview of men. Women reformers, even as they sought to promote women's economic opportunities in wartime, persisted in calling for protective labor legislation for workers whom they routinely called the future "mothers of the race." Government propaganda posters for the most part emphasized women's nurturing roles in supporting the war effort. Although many war films featured brave women, the most pervasive motif was one that pictured women as vulnerable to rape and assault by vicious enemies. They were objects for male protection, not agents themselves.

Despite contemporary observers' sense of the war being transformative for women, these attitudes meant that the war did not produce profound change in gender relations or women's status. As many scholars have argued, this was true not only for the United States but also for other combatant nations.[5] More accurately, the war accelerated developments already under way and heightened awareness of an emerging "new woman." What made these changes possible was the intersection of strong women's rights and feminist movements of the era with the demands of the war mobilization process. Thus, in assessing the war's impact on this new woman, this book follows two lines of analysis. On the one hand, it explores the exciting opportunities the war offered women to take on new and more modern roles and responsibilities. On the other, it asks why these dramatic possibilities were so imperfectly realized. In so doing, it offers a lens for exploring both the contours of change and its limits in early twentieth-century America and more broadly suggests why the struggle for equal rights has been such a long one.

Not only did the media attention to the war's "new woman" exaggerate the extent of change; it also obscured the diversity of women's experiences. Poor immigrant women were largely ignored, except as the object of Americanization drives and fund-raising efforts. While young college women who joined a "land army" to help harvest crops were widely touted, black and immigrant women, who constituted the majority of female farm labor, were largely invisible. *The Second Line of Defense: American Women and World War I* pays particular attention to African American women and especially the impact of the Great Migration from the rural South to the urban North and Midwest, which created new work opportunities in factories. In addition, black middle-class women seized upon the war to challenge formidable racial barriers. Active in a variety of voluntary associations that allowed them to demonstrate support for the war and their good citizenship, these women also protested discrimination and racial violence. For them, the war meant possibilities not just for new womanhood, but for the "new negro," the term used at the time to describe rising militancy and increased racial pride in the war years and their aftermath. Ignored by mainstream media, they were nonetheless broadening the definition of "new" womanhood.

Even as it constructs a more inclusive definition of the new woman, *The Second Line of Defense* challenges the very concept of "newness." Contemporaries during the late teens and 1920s widely believed that the war created the "new woman" of the 1920s, one who embraced expanded public and economic roles as well as enhanced personal and sexual freedom. Americans in the 1920s frequently invoked the phrase "since the war" to explain the dramatic changes in all aspects of life they witnessed. Their notion, however, flies in the face of what historians know: many of the changes so evident in the 1920s had been in the works for decades. The new woman was hardly new. In 1913, a popular journal announced that the nation had struck "sex o'clock," reflecting on the sense of changed sexual mores among young women. By 1910, there was a significant upswing in women's participation in the labor force and especially the expansion of white-collar work. Moreover, the progressive reform era heightened the civic involvement of many women, and, most important, the suffrage movement heated up in the prewar years. By 1914, eleven states had granted women the vote. And beyond suffrage, the feminist movement emerged in the prewar years and challenged conventional expectations about women's economic and familial roles. Thus the war continued and intensified, but did not create, the debate over changes in women's roles that characterized the early twentieth century.

Indeed, we can understand World War I's impact only by appreciating what came before. One way to provide historical context and bring the prewar new woman into focus is to consider striking garment workers in the early teens. In one of the most dramatic stories in twentieth-century American history, the so-called uprising of the women, between 20,000 and 30,000 hard-pressed garment workers, mostly Italian and Jewish women, struck in New York City in a wave of strikes beginning in 1909. They took to the streets and mounted picket lines, a shocking violation of norms of respectability, which newspapers exploited and illustrated. While the women sought to publicize their impossibly low wages and harsh working conditions, some commentators were skeptical, noting that the newspaper images revealed the strikers to be nicely dressed with elaborate hats. Critics of the strikers saw women dressed above their station, behaving in unladylike ways on the public streets, but the strikers saw themselves as attractive, modern young women, willing to fight for their rights and a decent standard of living.

These working women, whose labor contributed significantly to the world of fashion, wanted to participate in the growing consumer culture. Although factory work could be harsh and exploitative, they found sociability with their female peers in the workplace. And for male companionship, many turned to new urban pleasures found in dance halls and amusement parks. Such leisure sites stood in sharp contrast to the discipline of the factory and the restraint of their crowded homes and restructured courtship patterns and sexual behavior.[6] Movies, too, especially dramatic serials such as *The Perils of Pauline* (1914), featuring female heroines that were specifically marketed to working-class women, created new and exciting leisure opportunities that took women into public spaces that again challenged notions of respectability. As these young immigrant women peopled the city, so too did other women workers. Telephone operators and department stores saleswomen became a significant part of the workforce, as did clerical workers, who invaded what was then the masculine space of the office. Streaming into the streets, eating in cafés and cheap restaurants, riding streetcars and buses, strolling in shopping areas, these young women, like the strikers, seemed to epitomize growing female independence.

While young working women were changing the geography of the city in the years before World War I, contemporaries, especially women reformers, were aware of the hardships that most working women and their families faced. Wages, even for clerical workers, were so low that relatively few women could support themselves, and most lived with their families and contributed to the "family wage" that was necessary for working-class survival. Particularly in the case of factory workers, reformers feared that in the context of the freedom of urban amusements, poor wages led not just to employer exploitation but to prostitution as well.

Concerns about the urban poor, who presented such a challenge to the cherished notions of American opportunity and democracy, contributed to the progressive reform movement of the early twentieth century. The progressives included many elite and middle-class white women, who themselves exemplified aspects of the new womanhood as they entered the political arena in what they often called "social housekeeping," reforms that linked the concerns of the home to public policy. White women supported social justice reforms through a far-flung network of clubs and associations. Settlement houses, like Jane Addams's Hull House, became progressive agencies for lobbying state and municipal governments for factory and slum housing regulations, pure milk supplies, and public health nursing. Legislation to control the hours and wages of women workers and to eliminate child labor was at the heart of what historians often call "maternalist reforms," a fluid concept that is used here to refer to the idea that women's nurturing roles in the home could be brought into the public arena to implement social reforms, especially those concerning poor women and children.[7]

These progressive reformers were often wealthy women who could volunteer their labor in behalf of social justice. But increasingly in the early twentieth century, there appeared a new cohort of educated middle-class women. They were employed as lawyers, like Madeleine Z. Doty, who became an expert on juvenile and women prisons; as factory inspectors, like Florence Kelley, a Hull House resident who went on to press for protective labor legislation for women and children; or as mainstays for charitable foundations, like Mary van Kleeck, who worked for the Russell Sage Foundation investigating industrial conditions. Exemplars of the educated new woman, determined to participate in public policy yet excluded from male-dominated political parties and patronage, these women formed a political culture separate from men that offered them opportunities for influence and leadership.[8]

This network of reformers consisted almost exclusively of white women, and the focus of progressive social justice reforms largely ignored African Americans, who still lived overwhelmingly in the South, where progressivism was weak. But African American women nonetheless engaged in their own reform efforts. Black women avidly supported reforms in their communities, working especially through the National Association of Colored Women (NACW), founded in 1895, which flourished in the early teens. They created kindergartens and mothers' clubs, old-age homes and neighborhood clinics, job training programs and black branches of the segregated YWCA. African American women were also active in a burgeoning civil rights movement embodied in the 1909 founding of the National Association for the Advancement of Colored People (NAACP). Through both the NAACP and the NACW, black women emerged as local community leaders. Women like Ida B. Wells-Barnett, Nannie Burroughs, Addie Hunton, and Mary Church Terrell had national recognition as well. Their "new womanhood" was measured through their outspoken commitment to racial uplift and racial justice.

Perhaps nothing epitomized the pre–World War I new woman more than the seemingly omnipresent suffragist, who insisted upon women's equal political rights and increasingly took her argument to lecture rostrums, soapbox platforms, and city streets. The suffrage movement, which had had some success in the 1890s and then weakened, flourished in the early twentieth century. Although black women ardently supported suffrage, they did so in their own organizations, having been largely excluded from the ranks of white suffragists in the National American Woman Suffrage Association (NAWSA). Despite its success, NAWSA was rife with tension as its major leaders, Carrie Chapman Catt and Anna Howard Shaw, grappled with challenges posed by young militants such as Alice Paul and Lucy Burns, who had been given charge of NAWSA's long inactive Congressional Union (CU) in 1913. Burns and Paul almost immediately began to agitate for a national amendment instead of pursuing the state-by-state approach favored by NAWSA.[9]

But far more than the stance in regard to a national amendment separated what would by 1916 become the two wings of the white women's movement. Burns and Paul had been active in the British suffrage campaign, which involved them in radical and unconventional tactics of public protest and street theater. This paralleled efforts in the United States on the West Coast and in New York to draw upon both the British example and patterns of working-class women's protest, especially the use of public space for parades and street-corner speaking and other attention-getting tactics. One particularly effective publicity gambit was a massive suffrage parade in Washington, D.C., organized to coincide with Woodrow Wilson's 1913 inauguration. At least 5,000 suffragists marched in an impressive visual spectacle before an estimated crowd of 250,000. But, despite the presence of mounted policemen, the hecklers in the crowd stormed the marchers in what was described as a "near-riot." Ironically, the parade's greatest contribution to the suffrage cause may have been the disruption. Newspapers all over the country condemned the rowdy crowds as well as the police for failing to protect the marchers. The debacle led to a congressional hearing, which the suffragists skillfully exploited to generate favorable publicity.[10] The tactical use of suffrage parades more broadly signaled the way in which militant women like Paul and Burns were challenging notions about respectable behavior. Their transgressions in occupying public space for their campaign, like that of immigrant women's seeking urban amusements, embodied the modern new woman, one that would reverberate during the war years.[11]

The fascination with the "new woman" before the Great War was further fueled by the emergence of the small but compelling "feminist" movement. The term itself appeared in the early twentieth century and, although rarely precisely defined, conveyed a commitment to challenging the strictures that limited women's pursuit of individual self-realization. Beyond the political rights sought by the suffrage movement, feminists demanded economic independence and more modern sexual relationships and marriage. Women across the United States were attracted to urban areas, where they found jobs as lawyers, journalists, and social workers and experimented with heterosexual and lesbian relationships. New York's Greenwich Village was undoubtedly the center of American feminism. Here, in 1912, twenty-five feminists organized Heterodoxy, a club so named because it "demanded of a member that she should not be orthodox in her opinions," and staged in 1914 "the First Feminist Mass Meeting."

Heterodoxy and the broader feminist circle included liberal reformers, suffragists, trade union organizers, and socialists. Feminists tended to be young college-educated women who worked for a living and who delighted in their sense of freedom from the restriction of convention and the patriarchy of the family. As one Heterodoxy woman described them, they were "fine, daring, rather joyous and independent women . . . women who did things and did them openly."[12] Feminists supported suffrage, certainly, but they also embraced the cause of birth control, joining in a campaign to challenge New York State's suppression of birth control pioneer Margaret Sanger's contraception clinic and publications. The emphasis on birth control was part of a broader eclectic free speech movement of the era that featured protests against the suppression of radical unions like the Industrial Workers of the World and against censorship of art and literature. The birth control movement had particular meaning for feminists—it was the key to women's ability to achieve economic independence without sacrificing sexuality. Although feminists embraced a wide range of issues, this theme of sexuality, coupled with economic self-determination, certainly made them "modern" and captured the radical potential of "new women" seeking to break down barriers.

In her various incarnations, the new woman of the teens evoked enthusiasm and anxiety, fascination and fear. She set the context for understanding what was novel—and what was not—about American women's experiences during World War I and helps us to view the war not so much as the root cause of transformation, but as an accelerator for changes already under way. *The Second Line of Defense* traces war's impact on pacifists, left-wing radicals, civil rights activists, and suffragists, as it examines their demand for an increased voice in politics and policy. It explores developments in the workforce, especially for professional women and clerical workers. It charts the continuation of maternal reform activism as well as the agency of reformers themselves. It grapples with a somewhat elusive aspect of the "new women"—the way in which they were carving out more personal freedoms as they broke with conventions about women's proper behavior. This was embodied in YWCA workers who served near the front in France and reporters who covered the war and the Russian Revolution. It appeared graphically in ubiquitous images of defense workers and Red Cross volunteers, clad in overalls or uniforms, as well as in films in which modern women starred, like actress Mary Pickford's character in *The Little American* chastising a Germany submarine captain and saving herself and her fiancé from enemy bombs. In exploring these changes in the context of war, the book charts the development of a new modern woman, whose presence the war magnified in dramatic ways while keeping in focus the limits to this presumed liberation.

The Second Line of Defense brings the war front and center to examine early twentieth-century women's history, but it also explores the nature of war mobilization. Although military and traditional political history still dominates the historiography of war, scholars increasingly have incorporated gender into their analysis of war and warfare. This book fits squarely into this trajectory by examining not just war's impact on women, but also women's impact on war. A gendered approach to war, as opposed to that of military or (most) political historians' framework, allows for a more complex rendering of the ways in which the nation mobilized for war and also allows us to see clearly the continuities in war's wake, as well as the changes. If military historians ask "Why do soldiers fight?" I ask why (and how) do civilians and more specifically women citizens support a war? At the heart of unpacking the issue of gender and war is the notion that military service, traditionally limited to men, defines citizenship. And, moreover, the prevailing assumption in World War I America was that men willingly took up arms to defend their dependent wives and children. Throughout the book, I explore these ideas and analyze the ways in which women activists in contrast staked their claim to loyal citizenship by framing women's war work as "the second line of defense."

This raises a broader issue: in what ways was World War I a modern war? This modernity can be defined in many ways, but one compelling aspect of the "Great War" was the role of civilians in its prosecution. More so than in previous wars, civilians in Europe, but not in the United States, faced danger: aerial bombardments, forced labor and migration, and serious food shortages. But civilians, including women, also worked for the war effort in their various countries. Indeed, it was in this conflict that the term "home front" came into use. While combatant nations privileged the role of the men as soldiers on the battlefront, women on the home front nonetheless contributed significantly to their countries' war aims. They worked in munitions factories and served as nurses and other aids to the military machine. To be sure, women had been camp followers, cooks, and nurses in previous wars, but now their efforts were formalized and tied to the bureaucratic organization of the modern state. In varying degrees, national leaders also turned to voluntary associations, especially those of middle-class and elite women, to disseminate propaganda, raise funds, and conserve food and matériel. This was especially true in the United States, where women's voluntary war work reveals the complex interplay between the federal government and voluntary associations in war mobilization. Thus the ways in which American women supported the war effort were part of the very definition of how a global, modern war must be fought.[13]

The iconic Rosie the Riveter image that symbolized women's defense labor in World War II remains vivid in contemporary memory in ways that highlight the civilian role in mobilization. World War I historians, but rarely the general public, can also summon up powerful images from propaganda posters featuring housewives conserving food or from compelling photographs of women war workers dressed in overalls and posed with railway engines or heavy machinery. Perhaps more so than in the Second Great War, during World War I the American public was constantly exposed to the role of women in "the second line of defense." A vibrant woman suffrage movement as well as a national network of women reformers and clubwomen persistently kept women's contribution to war before the public eye and helped to create a popular — and exaggerated — perception that the war would usher in significant changes in women's economic and political opportunities.

A wide variety of women contributed to the national effort in World War I: from munitions workers in New Jersey to elite clubwomen in Los Angeles, from African American civil rights activists to "Hello Girl" telephone operators in France, from movie star Mary Pickford to suffrage leader Alice Paul, from Japanese American Red Cross workers to jailed radical pacifists. This underscores the diversity of American women. Class and racial differences were powerful markers. So too were ideological differences. Maternalist reformers' protective stance toward working-class women emphasized women's difference, for example, while feminists articulated a fundamental equality between men and women. The debate over what was popularly called the "woman question" was thus many sided, and the tension about women and among women pervaded the teens and persisted through the war years. World War I fueled a cauldron of anxieties about the nation's ethnic population. Potential disloyalty about "hyphenated" Americans brought long-standing tensions over the definition of American identity to a boil. The same could be said about the woman question. As working women, political activists, and volunteer war workers poured into public spaces and staked a claim for full citizenship, they threw into sharp relief the excitement, as well as the tensions, surrounding the modern "new woman" as she emerged in the early twentieth century.

ONE

Women, Politics, and Protest

> It is impossible to think that [women] should be asked to wage war for the principle of self-government and to protect it and make great sacrifices, most supreme sacrifices, without having some part in the Government.
>
> *Elizabeth Selden Rogers of the National Woman's Party testifying before Congress, 1917*

In July 1917, four months after the United States entered World War I, African American women participated in the historic silent march of 10,000 men and women in New York City to protest the "East St. Louis Massacre," a particularly vicious white assault in black neighborhoods that left at least forty African Americans dead. The notion of using public space to demand justice and claim citizenship has a long history but became particularly important in the early twentieth century as American suffragists, beginning in 1910, staged a series of stunning parades to publicize their cause. Taking to the streets, even in an orderly fashion, was a challenge to notions of respectability, as these events drew enormous crowds eager to see a mass violation of ladylike norms. For their parade, black women chose to march in groups distinct from men, a decision that speaks in part to their political consciousness that organized black womanhood had a role to play in the fledgling civil rights movement of the war era. Although concerns about appearing unpatriotic limited African American women's militancy during the war, they did view the war as an opportunity to demonstrate their claim to citizenship and to protest discrimination and violence.

This chapter on politics and protest examines the intersection of war and women's political activism by looking at four groups that challenged conventional notions of women's proper behavior and place to protest about a range of social justice issues. Three of the groups were composed almost exclusively of white women: the antiwar women who dominated the American peace movement between 1914 and 1917; radicals associated with the Socialist Party and the Industrial Workers of the World (IWW); and the suffrage organizations, the National American Woman Suffrage Association (NAWSA) and the Congressional Union (CU), which later folded into the National Woman's Party (NWP). While African American women leaders were adamant supporters of suffrage, in contrast to white women they rarely conjoined their war activities to the suffrage campaign. Instead, African American women, the fourth group considered here, consistently linked black civil rights to the "war to preserve democracy" abroad.

Significant differences distinguished these women, and indeed the war exacerbated divisions among women activists. Some cast their protest in highly gendered terms. Many pacifists, deeply rooted in maternalist reforms of the Progressive Era, legitimated their claim to speak out against war on the grounds that women, as nurturers/protectors of children, had specifically female reasons to abhor war. Left-wing radical women, most of whom were also feminists and pacifists, rarely discussed the war in gendered terms but instead invoked class oppression and imperialist designs. Although African American women consciously spoke as women, they generally privileged racial concerns over those of gender. White suffrage women warred over appropriate tactics for securing a national amendment for enfranchisement, a dissension that to some also reflected different ideas about women's claim to citizenship, with the NWP stressing themes of equality while NAWSA took a broader path of staking the right to vote on both equality and self-sacrificing service to the nation. The groups also differed in the viability of their protests. Only suffragists could claim true success. The war—and their tactical use of it—undoubtedly hastened the passage of the Nineteenth Amendment.

Despite these differences, women did share their commitment to shaping politics in this era. And most did so through voluntary associations in which they drew upon female networks and shared commitments to social reform. The war climate made their efforts particularly challenging, as notions of men's superior citizenship are generally reinforced by their exclusive obligation to bear arms in defense of their country. Yet American women implicitly or explicitly recognized that modern "total" warfare meant that civilians, too, defended their country. As suffragist Anna Howard Shaw wrote in the *Ladies' Home Journal*, "Preparedness for war is not limited to the mere equipment of soldiers in the field, but concerns the whole of the nation at war."[1]

The war did not create these women's commitment to activism, but because it focused attention on questions of citizenship, patriotic service, and democratic rights, it did offer them a particularly auspicious time to make a claim for an enlarged sense of citizenship. Despite being largely disenfranchised when the European war began in 1914, the women in these four groups all insisted upon their own agency—a political voice—and demanded a more inclusive democracy. In doing so, they physically—through parades and public protests—and metaphorically transcended barriers that served to contain women's power and limit their citizenship. If they did not fully overcome these barriers, they nonetheless powerfully represented the new woman's emergence on the national scene in the early twentieth century.

WOMEN PACIFISTS/WOMEN PREPAREDNESS ACTIVISTS

When war broke out in August 1914, most Americans assumed that the European conflict was no real concern of theirs. Some leaders, however, with an eye to issues of international power and influence, began to call for the United States to embark on a program of military preparedness. At the other end of the spectrum, antiwar internationalists mobilized a campaign to end the war. The male-dominated prewar pacifist movement had focused on promoting institutional structures to defuse European militarism and to spread American-style democratic institutions. But when the Great War began, U.S. antiwar activists created a new movement, one that was heavily influenced, even dominated, by women and closely aligned with the Progressive reform movement. Although American women participated in a number of peace organizations, the most significant were the Woman's Peace Party, founded in 1915, and the mixed-sex American Union against Militarism (1916).[2] A handful of African American women participated, including Mary Church Terrell and Addie Hunton, but the pacifist movement was predominantly white. Both institutions attracted a wide range of social workers, feminists, socialists, and suffragists and built upon female networks of friendship and organizational ties.[3] They not only opposed the war but hoped by bringing women's values to the international arena to change the nature of diplomacy itself.

To justify entering what was a male world of diplomacy, antiwar women varied in their explanation as to why war should be a woman's issue, but the most common line of analysis stemmed from maternalist ideology. Women as mothers had a special interest in working for peace and assuring that their sons would not be sacrificed pointlessly on the battlefield. Less specifically, they argued that women and children were invariably the most damaged by war and thus that women were particularly invested in working for peace. As NAWSA leader Carrie Chapman Catt expressed it, "When war murders the husbands and sons of women, destroys their homes, desolates their country and makes them refugees and paupers, it becomes the undeniable business of women."[4]

Most pacifist women were also suffragists, and their arguments about women's right to vote pervaded peace rhetoric. They countered the claim that male physical strength and the ability to participate in battle to defend the state was the basis for claiming men's exclusive right to vote with the contention that modern life and industrialization had diminished the role of physical force. Jane Addams explained that "the entire structure of the modern world is built upon a groundwork of industry, and the problems that concern it are in the main those of industrial well-being, and of national, state and city housekeeping."[5] Thus both women *and* men served the modern state and economy. Pacifist suffragists also emphasized that women were inherently nonmilitaristic and that their disenfranchisement had promoted war by denying them a role in influencing public opinion and policy. Universal, international, woman's suffrage, they argued, would bring a more peaceful world order.

Not all women peace activists, however, built upon such explicitly gendered interpretations of their actions. Younger, more militant women tended to eschew maternalist ideas while still emphasizing the devastation war brought to the pursuit of social justice. Socialist women leaders stood out for their rejection of more traditional notions of female nature. Historian Kathleen Kennedy has demonstrated that male socialists seeking to attract women to their antiwar stance traded on the idea of mothers of sons' natural affinity to the peace movement. In contrast, most women leaders on the left instead focused on the war as a form of capitalist oppression. In its diversity, the peace movement reflected the ferment of women reformers, feminists, radicals, and suffragists of the era. While peace activism initially attracted a wide range of women, from genteel club ladies to socialist firebrands, it ultimately proved an unstable alliance. But in the tense moments leading up to the American entrance into World War I, their voices were significant in resisting the momentum toward war and in articulating a democratic vision of the international order.[6]

The first effort to rally American women to the cause of peace was New York City's August 29, 1914, Peace Parade. Taking a page from the suffragists' notebook, 1,500 women marched down Fifth Avenue to express their profound opposition to war. Wearing all black or white with black armbands, they were silent, with the dramatic exception of muffled drumbeats. No permanent organization emerged from the event, but a movement gathered steam. In January 1915, encouraged by a diverse group of women, including European suffrage and peace activists, Jane Addams, the most distinguished American woman of her time, and Carrie Chapman Catt invited prominent women and representatives of their key voluntary associations (including the Woman's Christian Temperance Union, the General Federation of Women's Clubs, and the Daughters of the American Revolution) to a meeting in Washington, D.C., where they established the Woman's Peace Party (WPP). Addams was a natural leader for the new organization. Revered for her social reform work associated with Hull House, she had also been active in prewar peace organizations. She also had the tact and managerial skills to oversee the creation of a platform that most of the seventy-six delegates could support.[7]

That platform had numerous components, the most significant of which called for a convention of neutral countries that could mediate between combatants; arms limitation; resistance to militarism in the United States; the "removal of economic causes of war"; a government commission in the United States, composed of men and women, to "promote international peace"; and "the further humanizing of governments by the extension of the franchise to women."[8] These goals embodied the belief that unified women could help create a new diplomacy that would promote international justice and human rights.

Since a key aspect of the WPP's platform was neutral mediation, WPP leaders were pleased to be invited to attend the April 1915 International Women's Committee of Permanent Peace meeting at the Hague. Over forty American representatives from several groups, including the WPP, traveled to Holland. Notable among them were women with distinguished careers in social work: Lillian Wald, Grace Abbott, Sophonisba Breckinridge, and Emily Greene Balch.[9] The 1,000 delegates protested against "the madness and horror of war" as well as "the odious wrongs of which women are the victims in time of war, and especially against the horrible violation of women which attend all wars."[10]

The convention urged the establishment of a conference of neutral nations, which would set up a process of "continual mediation" as the war ground on. The platform, which particularly reflected the WPP's influence, also included a rejection of the transfer of territory without a people's consent, a call for democratic institutions, and creation of a system of international arbitration, all of which would subsequently feature in Woodrow Wilson's Fourteen Points. Finally, as was the case with the WPP, the international group insisted upon universal woman suffrage.[11] In addition, it charged a group of women with the responsibility of meeting with foreign leaders to urge that they adopt their platform. Thirteen women, including Addams and Balch, a one-time settlement house founder and a professor of economics at Wellesley College, met with a series of European leaders, in the process visiting fourteen capitals. Although they were not successful in bringing neutral nations together, their activities, widely publicized in the media, highlighted American women's novel role in international activism. WPP women also met repeatedly with President Wilson, with Jane Addams seeing him six times in late 1915, a testament to Addams's national stature more than Wilson's amenability to her proposals concerning mediation.[12]

The other major peace organization in which women played a crucial role, the American Union Against Militarism (AUAM), emerged from the New York City Henry Street Settlement House in late 1915, first as the Anti-Preparedness Committee and then as the AUAM in early 1916. Key female figures included Jane Addams, Florence Kelley, Lillian Wald, and Alice Lewisohn, all noted for their connections to settlement work. Reflecting its founders' criticism of U.S. imperialistic ventures in Asia and Latin America, the AUAM adopted a platform that called for improved Asian-American relations and the creation of a Pan-American organization that would repudiate the Monroe Doctrine.[13] Particularly influenced by socialist Crystal Eastman, the AUAM became what one historian has called "America's most important radical internationalist organization."[14] Other indications of its far-reaching critique included a call for levying income and inheritance taxes to pay for armaments. Like the WPP, the AUAM worked for a mediated peace, but increasingly, given President Wilson's resistance, it urged the creation of unofficial commissions and conferences.[15]

As tensions rose in the United States over German submarine actions, with the first major crisis being the sinking of the neutral ship the *Lusitania* (with 1,195 lives lost) in 1915, pressure mounted on President Wilson. "Preparedness" advocates urged the president to increase army and naval forces and to institute universal male military training. Both the AUAM and the WPP launched a counterattack, using lobbying and publicity campaigns to forestall military buildup, conscription laws, and compulsory military training in the schools. In keeping with the social work connection to the peace movement, they argued that the attention and cost of an enhanced military undermined social reforms and reflected corporate interests that exploited working people.[16]

One of the most significant groups within the peace movement that fought military training in the public schools was the American School Peace League (ASPL). An older organization (founded in 1908), it became much more militant in the teens, as young activist schoolteachers, many of them aligned with the suffrage and other reform movements, organized campaigns to oppose the militarization of the schools. As one member of the ASPL described the Buffalo, New York, branch, "One is the President of the local Woman Teachers' Association; another is the leader of the teachers' suffrage party. Others are radical, strong women of the younger type." These younger activists struggled not only with their militarist opponents, but also with the president of the organization, Fannie Fern Andrews. Although she was a suffragist, Andrews took a conservative approach and often resisted the direction the teachers at the grassroots were taking the ASPL, a fitting example of the tensions that bedeviled women reformers and activists in the era. Historian Susan Zeiger notes that in part the preparedness emphasis on school military training reflected a widespread sense of a crisis of masculinity in the early twentieth century, a crisis that critics argued was brought about by the feminization of the teaching profession and the spread of pacifism.

As local school boards, state legislatures, and even the federal government considered adopting compulsory training for boys, these teachers swung into action, lobbying within their communities and among teachers' groups to block these schemes. They based their critique on the damage such militarism posed to children. Katherine Devereux Blake, one of the main leaders of the anti-preparedness movement within the ASPL, said that even during the war the organization should use "its every endeavor to safe-guard the children from the dangers of war, namely exploitation of labor, undernourishment, under-education, and legacy of hate that war engenders." The teachers' campaign succeeded. Only in New York State did military training become compulsory in the schools.[17]

Preparedness intensified in the spring of 1916 and became the mantra for a wide range of politicians, voluntary associations, patriotic organizations, and business groups. Women formed a notable part of the preparedness campaign. Most groups emerged out of American women's efforts to raise funds for aid to Belgium, France, and England. But as the preparedness movement heightened, they took this cause on as well. They worked primarily through auxiliary organizations to male groups, especially the Woman's Section of the Movement for Preparedness, the Women's Department of the National Civic Federation, and the Woman's Section of the Navy League (WSNL). Preparedness women, like their male allies, tended to be elite, with links to the conservative wing of the Republican Party. Patriotic organizations such as the Daughters of the American Revolution (DAR), which had moved away from its earlier pacifism, and the United Daughters of the Confederacy supported the movement as well.

Although these organizations did not specifically embrace the cause of antisuffrage, the National Association Opposed to Woman Suffrage did find common cause with preparedness groups, as both vehemently excoriated feminist pacifists for their lack of patriotism. In criticizing peace activists, the preparedness women turned the pacifist maternalist rhetoric on its head and argued that a strong military protected their sons. Annie Cothren Graves of the WSNL insisted that young men would be eager to fight for their country and that their mothers would want them to have "great ships and great guns, equipped for service and victory" so that they would not be "like sheep to the shambles to be slaughtered in unpreparedness by the disciplined and more numerous ships and soldiers of a prepared foe."[18]

Like pacifist groups, women who supported preparedness held conferences and lobbied politicians. They also participated in preparedness parades, with at least 4,000 women marching in New York City's 1916 event and similar numbers turning out in other cities such as Chicago and Providence. Women's participation in these parades had a certain irony, since the New York woman suffrage parade had provoked a storm of criticism from conservative women.

The dilemma of maintaining that women's novel activities in behalf of preparedness did not jeopardize traditional notions of femininity emerged in the justification for the series of quasi-military training camps that the WSNL established in a number of cities during 1917 and 1918.[19] The WSNL drew its idea for these camps, called collectively the National Service School, from the Plattsburgh movement, a program of volunteer military officer trainings camps in 1915 and 1916. Hundreds of women, many of whom were young elite socialites, participated in the series of two-week camps. On the one hand, reports explained that the women "will study military calisthenics, surgical dressings and bandage-making, dietetics, invalid cooking and scientific bed-making," suggesting that the camps built upon women's domestic and nurturing skills. On the other, as one young woman participant noted, the classes on "mechanics, the wireless, and ordinary telegraphy seemed to arouse more enthusiasm than any of the other courses." She hinted that the training could appeal to "new" women eager for novel opportunities in the face of war. The tone of press coverage of the camps varied. The first camp, in Baltimore, outside of Washington, D.C., drew extensive and respectful attention because President Woodrow Wilson addressed the women on the subject of preparedness. While subsequent accounts, usually illustrated with a photograph of women in uniform drilling, often praised the women's patriotism, more commonly they injected a note of jocularity at the prospect of privileged women roughing it as make-believe soldiers.[20]

The camps helped spur the popularity of the WSNL and reflected the growing enthusiasm for preparedness and the rising tide of nationalism. Tensions over preparedness and peace activism disrupted women's groups, and during 1916 peace organizations like the WPP and the AUAM saw many older, more conservative women, often uncomfortable with the more militant approach of younger women, retreat from their commitment to peace. Those who remained active redoubled their efforts. In February 1917, when the United States broke off diplomatic relations with Germany over its resumption of unrestricted submarine warfare, Addams and other peace leaders called for a national referendum on war and kept up their publicity and lobbying efforts with renewed intensity.

But the women's peace movement was losing steam—most strikingly symbolized by the late February 1917 decision by NAWSA to pledge support to the government in case of war. The about-face reflected the priority of leaders like Catt on suffrage and an unwillingness for the cause to be linked to that of the increasingly unpopular antiwar sentiment. The CU took no public stance on the war and criticized NAWSA for acting out of expediency rather than principle. At the same time, many women reformers, originally attracted to antiwar activism by social justice concerns, distanced themselves from peace organizations, feeling that criticizing the government at this point would damage their legitimacy and undermine their ability to promote reforms.[21]

The dissension among women about their stance toward war had particular meaning for the newly minted first woman congressional representative (1917), Jeannette Rankin, a Democrat from Montana. Rankin's pacifism reflected both her maternalist ideas and her populist reform sentiments. She argued that "it was women's work that was destroyed by war. Their work was raising human beings, and war destroyed human beings to protect profits and property." When Congress considered President Wilson's war message in March 1917, many of her suffragist friends and supporters insisted that a vote against the war resolution would damage the suffrage cause. Yet Rankin also had close ties to the CU and Alice Paul. As a Quaker, Paul was opposed to war but did not participate in the peace movement or speak publicly against the war. Nonetheless, she privately urged Rankin to vote against the war. Ultimately, Rankin stood by her pacifism. One of fifty representatives to vote against the war resolution, she declared as she cast her vote, "I want to stand by my country, but I cannot vote for war. I vote no."[22]

WOMEN, WAR, AND THE DRIVE FOR 100 PERCENT AMERICANISM

Jeannette Rankin paid for her principled stance: she was vilified in the press for her lack of patriotism, as were other pacifists. She was not reelected to Congress until the 1940s, when once again she cast a vote against a congressional declaration of war. The World War I attack on Rankin formed part of a broader hypernationalism that quickly flooded the country and in which women played a part, as both perpetrators and victims of the war-born hysteria. Nations predictably insist upon patriotic loyalty from citizens during times of war, but in the United States this demand was deeply rooted in prewar anxieties about the growing pluralism of the nation. Old-stock Americans worried about the presence of so many immigrants and their influence on politics and culture, leading to periodic demands for immigration restriction and Americanization programs. The growth of labor radicalism, both the modest political success of the Socialist Party and the high visibility of the IWW in leading successful strikes and drawing attention to class inequalities, also fueled concerns. So, too, did the emergence of the "new woman," which in the public mind was often conflated with pacifism, suffrage agitation, and "free love."

Moreover, after 1914, the nation divided over the issue of U.S. intervention, and the Wilson administration rightly understood that many Americans were ambivalent about the U.S. decision to go to war. Part of the process of mobilization, beyond raising troops and manufacturing war matériel, was to publicize war aims and promote patriotic nationalism. The major federal vehicle for this, the Committee on Public Information (CPI), used modern advertising techniques to disseminate war information and keep Americans emotionally engaged in a war fought thousands of miles away. One of its techniques was a speakers' bureau of "Four Minute Men," for which local businessmen spoke on prepared topics for four minutes. In many communities, women speakers, dubbed "Three Minute Women," addressed virtually any large gathering of people: "factory lunch crowds, department store customers, community playground users, and school groups."[23] Although the CPI's stated goals were educational, it quickly became a propaganda machine that encouraged mindless nationalism, with many women getting caught up in the spirit of patriotic excess.

The political climate that made it so easy to label someone as un-American was stimulated not just by the CPI's propaganda, but also by wartime federal laws that made the era a nightmare in terms of civil liberties. The June 1917 Espionage Act, reinforced later by the Sedition Act, offered wide latitude for the suppression of the press (particularly the radical and foreign language press) and of free speech. Often, criticism of the president or commentary about the draft was enough to land nonconformists in jail. And in many communities, local prosecutors used the federal legislation to continue their war on labor radicals, especially those associated with the Socialist Party and the IWW. Not surprisingly, given this, of the roughly 2,000 people indicted under the Espionage Act, none was accused of spying.[24] The government also required German aliens (meaning unnaturalized German immigrants) to register with local federal authorities, and both men and women were rounded up and fingerprinted, thus legitimizing suspicion about immigrants in the nation's midst.

At the same time, the conscription law, which offered few possibilities for exemption on moral or conscientious grounds, spurred massive "slacker" raids in the nation's cities. Although women rarely had a part in them, the hunt for the slacker was suffused with gendered rhetoric. Men who avoided the draft were not merely disloyal, but feminized, and were failing to do their duty in protecting women and children. Moreover, in popular culture, mothers were repeatedly criticized for their unwillingness to encourage their sons to military heroism, a theme that was tied to fears that pacifist women presented a threat to the nation's security.[25]

Between the CPI and the legislative basis for the repression of dissent, the war era reverberated with the demand for conformity and often reflected anxiety about the gender order. At one extreme was vigilantism—violent mob attacks on perceived traitors or slackers- such as the horsewhipping meted out to socialist and pacifist Herbert S. Bigelow in October 1917. Bigelow's masked attackers in Florence, Kentucky, kidnapped him, stripped him, and then viciously whipped him. Exclaiming they acted "in the name of the poor women and children of Belgium and France," the mob implicitly equated Bigelow's pacifism with his unmanliness. Men were the primary victims of such violence, although there were some reports of women being physically abused. In Michigan, for example, twenty women tarred and feathered Mrs. Harley Stafford "for alleged unpatriotic utterances." A "vigilance committee" sworn to make "Vicksburg and Warren County [Mississippi] 100 percent

American" tarred and feathered two black women, Ella Brooks and Ethel Barren, who allegedly had boasted that they did not have to work. They were released after they promised to seek immediate employment. Later, the six men of the "committee" were themselves arrested. Although extreme, the insistence that they work in the fields during the war reflected whites' expectations about black women's proper roles.[26]

Less draconian, but still with a coercive component, were the demands for conformity to "100 Percent Americanism." The mayor of Oakland, California, for example, demanded that all shop windows display the American flag and threatened those who refused with jail. In many areas, local leaders decreed that "sauerkraut" should be labeled "liberty cabbage" and banned the speaking of German or the playing of German music in public places, policies that the DAR enthusiastically endorsed.[27] Americanization programs intensified, many of them organized by various women's groups and clubs. The programs that women's groups implemented were less hostile than those that men's groups proposed. Yet it is reasonable to ask whether the immigrant women and men who attended such language and citizenship classes during the war were there completely voluntarily or felt compelled to attend, lest they be labeled disloyal.

The Wilson administration frequently took up the issue of coercion. It emphasized how much of the war effort was organized through voluntary associations, thereby avoiding the governmental "Prussianism" of its enemies. Yet, in the hypernationalist climate of World War I, volunteerism could become coercive as well. When clubwomen went door to door asking housewives to sign pledges to conserve food or support Red Cross fund drives, they commonly understood themselves to be engaged in patriotic civic service. But they were also part of a widespread network of volunteers demanding patriotism from their fellow Americans. When they met with resistance, they often interpreted it as disloyal and in many instances submitted names "to authorities." In Fort Wayne, Indiana, for example, the names were collected and turned in so that they might "induce slackers to become Americans in war service," a comment that expanded the meaning of war service to include women on the home front engaged in food conservation and other war-related activities.[28]

This climate of suppression and conformity was further encouraged by the CPI's request, published in magazines like the *Saturday Evening Post*, that citizens "report to the Justice Department 'the man who spreads pessimistic stories . . . cries for peace, or belittles our efforts to win the war.'"[29] More systematic volunteer hunts for spies came from the American Protective

League (APL). The APL consisted of private citizens, mostly businessmen, although some women apparently participated. Organized in major cities, its members assisted the Justice Department in investigating individuals suspected of disloyalty and particularly of draft evasion. Volunteers, they nonetheless had a quasi-governmental standing that gave them broad powers to examine the activities of people in their communities. In some communities, women accused of operating brothels or being prostitutes came under attack by the APL on the grounds that prostitutes endangered soldiers' health and undermined the war effort. In New Orleans, the APL led police to arrest five women on the grounds that there was "much evidence . . . showing willful and flagrant violation of the laws to protect the soldiers and sailors from the danger of the underworld."[30]

In some communities, local women's groups got so caught up in the hunt for disloyal citizens that they actively ferreted out allegedly disloyal women in their own organizations. Historian Christopher Capozzola has noted that the New York City Federation of Women's Clubs' 1918 annual convention was electrified when Mrs. Thomas Massey informed a luncheon meeting that she had overhead "strong pro-German sentiments" from club members. She explained that she found out their names and turned them over to the police. She insisted, "We must put all traitors out of our clubs." The gathering passed resolutions that any member who expressed disloyal statements would be turned over to the executive board. Only two women remained seated when the assemblage rose to vote approval. Both were suffragists, and one,. Ella O. Guilford, had been arrested for picketing the White House, raising the intriguing question as to whether Massey was in part targeting a militant suffragist for her "disloyalty."[31]

It is unlikely that many clubwomen found themselves ostracized or punished for un-American sentiments, but a small group of women did find their lives profoundly disrupted. Public schoolteachers were particularly vulnerable. Firings and forced resignations of dozens of schoolteachers made the newspapers. Idaho officials compelled one to resign because she would not promote the sale of thrift stamps. San Franciscan Dora T. Israel lost her job when she told the "board of education she could not teach children to honor the flag, which she said meant nothing to her." These women's experiences were reinforced by the decision of many school boards to require loyalty oaths, which underscored the limits to educators' ability to express themselves freely in the classroom.[32]

Despite the danger inherent in dissenting during World War I, some women found ways not only to resist the hypernationalist insistence on conformity, but also to criticize the war effort. Left-wing women associated variously with anarchists, socialists, and the IWW spoke out openly against the war and ran afoul of the Espionage and Sedition Acts. A handful of dedicated pacifists sought other means to maintain their commitment against militarism, most importantly through agencies established to protect the civil liberties of those who resisted conscription or challenged government restrictions of free speech. Neither women civil libertarians nor radical agitators tended to frame their activism in terms of their gender, although in both cases they implicitly claimed the legitimacy of women's political voice. Their critics, however, interpreted their failure to support the war as evidence of their failure to be respectable women. These dissenters exacerbated both war-related anxieties and long-standing tensions over challenges to the gender order that the emerging new woman represented.

During the war, two major organizations emerged to oppose governmental repressive practices toward immigrants, radicals, and conscientious objectors. Women proved crucial to both the Civil Liberties Bureau (CLB, which eventually became the long-standing premier civil rights agency in the United States, the American Civil Liberties Union) and the Bureau of Legal Advice.[33] Roger Baldwin, a conscientious objector who would be imprisoned for his stance, was a dominant force in the CLB, but Crystal Eastman was also a significant leader in the organization in its early days. Although she was a lawyer, Eastman did not participate in any CLB litigation but instead contributed to the organization's publicity campaign, a crucial part of its agenda.[34]

The Bureau of Legal Advice (BLA) is less well known than the CLB, in part because it did not become a permanent organization, but also, according to its historian, Frances Early, because the agency was dominated by women, especially feminist socialist pacifists Frances Witherspoon and Tracy Mygatt, who were also life partners. Both women had been active in the New York branch of the WPP, and that agency had helped form the BLA. Although men worked for the agency and its litigating attorneys were male, women formed the mainstay of the organization. The agency assisted some women, particularly working-class immigrants whose sons or husbands had been drafted, leaving them with no means of support. For the most part, however, the bureau focused on free speech cases (usually concerning labor radicals) and on serving conscientious objectors (COs) in the New York area. The federal government exempted men who were congregants of established pacifist religions, such as the Society of Friends (though local draft boards sometimes ignored these regulations). Men who claimed CO status for moral or political grounds were still subject to the draft, and it was these men that the BLA primarily assisted.

The BLA was rarely successful in its efforts to get such men exempted from the draft, but it carried through by agitating for humane prison treatment for COs. Here too, women were central, serving as informal prison inspectors, often visiting men who were their husbands or partners and reporting back to the BLA. Their experiences highlight the centrality of gender in defining wartime roles. Imprisoned conscientious objectors were constantly subject to jeering attacks on their masculinity, reinforcing the way in which wartime rhetoric conflated military service with manliness. Alice Navard, who visited Fort Riley in Kansas, reported that the prisoners were "denounced as cowards, unmanly, good-for-nothings." At the same time, military officials viewed these women visitors, despite their care in choosing respectable lodging, as of dubious morality. A number of women reported attempted sexual assaults or other threats by officers. As Frances Early sums it up, "Women who shared the views of such men faced gender ridicule and also became potential 'bad' women and outcasts who could not depend upon the patriarchal, militaristic code of chivalry to protect them."[35]

These pacifists, while important to the history of civil liberties and left-wing radical movements in the United States, were exceptional. So, too, were the handful of women who were indicted under the Espionage and Sedition Acts, but they are significant because they also sought to break down barriers to their political voice and did so at a time when dissent was dangerous. The vast majority of people arrested and brought to trial on federal charges under the Espionage or Sedition Acts were men, but some women did come under federal scrutiny, and their cases are revealing. Most had been prominent in the labor or radical movements and had also been outspoken in terms of women's rights, including access to birth control. Given the way in which the fight for birth control access in the teens elided with the radical free speech movement of the IWW, it is not surprising that women who had been engaged in civil liberties battles before the war would also be active in resisting the restrictive civil liberties climate of the war years. Whether or not they took part in the earlier birth control campaign, the accusations against them and the language used in their trials suggested how contested was the new woman, radical or not.[36]

The most famous women to come to trial were anarchist Emma Goldman and socialists Rose Pastor Stokes and Kate Richards O'Hare.[37] Russian-born Goldman was the quintessential disorderly woman, who was portrayed as the epitome of the threat immigrant radicals posed to mainstream America. Having received national attention for her radical politics and unconventional lifestyle for decades, Goldman's activities leading up to the war included an outspoken campaign for birth control as well as a relentless critique of capitalism and the power of the state and the patriarchal family to undermine individual freedom. In May 1917, Goldman established a "No-Conscription League" for the "purpose of encouraging conscientious objectors to affirm their liberty of conscience and to translate their objection to human slaughter by refusing to participate in the war."[38] Although the league claimed it counseled only those who had already decided to be COs, it quickly ran afoul of the Espionage Act. After one meeting on New York's immigrant Lower East Side, Goldman was arrested, along with her longtime friend and one-time lover Alexander Berkman. Figure 1, a rather stolid photograph taken of Goldman on a streetcar shortly before her arrest, hardly captures the charismatic demeanor of Goldman, but it is notable for the ironic juxtaposition of Goldman, in the foreground, with the now-iconic Uncle Sam's "I Want You" recruitment poster in the background.

The immediate spark to the arrest—a violent disturbance at a meeting precipitated when police asked men in attendance for their registration cards—is interesting in itself. Lower East Side immigrant women, anxious about military conscription's threat to their families, attempted to block arrests of their sons and husbands, demonstrating their own unwillingness to be "patriotic mothers." Another highly publicized riot occurred after Goldman's arrest when several hundred women of the Women's League for the Repeal of Conscription, also from the Lower East Side, marched to the mayor's office demanding an end to the draft. Although the women were not specifically protesting Goldman's arrest, newspapers conflated the two issues, reinforcing the sense that Goldman was promoting civil disorder and encouraging other women to do so as well.[39]

Using articles from Goldman's journal, *Mother Earth*, No-Conscription League literature, and police transcriptions of her speeches, the prosecutors insisted that Goldman had encouraged resistance to the draft. In addition to evidence about Goldman's stance on conscription, the prosecutors as well as the press emphasized Goldman's threat to social order. Her charisma was so mesmerizing that she could sway crowds, particularly ethnic crowds, to revolutionary action. Critics also claimed that she dominated Alexan-

Figure 1. Emma Goldman, New York City, 1917. Library of Congress, LC-B2-4215-16. Photography by Bain News Service.

der Berkman, which suggested her ability to emasculate men and implied her unnatural femininity. Goldman clearly understood that her challenge to conventional expectations about women fundamentally shaped her trial. Allowed to ask prospective jurors questions, Goldman's queries included the following: "Would you be prejudiced against the defendants to know that Emma Goldman had devoted a large part of her life to the emancipation of women?" "Do you believe in woman's equality with man?" "Would you be prejudiced against Emma Goldman if it came out in the trial that she advocated birth control for the poor?"[40]

Although Goldman staked a claim to patriotism, arguing, "The kind of patriotism that we represent is the kind of patriotism that loves America with open eyes," both she and Berkman were convicted and sentenced to two years in prison. Released in September 1919, they immediately faced deportation proceedings, based on their anarchist beliefs and their lack of citizenship. Although Goldman's political radicalism prompted her indictment and later deportation, a major part of her crime was that she was, in Kathleen Kennedy's words, "the quintessential disorderly woman, one who used her influence to discourage immigrant men and women from fulfilling their duties as patriotic men and women."[41]

Rose Pastor Stokes, a Russian Jew, also found her trial for sedition framed in the context of her ethnicity, radical politics, and gender transgressions. Labor activist Stokes, a former cigar worker, married a fellow socialist, wealthy J. G. Phelps Stokes, in 1905. Newspapers routinely referred to her as a "millionaire socialist" and gave as much coverage to her decision to keep her maiden name as it did to her political activities. Before the war, she combined her socialism with suffrage activism and outspoken support for birth control. Moreover, she was a member of the WPP. Briefly she, along with her husband, supported the war and renounced socialism. But by 1917, she returned to her early antiwar stance and to the Socialist Party and took to the lecture circuit, critiquing the war as a capitalist one that oppressed the working class.

Her arrest came after a speech to a woman's club in Kansas City and a follow-up letter to the *Kansas City Star*, which had incorrectly stated that her speech included "unqualified support" of the government's war aims. In a published letter to the newspaper, Stokes denied that she had made such statements and insisted, "No government which is for the profiteers can also be for the people and I am for the people while the Government is for the profiteers."[42] The Justice Department indicted her on three counts of violating the Espionage Act, claiming that the letter and speech indicated that she intended to interfere with the recruitment of soldiers. Central to the prosecution's case, however, was her sympathy for the Bolsheviks, which in itself, prosecutors argued, endangered American soldiers and justified prosecution.

As in Goldman's case, the trial hinged on her failure to be a "patriotic woman." She was accused of failing to support the American Red Cross, an organization widely admired and understood to reflect womanly values of nurturing those in need. Her birth control advocacy, specifically linked to that of Emma Goldman, was also invoked to suggest her dangerous views.[43] The trial ranged far afield from what Stokes may or may not have said, as the prosecution constructed a gendered critique of her disloyalty. She was not just an antiwar radical, but a radical woman, who embodied the gender disorder so worrisome to conservative Americans in the early twentieth century.[44] Stokes was convicted but, unlike Goldman, never served time in jail. She appealed her case, and in 1920, the Supreme Court overturned the conviction.

A third case that reflected the fear of "scurrilous women and disorderly women" was that of Kate Richards O'Hare. O'Hare's socialist antiwar stance differed from that of many other socialist women in that she invoked woman's maternalism in her opposition to war. This aspect of her thinking appeared in her court case when she was indicted under the Espionage Act in June 1917. The Justice Department claimed that, in a speech in Bowman, North Dakota, to the Nonpartisan League (a left-wing but nonrevolutionary group that opposed the war), O'Hare had called American women "brood sows" whose purpose in war was to "raise children to get into the army and [be] made into fertilizer." O'Hare denied the charge, saying she was referring to European women. Her alleged argument that "war corrupted motherhood" became far more central to her trial than her anticapitalist critique of war. O'Hare's crime was to undermine "patriotic motherhood" by arguing that war "reduced women to vehicles for the reproduction of soldiers who in turn killed and were killed for the state."[45]

In contrast to Stokes and Goldman, O'Hare was native born and conventional in her personal life, but her radicalism appeared every bit as dangerous, an interpretation the socialist *New York Call* agreed with, calling her approvingly "a dangerous woman, a thinking woman . . . that stirreth up the people." The jury convicted O'Hare of interfering with the draft, but she was out on bail until 1919, when she lost her appeal. She served her time in a brutal prison whose inhumane treatment she exposed in a series of letters. After she began her sentence, defense groups worked tirelessly for either a commutation of her sentence or an overthrow of her conviction. The judge kept up pressure on the Justice Department to sustain her imprisonment, and further lobbying emerged from a group called War Mothers in North Dakota, as well as the American Legion and its female auxiliary, which argued that her release would be a "vile slander upon American womanhood." Nonetheless, Attorney General A. Mitchell Palmer commuted her sentence, noting that

O'Hare was herself the mother of four children and that her imprisonment was thus far harder than it would be for a man.[46]

Federal prosecutors also went after less famous radical women. In June 1917, a roundup of persons accused of undermining draft registration in Kansas included two women, Dr. Eva Harding, the first woman doctor in the state, who was well known as a suffragist and socialist, and Leonora Warneson Moore, another socialist and a teacher who had come to public attention earlier in the year for putting an antiwar slogan on her classroom blackboard. Most accounts of her arrest noted that she preferred to go by her maiden name of Warneson. The charges against Harding were dismissed, and Moore, unlike the men in her arrest cohort, was fined rather than sent to prison. Other women experienced harsher treatment. The trial of Dr. Mari Equi, a socialist and lesbian associated with the IWW, began after the war ended but at a time when anxiety about radicalism continued to be deep. The prosecution stressed her gender transgression, calling her an "unsexed woman," and insisted that "unless you put this woman in jail, the Bolshevik flag would soon fly over the United States."[47] Another woman associated with the IWW as well as the birth control movement, Louise Olivereau, was indicted on charges that she encouraged men to resist the draft. Acting as her own attorney, Olivereau mounted a critique on the way in which the state was suppressing civil liberties and demanding cultural conformity. As Kennedy notes, one of Olivereau's supporters explicitly linked her participation in a free speech campaign for birth control to her demands for civil liberties of dissenters in wartime. Yet her impassioned arguments came to naught. The jury convicted her in under thirty minutes, and she ultimately served twenty-eight months of her ten-year sentence.[48]

Civil libertarians like Witherspoon and charismatic firebrands like O'Hare and Goldman had long-standing commitments to radical visions of social justice. And most women considered here had connections to women's rights issues, especially those associated with feminism, such as birth control. In one way or another, they were all "new women," and certainly their opponents viewed them as "disorderly women." In the prewar years, despite being "disorderly," many of them could find some areas of common cause with more liberal social reformers like Jane Addams and Lillian Wald, who were more willing to work within the system. Indeed, the feminist ferment associated with New York's Greenwich Village was notable for attracting both left-wing radicals and liberals. And the widespread popularity of the peace movement had temporarily offered a sense of energized women united behind a call for a new diplomacy that would reflect women's democratic values in the international arena. The war and the drive for conformity and the hunt for subversives, however, severely undercut the possibilities for such diverse women to find common cause with one another. Even as it gave some women opportunities to make their political voices heard, the war drew much sharper lines between radicals and liberals, a process that would accelerate in the postwar era when an antiradical Red Scare further marginalized radical women and even demonized liberal reformers.

WAR AND SUFFRAGE

Tensions between white women activists during the war were especially rife in the suffrage movement with the CU and NAWSA sharply divided over tactics and ideology. NAWSA developed a two-pronged justification for votes for women. On the one hand, leaders like Catt invoked themes of justice and democracy to insist on women's right to the vote. But on the other hand, NAWSA also continued to build heavily on the maternalist notion that women were essentially different from men and would bring their particular values to the public arena in a form of "social housekeeping." In contrast, the CU, rather than emphasizing the reforms that enfranchised women might achieve for family, home, and nation, foregrounded themes of equality and natural rights.[49] Although African American women, who had their own suffrage organizations, began to interact more with the white women's organizations in the years before the war and their National Association of Colored Women formally endorsed the federal amendment in 1916, they do not seem to have been involved in the controversies that disrupted the white suffrage movement in the war years.[50]

Controversy among white women resulted in a sharp break in 1914. As the CU continued to press for a national amendment, NAWSA attempted to marginalize the CU, which split from its parent organization. The next year, Catt, as the newly elected president of NAWSA, introduced her "winning plan," which called for both a state-level approach and the national amendment, a change that reflected the pressure created by Alice Paul and her organization. Catt brought to NAWSA inspired leadership and organizational skill, which reenergized the organization.[51] Although the two suffrage associations now agreed on two key points, the federal amendment and the importance of convincing President Wilson to endorse it, they moved even further apart. The CU became even more militant in 1916 when Paul created the Woman's Party (WP, made up of enfranchised voters), a single-issue pressure group. The party called for using women's votes in the states where they were already enfranchised to oppose candidates of the Democratic Party, reasoning that the Democratic administration and Congress, which had refused to pass enabling legislation for a national amendment, would be shown women's potential power. The tactic drove a further wedge between Paul's group and NAWSA, which continued to insist that suffrage supporters be nonpartisan.

There were too many other issues in the presidential year of 1916 — U.S. intervention in the war among them — to evaluate the specific impact of the Woman's Party's insistence that newly enfranchised women vote against the Democrats and Wilson. Because Wilson ran on a slogan of "He Kept Us Out of War" and his Republican opponent, Charles Evans Hughes, was a preparedness advocate, many suffragists, even members of the Woman's Party, supported Wilson. Of the twelve states where women could vote, Wilson won eleven. But Paul claimed a victory nonetheless by drawing attention to the potential power of women voting.[52]

Perhaps what is most significant, however, is the underlying assumption framing the Woman's Party's approach. It rejected the polite though persistent lobbying on the part of the NAWSA — essentially begging men to give women the vote — and used political leverage to achieve its aim. As Paul said, it was "more dignified of women to ask the vote of other women than to beg it of men."[53] This, as well as their unladylike public demonstrations, deepened the sense of the Woman's Party as radical or militant suffragists and created an even larger gulf between NAWSA and Alice Paul's group, which the war would heighten.

NAWSA, *Suffrage, and the War*

During the lead up to U.S. entry into the war, members of both organizations were probably not that different in their attitude toward war. Catt, Shaw, and Burns were all pacifists and as individuals were members of peace organizations. But, unlike NAWSA, which officially endorsed the WPP, the CU — with the focus on its single issue — had never publicly embraced the pacifist movement and thus when war came continued to remain largely silent on the issue of war.[54] NAWSA leaders quickly shifted gears to pledge support for the war and offer women's services to mobilization. The decision was in large part pragmatic. Catt rightly understood that in the nationalistic climate of war, it would be dangerous for the suffrage cause to be associated with pacifism and might subject women to the charge of disloyalty. NAWSA leaders also realized that war service such as fund-raising for the Red Cross and Liberty

Loan or campaigns for food conservation could further their cause by demonstrating women's patriotism and civic virtue.

The federal government initially had little interest in tapping the nation's women in its mobilization drive. Faced with the Wilson administration's foot dragging in implementing a plan for women's service, women leaders, most notably those associated with NAWSA, took the initiative to push for the creation of a national women's organization, which they hoped would parallel the Council of National Defense, the male-dominated national committee instituted to coordinate civilian mobilization under the direction of the War Department. The Wilson administration finally established the Woman's Committee of the Council of National Defense (WCND) in April 1917, intending it purely as an advisory body. With ex-NAWSA president Dr. Anna Howard Shaw as the committee's chair and several notable suffragists on the committee, the federal government reinforced NAWSA's efforts to align suffrage with war service. This dismayed antisuffrage activists and the Women's Service League, who had assumed that their preparedness activities situated them as the official government agency for female mobilization efforts. NAWSA's dominance in the WCND gave NAWSA officials throughout the nation increased opportunities to link woman suffrage with woman's war service in the public mind.

Once the United States entered the conflict, most of the leaders of women's organizations would come out enthusiastically for war and would coordinate with the WCND on a wide range of war services. Whatever their earlier stance on war, many were caught up in nationalistic patriotic fervor as well as the hope that their war work could promote both women's rights and social reform at home. Motivations for support for war were complex, but NAWSA clearly tapped the prevailing sentiment among women's organizations. NAWSA's stance was the focal point of its approach to the suffrage battle during the war.

Throughout the war, NAWSA officials stressed women's, and especially suffragists', patriotism, defining citizenship's meaning as service to one's nation. Women working through the WCND in the states embarked on an ambitious census to register women for home-front service and engaged in Americanization programs that combined civic lessons with praise for women's contributions to the nation. Other activities included making surgical dressings and knitted goods for the Red Cross and massive fund-raising campaigns for both the Red Cross and the federal Liberty Loan drive.[55] Such well-publicized service proved invaluable to the New York suffrage campaign of 1917, as "members sold Liberty Bonds ($11 million in 1917), lobbied against relaxation of state laws for the protection of women and children in industry, sponsored public speakers' bureaus, and conducted house-to-house canvasses, letter writing campaigns, automobile tours, canning and preserving home kitchen demonstrations, and moving picture exhibitions on behalf of war and suffrage."[56]

NAWSA's *Woman Citizen* was another important vehicle for disseminating the war service message. Although NAWSA emphasized volunteer work conducted by suffragists and in particular highlighted service of local groups in their community, another part of war service it applauded were the contributions of paid women workers who aided the defense effort by taking on new types of jobs. Munitions makers, street car conductors, railway workers, and personnel managers for women workers were all presented as serving the war effort and demonstrating women's patriotism. And, reflecting the wider reach of the suffrage movement to include working-class women, the *Woman Citizen* also drew attention to the need to address safety and compensation issues for working women. And Catt made it clear that such service needed to be rewarded with more than the vote. In May 1917, she wrote 500 Chambers of Commerce throughout the nation calling for equal pay for equal work when women took on men's jobs in war mobilization, noting that "work performed, not the sex of the worker, should determine the rate of pay."[57]

Woman Citizen issues also reported on women serving abroad as medical professionals, canteen workers (who served soldiers refreshments), Red Cross officials, and telephone operators, among other jobs. The journal took particular pride in reporting on its suffrage "service flag"—an actual flag to which a star was added representing each suffrage officer in the United States who went abroad to serve in medical units, as Red Cross workers, or as YWCA canteen workers. It reported in 1918 that the flag had twenty-three stars and included such women as Mary (Molly) Dewson, "chairman of the Legislative Committee of the Massachusetts Woman Suffrage association," who was serving as a social worker in France, Lucille Ryan, the vice president of the Mahaska County (Iowa) Suffrage Association, who served as an accountant for the Red Cross in Italy, and Adah Bush, vice president of the Women's Franchise League, Indiana, who was working for the Young Men's Christian Association (YMCA) abroad. The idea of the flag is in itself interesting because it borrowed on the idea of men's organizations that had service flags to denote male members' military service, clearly suggesting NAWSA's understanding that war service abroad was a particularly significant example of women's citizenship that was on a par with men's.[58]

The *Woman Citizen* implicitly and sometimes explicitly argued that these types of service were akin to the work that men did for the war effort. The real challenge for suffragists in making this comparison was the assumption that, during wartime, military service became the ultimate example of citizenship, something denied to women. On occasion, the journal explicitly countered this understanding by arguing that in modern warfare, all types of service might be viewed on a par. An editorial in November 1918, as the war was about to end, reflected, "There have been wars before this, but never a war which has been so much in partnership between men and women all the world around. . . . Women have not in this war as in former wars served merely as inspirers of men, but have performed the actual war service, as well on the battle line as in the war industries."[59]

While NAWSA supporters focused a significant part of their suffrage argument on women's war service, a second theme appeared alongside it. The Wilsonian war message of a "war for democracy" seemed tailor-made for the suffrage cause. Clara Ueland of the Minnesota Suffrage Association insisted, for example, that "we are waging a war to make the world safe for democracy, and for the principle that those who must submit to authority should have a voice in their government." In a long essay, "War Messages to the American People," Catt spoke of the role of the United States as "the world leader in democratic progress." Noting that many other countries had already enfranchised women, she claimed that "the world expects America to be true to her ideals" and stressed that although representative government was the "mainstay of our progress," it "will only become representative when *all* of the people give consent to the representatives entrusted with the law-making and law-enforcing power of the land."[60]

The National Woman's Party and Disruptive Power

As NAWSA publicized women's war service and cast suffrage as a war measure that would extend democracy at home while the nation fought for it abroad, Alice Paul's group sought a different kind of publicity as it continued to focus on putting pressure on President Wilson and the Democrats. After the 1916 elections and shortly before the United States entered the war, the CU established peaceful pickets in front of the White House. As Paul and her comrades saw it (and NAWSA would have agreed), Wilson's endorsement of a federal amendment would be the turning point in the suffrage battle. Their tactic of pickets composed of peaceful, silent sentinels, as they called themselves, aimed at bringing pressure to bear on Wilson and attention to their cause. The use of picketing followed both the English radical suffrage tactic (although the latter included sporadic violence such as rock throwing) as well as the tradition of working-class women's strike behavior. First used in the United States by New York suffragists, it was a continuation of the novel approach of parades for the suffrage cause, in which women laid claim to public space and crossed barriers that defined women's proper behavior.

Momentously when the war began, Paul and her party (now the National Woman's Party [NWP], an amalgamation of the CU and the WP) kept the pickets in place. Tensions exploded in June 1917, when Russian delegates from the new revolutionary regime that had toppled the czar a few months earlier arrived in Washington, D.C., where Wilson hoped to convince them to stay in the war rather than seek a separate peace. The pickets met the Russians' arrival with a provocative banner, held aloft by Lucy Burns and Doris Lewis, that disputed the Wilsonian claim of universal enfranchisement in the United States. The banner named Wilson as "the chief opponent of their national enfranchisement" and urged the Russians to "tell our government that it must liberate its people before it can claim free Russia as an ally."[61] While the Russians apparently did not see the pickets, an angry mob, which included some women (one of whom yelled, "This is treason"), set upon the suffragists, tearing their banners down and creating what the newspapers called a riot. For the most part, the press blamed the women for the melee and newspaper coverage was hostile. The *Baltimore Sun* likened the suffragists to "Emma Goldman and other enemies of the country," a comparison that emerged repeatedly among critics of the picketers.[62] As historian Christine Lunardini has argued, "Newspapers such as the *New York Times* mixed anarchists, strikers, antiwar demonstrators, draft resisters, and suffragists, presenting them in such a way as to convey to their readers the implication that *all* dissent was equally meritless and harmful."[63] Undaunted, the WP continued picketing, using their signs ironically to juxtapose quotations from Woodrow Wilson about the war for democracy. In figure 2, an August 1917 photograph, Virginia Arnold holds a particularly startling banner. In labeling Woodrow Wilson as "Kaiser" and invoking Wilson's words criticizing the German government, the banner accused the president of hypocrisy. How, it asked, were the 20 million women who could not vote in the United States any different from the "poor Germans" who were not self-governed?[64]

Over a thousand women would participate in the White House picketing, most of whom found it an affirming experience. Some were socialist working-class women like Ernestine Hart, who explained her picketing by invoking her politics: "As a radical, I believe in justice." Most of the picketers,

Figure 2. National Woman's Party member Virginia Arnold holds a banner comparing President Wilson to the Kaiser as part of the party's White House picketing strategy, August 1917. Library of Congress, Prints and Photographs Division, Records of the National Woman's Party, Harris and Ewing Photographers: Digital I.D. http://hdl.loc.gov/loc.mss/mnwp.160030.

however, were elite women, one of whom claimed, "The fundamental rightness of it brings comfort to the mind and helps us to bear the rebellion that is rising in our souls."[65]

Their tactics continued to draw fire, including from NAWSA. Ida Husted Harper, a noted suffrage journalist, complained that "when the 'picketing' began in Washington last January, almost every newspaper in the United States held the entire suffrage movement responsible for it." NAWSA, she reported, sent out 250 letters condemning the pickets and insisting that NAWSA had always been nonpartisan and nonmilitant.[66] Similarly, the *Woman Citizen* in September 1917 proclaimed that the 2 million women of NAWSA "repudiate the methods of the Woman's Party and for more than forty-five years have appealed to Congress, always within the bounds of decorum and in a constitutional manner," a pithy comment that got to the heart of the distinctions between the two groups' tactics.[67]

Although initially the Washington, D.C., police periodically arrested and then released the picketers, in late July, sixteen of the women were brought before a court on charges such as disorderly conduct and obstructing traffic. When they refused to pay their fines, the judge sentenced them to jail. They served only three days, and the picketing continued, as did escalating violence against them, by both mobs and the police. More arrests followed, which led to thirty- to sixty-day sentences. Most went to Occoquan, a grim workhouse prison where they were held without visitors or access to lawyers. Their imprisonment was particularly significant because many of the women were well-connected politically and socially. Moreover, at least two of their husbands expressed their outrage to Wilson personally. Alison Hopkins's husband, a former campaign advisor to Wilson, urged the president to come out on behalf of the amendment immediately, as did Matilda Hall Gardner's husband, the journalist Gilson Gardner, who wrote Wilson warning him of the political ramifications of the women's imprisonment. Wilson, for his part, was disturbed that the police had overreached and helped make "martyrs" of the picketers.[68]

The police had played into the picketers' hands. On their release, they began an extensive drive to publicize their arrests and prison terms. Maud Younger was one of four NWP women who fanned out across the country to hold meetings to draw attention to their cause and highlight the brutal treatment they had received. The *Mississippi Gulfport Daily Herald* reported in October that Younger would speak to Gulfport audiences and tell them, from her "first hand knowledge," of the horrific conditions accorded women who were asking for "their political liberty." Vivian Pierce stressed the concept of a war for democracy when she told a New Orleans audience, "We knew we had got under the skin of the politicians, not because we were wrong, but because we were advertising to the country the inconsistency of a war congress that sends men abroad to fight for democracy and denies democracy to women at home."[69] Rather than be deterred, women from all over the country continued to join the ranks of pickets, and local newspapers reported when they, too, were arrested.

The violation of their civil liberties, freedom of assembly and freedom of speech, and their treatment in incarceration was shocking but in keeping with the tenor of war years when dissent was widely suppressed. And even more extreme treatment was to come. Alice Paul and Rose Winslow, imprisoned in Occoquan, embarked on a hunger strike on November 20, 1917, over being placed in solitary confinement because they had smuggled out a letter of protest to the Washington, D.C., commissioners. Paul was familiar with the tactic in England, where she had also participated in hunger strikes and learned their strategic publicity value. In addition to force-feeding her, prison officials also harassed her by threatening to commit her to an insane asylum. Adept at finding a tactical advantage, Paul and the other jailed women used their imprisonment and treatment to claim that they were political prisoners.[70]

Despite efforts to keep news of the hunger strike from the press, it became a major story. When they learned that the women were being fed through a feeding tube, some papers, which continued to be hostile to the pickets, accepted official reports that no force was being used. But others, like the *Elkhart Truth*, headlined the story: "Militants Forcibly Fed; Many Protest to Wilson," and reported that the White House was deluged with telegrams over the women's treatment. Newspapers also printed the account by Winslow of their treatment, which the *Macon Telegraph* sensationalized with the headline "Miss Mary Winsor [*sic*] Declares Prisoners Not Even Given Rights Accorded Murderers."[71]

Outrage over the prison abuse and the exposé of the women's mistreatment undoubtedly embarrassed the Wilson administration, despite the president's insistence that "no real harshness of method is being used." As former prisoners from Occoquan embarked on a publicity trip, more unfavorable reports filled the newspapers, leading Democrats to worry about the 1918 congressional elections. Alameda County, California, Democrats reported that Anne Martin's speech "did much harm," while other party officials, such as Illinois's state chairman, asked if Wilson could not arrange for the women's release and facilitate the federal amendment.[72] On November

27 and 28, without any explanation, all of the women were released from prison, and with the exception of a series of arrests the following August when the women were protesting in nearby Lafayette Park, they were allowed to continue their peaceful demonstrations, which lasted until January 1919, without harassment.

A new stage in the suffrage movement began shortly after the women's release from prison, when the blocked amendment suddenly began to move through Congress with the president's tacit approval. In December, the House of Representatives rules committee reported that it would finally bring the amendment out of committee to a vote, and on January 9, 1918, Wilson announced his support for a federal amendment enfranchising American women. The House passed the amendment, but in the Senate, despite the personal appearance of Wilson to urge passage, claiming that the amendment was "essential to the successful prosecution of the great war of humanity in which we are engaged," the measure failed by two votes. It was not until June 1919, under constant pressure from Wilson (and the NWP and NAWSA), that the Senate finally passed the amendment.[73] Fifteen months later, in August 1920, the Susan B. Anthony Amendment was finally ratified, after extensive work on the state level by both the NWP and NAWSA.

Given the timing of Wilson's decision, right after the barrage of bad publicity about the hunger strikes, we must credit the NWP's "disruptive power" approach as being instrumental in forcing Wilson's intervention.[74] Beyond the picketing, moreover, Alice Paul had constructed a potent tactic when she urged enfranchised women in 1914 and 1916 to vote against Democratic candidates as a form of protest. The Democrats were clearly worried about the 1920 elections, for when New York, with its 45 electoral college votes, passed woman suffrage in 1917 it meant that states where women could vote for president (six states let women vote in presidential elections only) totaled 184 electoral college votes, or 35 percent.[75]

As important as Paul's tactics were, however, the role of NAWSA and Catt must be acknowledged. NAWSA, often in conjunction with the WCND, widely publicized women's service to the nation in time of war and helped to articulate the link between the war for democracy at home and abroad. If it did not create the same sense of urgency that the NWP women did, it did offer a sustained and persuasive argument for enfranchising women. Its work in the states was crucial to creating the needed votes in Congress, and its behind-the-scenes lobbying of Wilson was unrelenting, if polite. More complexly, the two suffrage groups created an "insider-outsider" dynamic. Historian Lynda G. Dodd explains that "when Wilson and the Democratic members of Congress eventually decided to offer their public support for the federal amendment, Catt's role provided political cover, allowing them to praise her and publicly disclaim the influence of the NWP's political campaigning and acts of civil disobedience."[76]

The war years and the controversy over picketing versus lobbying widened the gap between the two wings of the suffrage movement. It not only reflected tensions within the suffrage movement but would also bedevil activist women in the 1920s as they sought to find ways to turn the vote into political power. Yet both understood that the war emergency could be turned to suffrage advantage because of the very nature of professed American war aims. As Catt quite rightly noted, the war made the suffrage amendment possible.

AFRICAN AMERICAN WOMEN AND THE WAR FOR DEMOCRACY

African American women leaders supported the suffrage movement, but the war crisis led them to concentrate primarily on the implications of war for the broad question of African American civil rights and racial progress. In this era, the National Association of Colored Women (NACW) maintained its role as a key association for middle-class black activists. By 1916, it had a membership of 50,000 women in thirty-six states and continued to focus on "lifting as we climb."[77] African American women reformers used their local clubs to promote racial uplift, focusing on such community-building efforts as settlement houses and kindergartens. But they also began to understand their organization's lobbying possibilities, with NACW passing resolutions in 1912 against Jim Crow railroad cars and lynching and in support of "full" woman suffrage.[78] At the same time, women in the newly founded NAACP (1909) joined in the fight against segregation and disenfranchisement. Attention to civil rights issues escalated during the war, even though the political climate made it difficult for black Americans to express dissent. Although men dominated the black press, many women race leaders found vehicles for expressing their understanding of the war and its meaning for black men and women. They spoke out against racial violence and discrimination yet were hopeful about the war's potential for promoting racial progress.

African American Women and Support for the War

As the United States moved toward intervention in the war, African American leaders, male and female, faced a dilemma. Racial violence against blacks was endemic in the South, and patterns of segregation and disenfranchisement had hardened. They could expect little from President Wilson, who had facilitated segregation in federal offices in Washington, D.C. How could they view the war as important to them or willingly undertake sacrifices for Wilson's war for democracy? Some openly commented that the war had little meaning for African Americans, and socialists like A. Philip Randolph and Chandler Owen persistently critiqued the war. Monroe Trotter of the National Equal Rights League, an organization that included many women, adamantly criticized the war and spoke out repeatedly about injustice against African Americans in the United States. Most black leaders, male and female, however, at least initially followed the lead of the NAACP *Crisis* editor, W. E. B. Du Bois. Du Bois called for "closed ranks," meaning that African Americans should loyally serve in the war with the expectation that they would strengthen their claim for civil rights at war's end as reward for their patriotism. The decision to support the war stemmed to some extent from genuine support—many black leaders believed with Du Bois that colonialized people of color worldwide would be better off with an Allied victory than a German one. Others supported the war in the hope that service could earn citizenship rights, in much the same way that women in NAWSA saw war service as a vehicle to obtain suffrage.

African American women leaders generally supported the war and sought to highlight women's contributions to the effort, but they also saw it as an opportunity to press for recognition of all African Americans as citizens. In a stunning short play printed in the NAACP's *Crisis* in 1918, poet and journalist Alice Dunbar-Nelson told the story of a young black man, Chris, who receives his draft notice but tells his sister and crippled brother that they need him. Besides, he will not go and fight "for the nation that let my father's murder go unpunished." As Chris insists that the war is not *their* war, both his sister and his brother insist that African Americans have always served their country in time of war. By drawing parallels between the Germans' brutal treatment of women and children in Europe and the violence visited on blacks in the United States, they finally convince him that he must go. Sister Lucy points out his duty to the nation and the race: "Yes, we do, Chris, we do need you, but your country needs you more. And, above that, your race is calling you to carry on its good name, and with that, the voice of humanity is calling to us all—we can manage without you, Chris."[79] Other women leaders who encouraged support for the war also insisted, like noted educator Nannie Burroughs, "that the race would be patriotic in every instance, but must at the same time contend for a democracy at home that will include them." Speaking before the Baltimore Women's Co-operative Civic League in February 1918, she denounced advocates of segregation measures as German propagandists whose racism had made "some colored people less inclined to patriotically support their government."[80]

As Burroughs's comment indicates, African Americans knew that whites suspected them of being potentially disloyal. Throughout the South, but especially in regions where blacks outnumbered whites, local white leaders claimed that Germans were sowing propaganda that might lead not merely to traitorous ideas but even to violent uprisings. Rather than acknowledge that any potential disaffection stemmed from pervasive racial discrimination and violence, they alleged that blacks' inferior mental capacity made them susceptible to German provocateurs. South and North, black leaders were often subject to surveillance and suspicion.[81] Not surprisingly, then, most African Americans voiced support for the war and were usually restrained in their criticism of African Americans' treatment during the war.

Although for the most part black women leaders discussed the patriotism of African Americans as a group, many were eager to stress the specific contributions of women to the race and to the war.[82] Often black women stressed the ways in which they contributed to the war effort in their role as housewives. Martha E. Williams, a Kentucky club leader, explained that the government had asked women to do their fighting "with the knife and fork by eliminating waste" and urged black women not to be "slackers, but measure up on the foremost line with the women of the world in this battle. We can win and come off the field with flying colors and we must win."[83] Black women also constantly cited their efforts at knitting, raising funds, and working for the Red Cross, YWCA, and WCND as examples of their good citizenship. Beyond praising such volunteer work, African American YWCA leaders emphasized the way in which black women factory workers supported the national defense.[84]

A strikingly visual way of expressing black women's contribution to the nation appeared on the March 1917 cover of the African American journal *Half-Century Magazine* (fig. 3). For the mainstream media and government propagandists, Lady Liberty, representing as she did the nation, was invariably and inevitably white. *Half-Century Magazine* challenged the convention. The use of the phrase "Maid in America" added to its commentary. "Maid" might refer to a young woman or to the domestic work relegated to African American women. The editor made clear that it was also a pun on "made," a

Figure 3. "Maid in America," an African American Lady Liberty. *Half-Century Magazine*, March 1917.

statement that reinforced the image that African Americans insisted upon claiming American identity and indeed that their loyalty to the United States was greater than "hyphenated" immigrant Americans.[85]

Although they were similar to white women in stressing their war work on behalf of Liberty Loans, the Red Cross, food conservation, and in defense factories, much of their energies focused on serving blacks in their local communities. They equated war work with the racial uplift that was so much a part of black women's activism. Thus when they provided entertainment and comfort kits for black soldiers and lobbied agencies like the YWCA to establish facilities for women and girls laboring in industrial defense work, they expressly understood it as serving their own communities. Charlotte Hawkins, of Sedalia, North Carolina, urged African American women to support the united war work campaign in November 1918 because of the service given by the YWCA and YMCA to black soldiers. She specifically noted the need for social work for young black women working on war orders in factories, arguing that many "are working under new conditions and strange environment, and all at top speed. They must be comfortably housed, and given recreation, sympathy and comfort."[86]

African American Women and the Protest against Discrimination

Despite the "closed ranks" imperative and the eagerness to demonstrate good citizenship, many black women protested against discrimination. Margaret Black, writing in the *Afro-American,* resented that blacks were "being snubbed, jim-crowed, thrust aside wherever possible, even by those who should at present time throw prejudice aside, and still we are asked 'To do our bit.'" Nonetheless, she encouraged her readers to do all they could to support the war.[87] Recognizing the power of military service for staking a claim to democratic rights, some black women criticized the lack of respect accorded black soldiers. About 360,000 black troops served during World War I, and 200,000 of these served abroad in the American Expeditionary Force (AEF). In the context of contemporary notions of gender, warfare, and citizenship, it is not surprising that many white leaders resisted drafting African Americans. Mississippi senator James Vardaman was explicit. Being in the military would encourage the black man to believe "that his political rights must be respected, even though it is necessary for him to give his life."[88] So pervasive was this attitude that at the beginning of the war, Kathryn M. Johnson, editor of *Half-Century,* a magazine targeted to black women, predicted that few black men would be allowed to wear the uniform but hoped that they would find other meaningful ways to contribute to the war effort and that "the time will surely come that conduct and not color will be the measure of manhood in the world."[89]

Although black men were drafted, the military maintained a strictly segregated army, and most black men witnessed the war in labor battalions, not as combat troops. A small cadre of officers was commissioned, and they too served in a Jim Crow army. Limiting blacks' exposure to combat reflected the military's attitude about blacks' aptitude in battle. Equally important was the desire to keep them as second-class soldiers whose access to heroic achievement and claims on citizenship were circumscribed. African American newspaper accounts of black troops abroad, however, generally referred to them as "fighters," and the black public might not have been aware of their limited opportunities for combat heroism.[90]

For black women, the Red Cross military nurse became the analogy to the soldier's claim to citizenship. African American women leaders complained about the discrimination they faced in various war agencies, including the WCND, the Red Cross, and the YWCA, but of particular concern was the nursing profession. In the preceding decades, white nurses ostracized black ones, whose access to training programs was limited. African American women founded their own professional organization, the National Association of Colored Graduate Nurses (NACGN), in 1906, and worked within a segregated system of education programs and hospitals to become qualified and to serve their communities. Unlike white nurses, who battled again sex discrimination, African Americans focused on race discrimination, especially in access to training, jobs, and state certification.[91]

As war approached, they were particularly concerned because the American Red Cross, which was the primary conduit for military nursing, barred African American nurses. The NACGN lobbied both the Red Cross and the surgeon general for months without success. The black press was incensed at the insult. The *Savannah Tribune* contrasted the numerous ways in which African American women had supported the war effort with the government's refusal to "honor and reward the Negro wing of this service by the recognition which comes with opportunities for field and overseas service." The newspaper explicitly argued that service abroad was the most significant form of patriotic duty. "Our women . . . want the chance to serve the soldier directly and to face with him the dangers of shot and shell. . . . Our women want the chance to risk their lives on the battlefield in the hospital service, like other women. They want the chance to die, if need be, for if they do not participate in this feature of the work they lack just so much of being full-fledged Red Cross workers."[92]

Extensive protest, on the part of the NACGN and the NACW as well as other black leaders, in addition to the devastating flu epidemic of 1918–19, eventually led the Red Cross to accept African American women, in July 1918. However, it made no commitment to send them overseas, which the *Savannah Tribune* felt deprived them of their ability "to register full participation in the great war in behalf of the Negro race" and democracy. Eighteen black women were accepted in the Army Nurse Corps in December 1918, after the Armistice, but no African American nurses served in Europe.[93]

Confronting Racial Violence in the Great War

African American men and women were discouraged by the discrimination meted out to their soldiers and nurses, but the persistence of racial violence during the war proved even more disheartening. The worst of the eighteen riots that occurred between 1915 and 1919 took place in East St. Louis, Illinois, an industrial city that received substantial African American migration in this era. Tensions were high, especially because white union organizers blamed the ample supply of African American laborers for the failure of strikes and the ability of employers to suppress unions. A brief riot had erupted in May 1917, but the full force of white violence against blacks began on July 1. After white men in cars drove into the black part of town and fired on African Americans, blacks retaliated, killing two plainclothes policemen. With that, white mobs invaded the black community, viciously beating and killing indiscriminately and torching the neighborhood, while the police stood by. By the next day, when peace was finally restored, at least thirty-nine blacks and eight whites were dead, and African Americans were fleeing the city en masse. East St. Louis had hardly been the promised land—blacks were heavily discriminated against, and despite a law prohibiting segregation, the city was as segregated as southern ones. African Americans had initially been optimistic about the possibilities of living and working in the North. The riot in East St. Louis was a bitter blow, made all the more discouraging in the context of their hopes that World War I would bring democratic change.[94]

The riot and the failure of authorities to stop the violence outraged the African American press and leadership. Predictably they emphasized the ironic juxtaposition of a "war for democracy" abroad with the outbreak of "atrocities" at home. Kathryn M. Johnson reported on her investigative trip to East St. Louis and the riot in the broad context of "ninety million whites" who have taken "vicious advantage of ten million Colored people . . . through numerous riots and lynchings," and yet "have no hesitation in asking them to fight to preserve and defend the same government that permits such atrocities." Margaret Black, writing in the *Afro-American*, praised black leaders who were determined to protest and send petitions to Washington, but she also concluded that "every man, woman and child over fourteen should know how to handle a gun, and not only know how to shoot but to shoot straight."[95]

Black women played an unusually important role in framing black response to what they routinely called a massacre. The NACW urged its members throughout the nation to turn to a familiar means of coping with crises: local prayer meetings designed to convey black women's spiritual and moral strength. But at the same time, the NACW started a petition drive to demand congressional action, a tactic that reflected the influence of the NAACP's determination to use lobbying and African Americans' increased voting power to influence legislation. The *New York Age* reported that black women in Washington, D.C., issued a call to prayer and protest. It urged them to not "stop praying until the voice of Negro women is heard and their petition for the suppression of mob violence is accepted by the American people, and lynching and slaughter of human beings be made a crime." But even as they rallied against mob violence, the women were careful to express their loyalty and service. "We propose to fight for our country to help against foes at home and abroad, to conserve food and fuel supplies, and we believe that the fight for Democracy must begin at Jerusalem (at home)."[96]

When the *Winston-Salem Journal* reported on the prayer meeting tactic, it acknowledged the role of NACW president Mary Talbert in the prayer/petition campaign but also emphasized that the "indefatigable" Nannie Burroughs was the driving force behind these efforts. Burroughs, a well-educated women noted for her powerful oratory, was best known for having established the National Training School for Women and Girls in Washington, D.C. In the wake of the riots, she used her position on the NACW's committee for the suppression of lynching to spring into action. Black newspapers carried accounts of her speeches and written comments about East St. Louis. As Burroughs publicized the crisis, she also promoted the petition drive and claimed to have presented over 10,000 signatures from thirty-six states to the Congressional Rules committee, where she, along with another woman, "made a plea for federal investigations and the passage and enforcement of laws that would make America a safe place in which the Colored American may live and labor." Burroughs was insistent on being recognized for her leadership and in particular criticized unnamed, but presumably male, leaders who tried to claim credit for the petition drive.[97]

Ida Wells-Barnett spearheaded another protest effort about the East St. Louis Riot. Wells-Barnett had long been recognized for her pioneering role in publicizing and analyzing lynching. Researching reported lynchings, she argued that the claim that black men had assaulted or raped white women rarely stood up and that white mobs targeted men who had achieved political or economic gains. In 1917, Wells-Barnett, along with her husband, Ferdinand Barnett, was a leader in black Chicago, although a controversial one, as more conservative black leaders felt that both husband and wife were too militant in their protests against racism and racial violence. The East St. Louis Riot galvanized Wells-Barnett. She made two investigative trips to the city and produced a pamphlet, "The East St. Louis Massacre: The Great Outrage of the Century," which detailed the vicious attacks on African Americans in great detail. Beyond publicity about the tragedy, she organized and led a delegation to Illinois governor Frank Lowden. Representing the National Equal Rights League, a militant civil rights organization that unrelentingly criticized discrimination during the war, she also traveled to Washington, D.C., where she presented a statement calling for a federal investigation of the events in East St. Louis. The document included a long list of other grievances and asked President Wilson to end racial segregation in federal offices and in interstate travel, and to enforce the Fourteenth and Fifteenth Amendments to the Constitution, "which forbid peonage and disfranchisement, thereby restoring to millions of Americans their civil and political rights." In keeping with wartime civil rights rhetoric, Wells-Barnett's petition invoked black patriotic service, claiming that "as American Citizens our lives are subjected to the Nation's call, and at no call have we faltered or failed. As American citizens we call to the Nation to save our lives; to that call will the Nation falter or fail?"[98]

A final example of protest about East St. Louis was the parade in New York City described in the opening of this chapter. In choosing an iconic venue, New York City's Fifth Avenue, protesters staked their claim as citizens to occupy an important public place. To emphasize the dramatic import of their protest, they marched silently to muffled drumbeats. Men and women marched separately. The women decided to wear white, which they explained symbolized "purity." Between 5,000 and 10,000 people marched on Fifth Avenue, carrying banners proclaiming African American patriotism and decrying racism and lynching. Although the parade was organized primarily by the male-led NAACP, hair and cosmetic entrepreneur Madam C. J. Walker had been central to promoting the event. A number of other cities subsequently staged similar marches in which women also played a notable role.[99] Speaking about a planned parade for Jersey City, Helen B. Pendleton, who was an organizer for the New Jersey State Negro Welfare League, said, "I want this parade. I want it to touch the hearts and reach the consciences of white people as to their attitude toward the negro. It will be a dignified and inspiring showing of the solidarity of the race, and their loyalty to our country's flag. . . . I hope every white man and woman will see it." She added, "It will bring home to them the fact that the negro doesn't get a square deal, especially in the way he is forced to live."[100]

The day after the New York parade, Walker joined several men in traveling to Washington, D.C., where they believed they had been promised an audience with the president. In the end, they had to settle with a meeting with Wilson's secretary, Joseph Tumulty. The group presented a petition that emphasized African American patriotism and, in particular, black men's willing response to the draft and "implored the President to 'use his great powers' to assist lynching victims and to use 'his great personal and moral influence in our behalf.'" The petition also argued, "No nation that seeks to fight the battles of civilization can afford to march in blood-smeared garments." Fifteen men and Walker signed the petition. The next month, Walker staged a convention of her sales agents. The Madam C.J. Walker Hair Culturists Union met in Philadelphia and, in addition to addressing issues connected to their product and telling their success stories, the women sent a telegram to President Wilson, protesting the racial violence and calling for an anti-lynching bill.[101] Walker used her national network, as well as her significant influence as a successful entrepreneur, to promote racial pride and to swell the ranks of women protesting lynching during World War I.

Barely recovered from the crisis of East St. Louis, African Americans faced another trauma in late August when black soldiers in Houston rioted, killing seventeen whites and wounding another eleven. The soldiers were part of the regular army—not draftees—many of whom had served in the Philippines during the insurrection against the United States in 1906–8, and they had a clear notion of military service having secured them rights as well as reinforcing their claims to "manhood." When the members of the 3rd Battalion of the 24th Infantry were stationed in Houston, however, problems began immediately. Whites resented "uppity" uniformed blacks, over whom they had relatively little control, and skirmishes between whites and black soldiers multiplied.

Tensions erupted on August 24 when two white sheriffs harassed a black woman in her home and treated her roughly as they arrested her for daring to protest their search. Calling Sara Travers "one of these biggity nigger women," the policemen refused to even let her dress properly before dragging her down the street, a clear affront to her respectability. When a black soldier in uniform, Private Alonzo Edwards, attempted to intervene, one of the policemen repeatedly pistol-whipped him. Corporal Charles Baltimore, an African American member of the Military Police, subsequently attempted to find out what had happened, and he too was beaten. False rumors swirled around the army base that Baltimore had been killed and that a white mob was assembling (neither was true). Eventually, armed black soldiers followed the lead of Sergeant Vida Henry into town. As historian Adriane Lentz-Smith put it, "Having established their civic manhood by fighting enemies outside the nation's borders, they would defend it by attacking the enemy within."[102] The riot, technically a mutiny, lasted two hours. The government quickly moved the 3rd Battalion out of Houston and court-martialed sixty-three members of the battalion. Thirteen were hanged in secret, forty-one received life prison terms, nine received lesser jail time, and five were acquitted.

African American leaders regretted the violence, but few condemned the rioters wholeheartedly. Most stressed the patterns of insults and violence African Americans faced and implicitly honored the soldiers for standing up for "their manhood." As the *Savannah Tribune* put it, the black rioters "were more sinned against than sinned."[103] Some women's voices emerged about the issue. In Chicago, the Federation of Women's Clubs passed a resolution to send to President Wilson requesting a thorough investigation of the soldiers who had been imprisoned, concluding that "we pray and demand that justice be meted out to those prepared to shed blood for the preservation of the flag."[104]

Carlotta Bass, activist and owner/managing editor of the *California Eagle*, visited Houston shortly after the riot and interviewed a number of African Americans, including Sara Travers. In a lengthy article, Bass excoriated the treatment accorded black soldiers and civilians in Houston. She defended the soldiers who rioted, reporting that some of them had "stated that their only reason for their behavior upon this occasion was to convince that rough white element, who no doubt would have invaded the camp that very evening that they were prepared to defend their rights as American citizens." Implicitly equating the Houston violence with East St. Louis, she announced that "the colored people of the west must get busy and with the race men and women of the east and demonstrate that, as law abiding American citizens through the medium of grand silent parade we resent the present treatment of White America against Black Americans all over this country."[105]

The most remarkable published comment by a black woman appeared in the *San Antonio Inquirer*. Texas teacher Clara L. Threadgill-Dennis, a "guest contributor," wrote an impassioned article that placed the uprising squarely in the context of gender, maintaining that the black soldiers had "dared protect a Negro woman from the insult of a southern brute in the form of a policeman." Although she expressed regret that the mutiny had taken place and that innocent people had died, she insisted that "it is far better that you be shot for having tried to protect a Negro woman, than to have you die a natural death in the trenches of Europe, fighting to make the world safe for a democracy that you can't enjoy." Complaining about the insults black women constantly encountered to their respectability, she concluded by praising the court-martialed soldiers, explaining that they had died "for the most sacred thing on the earth to any race, even the southern white man, his daughter's, his wife's, his mother's, his sister's, his neighbor's sister's protection from insult."[106]

Threadgill-Dennis's comments encapsulated many of the grievances of African American women. She expressed outrage over the treatment of soldiers, certainly, but she also highlighted the vulnerability of African American women and the difficulty black men faced in protecting them. By referring to white men's desire to protect their women from "insult," she also implicitly acknowledged the irony of white society's concern for white women's virtue when in fact African American women were far more vulnerable to sexual attack and insults to their respectability. Such outspoken language justifying the mutiny was dangerous, and it is not surprising that there are so few public statements by women. Both Threadgill-Dennis and the editor of the paper were arrested by federal authorities, although apparently only the editor was found guilty under the Espionage Act and imprisoned.[107]

Ida B. Wells, too, drew federal attention for her response to the Houston uprising. She began selling buttons reading, "In Memoriam, Martyred Negro Soldiers. Dec. 11, 1917." She reported that her husband worried that she would "get into trouble," but she countered by noting, "No one can criticize me as disloyal. I have helped to send hundreds of comfort kits to our Negro soldiers at Camp Grant. No Negro soldier has ever been shot as a coward." Visited by U.S. agents who accused her of "treason," she reported in her autobiography that she said, "I'd rather go down in history as one lone Negro who dared to tell the government that it had done a dastardly thing than to save my skin by taking back what I have said." Moreover, she refused to stop selling the buttons. The government resolved the button sale by pressuring the button manufacturer to agree to stop supplying Wells-Barnett.[108]

A more isolated protest staged by black women about another violent episode sums up in many ways the sentiment of black women activists seeking to claim their democratic rights and indeed their humanity in the context of the world war. In May 1918 in Valdosta, Georgia, a particularly horrific lynching "orgy" took place, in which at least eleven African Americans were killed. One of them was a woman. When Mary Turner, eight months pregnant, protested the murder of her husband, she, too, was brutally murdered. Black women in nearby Augusta called on women of their city and state "to unite in a service of humiliation and prayer as a protect against the awful lynchings that recently disgraced our state, especially that of Mary Turner."

Instead of meeting at a church, the women, who had just created a federation of City Colored Women's Clubs, chose to convene at the Toussaint L'Overture Branch of the American Red Cross. Choosing the Red Cross as their venue suggests their determination to frame themselves as loyal citizens serving the nation, yet the decision to name the branch after Haitian revolutionary Toussaint Louverture also reveals an insistence upon honoring a history of black resistance to injustice. After their prayer service, the women passed a resolution that they sent to President Wilson, Governor Hugh Dorsey, and the presidents of the state and local white women's club federation. The document explained that the black women of the state "were aroused by this unwarranted lawlessness and are discouraged and crushed by a spirit of humiliation and dread," and urged that "you use all the power of your great office to prevent similar occurrences and punish the perpetrators of this foul deed and urge that sure and swift justice be meted out to them."[109] Although the women's resolution emphasized black men's contributions to America's war as soldiers, it also acknowledged women's labor in an unusual way. Reflecting their southern agrarian context, they honored black women who worked in the fields, valorizing them as serving the national interest.

The Atlanta women did not refer specifically to the broader question of the sexual threat to black women's bodies that was so evident in Threadgill-Dennis's letter, but the focus on Mary Turner's lynching does highlight their concern about black women's vulnerability. Not only did the women send protests to government officials, but they also addressed white clubwomen in Georgia. Having just established their own city federation for black clubwomen, which immediately followed a meeting in Savannah of Georgia's state federation of black clubwomen, the meeting at the Red Cross headquarters suggests the way in which African American women were looking to organizational strength of women's clubs as a means of strengthening their community and expressing their protest.[110]

This effort signals a key aspect of the impact of World War I on black women leaders. While clubwomen were still interested in the themes of racial uplift through moral reform and community service, many became more militant in their defense of civil rights. The war, as well as the Great Migration, would raise African American expectations. Disillusioned by continued discrimination and a wave of race riots in 1919, many black men and women race leaders became more militant in the 1920s, calling for a "new negro." Although the militant new negro, much celebrated in the black press, was held up as a masculinized ideal, black women too sought to be part of the enhanced campaign for racial justice. Continuing their commitment to fighting racial violence, for example, a group of women in the NACW organized the Anti-Lynching Crusaders as part of the NAACP in 1922 to lobby and raise funds for the Dyer Anti-Lynching Bill. Armed with the suffrage amendment, they also developed grassroots organizing skills in their campaign to get black women to register to vote in southern states where African Americans had been disenfranchised for decades. More successfully, they urged northern black women to vote, which gave them limited traction with the Republican Party. Although these campaigns met with relatively little success, they persisted in their political activism in behalf of racial justice.

African American women leaders had based their claim for political agency during World War I on their loyalty and patriotic service. Faced with persistent discrimination and violence, they used the war and the nation's professed democratic aims to bolster their call for racial and human justice. Although white suffragists' experiences were significantly different from those of black women, they similarly used America's war for democracy to further their campaign for the vote and political power. Black women saw few tangible results from their wartime protests, but there is no question that World War I was instrumental in accelerating the passage of the Nineteenth Amendment, making it the most enduring legacy of World War I for American women.

In other ways, the war era facilitated woman's movement into the political arena. Women pacifists, drawing upon maternalist ideas about women's voice in decisions about war and peace, as well as upon reformers' concerns about the damage war would do to progressive social justice reform efforts, worked tirelessly—if unsuccessfully—to influence international politics and the nature of diplomacy itself. Opposing them, female preparedness advocates might have expressed conventional notions about women's proper role in the home, but they nonetheless challenged those ideas as they, too, sought to shape the nation's stance toward war. This division between conservative women and liberal reformers and pacifists would continue to shape and constrain postwar American women's political activism.

Most women activists during World War I maintained a relatively genteel demeanor, despite their call for political power. African American clubwomen, who had a long history of stressing their respectability, might have been outspoken during the war, but they rarely challenged expectations about women's public persona. And many white women associated with NAWSA similarly adopted conventional public behavior despite their insistence upon women's equality. Even these women, however, hinted at behavioral changes. Before the war, the suffrage parades had evoked scandalized comments. But in the context of patriotic displays of martial enthusiasm, even preparedness women marched in public, representing a symbolic encroachment of women into public and indeed political space. The same is true for the silent protest marches of African American men and women. If this occupation of public space did not accord women significant political power, it did signal evolving notions of women's respectability and civic participation.

More dramatically, the war also witnessed the spectacle of "disorderly" new women. The way in which antiwar radicals like Emma Goldman and Rose Pastor Stokes were vilified, as much for their challenge to the gender order as to the political order, suggests how great a challenge the "new" woman presented to mainstream America. Perhaps even more alarming were the militant new women of the NWP who transgressed against genteel womanhood when they so spectacularly picketed the White House and welcomed arrest as ammunition for their cause. As the following chapters will argue, World War I and the nation's need for citizens' participation in mobilization efforts offered many American women opportunities for challenging the barriers that constrained their behavior and for pursuing their political and personal agendas, mostly in the name of patriotic service. The long-term meaning of these challenges was mixed, but, at least in the short run, many women would find new agency in the midst of war.

TWO

Channeling Womanpower

Maternalism and World War I Mobilization

> You cannot meet a woman today who looks to a return to the pleasant dilettantism of prewar days. . . . They have sipped the nectar of the reward of achievement. They have discovered themselves, their capacity, their possibilities, and, above all, their amenity to united action, once deemed foreign to the sex. And they have tasted the flavor of power—that power that comes from united cooperation by which miracles can be performed.
>
> *Mrs. Herbert Cable on postwar expectations for American women*

The sense of agency—the "flavor of power"—that many women activists experienced during World War I was made possible in large part by the very nature of the war itself. Modern global wars have required extensive civilian mobilization and raise a vital question. How does a nation-state convince its citizens to support a war? While the question, "Why do soldiers fight?" is a compelling one, equally intriguing are related queries. How and why do civilians on the home front contribute to the nation's mobilization? And, more specifically, how and why do women citizens support a war? During World War I, why did Slovakian American women roll bandages for the Red Cross? Why did African American women engage in protective work for black soldiers and women defense workers? Why did white women reformers cast child health programs as war measures? And why did millions of women knit socks for soldiers, raise funds for the government's Liberty Loan drive, and sign food conservation cards that made them part of the "kitchen army?"[1]

The answers are complicated, encompassing many variables, ranging from preexisting cultural norms and instruments of state power to the nature of a specific war. During World War I, all the major combatants relied upon coercion to suppress dissent and corral support, but in varying degrees they also turned to voluntary associations, especially those of middle-class and elite women, to disseminate propaganda, raise funds, and conserve food and matériel. This was especially true in the United States, where women's voluntary mobilization reveals the complex interplay between the federal government's drive to pursue its war aims at home and abroad and citizens' desires to define and shape their contributions to securing victory. And as women leaders constructed their war service, they used it to promote their prewar agendas and especially to legitimate their claims to citizenship and political agency.[2]

This chapter has two goals. One is to explore the process of war mobilization among representative women's organizations to illuminate the mechanisms by which voluntary associations mediated between nation and citizens to create support for the war. Americans in cities mobilized for the war effort through a network of diverse organizations that drew their membership into a wide variety of programs. The Chamber of Commerce, Red Cross, Young Men's and Young Women's Christian Associations, and fraternal orders like the Freemasons or the Knights of Columbus all adapted their organizations to war work. Such groups became vehicles for disseminating the messages created by the powerful wartime propaganda office, the Committee on Public Information (CPI).[3] Crucial to this voluntarism were women's organizations. There is some evidence of activity among Asian, Mexican, and European immigrant communities, and this chapter specifically explores the mobilization work of black middle-class women, but for the most part white middle-class and elite women dominated the volunteer effort. It is also this group that has left behind the most extensive record of its efforts. Members represented only a fraction of American women, but their war activities nonetheless constituted a vital component of mobilization that underlines the role of voluntary associations in creating support for the war.

In addition to examining the federal government's use of women's voluntary associations as instruments of the nation-state, the second aim of this chapter is to explore the ways in which women activists conjoined the war emergency to their own goals of staking their claim to full citizenship, maintaining the vitality of their organizations, and continuing their reform agendas begun in the Progressive Era. The context of the suffrage movement was crucial to their participation in war mobilization. But so, too, were maternal reforms, evident in the way in which white women articulated a gendered justification for supporting the war that emphasized the instrumental role that women citizens played in protecting the family in the midst of the crisis of war. African American activists similarly emphasized the centrality of women citizens, but did so in the specific context of racial uplift. The emphasis placed on the family led women reformers, white and black, in two somewhat contradictory directions. The activism and the accomplishments of the reformers signaled a "new" woman citizen, who was taking her place in a modern world. Yet their maternalist ideology, which stressed women's role in the family, reinforced conventional notions of women's proper place and reflected the challenges women faced in breaking down barriers to greater equality in the war and in the postwar years.

THE WOMAN'S COMMITTEE OF THE COUNCIL OF NATIONAL DEFENSE

Once the United States entered the war, as we have seen, most women reformers and suffragists proved eager to contribute to mobilization, although they expected to do so on their own terms. The federal government intended the Woman's Committee of the Council of National Defense (WCND) purely as an advisory body, but the committee members, headed by former NAWSA president Anna Howard Shaw, had their own conception of making their organization a "channel" for delivering woman power to the war effort. Shaw anticipated that the WCND would facilitate this work through the major national women's organizations, which would in turn promote coordination on the local level of cities and states. To this end, it created an Honorary Committee of over seventy organizations that represented groups ranging from the International Federation of Catholic Alumnae to the Council of Jewish Women, from the Women's Trade Union League to the Woman's Christian Temperance Union, from the National Association Opposed to Woman Suffrage to the National American Woman Suffrage Association, from the United Daughters of the Confederacy to the National Association of Colored Women. Although black women were included in the honorary committee, for the most part African American women and women of color in general were marginalized in the WCND. As we will see below, women who were part of racial and ethnic minority groups did find ways to participate in war mobilization, as did working-class women, but for the most part women's mobilization, especially within the WCND, was dominated by white leisure class women, and the following discussion of the committee's activity focuses on this group.[4]

It is not surprising that affluent, educated women would be at the center of local citizen mobilization. First, they constituted the most leisured segment of the population, and only people with a degree of time on their hands or significant personal resources could devote much time to unpaid war work. For all the World War I rhetorical enthusiasm for voluntarism as a means of fighting a war democratically, voluntarism was of course constrained by and even defined by class. And it was shaped by gender. While men certainly formed a significant part of the volunteer cadre during World War I, the federal government, just as it had done in the Civil War, drew heavily upon the unpaid labor of white elite and middle-class women to implement scores of programs in support of the war effort.[5] A second reason for women's high visibility was that they were already organized in numerous clubs and organizations. In most cities, white clubwomen participated in a national network of like-minded women, a network that is crucial to understanding the way in which women tackled mobilization and the way in which the WCND operated.

Organizing Women for War Service

Having established its national framework, the WCND set up state and local branches. Dividing its work into departments, which included specific war concerns such as food conservation and Liberty Loans, it also had units focused on social welfare issues that women reformers had embraced during the Progressive Era, including "child welfare," "maintenance of existing social services," and "women in industry."[6]

Although these women had assumed that they would coordinate female volunteers throughout the country, they found that they had little power or decision-making authority. Federal departments—the Treasury's Liberty Loan campaign or the Food Administration, for example—often ignored the WCND's organizational framework, creating separate bureaucratic structures that frustrated the WCND's efforts at efficiency and influence. In numerous states, men who controlled the state Councils of Defense refused funding for women's activities and were resentful because so many local women's WCNDs preferred to take direction from their national leadership rather than the men who ran the local and state Councils of Defense. Dismayed by the hostile attitude of both national and state male leaders in the Council of National Defense, the national leaders were critical of the male bureaucracy, which they believed did not know how to approach women effectively, and which they felt often was mired in confusion.[7]

But women's groups also made their own mark on institutional confusion. Both nationally and in many communities, conflicts erupted between women's groups over responsibilities and activities that created ill-feeling and duplication of efforts. A major problem for the WCND was that the month before the United States entered the war, a group of women created the National League for Women's Service that aimed to do precisely what the government expected of the WCND. Popular especially in the Midwest and on the East Coast, the league sometimes worked well with the WCND but often set up programs that conflicted with the central leadership the WCND women hoped to establish. Suffrage and antisuffrage sentiment also troubled the national WCND, which was dominated by suffrage proponents but included women lukewarm or hostile to suffrage. And, finally, the ability of women to organize effectively varied by state. States where women were already enfranchised, such as Illinois and California, and thus with a history of political activism, were the ones most likely to make a success of the ambitious programs women sought to implement.[8]

Yet despite tensions, state and local activities of the WCND indicate that women's mobilization efforts as a whole were remarkably successful. One key aspect of their service were programs specifically designed to respond to government requests for women's participation, such as fund-raising for the Liberty Loan and Red Cross campaigns and the push for food conservation. As they mounted their efforts, WCND leaders on the local and national levels always conjoined their descriptions of women's activism to a notion of female citizenship that had as its special obligation the protection of home and family in the context of the disorder of war. And they aimed to show the efficiency and competency of this citizenship.

A close look at the organization of Los Angeles's WCND offers insights into the dynamics of the drive to meet government expectations for war mobilization. California women were particularly active in the state and local branches of the WCND. In Los Angeles, published reports and private correspondence reveal a strong sense of accomplishment on the part of the members for their committee, which they described as "a clearing house thru which the war activities demanded by the United States government of the women of Los Angeles have been largely conducted." The city committee, which was a subset of a Los Angeles county organization, relied on an elaborate system of door-to-door canvassing, a procedure used elsewhere in the state that was described, tellingly, as the "woman's army."[9]

The women created an impressive organizational structure. They divided Los Angeles into 800 precincts, with a committee for each. In addition to this geographical framework, the city committee, much like the WCND, drew extensively upon already-established women's clubs, by sending out a message to 350 women's organizations, asking them to send representatives to a planning meeting. No list exists of that entire group, but the board members elected suggest a degree of inclusiveness. In addition to women who represented elite groups like the Friday Morning Club and Ebell were those identified as associated with "Catholic Women of Los Angeles," "Jewish Women of Los Angeles," and "Labor Organizations," although references to the latter did not appear elsewhere in the WCND's records and few details exist about Catholic or Jewish women's contributions. Inclusiveness had its limits, moreover; no women of color were part of the board, although it is possible that some were rank-and-file participants. If so, they are invisible in the historical record. In many other cities in the country, as discussed below, black women had more representation in the WCND but almost always participated in a segregated context.[10]

The majority of over 29,000 women listed as active in the Los Angeles branch of the WCND apparently participated through their club memberships, and the fact that Los Angeles women's prewar organizational life was so strong may well explain the apparent success of the local WCND. The significance of the women's club framework cannot be overemphasized and provides an important clue to understanding the dynamics of war mobilization across the country. So much a part of civic-minded women were their voluntary associations that government agencies almost automatically viewed them as the representative institutions of all female citizens, a point WCND historian Emily Newell Blair made when she noted that "there seems to be a general acceptance of the idea that when you deal with women, you go to their organizations, when you deal with men you go to the governor or a legislature." "In effect," she added, women "could not, under the political system, function directly through the government."[11]

If the government reinforced the role of women's organizations by turning to them for home-front service, women's club officials seized the opportunity to further promote the prestige and influence of their institutions. They frequently discussed war work as a means of building interest in their organizations and eagerly sought publicity for their contributions to mobilization. Newspaper reportage was usually framed in terms of specific contributions of local women's clubs. This dynamic of voluntarism helps to explain how the federal government could achieve so much success through the use of voluntary agencies in its wartime drives for citizen mobilization. In peacetime, a major role of voluntary association leaders was to maintain the membership's interest in order to keep their associations vital. Always eager to find meaningful work with which to associate their organizations, during wartime, club officials promoted activities that enhanced institutional pride while stimulating patriotic service. This dynamic was not limited to women's organizations but could be seen as well in men's groups, such as the Chamber of Commerce, fraternal organizations, and labor unions. Both male and female organizations across the nation adopted their institutions' patterns to the war effort.[12]

Women's participation in war work and in civil life was different than men's, however, for the recent success of woman suffrage in California and New York notwithstanding, political opportunities for women were still circumscribed and they were very conscious of the need to demonstrate their sense of civic responsibility. In June 1917, Mrs. Shelley Tolhurst, speaking at the Los Angeles City Club about war service, proclaimed that "for the first time . . . women are being recognized as citizens in the government."[13] Tolhurst's comment could have been heard in any city or town in the nation. For many women, especially those active in suffrage or reform efforts before the war, this new sense of citizenship was thrilling. Mrs. A. Merrick of Michigan wrote to the WCND that "I take an almost indecent delight on my appointment to the government," and, repeatedly, WCND officials at local, state, and national levels of leadership invoked this new sense of citizenship to spur women on to greater service but as well to insist upon respect for women's contributions to the country in time of crisis.[14]

Women Citizens Register for War Duty

The political implications of women's war service emerged quite clearly in the campaigns to register women for war service. These predated the founding of the WCND, as both the National League for Woman's Service and the Women's Section of the Navy League began programs to mobilize women in February 1917 as part of a broader commitment to preparedness.[15] By the time the WCND was established, hundreds of thousands of women had signed up under various auspices, and the new organization stepped in with the hope of bringing order to the process. It created a national card for service that asked women for basic identifying information and then provided boxes to be checked for types of volunteer and paid labor and for expressing interest in various types of training. But rather than attempt national coordination, it left the decision and mechanisms for registration to the states. Figure 4 suggests why Louisiana was so successful. The New Orleans WCND and Women's Liberty Loan Committee ran compelling ads like this one that

Figure 4. Registration drive: women answer the call of Columbia. *Times-Picayune*, October 17, 1917, 31.

invoked the iconic patriotic imagery of "Columbia," attracting a long line of women eager to serve the nation by buying Liberty Bonds and registering for war service. As Chapter 5 argues, the snappy military look of the women's outfits also suggested a link between women's participation in the war effort and men's military service. Louisiana's enthusiastic effort may have been exceptional. Only about half of the states proceeded with registration. In fourteen of them, governors specified registration days, and some states had enabling legislation requiring the census. Some states—Michigan, Illinois, Pennsylvania, and Louisiana—were well organized and turned out significant numbers of women registrants. But others met with very weak response. In South Carolina, for example, only 1 percent of women registered. By the end of the war, over 4 million women across the nation, however, had registered for service.[16]

Accounts of the WCND efforts on the state level to promote women's registration suggest some of the dilemmas attending the mobilization of voluntary effort in time of war, especially the potentially controversial entry of women into the public sphere. Resistance to registration stemmed from numerous causes. Some questioned the utility of registration. Others worried about its coercive implications, and, repeatedly, leaders reassured potential registrants that making oneself available for service was voluntary. According to officials, as well as newspaper accounts, the fear of involuntary service was particularly evident among foreign-born women and rural dwellers. In addition to the fear that women might be conscripted was the fear that, by registering, women might endanger their husbands' draft exemptions.[17]

Yet another source of resistance was the belief that registration was tied to the suffrage movement. In northern Louisiana, one historian reports that "a number of men concerned with a false report that the registration was somehow connected to the women's suffrage movement, threatened to 'kick up an awful row within the shadow of the family hearthstone.'" There and elsewhere, women leaders hastened to reassure the public that there was no connection between the registration and the campaign for votes for women. These disclaimers may in some cases have been disingenuous. In Montgomery, Alabama, an irate letter to the editor claimed that the city's low registration figures were not a result of a lack of patriotism but rather that the process, and indeed the WCND itself, had been co-opted by the suffrage movement. The writer insisted that, in refusing to register, local women were expressing their resentment of the "attempt on the part of the suffrage organization to capitalize on the patriotism of Alabama women to further their propaganda." And, indeed, in Alabama, the organizing force behind the registration drive was not the WCND per se, but rather a suffrage organization, which, according to a sympathetic newspaper, had charge of the work because the government recognized that the suffrage organization was "the only one in Alabama which covers the entire State and the only body of women sufficiently organized to efficiently take hold of the big job."[18]

The linkage between registration and the suffrage movement appeared in other states as well. The connection between encouraging women to register for service and the hope that women might soon be registering to vote emerged in the way many cities' registration process and vocabulary underlined the relationship between the two types of registration. States varied as to how and where women registered, with some locales using department stores and women's clubs as sites for women to sign up. But it was also common to use existing political machinery. In Missouri, the registration process mimicked the state's electoral one, where precinct polling places as well as schoolhouses were used for the drive. The *Kansas City Star* explicitly reported on the registration process using electoral terms and comparisons to male voting: "The Office of the election commission was going full click and figure last night. But there were no black cigars, no profanity, no solemn expectoration, . . . and but for pink shirtwaists and an occasional dab of powder on the nose, it might have been any election night." Many observers and women themselves, then, could view the registration process as a symbolic entry into the political arena.[19]

This theme appeared in another comparison as well. In a number of instances, reporters likened registration to a female version of the draft. In Illinois, the *Belleville News Democrat* headlined that there was a "Military Air about Women's Registration: Captains, Lieutenants, and Sergeants for War Council Organization." And in Ohio, the *Cleveland Plain Dealer* commented on the possibility that women's registration might take place on the same day as men registered for the draft, noting approvingly that "conscription registration day may be given added color by the sight of Ohio mothers and daughters moving 'forward, a bright brigade,' to the school houses of city and hamlet to place their names and capabilities on the record."[20]

The vocabulary surrounding the registration drive suggested the way in which women could claim a symbolic expression of citizenship and service in time of war, especially important when male citizenship was so clearly tied to the ultimate sacrifice of giving one's life for one's country. But what of its practical use? In some states, government employment bureaus attempted to seize registration lists from the WCND to assist them in their compilation of a federal job registry, a move that created enormous tension between the Department of Labor and the WCND in many localities, but which suggests that registration had clear value.[21] Certainly, in states where turnout was high, there was an extraordinary enthusiasm for what women organizers had accomplished and how they had done it. In Louisiana and Illinois, for example, newspaper reports indicate a high degree of coordination and systemization, using phones, cars, and messengers. The WCND organization facilitated success with the foreign-born, a group of women viewed as resisting registration. And despite the general unwillingness of white women to work with African Americans, these states also reported significant enrollment on the part of African American women. In so doing, they may well have proved the claim that registration had the potential for engaging a wide range of women citizens in understanding their role in supporting the war effort.[22]

THE WCND AND MATERNALIST SOCIAL REFORM

When reporters and women officials described the registration drive, they frequently invoked the claim that "the government" wanted or even required women to register, thereby obscuring that the root of the drive was the women who clamored for registration as part of defining women's citizenship in the context of war. That women leaders pursued their own agendas while mobilizing support for war was particularly evident in the priority the WCND and other women's agencies assigned to maintaining the prewar trajectory for women's support for maternalist social reform, which for decades had been central to the way in which women reformers and suffrage activists had been framing a view of women's civil roles. Excluded from male-dominated political parties and patronage, these women formed a separate political culture that offered them avenues for influence and leadership, opportunities that the war enhanced.

Operating on the margins of political power encouraged many women reformers to be more willing than many men of their class to embrace expansion of the state for social purposes, seeing in agencies like the Children's Bureau institutions they could influence and use for maternalist reforms. This federal agency was created in 1912, largely through the lobbying efforts of female reformers in settlement houses and in organizations like the National Child Labor Committee and the National Consumers League, assisted by a far-flung network of women's clubs, most notably the General Federation of Women's Clubs. Women's groups throughout the country assisted the bureau. In effect, voluntary associations became an administrative arm of a federal agency. Historian Robyn Muncy has dubbed the women's groups associated with the Children's Bureau "the female dominion of reform," a term that may also be used more broadly to describe Progressive Era white women activists.[23]

While prewar pacifism muted some women's enthusiasm for the war and the nationalism that accompanied it, others, including the majority of the women who headed up the WCND, could view the war and the expansion of the power of the federal government as vehicles for promoting both the female dominion's social reform goals and woman suffrage. Thus primed for civic service, exposed to the Children's Bureau's model of volunteer/government cooperation, and amenable to notions of a benevolent state, these leaders seized on the opportunity to demonstrate their citizenship in partnership with a suddenly more powerful and expansive federal government. While women activists indicated their willingness to follow federal directives, they also revealed a commitment to define the nature of women's voluntary war service. Although maternalism emphasized women's difference based on their reproductivity and thus implicitly undermined their claim to equality with men, reformers were rarely troubled by this potential inconsistency. They framed women's war service in gendered terms that they felt empowered women by emphasizing their role in protecting the home and family. The WCND signaled its determination to continue maternalist reform efforts, despite the war, through its creation of a committee on existing social agencies, designed to encourage vigilance in maintaining social welfare programs and legislation, particularly those connected to women and children. Most state committees had similar agencies, but they varied in the level of attention given to protecting women and children. In well-organized states, however, WCND women took this aspect of their charge seriously, devoting particular attention to the Americanization of immigrants, the conditions of women in industry, and the promotion of child welfare programs.

Women and Americanization Programs

Given the widespread fear about "hyphenated," and thus potentially disloyal, Americans, it is not surprising that reformers interpreted immigrant outreach programs as important to war mobilization. Well before the war, urban white women's clubs, reflecting anxieties about unassimilated immigrants and the social problems clubwomen felt they engendered, had supported projects to facilitate immigrant education and assimilation.[24] During the war, the WCND was only one of several women's institutions that viewed Americanization as especially vital. In the states the WCND women frequently worked with the YWCA and the DAR. The DAR was particularly intent on what it called establishing an "All-American America" and created clubs to inculcate "real" American values for immigrant women. Its leaders called for mandatory attendance at public schools and enforced acquisition of English and even of the words to the *Star-Spangled Banner*.[25] But as noted in Chapter 1, WCND women, too, frequently insisted upon a zealous conformity to 100 percent Americanism. And, indeed, so many local WCND engaged in hunts for dissidents that the WCND felt compelled to issue a warning against "vigilantism."[26]

In contrast, some WCND Americanization efforts indicate a much more tolerant approach to the foreign-born. Unlike the anxious nativist sentiments expressed frequently in the *Los Angeles Times* and among businessmen of the city, for example, the Los Angeles WCND approach to immigrants was sympathetic, if condescending. The state's WCND created an Americanization department charged with investigating immigrant life in terms of "housing, industry, recreation, child welfare, education, citizenship, patriotism." That the state WCND viewed Americanization work as part of a broader pattern of social reform was further indicated by its postwar report, which insisted that assimilation required "industrial justice in wages, hours and sanitary surroundings, and safety conditions in shops and camps." And, in language that clearly set the WCND in opposition to conservative Los Angeles businessmen, the report concluded that "no amount of English education will overcome un-American conditions offered by employers."[27]

Although the original goal had been to improve the quality of life of immigrants while encouraging them to see themselves as "part and not an adjunct of America," the exigencies of war meant that the major attention to immigrants came in the efforts to draw the foreign-born community into support for the war. Thus, throughout the nation, WCND committees paid special attention to alerting immigrant families to the need for food conservation, an area where, according to one report, "it needed only interpretation to an intelligent conservation in which the foreign born women held their own in understanding and in the contribution of valuable suggestions." According to WCND reports, local immigrant communities eagerly responded to the call for food conservation and home gardens.[28]

The WCND focused specifically on immigrant women, and the tone of its descriptions reflects the belief that women reformers could create special bonds with immigrant mothers and facilitate their Americanization. When the Los Angeles WCND organized English classes for foreign-born women in the summer of 1917, it reported, "When the school is a social event, accompanied occasionally by light refreshments, and when the young teachers who preside over it act more in the capacity of genial hostesses than stern pedagogues, the school begins to take on the nature of a neighborhood recreation." Laden with ethnocentrism and condescension, these women's approaches to Americanization nonetheless suggest that many women reformers who supported the war consciously countered the illiberal nativism of the war era by portraying immigrants in a positive light and did so from a distinctly female point of view.[29]

Protecting Working Women

An equally urgent social problem was women's influx into war-related jobs. The context of reformers' concerns was the years of reform activism that had led to wage and hours legislation in the states for women workers. This legislative campaign stemmed from concern about the economic hardships working-class women endured, as well as the deleterious effects of industrial labor on women's health. The catchphrase "mothers of the race" captured the belief that as potential mothers all women workers were put at reproductive risk by long hours in unhealthful conditions. Weak women would produce weak children. Factory women who were single risked potential children's health, while working mothers damaged the children they already had.

Nineteen states passed new hours legislation between 1909 and 1917. Although women's health may have benefited from restrictions (where employers did not find ways to avoid obeying the law), the downside was that women's wages often suffered from reduced hours, setting up a tension between working women and reformers. At the same time, seven states by 1917 severely restricted women's night work, drawing especially on the argument that such work attracted impoverished married women, who, exhausted after a night at the factory, could not properly care for their children in the daytime. Laws also commonly prohibited women from working in saloons or as messengers, for fear that such labor exposed them to sexual danger. As with the case of hours limitations, these restrictions often closed doors for working women. Finally, a push for minimum wage laws met with some success in a few states before the war but had limited impact on women's income.[30]

Many of the reformers (and the many working women who supported protective legislation) embraced maternalist ideas about women's physical vulnerability but also viewed hours and wage legislation as an opening wedge that would improve conditions for both male and female workers. For them, the emphasis on difference was more pragmatic than ideological. Nonetheless, the thrust of maternalist protective legislation was to reinforce the idea that women were secondary wage earners. The laws and the rhetoric around them of "mothers of the race" reinscribed ideas about physical difference and, indeed, weakness and assumed that most working women were young and unmarried temporary workers whose future reproductivity needed to be protected, even if such efforts limited women's opportunities to find equality in the workplace.[31]

Once the United States entered World War I, reformers quickly recognized that the pressure for defense industrial production might endanger these hard-fought gains in protective legislation. They repeatedly cited the British example, where men and women early in the war worked to the breaking point, with absenteeism, poor work, and accidents rampant, leading the British government to establish regulations regarding hours and conditions. They worried, too, that employers would exploit women by using them to bring down wages and thus clamored for "equal pay for equal work" so that women would not undercut the male wage structure, a reflection—at least initially—of fears for the working-class family as much as for individual women workers.

Although many WCND women were overtly hostile to the idea that women might take on heavy industrial work during the crisis, the national committee, recognizing the inevitable, was determined that such women be protected in their labor. In 1917, it issued a statement, "Standards for the Employment of Women in Work on War Supplies," in which it called for no piecework in the home; no child labor; no employment of women two months before and after childbirth; equal pay for equal work; eight-hour days, unless suspended by federal order; no night shifts; the restriction of "extra heavy and extra hazardous occupations"; and no work in "dangerous trades." Despite a call for equal pay for equal work, the overarching theme of the WCND approach to women's work was decidedly maternal—with the insistence that as potential mothers, women were in need of protection. Thus, even as reformers expressed their own claim to an equal political voice, they reinforced women's essential difference, based on their reproductive qualities.[32]

The WCND worked closely with the federal agency, the Women in Industry Service within the Department of Labor, which was established to address war needs. Its director, Mary van Kleeck, was a well-known and highly respected labor reformer who routinely communicated with the WCND leadership and conducted speaking tours in the states as well. Van Kleeck's agency in many ways paralleled the way in which the Children's Bureau drew upon the white women's dominion of reform. For its part, the WCND urged its state councils to be vigilant in enforcing protective laws for women in the various states and addressing the question of suitable work for women in view of the labor shortage. States varied as to how deeply engaged they were in the issue. Those with significant industrial presence did see a fair amount of activism on the part of WCND women.[33] For the most part, however, these state efforts seem to have been primarily investigatory, with parallel efforts at lobbying to maintain or enact protective legislation.

Enforcement of laws and attention to hazardous conditions and crowded living circumstances were perennial sources of complaint during the war. A survey of the Frankford Arsenal in Pennsylvania, for example, reported that women's wages lagged behind men's. In Connecticut, WCND activists were militant in their insistence on equal pay for equal work, a stance that infuriated the men's Council of National Defense of that state. Maryland's committee for industry, frustrated because canneries refused to cooperate with their investigation, felt forced to stop assisting them in placing women workers in jobs there. In Chicago, Mary McDowell, connected to the University of Chicago Settlement House and chair of the state's WCND committee on immigrant women in industry, reported on foreign-born women in the packinghouses who worked the night shift. The majority had children, she reported, and "none get more than four hours' sleep. The chief reasons for working are the insufficient pay or illness of the husband." McDowell happily reported that she persuaded four Chicago packers to agree not "to hire women with children under six years." In October 1917, the *Chicago Tribune* quoted her as saying, "We want women to do anything they are able to do that will not injure them physically or morally or unfit them for motherhood. . . . Because women are of the mother sex, they must have some protections not necessary for men."[34] McDowell's comments get to the heart of the WCND agenda for what it called "maintenance of standards." They reflect the ambivalence about women, especially mothers, as industrial workers. But they also reveal the commitment to not letting war undermine the gains made in protective legislation for women.

The WCND and the Children's Year

Perhaps the most ambitious wartime reform effort—participation in the national Children's Year program of 1918—provides an excellent example of the female dominion of reform in action and the way in which women appropriated the war crisis to their prewar agendas. The WCND, working in tandem with Julia Lathrop and the Children's Bureau, offered an elaborate program of child welfare measures that they successfully presented as part of the war effort. Children, as the future of the nation, needed to be protected as a patriotic measure. One poster graphically expressed it, with Uncle Sam, ledger in hand, "taking an inventory of his wealth" and the crowd of children clustered around him. "We Register Voters and Soldiers/Lands and incomes/ Automobiles and motorboats," the poster stated, and "Why not babies?"[35]

A particularly important part of the national focus of Children's Year was infant mortality. Officials drew explicit comparisons to European combatants' concerns about unnecessary deaths of children, pointing out that England, France, and Germany had embarked on campaigns to improve infant health. "These precedents of foresights added to our own investigations already mentioned were warrant for the challenge to save 100,000 babies for the nation when life must be used up on the field of honor," Jessica Peixotto of the Children's Bureau explained.[36] The bureau assigned each state a quota of babies to be saved by reducing their infant mortality rate.

Although saving babies as a measure of patriotic service was a crucial part of the Children's Year, a broader maternalist reform agenda dominated the campaign. The National Child Welfare Association distributed an oversized illustrated flyer entitled, "Publicity Posters and Exhibit Panels Are Essential to the Success of Your Children's Year Campaign," which emphasized the reform agenda. Aside from a poster featuring Uncle Sam, the others ignored the war effort altogether and instead focused on general themes of child health that had characterized Progressive Era calls for communities to expand their services for poor children and their families. A poster headed "A Living Wage" also spoke to reformers' belief that improved wages for male workers would make for healthier wives and children. This reform mentality clearly went beyond concerns for children's health. The Children's Bureau urged its supporters to assert influence locally to prevent the establishment of nurseries in factories and to promote widows' pension laws and other programs to enable poor women to remain at home with their children.[37]

WCND women in many communities worked hard to fulfill their Children's Year responsibilities: weighing and measuring children; ensuring that state birth registration laws were implemented; lobbying successfully for pure milk regulations and for public health nurses and their training; and helping to distribute the reams of information that flowed from Washington. In Cleveland, a large army truck, refitted as a "Baby Saving Special," went to the city's different wards to conduct the weighing and measuring program, paying particular attention to "slum sections." Sick children were sent to a hospital for free treatment, and mothers were encouraged to attend free sessions on child health and child care. In Boston, a cottage on the Boston Commons was designated as a health center, where public health nurses demonstrated proper baby care and posters explained appropriate diet and healthful recreation. Immigrant communities received careful attention. Concerned about what they called the "Japanese problem," Los Angeles women called for a "thorough standardization of Japanese midwives" and worried because Japanese children were "not up to the standards of American weights" and not adequately supplied with milk. Securing the services of Dr. James Hara and a Japanese nurse, the group weighed and measured 795 Japanese children and offered "advice to the parents."[38]

Just as the prewar Children's Bureau had ingeniously marshaled the services of thousands of unpaid workers in communities all over the country, during the war it continued to orchestrate a wide-ranging program of child welfare and lobbying for legislation concerning children's health and education.[39] With the war emergency as justification, the Children's Year brought mothers and their families into unprecedented connection with the state and federal governments through the medium of a voluntary association, the WCND. The program perfectly illustrated the way in which women activists tied war mobilization to using women's influence to support their maternalist reform agenda.

The Children's Year campaign offers yet another insight into the context of these women's war efforts. As Robert Westbrook and other scholars have noted, the United States, with political ideals that emphasize individual liberty and freedom from state interference, faces a dilemma in mobilizing for war. The necessity of citizens risking their lives to protect the state could imply that the state had failed to fulfill its fundamental obligations to safeguard individual life and liberty. Thus, as a more compelling and acceptable alternative to an appeal to protect the abstract nation-state or a political community, twentieth-century Americans during wartime have been encouraged to "defend *private* interests and discharge *private* moral obligations." War aims have tended to be cast in terms of familial obligations. Certainly World War I propaganda invoked ideals such as democracy and freedom, but even the most casual perusal of U.S. government war posters reveals the way in which protecting women, children, and the home became defined as the preeminent goal of American victory, a goal that could mobilize a wide range of civilian supporters. Although its focus was on domestic reform, the Children's Year campaign both reflected and reinforced an understanding of the war that made it immediate and personal, rather than abstract and political.[40]

These activists' engagement with family rhetoric in support of World War I gave a different spin to the pervasive tendency of the government and popular culture to interpret war goals as including the protection of women and children. Implicitly, women activists suggested that the war potentially *endangered* children and the family. And, rather than portray women as passive recipients of the protection soldiers offered them, they extended the maternalistic rhetoric that justified social reform efforts to legitimate women's vital role in protecting the home front. In the process they challenged wartime rhetoric that privileged male military service as the epitome of citizenship.[41] This is not to suggest that women reformers were engaged in some sort of counterhegemonic activity, for the thrust of their efforts reinforced the power of the state during wartime. Their emphasis on protecting the family from the dangers of war was not a criticism of the war. Rather, because the war created disruptions, it was all the more necessary to support the government's mobilization drive to ensure victory. Women may have appropriated the war for their reform purposes and used it to justify women's claim to equal citizenship, but at the same time their efforts reinforced the government's goals of engaging citizens' support for war.[42]

THE YWCA AND THE WCTU AND MATERNAL REFORMS

Similar processes that blended women's reform agendas with a support for mobilization that undergirded the interpretation of war aims as the preservation of home and family emerged in the activities of two major national women's organizations, the Young Women's Christian Association (YWCA) and the Woman's Christian Temperance Union (WCTU). Both refashioned their traditional programs in the context of the war and worked closely with the federal government in support of both their reform agendas and "victory."[43] Their activities may have served their own prewar goals, but they also potently signaled the role of women in home-front national defense.

The YWCA and Protective Work for Women

Through its War Work Council, the national headquarters of the YWCA quickly found a way to mesh the traditional YWCA program of Christian service on behalf of young working women with the nation's wartime needs. Before the war, the YWCA focused on protective services for young women workers, including dormitories, housing registries, educational and training programs, and recreational clubs. The YWCA program promoted social and sexual morality but also lobbied on the state level for "industrial standards"—the eight-hour day, prohibition of night work, equal pay for equal work, and similar progressive goals that had also been supported by the

WCND. The YWCA served African American women in segregated branches (as discussed below), but the majority of the women were white.

One program the YWCA expanded to meet wartime needs built upon its tradition of urban Immigrant Institutes, first established in 1910 as Americanization agencies. These became the basis for a translation service to assist immigrant women and their families with such issues as alien registration, draft registration, and food conservation. To help the families of enlisted men, the YWCA provided multilingual workers in some munitions and other defense industries as well as in some army camps. Apparently, in some locations, visitors went to the homes of foreign-speaking soldiers, "to explain why their men have been called to the colors and to teach English and Americanize the home-life." Californians also reported that they established Americanization classes for Mexican women, who were part of a significant migration from Mexico to work in California food-packing industries. In addition, the YWCA created programs for assisting war refugees, a process that continued into the postwar years.[44]

The key component of the YWCA's War Council's work, however, was its focus on women who worked in defense industries. Its Women's Industrial Program offered training to prepare young women for new positions in jobs formerly occupied by men and provided housing and recreation for girls working in defense-related jobs. This effort was the basis for a massive fund-raising drive, as well as expanded training programs for YWCA workers, whose numbers increased during the war. The YWCA established thirty-six "industrial service centers," for example, to serve women in munitions plants and other defense-related industries. These offered recreation facilities and, in some cases, room registries, dormitories (less often), and low-priced cafeterias. The goal, according to a report issued after the war, was to "sustain the morale of the industrial army by steadying the girl workers and by contributing to their health and enjoyment."[45]

War Work Bulletins, issued monthly, offered illustrated accounts of women working in defense industries and the programs the YWCA had devised. So, for example, the August 1918 issue featured munitions workers in the DuPont factory in Penniman, Virginia, where the YWCA had established a center that contained a dormitory, cafeteria, gymnasium, shower room, and attractively furnished living room. The article was illustrated with photographs of women relaxing at one of the regularly scheduled beach parties and enjoying the healthful effects of a weekend camp.[46] Other recreational activities included military-style drill teams in which young women engaged in exercise while twirling ersatz guns. YWCA leaders, reflecting reformers' concerns about the demoralizing effects of commercial urban leisure, took particular pains to create opportunities for healthful "play" for hard-pressed young working women.

YWCA war reports also indicate that YWCA leaders attempted to work with employers to facilitate good working conditions and adherence to state laws governing women's hours and night work. A report on industrial work in southern mill and mining towns was enthusiastic about the success of YWCA programs. It pointed out that federal contracts mandated improved working conditions and wages and that defense work had thus, with further encouragement from YWCA leaders, helped to bring progressive reforms to areas that had largely ignored it. The same report claimed that YWCA work in the canning industry and fisheries of the Pacific Coast was furthering efforts to regulate hours, conditions, and wages for seasonal and migrant workers and, indeed, that the work was so vital that the YWCA planned to continue its program in the postwar period.[47]

The YWCA was part of the women's dominion of reform, and its approach to women workers was clearly protective and maternalistic. It was insistent that women not be placed in work that was inappropriate for them on moral or physical grounds. So women under twenty-one should not be employed in "the public messenger service, in street car, elevated, and subway transportation service, as elevator operators, as bellboys in hotels and clubs," because it exposed them to sexually inappropriate behavior. It also discouraged the employment of mothers of young children. Yet, despite this protective stance, the YWCA championed young women workers and insisted on their reliability and productivity and called for public recognition of their service in wartime.

YWCA leaders routinely called industrial workers "the second line of defense," and the logo for the Women's Industrial Program featured a woman in uniform. Defense workers participating in YWCA programs were not required to be YWCA members but were required to sign a pledge that read in part, "It is my desire to serve to the best of my ability in the ranks of the Women's Industrial Army, 'A Second Line of Defense.'" Spurred on by women's war employment, YWCA leaders were recognizing that working-class women were not merely vulnerable girls subject to exploitation but also "new women," whose work was valuable. A postwar report was explicit on the issue, noting that the older concern of protecting women workers because of their role in "propagating the race," had given way to viewing them as a "great social asset." As such, the "nation cannot maintain its status in the civilized world if the health, mentality and capacities of its women are suffered to decline or are wasted through lack of general recognition of their social worth or through neglect to establish proper safeguards of that work."[48] Not all YWCA leaders embraced this vision of a new working woman, and even those that did continued to stress the need for protecting women workers, who seemed inherently vulnerable.

YWCA leaders may have been coming to a more modern notion of working-class women, but their approach to issues of sexual morality continued to be conservative. This theme was paramount for the YWCA during World War I. It led to participation in a nationwide effort to stamp out venereal disease, in itself a project of extraordinary partnerships among organizations like the YWCA, the YMCA, and the federal government. The cooperation was institutionalized in the Commission on Training Camp Activities (CTCA), a federal agency that gave official status to the work of the YMCA and the YWCA, making both associations what historian Emily Rosenberg has termed "chosen instruments" of federal policy. While the military's focus was primarily on making soldiers "fit to fight," others in government shared with groups like the YWCA a belief in fostering behavioral norms that would hold both men and women to the same high single sexual standard, a goal that stretched far beyond the specific wartime concern regarding disease.

The context of this cooperation was the widespread prewar anxiety about what was often called the "girl problem," a euphemism for sexually active young single women. During the Progressive Era, male and female moral reformers had been concerned about prostitution and its effect on the home and social order, as well as the plight of the prostitute herself. These anxieties took place in the context of shifting notions about prostitutes and "charity girls" (women who offered sexual favors, often in exchange for gifts and entertainment). Increasingly, a new class of professional social workers viewed "fallen women" less as helpless victims of male lust and more as delinquents with their own sexual agency. They also worried about working-class girls and the opportunities new urban leisure sites (such as dance halls and amusement parks) offered for illicit sex. In addition to rehabilitating sexually active young women through the juvenile court and reformatory system, reformers wanted to shut down red-light districts and regulate dance halls and other sites of urban "cheap amusements."[49]

The advent of war made the issue of vice even more pressing. With hundreds of thousands of soldiers in training camps across the nation, the likelihood of unrestrained sexuality loomed large. Government officials often expressed the concerns of reformers that soldiers' exposure to immorality damaged the nation's moral fiber. But, more pragmatically, they feared that sexually transmitted diseases would undermine soldiers' health and military readiness. For their part, women reformers usually concentrated on the danger to young women of the "lure of the khaki." In particular, they recognized that the presence of soldiers on leave with money in their pockets would expand the practice of "treating," according to which working-class girls exchanged sexual favors for gifts and access to places of public amusement.[50]

The CTCA coordinated with local officials to shut down brothels and saloons near military camps. Closing down red light districts, however, just sent prostitutes undercover. In response, the CTCA sought to get all sexually promiscuous or potentially promiscuous women off the streets. It targeted prostitutes as well as charity girls, who were particularly problematic. Raymond Fosdick, head of the CTCA, explained this decision: "We are confronted with the problem of hundreds of young girls, not yet prostitutes, who seem to have become hysterical at the sight of buttons and uniforms."[51] The CTCA's Committee on Protective Work for Girls developed a program of enhanced policing, usually involving the novelty of hiring women police officers and social workers to identify female sexual "delinquents." In many cases, social workers sought to counsel young women about their dangerous behavior. This was the case in New York City, for example, where social workers drew sharp distinctions between prostitutes and charity girls, whom they viewed as naive and misguided. Alarmed by the overt displays of sexual activity in public spaces, especially commercial entertainment venues, as well as by the increasingly young age of girls in the company of soldiers, social workers sought to offer them the maternal guidance that they believed their working-class mothers had failed to provide.[52]

In some localities, however, the CTCA program apparently minimized the differences between prostitutes and charity girls. Women and girls suspected of posing a danger to soldiers were arrested and subjected to medical exams. If they were found to have sexually transmitted diseases, they were incarcerated in hospitals, jails, or special facilities built to house them and held until they were free of disease. Many local WCND groups endorsed this coercive approach and lobbied municipal officials to hire policewomen and build reformatories to house infected women. In Kentucky, the chair of the WCND's Child Welfare Committee was so committed to the program that she personally "patrolled the streets" in her car until an officer could be provided. An estimated 30,000 women were arrested for sexual offenses during the years 1918 to 1920, and while first-time offenders were likely to be released on probation, 18,000 spent time in some sort of detention facility.[53]

Although local WCND groups participated in this draconian program to keep diseased women off the streets, the YWCA focused primarily on less coercive approaches to the "girl" problem. It created a "patriotic league" for young women, which focused on working girls and young "business women," and organized recreational activities as well as patriotic war service, such as knitting for soldiers. The aim, as a Los Angeles YWCA official explained it, was "to provide a constructive outlet for patriotism," which was a euphemistic way of referring to the challenge of maintaining sexual morality when so many young women were "naturally stirred by the presence of so many Knights about to set forth on a crusade."[54] The YWCA also worked with the CTCA to promote sex education for men and women, as well as the channeling of sexual energies into social events and patriotic activities. Throughout the nation, reformers interested in promoting moral reform, specifically red-light abatement and Prohibition, eagerly embraced the CTCA plan to create camp canteens for wholesome recreation. They were so enthusiastic that Fosdick reported, "I confess that this canteen business is becoming a veritable nuisance. . . . I am besieged by women's delegations and others, asking the privileges of running combination canteens and clubs in the vicinity of Army camps." To prevent duplication, the CTCA authorized the YWCA exclusively to construct "hostess houses" adjacent to army camps.[55]

The CTCA's focus was on protecting soldiers from sexually dangerous women, but the YWCA understood its work with the CTCA as an extension of its protective work for women. Mary Alden Hopkins noted in "Conserving Woman Power in War Time" that the hostess houses "are designed for the comfort of the wives, mothers, and sweethearts who come to the great camps to see their soldiers."[56] Eventually, 124 houses were established, many of them staffed with multilingual speakers and 17 set apart for African American troops, which provided a chaperoned environment for men to meet with sweethearts and female relatives, where they could enjoy wholesome refreshments and modest entertainment.

To further encourage what they viewed as a high standard of morality, the YWCA continued its long-standing campaign for sexual reform among young women. To promote sexual abstinence in wartime, the YWCA's National War Work Council sent out lecturers on "social standards." By the end of the war, 60 lecturers had given 2,261 talks in 229 communities to an estimated 387,000 "mothers, teachers, high school girls, and business women." In California, "in every War Camp community a series of talks by a physician selected for her approach to girls and young women was given to supplement the teaching of social morality to men in uniform." This program was considered so useful that it was adopted by the CTCA, which employed former YWCA lecturers. Under government auspices, the federal approach was much less sympathetic to young women, choosing instead to scare them into "chaste behavior by demonstrating the horrible illnesses, physical deformities, and terrible social consequences that could result from venereal disease." CTCA and YWCA lecture programs may well have served the purpose of introducing sex education to young women, but it is doubtful that they succeeded in promoting sexual abstinence. Historian Elizabeth Alice Clement argues that the increase in wartime treating accelerated the development of more sexualized patterns of courtship that would become increasingly evident in the 1920s among working- and middle-class young women.[57] YWCA officials like Ruth Southwick understood that the issue was not a new one and not one that was likely to disappear at war's end. She insisted that "the girl problem in war was the same as in peace, except that in war it was raised to fever heat."[58] What YWCA leaders did not seem to realize, however, was that their approach to the sexual lives of many of the young women they hoped to serve was becoming outdated.

Whether their focus was the lure of the khaki or the threat to protective labor legislation, the YWCA's wartime work never strayed very far from its agenda concerning the economic and social problems of young women, especially those of the working class. It had a two-pronged approach. It engaged in protective work for women in terms of their laboring lives. But it also focused on promoting moral reform, particularly the notion of a single sexual standard. Certainly, the YWCA activists worried that the war might undermine familial order, but they also were optimistic that their activities could have long-term results in protecting working-class women. By eliding the maternalist reform agenda with war mobilization, the YWCA's programs dovetailed with the prevailing propaganda that interpreted the war in the context of the social and moral order of the family.

The WCTU and Moral Order

In a similar fashion, the WCTU viewed the war through the lens of the social and moral order. Ever since the 1870s, when WCTU president Frances Willard announced that the organization's plan should be "to do everything" to preserve the home, the WCTU had had a wide-ranging list of reforms that it supported, including woman suffrage and anti-vice campaigns. The group's primary commitment to eradicating alcohol use was dramatically aided by the implementation of wartime prohibition measures, and throughout the war the organization continued its lobbying for the Prohibition amendment.

Even as it rallied behind food conservation, for example, it kept temperance in sharp focus. As one slogan went, "Bar the barley from the bar and bake it into bread." A related theme was another moral reform—the eradication of prostitution—and the campaign against venereal disease, which now had the imprimatur of the War Department, assisted communities in forcing prostitution undercover. Although Prohibition was the group's primary concern, like the YWCA, the WCTU had lobbied for labor legislation for women workers, and this continued to be on its agenda during the war.[59] The WCTU also continued its long-standing support for a suffrage amendment.

While persisting in its prewar agenda, the organization took on a variety of war work programs.[60] Support for the war effort was not without ideological complications. Many women in the WCTU were pacifists, and the organization had long maintained a "department of peace."[61] But despite this persistence of antimilitarism, the organization apparently bowed to the pervasive nationalist fervor and allied itself with the WCND. It created a Special Publicity Bureau to document its war work and reported after the war on the way it had loyally responded "to the emergency call for patriotic service." As Mary E. Woodard, an Indiana leader, explained their war efforts, "Our great organization has always stood for the peaceful settlement of all difficulties but in a crisis like this, is not a 'slacker.'"[62]

As was the case with the YWCA, the WTCU advocated a single sexual standard, or what it called "a white life for two" (with white referring to purity), and promoted sexual abstinence among young women and men. The organization sought to reach men through lectures and alternative chaperoned entertainment and through eliminating red-light districts to remove temptation. As to women, the hope was that young WCTU members—"white ribbon girls"—would set "a high social standard" that "exerted a restraining influence over those young women who foolishly failed to observe toward men in uniform the proprieties that prevail in times of peace." The work had a coercive side as well. The national headquarters coordinated with local WCNDs and the CTCA to secure the appointment of women police officers in camp areas to "protect the girls ignorant of danger, and, whether desired or not, to give help."[63] The Los Angeles branch, similar to those in other cities, reported that it had been "influential in securing the appointment of police women and social service workers," that it made investigations "of the moral conditions surrounding our army camps and [that] steps have been taken to safeguard the morals of young girls especially in localities near the camps." It further cooperated with the city's Morals Efficiency Association to help rehabilitate young girls.[64]

The WCTU also focused on young soldiers. It established "Home Centers" near military bases, designed to offer soldiers opportunities for wholesome relaxation, and placed a great deal of emphasis on the welfare of soldiers, beyond promoting temperance and sexual abstinence. One of its major projects was to make "comfort bags" to send to the troops. In addition to the usual toiletry items, the Los Angeles WCTU bags contained "an evangelistic letter, . . . a 'mother' letter, . . . seventeen different leaflets on temperance purity and anti-tobacco," and the Bible. It also provided soldiers with three cards with which they could pledge their abstinence from drinking, vice, and tobacco. A sense of personal connection with soldiers was furthered by work at the Home Center, which provided "home-made candy, flowers, individual bouquets," and assistance to soldiers in writing letters to their "mothers and friends."[65]

The WCTU's attention to soldiers indicates the way in which women's war mobilization centered on familial concerns. As scholar Susan Zeiger has shown, motherhood was a persistent theme in American war propaganda. She argues convincingly that this outpouring of sentimental depictions of self-sacrificing, loyal mothers and the soldiers who went to war to protect the sanctity of the family was designed in part to counter the pacifist inclinations of many women's groups in the prewar era.[66] In the case of the WCTU, the focus on soldiers' welfare offered a means of demonstrating patriotism while minimizing the challenge to their own pacifist values. Here, in contrast to the theme of protecting women and children that Zeiger notes, however, the WCTU's program empowered women by focusing on the way they nurtured young men who were called upon to fight the war.

White women reformers served the war effort out of patriotism, certainly, but they also served their own agendas. They promoted a range of social reforms—from protective labor legislation to immigrant Americanization, from the prevention of vice to the protection of children. These reformers built upon conventional notions of women's maternal functions, but they also represented the new woman of the Progressive Era, determined to participate in civic life and influence public policy.

BLACK WOMEN'S VOLUNTEER WAR WORK

African American women for the most part were excluded from these white women's reform associations, yet in their own organizations they clearly reflected the reform ethos of the Progressive Era, an ethos that was manifest in the ways in which black women leaders participated in war mobilization. In some ways, the experiences of African American volunteer war workers were similar to those of white women. Middle-class black women were already well organized into a variety of clubs, many of which were affiliated with the National Association of Colored Women (NACW), and these local organizations often became the springboard for war activity. And, like many white women, black clubwomen generally sought to continue prewar reform goals, including support for the family, in the context of war work. But the similarities quickly break down. African American women's goals were framed through the lens of racial uplift in their varying communities, and their efforts were constantly stymied by the racial discrimination black Americans faced as they sought to do their bit for the war.[67]

Jim Crow pervaded the organization of these volunteer efforts. The WCND included NACW president Mary Talbert on its national committee, and white national leaders did express concerns about the need to bring black women into war work. But the national operation explicitly refused to interfere with states' treatment of black women. Thus state and local NCWD committees, dominated by white women, made their own determination as to if and how they would use black women in volunteer work. Outside the South, most states had parallel organizations called "colored auxiliaries," which were subject to white oversight. Only Illinois, North Carolina, and Massachusetts attempted to integrate black women into their main structures.[68]

Black women did participate extensively in national drives such as the Liberty Loan and Red Cross fund-raising efforts. The *Chicago Defender* announced that Mrs. Bertha Montgomery was on the "honor roll of the fourth Liberty loan committee." Montgomery, described as a social worker and a "well-educated woman," was a "leader in politics among the women of the Second ward." As president of the Second Ward Liberty Loan committee, she raised $6,000 in bonds, which put her district 124 percent "over the top." A New York Red Cross worker reported on her auxiliary, commenting that despite the training necessary, "a large number of ladies are now genuine workers."[69] Even when black women worked within these national organizations, however, they did so usually in segregated and units, whose value white leaders rarely recognized.

In the South, organization of black women was spotty, and the national WCND office sent Alice Dunbar-Nelson, a well-known clubwoman, author, and reformer, on a six-week southern tour to investigate black women's contributions to the war effort. This decision was prompted in part by pressure from Emmet J. Scott, an African American special assistant to the secretary of war. Citing resentment of racism, Scott reported on a state of "restlessness" among the black population and insisted upon the need to improve African Americans' morale.[70] As Dunbar-Nelson conducted her survey of black women's war work, she also reported on alleged anti-American sentiment among the black population, while at the same time rallying black women to the cause. In addition to conducting personal interviews, Dunbar-Nelson gave speeches to African Americans on such topics as "the meaning of the war to the Negro," "what the Negro can do to help the war," and "the need of combined forces of colored women to help make the country a loveable place for the race."[71]

Dunbar-Nelson's correspondence provides an unusually rich account of the dilemmas facing black southern women in their efforts to contribute to war service. She found them eager to participate in Liberty Loan and Red Cross drives, food conservation, and child welfare. They were also energetic in the provision of knitted goods and kit bags for the troops, but, with a few notable exceptions, she found their energies underutilized. Her letters back to Hannah Patterson, resident director of the WCND, detailed the racism black women routinely encountered. In North Carolina, she discovered that the state agents for the Food Administration had denied blacks the opportunity to sign food conservation pledges. Women she interviewed in New Orleans complained that "government employment bureaus here recognize in every colored girl who applies for work only a potential scrub woman, no matter how educated and refined she might be."[72]

In Mississippi, the situation was particularly tense. On the one hand, the white head of the Mississippi WCND was eager to organize black women and had even personally financed a black organizer. On the other hand, Mississippi blacks were resentful of the racism they continually experienced. Dunbar-Nelson reported that a number of African Americans had been tarred and feathered, including one woman whose husband was in the army in France. Also in Mississippi, black women were denied membership in the Red Cross. Dunbar-Nelson dismissed the concerns about African American women's potential disloyalty by emphasizing their willingness to contribute, despite the frustrations they faced. She concluded that the problem "isn't German propaganda, either, it's American propaganda, that is working harm among the people."[73]

This overt racism also surfaced in the general lack of black women's participation at the state level of the WCND. Only two southern states, Florida and Maryland, systematically included African Americans on the Women's Committee. In most southern states, committees appointed black women when need for specific activities arose. This approach kept black women not only subordinate but also virtually invisible to the larger society. And, as Dunbar-Nelson's investigation proceeded, the national leadership was quick to reassure white southern women leaders that her investigation was not to be interpreted as a prelude to dictating racial policy to them.[74] In effect, during the war, black women faced the same mind-set that shaped the national suffrage movement—that of white national leaders unwilling to risk alienating white southern women even if it might expand the opportunities for productive war work.

Despite these insults, black women did organize extensive wartime contributions in the South. Eartha White directed the work of Jacksonville, Florida, women. The chair of that state's Colored Women's Section of the Council of National Defense, she was an organizer so impressive that the WCND invited her to speak at a national conference in June 1918, much to the dismay of a number of southern white women. In June 1917, just a few months into the war, the Jacksonville City Federation of Colored Women's Clubs reported that it was the first "colored society" to affiliate with the Red Cross. It detailed its work in food conservation, including having secured a "colored County Canning Demonstrator." Other accomplishments, sprinkled in their list of 1917 activities, were not specifically war-related but fit well with the tendency to promote community improvement as a war measure. Thus its leaders secured from the city a social worker as well as two nurses for the schools. They also "celebrated as usual: Good Health Week, Clean-Up Week, Baby Week, co-operating with white women's clubs." Later, Florida established a "Mutual Protection League for Girls," which had taken up the "unfamiliar work of elevator girls, bell girls in hotels and chauffeurs." This led to a "union of Girls in Domestic Service," which was to be extended after the war.[75]

The reform thrust of African American women's mobilization was evident even in the most traditional and "patriotic" activity, providing assistance to soldiers. Although they sometimes acted in concert with local WCND groups and with the Red Cross, African American women were more likely to operate through independent black organizations. This was especially true in the growth of organizations designed to offer material aid to the black troops. Most notable was the Circle for Negro War Relief, which began in New York and spread to cities throughout the nation, but especially in the East. It totaled over fifty units and had the goal of "promoting the welfare of Negro soldiers and their dependent families."[76]

Prominent black clubwomen participated in the Circle, including Alice Dunbar-Nelson, Margaret Murray Washington, Madame C. J. Walker, and Leila Walker Robinson, Walker's daughter. According to historian Nikki

Brown, the Circle specifically noted that black soldiers and their families were the least likely to get government assistance. One pamphlet argued that "the negro soldier's absence [from his family] will be felt more keenly than can possibly result from the service of any other soldiers in ranks, for it must be admitted that the colored troops represent the most impoverished class in the United States."[77] The perception that black soldiers and their families were at risk formed part of a broader vision of the African American clubwomen who spearheaded black war activity: their work followed patriotic lines, but also was a form of community service and racial uplift.

This theme was particularly potent in black women's experiences working with the YWCA. On the eve of World War I, the national YWCA had made minimal strides in incorporating African American women into the institution. Virtually all black women who participated in the YWCA did so in segregated "colored" branches, and few of these were in the South, where white women for the most part actively resisted expanding their work to black women. African American women had about eighty college or university branches and sixteen city associations. Generally, black associations in the South reported directly to the national board, thus sidestepping local white intransigence. Black activist Addie Hunton had been a major force in urging the YWCA to be more proactive in organizing blacks, and in 1918 the organization established its first permanent position of director of "colored work."[78]

At the urging of male and female leaders who stressed the country's war needs, the YWCA expanded its basic war programs of hostess houses, patriotic leagues, recreation centers, and industrial service centers to black women. In late 1917, the National Board authorized $200,000 of its $5 million budget for African American projects, and estimates are that the final figure for the war era was $400,000. The YWCA also expanded black women's representation on its war work council from one member in 1917 to twelve in 1918. While the YWCA's War Council controlled the purse strings, an African American woman, Eva Bowles, led the Committee on Colored Work. The YWCA war work brought a significant number of educated black women, many of them teachers, into YWCA programs. Organizers sent by the national YWCA trained new workers and cooperated extensively with local leaders, most of whom were well educated and members of the NACW. The linkage between the YWCA and the NACW allowed the YWCA access to the black community, while it gave African American women the opportunity to participate in a national program that both supported their own ends and furthered the nation's war aims.[79]

The need for hostess houses for African American soldiers and their families was a particularly pressing one. Like white reformers, black women were concerned about sexual immorality in the camp communities, but African American women viewed the need as even more crucial. NACW president Mary Talbert urged "women's organizations situated near the army cantonments to see that colored girls and women do not go near them, so that the social evil, usually so prevalent near war camps may not be attributed to our women in any way whatever."[80] Although leaders like Talbert wished to counter vicious stereotypes about black women's sexuality, they also recognized the particular problems African American men and their relatives faced in bases where racism was a daily fact of life and where African American soldiers had limited opportunities for recreation because neighboring communities were explicitly off-limits to them.

These problems were underlined in the difficulties that YWCA women faced in establishing hostess houses. They struggled to find suitable buildings for their houses and usually had to make do initially with substandard facilities. The first hostess house for African Americans, established at Ft. Upton (Long Island, New York), was a ramshackle building, where rain and snow seeped through the walls. African American YWCA organizers and local women created a total of sixteen hostess houses during the war, which they viewed with great pride as being attractive places of comfort, recreation, and rest. As was the case with the hostess houses for white soldiers, these facilities served meals, provided entertainment for men, and offered female relatives and friends a safe environment for visiting.[81] The posed photograph in figure 5 suggests the goals of these hostess houses: well-dressed women and children enjoy a pleasant interlude with their uniformed soldier relatives.

Descriptions of these camps reveal yet another motive behind them. Historian Nancy Robertson has argued that black leaders hoped that the genteel hostess houses they established would "show poorer African Americans what a 'proper home' should look like."[82] Jane Olcott made the point explicit in her postwar account of YWCA work among African Americans, noting that "the houses, their furniture, draperies and the whole method of life kept before the men, high standards of living and, in all too many cases, new standards to the men and women who were accustomed to being pushed off in squalid quarters of Southern cities."[83]

While black YWCA women hoped that the model set by hostess houses would endure, much of their long-term hope for change centered on the work with young women and girls. Black migration to the cities of the North and the South, as well as disruptions caused by "the lure of the khaki," made

Figure 5. Sunday at the YWCA Hostess House. From Jane Olcott, *The Work of Colored Women* (New York: Young Women's Christian Associations, 1919), 17.

black women particularly sensitive to the needs of young women in urban and industrial areas. They described their activities with recreation and industrial service centers as part of a patriotic war effort. Yet their goals were clearly to marry the war to long-felt community needs for social services. This drive, as well as their patriotism, led to strong support within the African American community for their programs.

As was the case with the hostess houses, black YWCA women found it challenging to find appropriate places for recreation or industrial service centers because of poverty and segregation. In Petersburg, Virginia, for example, which had grown dramatically during the war, from 15,000 to over 25,000 inhabitants, "the situation was serious as far as vice and housing were concerned. The only recreation centers were two dance halls and two parks, equally bad." Although residential segregation made finding a building difficult, by January 1918, a new center served over 500 girls, and it specifically devoted one day a week to a "day of fun and pleasure for industrial girls from tobacco factories."

The forty-five YWCA black recreation centers established in Washington, D.C., and twenty-one states focused on offering wholesome activities, including basketball, hiking, folk dancing, and community sings, for girls and young women. Although YWCA officials reported that war-related projects such as knitting took place in these centers, overwhelmingly the focus was on the young women themselves, not the war effort. As Jane Olcott reported in her postwar book on African Americans in the YWCA, in summarizing the accomplishments of the Richmond, Virginia, YWCA, "It must be remembered that the war work has been simply a part of the general Association work which had already been well established," a point also made by white YWCA workers.

Most African American recreation centers also attended to the issue of sexual morality, with "social hygiene" lectures a common feature. YWCA worker Sarah A. Blocker described the situation between soldiers and girls in Newport News, Virginia, as "so alarming that some hundred thoughtful colored women organized into 'block patrol'—each woman taking the responsibility for girls seen in her block." Such concern also led to extensive club work in the city, with about 300 girls enrolled in twelve clubs.[84] In Louisville, close to Camp Taylor, black YWCA women organized a group of women speakers to go into "factories, churches and other centers to educate the girls." At the same time, black leaders were instrumental in getting an African American policewoman appointed. The Louisville work was so successful that they were able to raise sufficient funds to enable the Phyllis Wheatley Branch to open a three-story building, "with fourteen rooms, including a reception room, assembly room and offices, dining room and kitchen, rest room, gymnasium, three bath rooms and six light, airy bedrooms, with running water, accommodating fifteen girls."

In most cases, recreation work went hand in hand with concern for the working concerns of girls and women. In large industrial centers, YWCA organizers generally began their work with surveys of industrial conditions, projects that reflected the organization's progressive-era social work orientation. Although some industrial service centers focused primarily on reaching working women for recreation purposes, others took a proactive stance in attempting to improve black women's working and living conditions. In St. Louis, the YWCA had created an industrial club for black women in 1913, and during the war it continued its former activities, including an employment agency, factory visits, and training. Jane Olcott made the poignant observation that "the girls did not wish to return to domestic work."[85]

African American YWCA leaders' industrial work reflects a shifting pattern among black women reformers as a group. Historian Dorothea Browder contrasts the racial uplift message of black clubwomen with a new style of leaders, such as Mary E. Jackson, the YWCA's national industrial secretary for colored work, who focused on helping black women to fight discrimination in the workplace. As they pursued their work with young black women, they conducted surveys and publicized often-brutal working conditions.

Forming alliances with the Women's Trade Union League (WTUL) and government officials, they sought to educate employers about the abilities of black workers and to encourage interracial cooperation with white women workers. Their activities, Browder argues, foreshadowed the way in which black civil rights activists in the postwar decades would incorporate civil rights unionism into their campaign for social justice.[86]

By the time of the published report on black YWCA activities, 12,000 African American women and girls had enrolled in YWCA clubs, and an estimated additional 25,000–30,000 had benefited from the centers. Although Olcott's assessment of the work for the most part took an upbeat tone that stressed its accomplishments, she nonetheless acknowledged repeatedly that blacks faced an uphill battle in the struggle to participate in the war effort, and in American society more generally. The report noted the dispiriting effect of riots in a number of cities. It detailed poor living and working conditions and frequently revealed the resistance to black workers on the part of employers and white workers.[87]

One of the most revealing aspects of the published report is the repeated commentary on the hardships facing the organizers themselves. Some of these stemmed from the difficulties of traveling in segregated states. One woman, Mrs. Wilder, found her work in Texas such a great strain that she was forced to discontinue the work. The report summed up the problems as including "traveling in Jim Crow cars, often having to sleep in them with her suit case for a pillow, with good restaurants closed to her, with the knowledge always that there was 'an undercurrent of race prejudice which is dangerous' and that 'one mistake means tragedy.'" But the women also were frustrated by the prejudice they faced from officials, especially white officers, who were dismissive of "colored women as leaders."[88]

The report on YWCA work celebrated the accomplishments of black women while noting the difficulties they faced, within the YWCA and outside of it. An even more trenchant account of the resistance black women faced in attempting to contribute to the war effort and their communities was Mary Church Terrell's assessment of her experiences as an organizer for the War Camp Community Service (WCCS). Created by the Playground and Recreation Association of America, in conjunction with the CTCA, the WCCS organized recreation for servicemen in military camps. The WCCS had asked Terrell, a founding member and first president of the NACW, to conduct a survey on the WCCS efforts on behalf of the black community. She began her work after the Armistice, but while the camps were still open and the WCCS was still active. Over a period of several months, Terrell traveled north and south in the states in the eastern part of the nation. She was appalled at the extreme neglect she found in terms of community services for African Americans. Her comments on Tennessee, her home state—put the optimistic YWCA reports of progress in perspective, as she noted that there were two YWCA workers for the black population of Chattanooga of more than 25,000. She reported further that the WCCS had done nothing for the black community, although soldiers themselves had created a club. The city had no recreation facilities for blacks, and no library or orphanage. As she described it, the conditions were poor for "the colored people from the standpoint of recreation, living conditions and education. There is almost nothing done for the colored girl."[89] For other cities, her report was a litany detailing poor living and social conditions.

Moreover, Terrell was exposed to repeated evidence of the WCCS officials' indifference, if not hostility, to working with and for African Americans. The racism was palpable. She found virtually no support for sending black WCCS agents to do work with girls. Even though she was originally a southerner, Terrell was nonetheless apparently shocked by the racism she encountered in southern states. Because she was light-skinned, on occasion her white contacts assumed she was white. She recounted a painful experience with a banker in Biloxi at length in her autobiography, *A Colored Woman in a White World*. He excoriated African Americans for wanting to be on the same level with whites and explained to her that "the nigger woman who came here would want to come to this bank, sit down in that chair where you are and talk to me as you are doing." Terrell reported that "an indescribable feeling of surprise, disgust and terror came over me."[90]

As objectionable as this and other southern experiences were, Terrell pointed out that the North was scarcely better. In New York City, the white woman in charge of all WCCS services for women in that city exclaimed, "I couldn't possibly do any work among Negro women. I know nothing whatever about the Negro mind and psychology, and I would never know when a Negro woman was telling me the truth." Terrell challenged her on this assessment, reminding her of the war just fought for democracy. According to Terrell, the woman responded flippantly: "The world is not ready for Democracy yet."[91]

Terrell's wry commentary about the white woman's response to her invocation of the war for democracy encapsulates the dilemma black activists faced. Though black women hoped that war service might prove a path to equal citizenship, they were repeatedly denied opportunities to demonstrate their patriotism and faced relentless discrimination. Nonetheless, they persisted, using the war emergency as justification for expanded community services for African Americans and their families and for economic opportunities for black women. Black women's enhanced presence in the YWCA, moreover, not only allowed them to work on behalf of their communities during the war, but also set the stage for increased influence in the organization in the postwar years. Like white women activists who pursued preexisting reform agendas, they framed their war work in the context of their longstanding agenda for racial uplift and community service.

THE RED CROSS AND AMERICAN WOMEN

Although much of women's wartime energies reflected political goals that predated the war, many millions of women outside the network of social reformers supported the war in response to immediate patriotic appeals to do their bit to win the war. But here, too, war and the protection of the family merged.[92] A major vehicle for their activity was the American Red Cross, whose activities exemplify the way in which the nation relied upon voluntarism in pursuit of its war aims. Rooted in both the Sanitary Commission of the U.S. Civil War and the International Red Cross, established in 1864, the organization, founded in 1881 by Clara Barton, was designed "to furnish volunteer aid to the sick and wounded of armies in time of war" and to provide relief in times of disaster. It participated in the Spanish American War and shortly afterward, in 1905, received a charter by Act of Congress, which made it subject to federal supervision and a yearly audit. To further emphasize its quasi-official status, it made the president of the United States the organization's head.

In 1914, the American Red Cross mobilized to offer humanitarian assistance to all combatants in the European war, but when the United States entered the conflict, it limited its aid to the Allies. At the request of the federal government, it took on the responsibility of providing base hospitals abroad, equipping them with materials and staffing them with nurses. During the war years, the Red Cross enrolled over 20 million members and raised approximately $400 million through voluntary subscriptions, campaigns in which women were active participants. In explaining why "work of such magnitude and consequence should not be an object of Government instead of private endeavor," a 1919 Red Cross publication reported that this method was not only more efficient and economical, but also that participating in the Red Cross gave men, women, and children who could not go to the front an opportunity to express the vital "volunteer spirit." The report emphasized that through the Red Cross, "one-half the nation, namely, the women, can most effectively serve their country in the war emergency."[93]

The Red Cross was not exclusively a women's organization: both men and women joined the almost 4,000 chapters located throughout the country. Although men may have dominated the leadership of the national and local organizations, women were a highly visible presence. In Los Angeles, for example, they constituted half of the board of directors and headed up the committees that were concerned with marshaling women's activities. Red Cross officials helped to articulate a specifically gendered vision of women's war mobilization, which did not focus on reform but was in keeping with the maternal familial thrust of other women activists.

Women's central presence in the Red Cross was graphically depicted in one of World War I's most ubiquitous and famous posters, featuring a Red Cross nurse and the caption, "The Greatest Mother of Them All."[94] This sentimental vision of a nurturing woman belied the hard, dirty work of caring for wounded near the front, but it captured the Red Cross's emphasis on women's maternal desire to support the nation's soldiers. Far more numerous than nurses were women on the home front who donned Red Cross uniforms to sew or knit garments; make bandages; assemble comfort bags; or serve coffee and doughnuts at railway station canteens.[95] That women were central to the Red Cross effort was symbolically expressed at the enormous May 1918 parade in Los Angeles, which garnered 10,000 marchers, the majority of whom were women, and which the *Los Angeles Times* described as a "Seven Mile Tribute to Women's Work in War." "Never in Los Angeles has there been a parade where its womanhood took such a conspicuous part."[96]

In Los Angeles and elsewhere, women joined the Red Cross chapters of the region as individuals in geographically determined branches but also allied in auxiliaries associated with their clubs and other social groups. Elite women's clubs hosted balls and other fund-raisers, which became an important part of wartime social activities and a source of much heartfelt rivalry among women's groups. According to the *Los Angeles Times* report, "competition in patriotic zeal is rife."[97]

Red Cross activity was easily adaptable to the leisured women's club world, but it may also have offered the widest possibility for diverse women to participate in the war effort. In Syracuse, New York, Slovak girls made bandages and raised money. In Chicago, African American women were Red Cross canteeners, who, according to an illustrated article in the *Chicago Defender*, met trains to "serve sandwiches, chocolate and coffee to the troops." In Los Angeles, Japanese immigrant and Jewish women had their

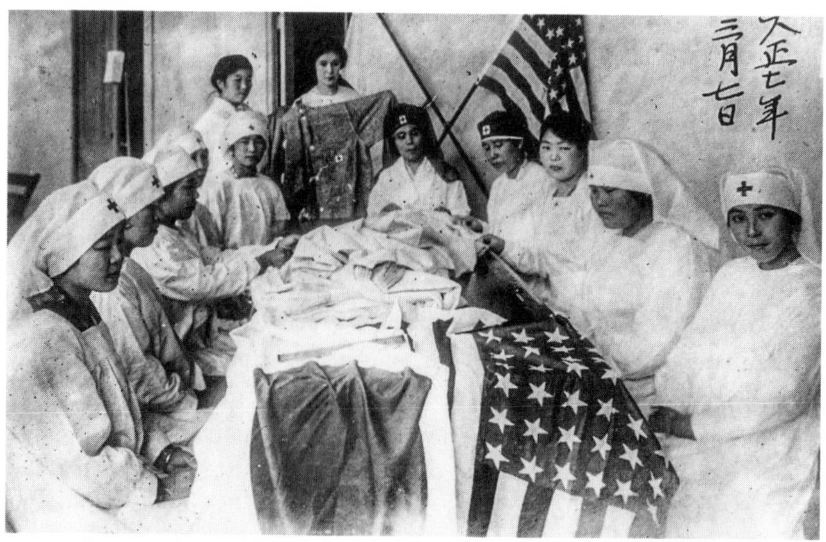

Figure 6. Los Angeles Japanese Women's Red Cross Auxiliary. Courtesy of the Seaver Center for Western History Research, Los Angeles County Museum of History.

own auxiliaries; and Mexican women worked for the Red Cross at Brownson House, a Catholic settlement house. Figure 6 shows members of the Japanese Women's Auxiliary to the Los Angeles Red Cross as they prepared supplies for the troops. The uniforms were typical of Red Cross workrooms. The presence of American flags was common too, although the two flags shown here suggest the women's eagerness to show loyalty to the United States, a point reiterated in a report after the war by "the Japanese committee" forwarded to the county's war history committee by the Japanese consul. The account claimed that the majority of Japanese in Los Angeles joined the Red Cross, but that the "most consistent war work . . . was the praiseworthy contributions of their women."[98]

A history of the Pittsburgh Red Cross during the war contained a list of over 150 auxiliaries, complete with membership rolls. Here, too, the diversity is striking. Most were organized through religious institutions, including Catholic and Jewish groups, but also through ethnically or racially based organizations, including Italian-, Slovak-, Swedish-, Polish-, and African American–sponsored units. Pittsburgh auxiliaries numbered several associations defined by employment, such as the women working at Rosenbaum Company or the Frick Building. Finally, one of the largest auxiliaries was the Woman's Suffrage Auxiliary.[99] Further indication of the diversity of Red Cross volunteers appears in accounts of Red Cross parades throughout the country (see Chapter 5), which duly note the presence of elite clubwomen but also report on participation by working-class, African American, and immigrant women.

Red Cross work offered women a communal activity in which they donned Red Cross uniforms as a visible symbol of their membership in a cadre of women serving their country and specifically addressing the needs of soldiers. Because of its specific association with caring for soldiers, the Red Cross activity of making bandages or knitting garments also brought women symbolically close to men on the field of battle. There was nothing new about this process. It followed a long-standing tradition in the United States of women fashioning garments for the troops, first begun by Sarah Franklin Bache and Esther De Berdt Reed, who organized Philadelphia women to sew shirts for General George Washington's Continental Army.[100] Like women in other combatant nations, Americans focused on knitting socks, mufflers, sweaters, and other warm items. The Red Cross alone counted a total of 24 million military items produced.

Knitting became such a central motif for women's war work that it is worth exploring at length. Knitted goods were welcomed by the military, at least initially. Tensions about the flood of socks and mufflers soon emerged, however. Was hand knitting really necessary and the best use of time and available wool, some asked. As a *Brookline (Massachusetts) Chronicle* letter-to-the editor taunted, "For God's sake, wake up and stop this hand-knitting by which at least 20,000 pounds of scoured wool has already been wasted at a time when the Huns are at our gates."[101] Others critics lampooned the knitters as socialites pursuing a fad. One feminist, frustrated by emphasis on domesticity, suggested that knitters be "legally restrained."[102] Eventually, a number of Red Cross units compromised by using knitting machines, with a handful of skilled knitters for finishing work, and later in the war, when wool supplies became scarce, they requested that women provide knitted socks only.[103]

But whether or not hand knitting was something the army valued, women were clearly insistent on keeping their needles busy, and, as with other women's war activities, their efforts suggest women's desire to define the nature of their war contribution. The papers of Pasadena, California, clubwoman and former high school principal Virginia Hunt offer unusually detailed reporting on the way in which knitting became an organized and contested activity during the war. Hunt headed up the Pasadena Women's Section of the Navy League, a group that had promoted preparedness before the United States entered the war. To systematize these women's knitting efforts, Hunt created an elaborate card file system that enabled her to report at length on the process of buying and distributing wool and keeping track of the knitted goods as they made their way to soldiers. Hunt clearly drew upon a military model, dividing her more than 2,000 knitters into squads of eight women, headed by a sergeant, with four squads to a platoon, headed by a lieutenant, and so on up to regiments headed by a general. As she explained it, "Officers are promoted as they show organizing ability."[104]

Hunt's knitters reveal the importance of giving women a sense of direct connection to soldiers. They did not produce garments for an abstract military but rather assumed that their socks and mufflers would go to Pasadena "boys." A major knitting controversy in the early months of the war, however, revealed the way in which national priorities impinged upon these local women's autonomy. In August 1917, Secretary of the Navy Josephus Daniels became embroiled in a serious conflict with the male national Navy League's leadership. His efforts to rein in that group also affected the women's branch of the Navy League, as he insisted that only one agency—the Red Cross—should distribute knitted goods. The directive sent Hunt and her group into a tailspin. They did not want to give up their autonomy, much less their socks. In a private letter, Hunt expressed her anger in specifically gendered terms, noting that "as a woman citizen, I am anxious to support the government in every possible way, but I consider that the government owes something to the women."[105]

Despite her sense that the government was slighting women's service, Hunt and the Pasadena women eventually agreed to work through the Red Cross, but then other issues emerged. Though state-based national guards existed during World War I, men and officers in the California National Guard who served at the front were integrated into national army units. The Pasadena women were dismayed to discover that they would have to give up their effort to supply local men directly with goods. "We will not be able to distribute to our Pasadena boys as we will have to meet the necessary red tape," Hunt explained.[106]

Hunt's knitters reflect the eagerness of women to take up a traditional female skill that would create a personal, supportive link to the young men who were fighting for their country. The nature of their contributions was their choice, not the government's. By maintaining this intimate connection to local men, they were attempting not only to sustain maternal protective roles on behalf of young men, but also to negate the depersonalizing qualities of modern armies and modern warfare. Yet this nurturing system for knitting and distributing goods of which Hunt was so proud was transformed by the wartime cult of efficiency. It was also transformed by the presence of a national organization—the Red Cross—and by the intervention of Secretary Daniels. Women may have sought to define their war roles, but ultimately they faced limits imposed by the federal government.

The concern about challenges to localism and the desire to maintain more intimate connection to soldiers was evident in yet another Red Cross program, a Home Service department designed to help dependents of soldiers cope with the absences of their loved ones. As the Red Cross placard displayed in the nation's railway stations put it, "We keep your home safe while you fight to keep the world safe." By the end of the war, 3,620 Home Service sections served 10,000 communities. The Red Cross estimated that it had spent close to $6 million on assistance to 450,000 dependent families. On the surface, this Red Cross program seems superfluous, for through the War Risk Insurance Bureau, Congress had provided direct monetary payments to enlisted men's families. However, the Red Cross goal entailed far more than just financial assistance, although it did distribute some funds to needy families, which it insisted was not charity but "compensation in exchange for war service." Red Cross workers routinely helped families file their claims for federal allotments, thus acting as a mediator between nation and local citizen.[107]

Beyond financial assistance, Red Cross service units attempted to address family anxiety and disorder in the face of an absent husband and father. At times, Home Service sections prevailed upon local businessmen, doctors, and lawyers to provide their professional services. But much of the activity was social welfare work, a reality the Red Cross acknowledged when it established forty-four institutes for training volunteers in social work practices. Curriculum topics included "The Unstable Family," "The Racial Equation," "War Risk Insurance Law," "Child Welfare," and "Employment of Women and Children." The Home Institutes thus reflected the engagement with social work so evident among many women reformers of the era and the desire to use the casework approach to alleviate familial disorganization in the face of war disruptions.[108]

The Kitchen Army: Food Conservation and Voluntarism

The examples of Red Cross volunteers, as well as clubwomen and reformers, reveal the means by which women sought to define meaningful war participation for themselves as "competent women" protecting the family and home front. A final example of ways in which women were mobilized to support the war, the federal government's food conservation program, entailed slightly different dynamics as this campaign was orchestrated by the government, with women leaders being more reactive than inventive. Far more than the preceding examples, the food campaign reflects an intrusive federal presence, but here, too, the mobilization of women reflects popular notions of women's familial role applied to the war effort and demonstrates the ways in which such gendered voluntarism could be harnessed to achieve governmental ends.

The food conservation drive proved to be one of the most successful examples of the use of voluntary associations to mobilize for war. Herbert Hoover, who headed up the Food Administration during the war, had a passionate commitment to voluntarism, announcing, "We propose to mobilize the spirit of self-denial and self-sacrifice in this country."[109] This belief, coupled with a hostility to federal bureaucracy and a commitment to individualism, led Hoover to reject the idea of food rationing and opt instead for voluntary conservation, to be accomplished by a massive effort to enlist American housewives in the campaign.

The way in which the government depicted women's conservation efforts reflected mixed messages about women's traditional role in the home. On the one hand, posters routinely featured feminine women at work in their kitchens. But on the other hand, government officials like Hoover repeatedly invoked the metaphor of a women's "kitchen army" and dignified women's contributions by arguing, "Women . . . are as much a part of the national army as are the men fighting at the front." This approach emerged quite clearly in the plan of California's federal food administrator, Ralph Merritt, to create teams of women to conduct a conservation pledge-signing campaign. Each "private" was to be given a "dainty emblem of the organization (an enameled United States shield, surrounded by a golden wreath of wheat) that she may be known as an enlisted soldier in the service of the government, and not a 'slacker.'" Next, she was to enlist eight other privates—to sign a food pledge card themselves and then go on to enlist others to make up a squadron, which advanced her rank, and then on to platoon, and so on. Merritt explained that the rationale for the proposal was to create "an actual ARMY organization, so that behind every man in the trenches, will stand a woman by the fireside."[110]

Hoover appointed federal food administrators like Merritt to oversee the conservation drives in the states. These men in turn appointed local directors, who worked with wholesalers and retailers to implement Food Administration guidelines and with farmers to stimulate production. They also were charged with coordinating the efforts of women's food conservation committees, which were commissioned to promote housewives' conservation efforts. Despite Hoover's aversion to bureaucracy, his agency issued thousands of directives, correspondence, and regulations. To promote its conservation measures, women's groups came under the purview of this bureaucratic structure as the agency sent a constant stream of posters, recipes, and letters to representatives of the WCND, women's clubs, librarians, and teachers. The national WCND had been keenly disappointed that Hoover chose to create his own food administrators and committees rather than draw upon the structure the WCND had already established among women in the states and localities. Nonetheless, it urged full cooperation with whomever Hoover chose as "food dictator" for their state, noting the importance of the task ahead of them: "This war may be won or lost as much through the saving of the American housewife as through the courage and skill of her husband, her brother, or her son in the fighting armies."[111]

State WCNDs varied as to their working relationship with federal food administrations. In some areas, the partnership was tense, but others proved quite successful. In Los Angeles, the woman chosen to head up the conservation effort, Mrs. J. T. Anderson, was also the head of the local WCND, so in this instance the food effort was consolidated with other activities already undertaken. Anderson enlisted the cooperation of 300 clubs and used a precinct system. During a three-month period in 1917, her group reported that it had orchestrated 172 food demonstrations and 94 home economics lectures; distributed 24,000 pamphlets and 48,000 mimeographed recipes; and held four meetings in each of 800 precincts, with a total attendance of 128,000. It held an "almost continuous chain of lectures and informal talks" and also successfully promoted "victory gardens" throughout the city.[112]

In many cities, WCND women labored to bring the message of conservation to a wide cross-section of the community, including immigrants and African Americans. The Los Angeles committee focused some of its demonstrations in locations that would reach "Italian, Mexican, Russian and other foreign-speaking people of foods suitable for their menus." Without irony, the report noted, "These foreigners were found, with very few exceptions, to be free from the treasonable crimes of waste." The WCND was so impressed with Russian women's use of rye bread that it scheduled demonstrations "to their American sisters" and reported that "the Russian women are delighted to have the opportunity and the committee feel that it will be a valuable piece of Americanization work."[113] A similar turnabout took place in Chicago. In March 1918, the *Ladies' Home Journal* featured a picture of "colored mammies" in white uniforms serving white Chicago women cornmeal cakes and bread. The picture reinforced racial hierarchies, yet it did acknowledge that African American women's expertise with cornmeal made them valuable resources in food conservation.[114]

For their part, African American women seemed eager to participate in the food conservation drive, although the white WCND women organizers often ignored them. Terrell sought to draw attention to the value of reaching out to African American women by writing to Anna Howard Shaw, the national head of the WCND, that since "the greatest conservation of food is in the kitchen, where so many of our colored women are employed as cooks, you will readily agree with me that they are playing a very important part in this war."[115] In areas where black women were well organized, local leaders reported great success with canning projects, gardens, and demonstration kitchens. Southern black women were particularly interested in using the food conservation drive to promote good nutrition as part of their broader project of using the war to promote public health.[116]

At the heart of the federal program was the drive to have housewives sign pledges that read, "I am glad to join you in the service of food conservation for our nation and I hereby accept membership in the United States Food Administration, pledging myself to carry out the advice and directions of the food administrator in my home, insofar as my circumstances permit." Working with the WCND, the national Food Administration mobilized close to 500,000 workers who obtained 15 million signed cards. In California, a local WCND proudly reported, "The windows of Los Angeles homes bore for the first time in history a card testifying to the passer-by that the inmates of this home were pledged to support the Government, the Food Administration, the cause of Americans, and the Allies at the front." Each housewife who signed the pledged was given "home cards," which had information on foods to be conserved (wheat, meat, fats, and sugar). The Food Administration urged that the cards "be hung in the kitchen where they might serve as a daily reminder" of their pledge.[117] It would also serve as a daily reminder of their relationship to the government and the war effort.

The federal Food Administration expended significant amounts of energy and drew upon the unpaid labor of thousands of women volunteers to implement a conservation program that did not involve legal coercion or formal rationing but was nonetheless a powerful check on the food habits of the nation's households. It resulted in an unprecedented incursion of federal power into the homes of Americans. The Food Administration relied upon women to drum up support for the war effort; and women were a crucial link in creating a climate of opinion that made hoarding and waste unpatriotic. Federal officials explicitly recognized that in drawing upon women in this way, they could mobilize the force of public opinion rather than the force of law.[118]

The conservation measures pushed by Hoover's Food Administration were hardly draconian. But by American standards, they did represent an unprecedented though short-lived invasive presence—which included not just regulations, but door-to-door surveys, inquiries, and checkups. Many women complained about the intrusion—resenting both home economists dictating housekeeping methods to them and the government requesting women to sacrifice while not asking men in charge of food distribution chains to do the same.[119] Emily Newell Blair, of the WCND, acknowledged the tension, writing after the war, "All tradition of housekeepers was against a government coming in to tell her what she should do there. Woman is suspicious of pledges of any kind, yet here she was asked to give a blanket pledge that might lead her anywhere, and ask anything of her." It might do "violence" to her motherhood obligation. Blair also pointed out that women resented "a stranger with no official badge or standing come nosing into her private affairs which tradition had told her were not connected with the public interest."[120] Yet housewives did respond—perhaps because the agents who brought the message to them were other women, perhaps because the propaganda of the Food Administration so clearly offered women a meaningful role in the successful prosecution of the war, a role in keeping with their maternal obligations.

As Blair's comments suggest, there were tensions connected to the expanded role of government during the war, despite the strong emphasis on voluntarism. Local and state groups were often frustrated in their dealings with the WCND and government agencies. They complained of mixed signals, weak lines of communication and authority, and general bureaucratic snarls. Women like Virginia Hunt resented red tape and the challenge to localism. Blair noted that women in the various states "stood ready to obey the word of command from Washington," but that they often "rebelled at the waste of time involved in conference between two appointees, or in making duplicate reports."[121] Private letters bristle with subtle and not-so-subtle complaints about duplication of efforts and delays in receiving material "that has been crippling to our efforts and maddening to our souls."[122]

Yet despite these frustrations, women leaders responded enthusiastically to the call for war service. In answer to the question posed at the beginning of this chapter—"How does a state generate the nationalist fervor necessary to sustain sacrifice on the home front?" — examining women's activities reveals the mechanisms by which voluntary associations and the federal government engaged women in a sense of the immediacy of war and the necessity of their support to wage a modern war. The WCND systematically fanned out to cover the nation's households, serving as conduits for the massive distribution of federal propaganda and information. In addition to fulfilling the federal government's requests for assistance in the Liberty Loan, Red Cross, and food conservation campaigns, women leaders in the semiofficial WCND, as well as the WCTU, YWCA, Red Cross, and local organizations, took the initiative in defining war work for women. As they catered to working women, infants, and children and to soldiers and their families, they cast their war activities in the context of maternal values taken into the public arena to counter disruptions to the familial order.

Their reason for engaging so wholeheartedly in war mobilization was not simply unalloyed patriotism, although certainly nationalistic patriotism formed the backdrop of war mobilization for most Americans. They also had their own agendas, which were in place well before the war — of enlivening their associations; supporting reform goals; conveying women's claim to full citizenship; and, in the case of African Americans, promoting racial progress. Yet these agendas dovetailed with the national priority of keeping Americans committed to a remote war. As these leaders articulated an active role for American women, they reinforced a broader connection between war aims and the preservation of the American family. If soldiers were to fight for home, women, and children, women were to mobilize to nurture the soldier at the front and preserve the family from the disorder of war. Although maternalist ideas on one level reinforced traditional notions of the gender order, women activists nonetheless sought to use the war emergency to demonstrate their status as competent new women and the legitimacy of their political voice. Their engagement in meaningful war work encouraged them to view the war as an opportunity to promote both long-standing reform goals and an enhanced role for women in public life.

THREE

Over There

Women Abroad in World War I

> The past week has been so full of thrills for me that it sometimes seems as if life couldn't hold any more, . . . and I sometimes wonder how we'll ever get along without a war when peace comes.
>
> *Charlotte Bannon, American Red Cross worker, 1918*

In a May 1918 letter sent from Paris home to California, nurse Elizabeth H. Ashe described some details of her work with French refugee children and exclaimed, "I am sure I will never be the same again."[1] Ashe was one of an estimated 25,000 American women who went to Europe during World War I. Some made their journey prior to the U.S. entrance into the war, doing volunteer work in aid of refugees or for wounded French soldiers. Once the United States became a combatant, the trickle of women became a flood. Virtually all the women abroad were white. Neither the government nor voluntary associations (with the exception of the YMCA) were willing to send African American women to serve in Europe. Thus, with one exception, this chapter analyzes the experiences of white women, who tended to be middle class or upper class and relatively well educated. While many were volunteers or earned only a modest stipend, others went as paid workers, including journalists, nurses, and telephone operators.

Diversity in the nature of their work and their class and educational backgrounds makes generalizations problematic, but we do know that those who left records described their war work as exciting, if not always the transformative experience Ashe recounted. Although it is difficult to gauge the long-term impact of war service on these women's lives, an examination of their varied experiences and the ways in which they viewed themselves and were viewed by officials and commentators offers insight into this book's broader questions. Women's roles abroad illuminate important aspects of the nature of war mobilization abroad, especially its gendered component. As was the case on the home front, moreover, many women's prewar agendas, including maternalist reform, shaped their contributions to war service abroad. They also inform our understanding of the war years as a culmination of expanding freedoms and opportunities for an emerging "new woman." War service abroad promoted a heightened sense of identity and capability but did not create it. Women who made the choice to go "over there" were already in many ways "new women."[2]

CIVILIAN RELIEF WORK: REFORMERS AND SOCIAL WORKERS ABROAD

The first cohort of American women who worked abroad before the U.S. entry into the war found a wide variety of war service opportunities. They followed in the steps of European women who created agencies to tend to wounded soldiers and to civilian victims of war—refugees, orphans, and others whose lives were upended by the battles that swept over their homes. The enormity of civilian disruption is part of the distinctive quality of modern warfare, which created a huge demand for volunteer agencies among the belligerent nations. Although men in these organizations also addressed the civilian crisis, women, drawing upon a female tradition of good works, played a particularly important part. American wealthy ex-patriates, as well as the wives and daughters of businessmen and diplomats stationed in the warring countries, joined European groups but also created their own agencies to provide for civilian relief, with their activities ranging from Germany to Belgium, from France to Serbia. These women were soon joined by others who made the perilous journey across the submarine-infested Atlantic to serve variously as nurses, doctors, social workers, secretaries, and ambulance or motor car drivers. American women signed up with foreign hospitals and organizations but also worked through newly established American agencies, including the American Fund for French Wounded (AFFW) and the American Relief Clearing House, as well as established entities such as the Society of Friends, the American Red Cross, and the YMCA.

Historians Dorothy and Carl J. Schneider termed many of these women "entrepreneurs" for the resourcefulness with which they found a niche for themselves, often drawing upon family friends and connections. They also frequently shifted positions as they sought more interesting work. Elizabeth

Putnam, a Bostonian of the Radcliffe College class of 1910, came to France to work for the American Ambulance (a hospital under the direction of American heiress Anne Vanderbilt) and did mostly clerical work and visiting with patients. In mid-July, the U.S. army took over her organization, and she felt thrilled to be part of "the whole machine." She next took a job as secretary for a major in the U.S. Air Service in Paris, a position she delighted in for the responsibility it gave her, writing her parents that "I shall consider it one of the most thrilling things I ever did." She concluded her war service working for the American Red Cross as a "searcher," interviewing soldiers to determine what happened to missing men, and at times acting as a nurse's aid.[3]

Marion Otis Mitchell, a Californian who came from a distinguished Berkeley-area family and attended Stanford University, related that she "was simply wild to apply" for a job driving ambulances at or near the front for the Red Cross. Mitchell was one of hundreds of young women who went to France, mostly privileged ones, paying their own way and often providing their own motorcars. The AFFW alone sponsored fifty drivers and motors. They were part of a cohort of young women who had already broken with convention by becoming accomplished drivers. According to scholar Kimberly Chuppa-Cornell, "Like most volunteers, the motor corps women were young, single, well educated, upper- or middle-class, and professionally experienced. Moreover, they possessed special linguistic and automotive skills, making them a distinctly qualified group."[4] Working mostly with displaced civilians near the front lines, Mitchell, an avid outdoorswoman and accomplished driver, found the work exciting and minimized the danger even as she described the sounds of bombs and the alarms of airstrikes. From Nancy, in France, which had been evacuated of all but essential people, she explained, "You never saw such activity, such convoys and batteries and troops going continually up to the front. I am out on that road every day and in the midst of it all. It is tremendously thrilling."[5] These volunteers wanted to be of service but also were clearly eager, like Mitchell, to "see the war," out of a thirst for adventure.

College Women and Social Workers "Over There"

Another important cohort of women who went abroad—college women's "relief units" and American Red Cross workers—focused primarily on assisting Belgian and French civilians whose lives had been derailed by the war. Although not immune to the excitement of witnessing the war and being part of the action, these women also reflected women's reform culture of the

Progressive Era. Not surprisingly, the maternalist reform ideas so evident among war workers on the home front played a part in the way in which these American women contributed to mobilization abroad. They also reflected the emergence of the professional type of "new women," who brought to war work abroad their experiences as settlement house workers, factory inspectors, librarians, youth recreation specialists, child welfare experts, social workers, and public health nurses.

By the late nineteenth century, both universities and colleges had become increasingly open to women (in 1890, women represented 40 percent of all college graduates), and in the new century, work opportunities for all college women expanded significantly. The most common career for these women was teaching, but social work was in the process of becoming professionalized and legitimated, in part because of the powerful influence of the settlement house movement. In the early twentieth century, the term "social worker" was a fluid one and could encompass women without a college education whose training had been relatively short or specifically oriented toward an institution, such as the religiously based YWCA. Elite college women continued to be volunteers in social work activity, but increasingly it was the purview of trained and paid workers. By war's start, this feminized profession, which allowed women interested in progressive reform efforts to find meaningful work, staffed charitable institutions such as the Russell Sage Foundation, as well as government agencies like the U.S. Children's Bureau. When World War I began, social workers flocked to war jobs, both at home and abroad.[6]

Although many college women went abroad as individuals working with various agencies, perhaps the most striking examples of educated women's war service were the relief units sent by Wellesley, Vassar, Smith, Radcliffe, Stanford, and Goucher to tackle the problems of devastated French villagers. Reflecting their mostly elite class backgrounds, these women served as volunteers, yet they embodied the emergence of a "new woman" eager to assert independence and demonstrate professional competence, and they did so in the context of Progressive Era reform culture. Of the groups of college women sent abroad by these institutions, the Smith College group was the only one to serve extensively during the war itself, with the others coming to address postwar reconstruction.[7] Smith, an all-women's institution, had been graduating students since the 1870s, and social work was an option of increasingly popularity in the war years.

The Smith unit originated with Harriet Boyd Hawes, a Smith alumna and archeologist, who had served as a nurse in both the Spanish American

War and the Balkan Wars of 1912–13. In April 1917, Hawes electrified a Smith College club meeting with her challenge to the alumnae to fund a group of Smith women to serve abroad in the field of civilian relief. The alumnae, who responded by raising a total of $200,000 over the years or by themselves volunteering to serve, undoubtedly responded to the idealistic urge to alleviate the suffering of French women and children, but their efforts were also shaped by a sense of proving their own competence. An editorial writer in the *Smith College Monthly* in October 1918, the same issue that featured an article on the relief unit, expected the war to open up opportunities, noting that "when the war is over, industrial and social conditions throughout the country will have to be readjusted, and many permanent positions will be open to trained and educated women."[8]

Negotiations facilitated by the American Red Cross, American heiress Anne Morgan's American Committee for Devastated France, and the AFFW convinced the French government to agree to a plan for Smith women to help dislocated peasants reconstruct their lives, communities, and agricultural production.[9] Seventeen women met a moderately rigorous set of requirements, which included some French language skills and the following attributes: "Proficiency either in motor driving (including the ability to make minor repairs) or in social service; we would like to have doctors, nurses, dietitians, experts in the care of children and the infirm."[10] Bringing with them supplies and motor cars and trucks, the unit set sail for France in July 1917. Among them were two doctors, a wireless operator, a carpenter, a social worker who had learned shoemaking, a journalist, a "farmer" (who had worked for the U.S. Department of Agriculture), four chauffeurs and mechanics, and four professional social workers. They were assigned to eleven (later fifteen) villages near Grécourt, an area of the Somme where a devastating German occupation had just ended. Because it was a major wheat-growing area, the French hoped that the Smith unit could reconstruct the villages sufficiently so that the peasants who remained (women, children, and older men) might restore their farming, even as the war continued to rage.

The once-prosperous villagers, as well as the unit, lived in extraordinarily primitive conditions. The Smith women used French-supplied portable buildings and parts of a ruined castle at their center at Grécourt, while the villagers made do in sections of shelled-out houses, barns, and cellars. A cold climate, intractable mud, and transportation malfunctions added to the challenges of reconstruction. American newspaper and magazine accounts—which were numerous—tended to play up the novelty of college "girls" (the women were all over twenty-five and several of them were significantly older) facing such harsh circumstances and doing rough men's work such as truck repair and heavy lifting. The *Cleveland Plain Dealer* described them as "breezy bonny girls" and depicted their work in sentimental, highly feminized terms, pointing out how they "met the need for women to console and hearten and feed and clothe the mothers and grandmothers and little children of the ruined French villages."[11]

The Smith women themselves viewed their tasks in an organized professional manner, understanding it in the context of social work. Louise Gaines, a member of the unit, would later write of their first impressions, "Destitution, overcrowding, insanitation, these are the familiar catchwords of social service everywhere."[12] To assist in restocking homes and farms, the Smith women established a "country emporium" but also became traveling peddlers, stocking a truck with items ranging from foodstuffs to blankets and then selling them at discounted rates to the peasants, who had French government financial assistance or had salvaged their own money after the Germans left. Child welfare experts set up schools and sewing or carpentry classes, as well as playtime activities and hygiene lessons. The farmer in the group, working with the French government, successfully arranged for seeds and plowing and also secured farm livestock, which the unit distributed to the villagers.

An important aspect of the Smith unit's social work was to help in distributing material goods, but the most compelling work as far as the women were concerned focused on children. Alice Leavens wrote to a friend about her efforts to establish "outdoor games, indoor games, French rounds, sewing and woodworking classes." More dramatically, Elizabeth Bliss, a child welfare expert, reported that "worst of all, the spirit of camaraderie and play has been stifled by the horrors of war."[13] This emphasis on children's play seems naive, even bizarre, in the midst of war, yet the same concerns motivated the American Red Cross, which included in its relief efforts a department of child welfare. These women could hardly have been unaware of the devastating impact of war on the people they sought to help, but both efforts demonstrate the way in which these social welfare reformers brought their domestic agendas and faith in healthy recreation with them to France.

Although their work was extremely difficult and the enormity of the task was daunting, the women's letters home brimmed with excitement and pleasure, a motif evident in almost all letters sent from France by American women. The farm specialist, Frances Valentine, wrote, "I am so thoroughly enjoying my work. I love to get out early & hear my roosters crow, feed the poultry & my horses, see that the cows & goats are all right, plan the farm work for the villages & ride about to see how it's going, and I don't mind being kept so busy. It really seems hardly right to be getting so much pleasure out of it all, when so near there is or will be such dreadful fighting." Similarly, Elizabeth Bliss described their crowded and difficult living conditions but concluded that "we are so happy to be needed we do not care."[14] The women found time for fun as well. Their letters recounted numerous social events with American and British officers, and romance may have flourished for some. Marjorie Carr, for example, later married a man she met at Grécourt.[15]

The Smith women's social work agenda had to be scuttled in March 1918 when a new German offensive broke through the Allied lines, forcing the villagers and the Smith women to evacuate. The relief unit performed heroically in getting its charges to safety and then working with wounded soldiers and refugees as the war raged around them. Newspaper reports announced that the "girls demonstrated admirable initiative and ability and the extreme coolness of the tried soldier."[16] The crisis meant that the unit could not return to Grécourt, and the women instead worked in small groups at ambulance, refugee, and other relief activities. Yet the Smith unit leaders were determined that they would return to their original goal of reconstruction, and in January 1919, four of the original unit as well as newcomers returned to the Somme and recommitted themselves to reconstructing "their" villages.

The postwar effort, even more than the early activities of the unit, reflected its commitment to a social work model. Historian Louise Elliott Dalby explained: "The Unit's work at this stage was more along the line of true social work than before," and in particular, the unit "concentrated on the establishment of permanent schools, of community centers, libraries, clinics, self-sufficient farms, and small shops."[17] Reflecting a clear desire to bring American social work practices to France, they also established a modern community center, which Gaines viewed as perfectly representing "the type of social work we were doing; we had the library, the cinema, the gymnastic classes, the public health nurses, and the dispensary. In short, we had at Grécourt from the beginning a social settlement."[18] It is doubtful whether the settlement house model had any long-term impact on French social services, but it is clear, according to historian Michael McGuire, that the work of the college units, as well as other agencies such as the American Friends and the AFFW, were significant factors in facilitating "interwar rural rehabilitation."[19]

The college units' efforts toward civilian relief and reconstruction had an aura of glamor about them, especially the pioneering Smith group, which received extensive publicity. But much of the relief work done by professional women in Europe was more mundane and framed by the much more bureaucratic structure of the American Red Cross, which had the dual goal of humanitarian aid for devastated civilians and medical care for U.S. troops. The Red Cross civilian work attracted nurses but also a range of highly competent professional or college women who served in administrative capacities for the Red Cross in Europe in one of its three main divisions: the Bureau of Refugees and Relief, the Bureau of Tuberculosis, and the Children's Bureau.[20] The work, which was shared by men and women, reflected American social work assumptions and training. As historian Julia F. Irwin summed it up, for these health and welfare professionals, "volunteering to help European civilians was but an extension of their social and political commitments to the international community."[21]

Two notable Red Cross workers were Molly Dewson and the woman who would be her lifelong partner, Polly Porter. Both ardent suffragists committed to progressive reform, they had experience as social workers. Historian Susan Ware argues that their motivation for going to France was not a romantic desire for adventure, but rather because "there was a war on, and they had no intention of leaving it all to men." Nor did they leave their enthusiasm for women's rights behind. Dewson reported that they were on a boat train to Paris when they heard that New York had enacted woman suffrage: "Our little car jambed [*sic*] with American social workers . . . nearly blew off the track with joy," an account that suggests that the two women found many like-minded suffragists in their work abroad.[22]

Dewson and Porter ended up handling administrative work, with Dewson in particular becoming highly successful, rising to director of civilian relief of a region that constituted about one-third of France. One of Dewson's reports summarized the background of women working for her. Although one assistant had "no special training," others included former employees of three major charity organizations; a superintendent of a large maternity hospital; a graduate from the New York training course for Home Service workers; and the executive manager of Children's Hospital in New York State. With such expertise, Dewson's staff addressed the material needs of thousands of refugees, who returned while the war still raged to their devastated homes, in dire need of homes, furnishings, and health care, a project that required finding the necessary goods and then transporting and distributing them, all the time working with both the Red Cross and French officials.[23]

As time passed, Porter and Dewson expressed frustration with their work. Both the French and the Red Cross imposed a great deal of bureaucratic control—itself a signal of the nature of modern warfare, which involved seemingly endless paper-pushing, and Dewson often expressed her exasperation with male officials. "Really these funny old business men all tricked out in uniform, running around ordering and counter-ordering, and saluting and Majoring and Captaining, are a perfect scream. I never thought men were any smarter than women, and I think their organizing ability is enough to make a dressmaker smile."[24] More telling, both women felt frustrated because they were remote from the battlefront. Although they took pleasure in helping individual French refugees, they longed to be part of the action. As Dewson recalled, "We were wild to go behind the front handing out doughnuts and cigarettes to the soldiers, but not for us. They appealed to us to stand by the ship." And, as Dewson's responsibilities increased, she had less personal connection to the satisfying work of personal interaction with refugees. She described her job as "getting to be a stupid old organizing job."[25] Her frustration stemmed not just from her boredom with bureaucratic work. American women abroad, like Dewson, repeatedly expressed their desire to work more closely with soldiers near the front, perhaps out of yearning for excitement but also because they sought more meaningful ways of contributing to the war effort.

This sentiment appeared repeatedly in the letters of American Red Cross worker Charlotte Bannon. A Smith College graduate and theater manager in Northampton, Massachusetts, Bannon was assistant to the head of Civilian Relief for the Red Cross in Paris. Her early letters enthused that she was having a "dazzling time." Bannon found the social life of Americans in Paris exciting, if at times exhausting, and she reveled in recounting the drama of the bombardment of Paris in spring 1918, even though she found it terrifying. Yet she was repeatedly frustrated by her desk job. When thousands of refugees fleeing a German advance poured into Paris in June 1918, the Red Cross sent scores of "doctors and nurses, auto trucks and chauffeurs, cooks and canteeners and interpreters" to assist them. Her responsibility was to "sit at a desk" and allocate assignments. Bannon, like Dewson, expressed an eagerness to work directly with American soldiers: "We all poured out money, sympathy and help to France and were happy in so doing, but when *our* offensive began and we saw our own men—nothing else but their welfare and comfort mattered."[26]

Elizabeth Ashe, like Dewson and Porter, was a social worker attached to the Red Cross. From a distinguished San Francisco family, Ashe had gone to nursing school in order to have the training necessary to establish the Telegraph Hill Settlement House, which she founded in 1905. She also pioneered at community public health nursing. At the age of forty-eight, Ashe went to France with the Red Cross as part of a contingent of child welfare nurses, and she soon became the head nurse of its Children's Bureau. The bureau's initial focus was on preventive care, and it set up an extensive program of child health education demonstrations that clearly reflected the influence of the stateside "Children's Year." But the nature of the war emergency meant that much of its energies went into assisting French agencies to address the needs of children facing the ravages of war. This included dealing with refugee children and repatriated ones those initially taken by the Germans and then sent back to France. Ashe spent a great deal of time in the field overseeing such efforts as children's homes, medical clinics, and maternity hospitals. She also helped to set up a school for French district nurses in Paris, a reflection of many Americans' optimistic hope that they could permanently shape French public health medicine.[27]

Ashe liked her work and took great satisfaction in its usefulness. Writing in December 1917 that "my work is intensely interesting, in fact quite exciting, as I have to fly from one spot to another adjusting difficulties," she was gratified to be "always welcomed with open arms which is a pleasant side of it." By the next month, as more American troops entered battle, Ashe became increasingly concerned about the needs of American soldiers, writing to a friend that "my deepest interest is with our boys."[28] So intent was she to serve soldiers that she requested vacation in order to work as a nurse in an army hospital, noting in a letter to a friend, "If I am shot at dawn for deserting I intend to look after our wounded instead of well baby clinics."[29] Military need for nurses became so pressing that Ashe also became responsible for sending women who had come to be children's nurses to the front instead. According to Ashe, all of them were eager to go and performed beautifully.

By August 1918, the pressure for military nursing subsided, and the Children's Bureau once again focused on long-term child welfare, with Ashe working on an infant mortality campaign. She had high expectations about the bureau's educational work, noting, "I feel that it will be the most lasting and real benefit that Americans will bring to France." In particular, she hoped that "the band of visiting nurses, whom we are training now, will have become a mighty army carrying their banners marked 'Hygiene' into every home in France."[30] It is hard to evaluate the long-term impact of the Children's Bureau, but one Red Cross historian has found lingering evidence of its success with the visiting nurses' plan and the educational outreach, especially in Lyons. The permanent impact fell short of Ashe's optimistic predictions, but overall the Red Cross and its agents certainly served to mitigate the suffering of the war emergency. About a sixth of its entire budget for French operations during the war—or $9 million—went to help 2 million French refugees.[31]

The YWCA: Professional Reformers "Over There"

Although individual women abroad, like Ashe, Dewson, and Bannon, got caught up in the desire to tend specifically to America troops, both the Red Cross civilian bureaus and the Smith College unit focused primarily on adapting American social welfare programs to the extraordinary circumstances of war-ravaged Europe. The European war work that YWCA women tackled was far more familiar to their long-standing reform agenda. Just as the YWCA had focused especially on wage-earning women at home, they did so in France and, to a lesser extent, in Russia, Belgium, Italy, Poland, and other European countries. Although the U.S. government authorized only male-led organizations (YMCA, Knights of Columbus, Salvation Army, and Young Men's Hebrew Association) to work abroad with soldiers, the YWCA found a niche in line with its traditional activities when French women who had already established some facilities for war workers requested aid for hard-pressed female munitions makers. In August 1917, the YWCA sent its first cohort of secretaries.[32]

The centers created for French women, called "foyer canteens," paralleled those for American women workers at home, and the ideas embedded in their approach seem virtually the same. YWCA leaders stressed the maternalist notion that a woman's organization was particularly appropriate for attending to the needs of these workers.[33] Anxiety to protect the morality of working women was also evident. Authors noted that French women's lives had been disrupted by war and further endangered by the presence of American soldiers. A prominent YWCA leader, Henrietta Roelofs, noted that there were "hundreds of American boys, who break loose from the seriousness of grinding work once in a while for a gay good time and hundreds of French girls also away from home and for the first time enjoying the taste of independence." Instead of allowing them to "throw themselves headlong at each other," the YWCA offered the young women alternative entertainment. Miss Alice Woolley, head of the foyer canteen in Tours, explained that the

YWCA center was "the only opposition to the streets, cafes and cinemas."[34] And although fears about sexual immorality were high on their list, YWCA leaders also hoped that their facilities would discourage alcohol consumption by offering attractive alternative places for meeting and wholesome recreation.[35]

YWCA foyer canteens were apparently appreciated by their clientele, as well as by the French government. For the French, however, the practical benefits of meals and quiet rest places, rather than the YWCA's larger reform agenda, were undoubtedly the attraction. YWCA leaders seemed to have worked with little interference from either American or French officials and to have enjoyed an unusual amount of autonomy, given the bureaucratic structures that shaped so much of war mobilization. Their success led to the French government requesting that their program expand throughout France. By the end of the war, YWCA women had created twenty-eight foyer canteens, six recreation camps, and four summer camps. Ultimately, approximately 339 women secretaries served overseas.[36] Eventually, YWCA secretaries would also take on responsibility for providing housing and services for American women abroad and for war wives, and they estimated that they had served over 20,000 French, American, and British women.[37]

While the YWCA war operations abroad suggest the way in which its leaders framed war activity through prewar ideology and controlled participation in war mobilization, the facilities are also revealing of the way in which they offered YWCA secretaries the opportunity to find meaningful war work in their professional capacity. As early as 1895, the YWCA began training its "secretaries" by offering graduate training in social services. In 1908, it began what would be called the National Training School in New York City. Graduates were dispatched to run YWCA programs both at home and abroad (the YWCA had an extensive missionary program in Asia at this time). While the school trained only a small proportion of YWCA secretaries, it speaks to the YWCA's understanding that its employees were professionals—"an executive of the Young Women's Christian Association must be a student of economic, educational, social and religious problems affecting the life of women and girls in all parts of the world. It is her function to devise and execute plans for the solution of such problems."[38]

It is not surprising that accounts of the secretaries in France repeatedly stressed their professional training and experience. Mary A. Dingman, one of the first YWCA secretaries to go abroad, had specialized in industrial work for women in New York City.[39] In Tours, Caroline Dow, who had been dean of the New York YWCA Training School for Secretaries, was in charge.[40] YWCA secretaries, at home and abroad, were part of a growing cadre of white-collar professional women, often college educated, who in the early twentieth century clustered in jobs connected to social services. Well before the war, they were making their mark, but the war offered them a unique opportunity to demonstrate their expertise and training.

SERVING SOLDIERS: YMCA CANTEEN WORKERS

The eagerness of Dewson, Porter, Bannon, and Ashe to cater to the needs of American servicemen was realized in the work of women who staffed "canteens" for soldiers overseas. While the army authorized several organizations (the American Red Cross, the Knights of Columbus, the Salvation Army, and, later, the Jewish Welfare Board) to operate facilities that provided soldiers with food treats, cigarettes, and (mostly) modest entertainment, the YMCA conducted the brunt of what was usually called "welfare" work, and will be the focus here. The Knights of Columbus did not use women in their canteens, but other agencies did. About half of the staff of canteens for the Jewish Welfare Board were Jewish women. The rationale for female participation stemmed from the same concern for moral order that had propelled the home-front drive to eradicate prostitution and control "khaki girls," and thus the YMCA work followed the trajectory of Progressive Era moral reform movements. Fears about venereal disease, heightened by a sense of European decadence, fueled the military's acceptance of the social hygiene reformers' notion that exposing soldiers to "respectable" American women as symbols of home and family would deter soldiers from sexual misadventure. The women would not only assuage homesickness, but they would also encourage sexual restraint that would keep men "fit to fight."[41]

Although this aspect of the military's campaign to control sexually transmitted diseases was well known, it also adopted a policy of abstinence education and, when that failed, mandated medical treatment. Social hygiene lectures, complete with graphic details of the physical results of sexually transmitted diseases, formed part of stateside training. The focus was a scientific, fact-based approach, rather than the moralism of the social reformers. More pragmatically, the AEF established prophylaxis stations throughout the war zone and made failure to visit these stations after sexual activity a court-martial offense. Despite the two-pronged attack of moralism and treatment, neither method was completely successful. The military estimated that at least 30 percent of men serving abroad were sexually active, and almost 400,000 cases of disease were reported at bases stateside and abroad, at an estimated cost of 7 million service days.[42]

While the scientific strand of progressivism was evident in the medical response to disease control, the moralistic one associated with both the military's promotion of abstinence and the YMCA canteen work was powerful in shaping the American approach to sexual disease among servicemen. The notion of the moralizing effect of women-staffed canteens also speaks to the nineteenth-century feminization of American culture.[43] Decades of women reformers' insistence on their gender's moral influence framed the discussion of women's value in serving soldiers near the front. Although the plan was not uncontested, the military's unprecedented decision to allow women to staff canteens abroad reflected a belief that such service was crucial to their men's welfare and the successful prosecution of the war.

Given their aims, not surprisingly, YMCA leaders made every effort to recruit women of high moral character. In addition to basic requirements such as age (a minimum of twenty-five, lowered to twenty-three after the Armistice), health, and no relatives serving abroad, the YMCA conducted interviews designed to ensure that only sensible, respectable women would represent it abroad. The organization almost completely excluded African American women. Only three were commissioned initially, and only nineteen served during the course of the war and demobilization. African American women served 200,000 black soldiers and had similar duties to white women, yet their work was much more stressful, in part because of the disparity in the numbers of men they tried to accommodate, but also because of the persistent discrimination they and the men they served experienced.

YMCA women workers were initially volunteers. Indeed, the first canteens were established by elite women (Mrs. Theodore Roosevelt Jr. and Mrs. Vincent Astor) and were staffed by Americans already in Paris. But as the need grew, YMCA women became paid employees. They were middle-class and, at times, elite women who were relatively well educated. Six women's college alumnae associations recruited and paid the expenses for their alumnae to go abroad; the Junior League also sent representatives from their local organizations; and the Federation of Women's Clubs financed two women from each state in their YMCA canteen work. Some were fluent in French; many had training as teachers, social workers, librarians, and kindred professions; others had worked as volunteers in charitable activities. Of the approximately 3,500 women who went abroad, YMCA reports indicate, only 649 were "unclassified" as to work experience. The most well-represented occupations were educators, secretaries, entertainers (the YMCA sponsored activities similar to the USO today), social workers, stenographers, and clerks. YMCA female workers, then, like relief agents, for the most part represented a generation of "new" women with an independence their education or work experienced had already engendered in them.[44]

Their experiences varied from place to place. Although the bulk of canteens were in France, some women served in Italy and Britain. Paris canteens, except those at the train stations, tended to be upscale dance and tea party events. The hours were long, and the duty was not without danger, given the periodic shelling of Paris. The YMCA also operated dozens of facilities at leave areas for enlisted men, who were not permitted to go to Paris or other cities on leave, for fear that they would succumb to sexual temptation.[45] For these men, the YMCA women organized social events and outings in gorgeous settings at former casinos and resorts for men on one-week leaves. The more arduous assignments were the YMCA "huts" near the front or in training areas, where women faced remarkable challenges in their job of maintaining morale.

Whatever their location, these women, or girls, as they were usually called, had as their official charge to serve men, literally serving them cocoa and cigarettes, but figuratively serving their spirits as well. African American and white women had similar work details, but their experiences were so different that I examine them separately here, with the African American story following that of the more numerous white women workers. These women clearly understood reformers' hopes that their presence would deflect men from baser pleasures. Frances J. Gulick's 1930 short memoir reported that on the boat across the Atlantic, they "listened to lectures about the 'beneficent influences' we 'wholesome American girls' were to exert upon the troops exposed to the 'perils and temptations' of foreign service."[46] In a letter from Paris, Violet H. Bennet wrote more earnestly to a friend, "It is hard for those at home to realize the struggle that the boys are making over here to keep [morally] straight for the sake of those they have left at home—and so they welcome the Y.M.C.A. and all it has to offer them—with open arms."[47]

Despite this all-important rationale, most YMCA workers' letters and memoirs soft-pedaled the reform aspect of their work and instead emphasized their role in helping men to cope with the stress of war and homesickness. Though seemingly less concerned with moral order, they, like YMCA and military officials, often presented their work in terms that emphasized their nurturing, feminine qualities. Some described enlisted men as "innocents" or as childlike, which may be part of a cultural stance that presented these women in nurturing positions. Their sentiments may also reflect class differences, as YMCA women's exposure to working-class men may have been limited prior to war, and the men's lack of polish may have made them seem immature. Marian Baldwin, for example, characterized the men she served as "adorably simple."[48] Finally, describing these men as innocents may have served to defuse issues of sexual attraction and harassment. Although undoubtedly women may have formed romantic or sexual attachments while serving abroad (especially, apparently after the war, when women continued to serve troops as they demobilized), these are absent from memoirs and letters. And there were no records of sexual assaults. Some women did express concern about the potential sexual threat posed by soldiers, but others commented on how safe they felt among the masses of men they encountered in their work. While it is tempting to suggest that lack of privacy and fear of military discipline were key factors in making YMCA women off-limits, it may also be that the sentimental commentators who waxed eloquent about how happy servicemen were to merely chat with wholesome American girls were accurate in their recognition that soldiers respected these women for their hard work and devotion and protected them.[49]

This devotion was impressive. YMCA work was arduous, even in the more pleasant venues such as Paris and leave areas. Nearer the front lines, YMCA women often arrived to find primitive living and working conditions and the circumstances disorganized. They had to convert spaces to their use, scour towns and villages for furniture, and locate sources of fresh provisions and fuel. YMCA male secretaries were present, although they tended to handle organizational and financial matters. While many women praised the YMCA men, others were critical of their incompetence and what we would now call their sexism. Frances Gulick wrote to her family about a new secretary who did not "know what to do with women around." He did not think ladies should do dishes, nor could they handle money. "The last week has therefore been taken up," she reported, "with demonstrating that we are of use otherwise than as ornaments."[50]

Once established, the women turned to the toil of preparing and serving food, coffee, and cocoa, making change (the YMCA charged a nominal fee for its products), mending uniforms, reading letters, and otherwise tending to homesick men. Their work was impeded by bitterly cold weather and ankle-deep mud. And given the large numbers of soldiers they had to serve, the pace could be frantic. Lucy Lester reported, " We are supposed to have off a day every week, several hours every day, but I can truthfully say that neither I nor my co-workers has had more than an hour free any day since we went to work. There have been days when the only time we sat down was at our meals."[51]

Although YMCA canteeners apparently were much appreciated by the soldiers themselves, the full extent of their responsibility and competence was often eclipsed by their disenchantment with the menial and tedious nature of much of their work. In addition, many chafed against YMCA male officials' lack of respect for them. Admittedly, the YMCA, which had first described their duties as "menial" work in the kitchens, increasingly emphasized their welfare work and changed their titles from canteen workers to the same classification as men, "secretaries," in an explicit recognition of the value of their work. Yet, despite this recognition, the overall public representation of the canteen worker stressed the nurturing woman who was extending woman's special capabilities to the European theater of war.

Even though the women themselves often adopted the language of nurturing their "boys," many YMCA canteeners defined their work in broader terms that revealed their own sense of being modern women. Although not viewing themselves quite as equals to the men they served, they often called themselves soldiers and stressed the significance of their uniform in distinguishing them as official parts of the war effort. Figure 7, which shows Frances Gulick dressed in her YMCA uniform posed happily in front of an army truck, hints at the pride women took in being part of the military world. When Marian Baldwin wrote home to her family that she received discounted train fare, she noted, "So you see, in more ways than one, it pays to be a soldier." After the war, Gulick recounted that during her canteen work with the First Engineers, the men gave her an ID tag, with "my name, my religion and '1st US Eng' stamped on it. I cannot tell you the pride I took in that dog tag. I belonged to an outfit." Even in the cloyingly sentimental postwar account of "My A.E.F.," in which author Frances Newbold Noyes thanked her soldier comrades for saving the world for democracy, Noyes recounted the camaraderie she enjoyed with "her" soldiers, which included, beyond the usual YMCA canteen activities, playing poker and shooting craps. In recounting a handful of army acronyms and slang, she proudly noted that "we are all citizens of the same far country and speakers of the same tongue. . . . We need no overseas ribbons to identify us; we all have the same password."[52]

But if the canteeners viewed themselves as "soldiers," the army most certainly did not and generally prohibited them from getting close to the battlefront. Yet many, if not most, yearned to be close to the front. Their comments are filled with the sense of enormous devotion they felt toward "their" men and determination to provide them with some minimal comforts as they

Figure 7. Frances Gulick, YMCA canteen worker. Library of Congress, Prints and Photographs Division, Photograph by Harris and Ewing. LC H261–30892.

prepared for combat or came out of it. And despite the prohibition, many did serve close to the front lines. According to a military account, during a crucial battle at Saint-Mihiel in October 1918, five YMCA women "worked in advance dressing stations, bathing wounded and distributing cigarettes and hot drinks." The same account reported that another woman, accompanied by a male secretary, got ahead of the ammunition trains convoy. Working under shell fire, they commandeered an abandoned German kitchen just behind the lines and "made hot chocolate all night, and after night carried it to various companies in thermos bottles." A number of YMCA women also joined their men in the march to Germany at the end of the war. Gertrude Ely had brought her own Ford "tin lizzie" to France. Given the order to move, according to one account, "she packed a lot of rations, a cook-stove, a boiler, chocolate, a fiddle, some maps," and other equipment. She set out ahead of the troops to the next destination, found a suitable place for a temporary hut, and then set up shop so the men would find her ready with they arrived in town. Even though the French did not approve of women near the front, Ely received the French Croix de Guerre for her service.[53]

The women's eagerness to continue their work near the firing line may be explained in part as an extension of the nurturing role they were supposed to fill. Yet many clearly chafed against the rules that limited women's participation and sought to prove their capability and also experience the drama of war firsthand. In wartime letters published after the war, Katharine Morse reported with much annoyance that the YMCA had sent her away from the front lines to Paris, a reassignment that was a disciplinary action for her success in getting near the front at Verdun. "I have, it seems, been guilty of conduct unbecoming a lady under shell-fire." Marian Baldwin's determination to stay with her men similarly got her into hot water. The first time she and a companion made a foray with supplies toward the front line at Verdun, she reported that "we started off ahead of the regiment with a certain feeling of thrill," but they were turned back by a colonel who told her that "this was no place for a woman." Less than a week later, Baldwin and three other frustrated rebels set off on their own, knowing roughly where the division headquarters were supposed to be and convinced that they were needed, "orders or no orders." She recounted an eventful process of driving, training, and trekking to get to headquarters, where the men were thrilled to see them. Having made a "triumphal entry," she exclaimed, "As long as I live I never expect to be so happy again." This time, officials allowed the women to stay. But she detailed continual resistance to women so close to the front and delighted in their success in managing to stay, commenting, "I don't suppose I have ever been as useful[,] and the experience is great."[54]

Baldwin may indeed have been a rebel, but her love of the adventure was a common theme. Many women wrote of their eagerness to get to the front. Edith Gratia Stedman, assigned to a leave area in Aix, reported that she was "anxious now to get my job here polished off—then go up to the Front." Later, having failed to get closer to the action, she did manage assignment to Paris, where the bombings had stepped up the danger. She described Paris as "a pretty good substitute for the Front. I can't tell you how grateful I am for the chance to be in this. War is awful but has its compensations."[55] These women who spoke so passionately—and often naively—about their desire to see the front suggest a different kind of modern woman than the social workers engaged in relief work. Their frustrations with YMCA and army restrictions based on their gender reflect the young new women's eagerness to break down barriers to personal freedom and to challenge the rigidity of the gender order that many male officials clearly wanted to maintain. Abroad, new women reflected the same diversity they embodied at home.

This diversity is especially evident in the experiences of the small number of African American women who saw service abroad in YMCA canteens. At first glance, their war service paralleled that of white women. They prepared and served food, wrote letters, sewed on buttons, and offered cheerful companionship to homesick young men. But black women abroad understood themselves not merely as "new" women enjoying the opportunity for service and independence, but as black women representing the race generally and black women specifically. As Addie W. Hunton and Kathryn M. Johnson noted in their 1920 memoir, "The authors have written because to them it was given to represent in France the womanhood of our race in America—those fine mothers, wives, sisters and friends who so courageously gave the very flower of their young manhood to face the ravages of war."[56] Hunton and Johnson, along with Helen Curtis, were the only black YMCA women secretaries to serve abroad during the hostilities, although in 1919, twenty more secretaries arrived to share their duties.

The three were quintessential "race" women. They were college-educated professional women, active in racial uplift and civil rights organizations, including the NAACP and the NACW. Older than most American women who went abroad (they were all in their forties and either married or widowed), they had significantly more life experience, and all three had traveled to Europe before as students or tourists. Curtis was apparently more outspoken than the other two and was almost sent home for having made comments critical of the treatment of African American soldiers. Hunton and Johnson tended to be more moderate in their racial politics, but historians suggest that their war experiences radicalized them, and like many other black leaders, they became more militant about asserting African American rights.[57]

While on the surface their responsibilities were the same as whites, their racial agenda led them to view their welfare work as an extension of racial uplift. By providing services to African American men, they understood themselves as continuing African American social workers' efforts to extend community services to blacks and to fight for equal treatment. In addition, both male and female black YMCA workers paid particular attention to offering their men educational opportunities, especially literacy training, in the YMCA huts, recognizing this as an exceptional opportunity for self-improvement. Hunton, Johnson, and Curtis served primarily near Saint-Nazaire, where African American troops were concentrated doing manual labor near the port of Brest, although they did have the opportunity to work briefly in the leave area of Aix-les-Bains and to visit Paris. Each was assigned to a different base, working with black male YMCA secretaries, but they were close enough to each other to offer some companionship and support. Their canteen work may not have been harder than that of white YMCA secretaries, but they keenly felt the disparity in numbers, reporting that the three of them were the only women detailed to serve approximately 200,000 men. The three—1 percent of YMCA women—served 16 percent of the AEF forces.[58] Figure 8 shows Hunton surrounded by a group of soldiers and hints at what Hunton and Johnson noted in their book: the delight of black soldiers to see one of "their" women as canteen worker.

Beyond the problem of inadequate representation, the three women witnessed more explicit racial discrimination from both YMCA officials and military personnel, noting that "the service of the colored welfare workers was more or less clouded at all times with that biting and stinging thing which is ever shadowing us in our own country." Hunton was first sent to Brest but was recalled almost immediately because the military decided that the men there were too rough to have YMCA secretaries, male or female, a decision that rankled with Hunton, who understood it as racially inflected. When the two women first arrived, they also discovered that Curtis was on the verge of being sent home. The news devastated them, making them question the value of their work. "Would blind prejudice follow us even to France," they later wrote, "where men were dying by the thousands for the principles of truth and justice?" And at the end of their service, they were insulted by the

Figure 8. Addie Hunton, YMCA canteen worker in France. Courtesy of the Kautz Family YMCA Archives, University of Minnesota.

poor shipboard accommodations for their return: all black YMCA women secretaries were placed on a floor below the white women, and male and female African Americans were "placed in an obscure, poorly ventilated section of the dining room." When the women protested, they were told that "southern white workers . . . would be insulted if the colored workers ate in the same section of the dining-room with them."[59]

As distressing as these insults were, most of the attention Hunton and Johnson gave to racial discrimination in their book featured the degradation black soldiers endured. For the most part denied the opportunity to serve in combat, these men were relegated to "Service or Supplies Units"—where they performed mostly manual labor. They were often refused access to YMCA canteens run by white secretaries, or if admitted, they received perfunctory attention. Even more disturbing was the knowledge that the military attempted to limit African American fraternization with the French by informing them that African Americans were not considered equals to whites and in some cases warning them that black soldiers were dangerous. For their part, the French tended to be welcoming to both the African American soldiers and the YMCA women. French courtesy, Hunton and Johnson explained, "furnished to some of us the first full breath of freedom that had ever come into our limited experience."[60]

Although Hunton and Johnson detailed their own experiences in France as well as those of black soldiers, the book conveyed a variety of tones. On the one hand, it celebrated African Americans' patriotism and service and justified their claim to full citizenship. On the other hand, although it acknowledged those white YMCA officials who sought fair play for blacks, it bitterly relayed the extent of discrimination both the women and the black soldiers faced. With this in mind, a comment in the introduction seems to have had a double meaning. "We were crusaders on a quest for Democracy! How and where would that precious thing be found?" Hunton and Johnson implied that they sought not just democracy in Europe, but democracy for African Americans in the United States. The book then, and their framing of their experience, was an extension of the crusade African American women leaders were pursuing at home. Hunton and Johnson protested injustice while demonstrating patriotism. And they constantly kept the needs of their community—in this case black soldiers abroad—at the forefront of their concerns.

While many of the women abroad discussed thus far often came up against military restrictions or regulations, they were part of the substantial machinery of war run by voluntary associations like the YMCA or the Red Cross. And, indeed, the fact that their employers or sponsors (in the case of volunteers) were nongovernmental agencies may explain part of the fluidity of mobilization that offered so many women a niche in the European theater of war. But a significant number of women worked abroad directly under the auspices of the U.S. government. Nursing accounted for the most numerous female employment in the military, but a few female doctors overcame stiff resistance to find their way to France, although many did so through voluntary associations. Additionally, the AEF needed clerical and other support staff. Medical personnel and white-collar staff came to their jobs as skilled professionals and workers who represented a range of education and at least some of the diversity that characterized the "new" woman's increased participation in the workforce in the prewar era.

Clerical Staff and the Signal Corps' "Hello Girls"

The need for clerical workers in government agencies and the AEF reflected the changing nature of warfare itself, with large-scale bureaucratic structures in place that needed administrative staff. One female YMCA administrator wryly noted that "she sometimes felt as though the war would be won by the stenographers."[61] But if warfare had changed, policy makers, especially in the War Department, resisted the idea of hiring American women to man the infrastructure of war. At home, military forces routinely used women staffers, and the Marines even permitted them to enlist as "yeoman," explicitly to free men for combat abroad. Still, the idea of women serving in uniform abroad was anathema to most officials, who felt they would disrupt military order.

One solution came by drawing upon the already-existing English Women's Auxiliary Army Corps (WAAC). Britain established the uniformed WAACs in 1917, amid controversy over the threat to women's femininity. As one woman reporter noted, her countrymen were fearful that when the WAACs came home from France, "the country will be overrun by cigarette-crazed, mannish, self-opinionated creatures with short hair . . . and a distaste for domestic life."[62] Early in the war, Elsie Gunther, who had an administrative job working on Wall Street in New York City and then organized the clerical force at a military training facility at Plattsburgh, New York, took charge of a program to bring hundreds of WAACs to France to assist the AEF in mostly clerical capacities. At the very end of the war, there was a brief flurry of anticipation that American women would be tapped for the same purpose—and apparently the government was flooded with applicants, who were disappointed when the plan was deemed unnecessary by military authorities, who felt that there were sufficient male draftees not suitable for combat who could fill the bill. But American women did find their way to France, working as stenographers, typists, and statistical clerks for U.S. military offices, most of them hired quietly without fanfare to minimize tensions over female military employment.[63]

Far more visible were the much-publicized Signal Corps "Hello Girls," as telephone operators were called in the United States. The need for American operators abroad arose when U.S. military officials realized that not only had the French telephone system been severely damaged by warfare, but also that French operators had neither the language skills nor familiarity with the American telephone system. Thus the call went out for experienced telephone operators who were fluent in French. Ultimately, of 7,600 applicants, 223 operators went to France between March and October of 1918, and others served after the war during the reconstruction period and the peace negotiations. The total number of women hired was 377, but many of these did not serve abroad. Those who did cross the Atlantic worked in Paris, Tours, and other cities, and in some instances at headquarters close to the front.

Most of the women and some observers apparently thought that the operators were actually in the army—they wore uniforms adorned with the official Signal Corps insignia. But, in fact, the women were civilian contract employees. Much ambiguity arose over their status, because most were inducted following military procedures and not offered civilian contracts. According to Oleda Joure-Christides, she "was sworn in exactly as my brother or any person enlisting in the U.S. Army." Signal Corps women found after the war that they were not entitled to veterans benefits or burial in military cemeteries, a status that was not changed until 1979. Aside from the disappointment over postwar treatment, the ambiguous status of Signal Corps women also served to constrain them. As historian Susan Zeiger notes, "Women, who believed they were enlisted personnel, behaved and were controlled like soldiers but received no military benefits."[64]

Military personnel file archives provide us with an unusually detailed statistical picture of the Signal Corps operators. Because the army had so much difficulty in finding operators who met its requirements, only about 25 percent of the women were both skilled operators and bilingual. A rigid language test narrowed the pool significantly, as did peacetime telephone companies' policies of not hiring women with accents. Those in the first group of women who went abroad were the most likely to be bilingual telephone operators. The AEF's response to the difficulty in finding suitable operators led to the decision to hire fluent French speakers (often teachers or college-educated women or women of French or Belgian descent) and then train them to operate a switchboard. Later in the war, when French fluency became less important than skill and speed, the AEF hired operators without language skills.

In many respects, the Signal Corps' Hello Girls were similar in background to canteen workers. They were white and relatively well-educated (43 percent were high school educated, compared to the general population figure of 16 percent, and 14 percent had college degrees). Most (87 percent) Signal Corps women had worked outside the home before their AEF experience, compared to 69 percent for canteen workers. Of the 303 women for whom historian Jill Frahm could identify employment, about 31 percent had been operators. The others were most likely to have been teachers or clerical workers. Like canteen workers, the vast majority were single (only 11 were married). But what is particularly interesting is how many of them—an estimated 57 percent—lived away from their parents, a significantly higher proportion than for the nation at large, where the percentage was about one-third.[65]

Although only about a third of the women had previous operator experience, the context of their domestic work patterns is instructive. The early twentieth century witnessed an expansion of women into clerical work, and what we now call pink-collar work—especially telephone operators, which had become an almost exclusively female position. Thus, when the military argued that women operators would take the place of men, who could then serve at the front, they were being disingenuous: Signal Corps women were filling positions already established as women's work (and, indeed, in France, women operators trained the enlisted men who took the evening shifts). Typical of other sex-segregated jobs, operators were viewed as doing "women's work," which meant that they were devalued and underpaid. Telephone operators had a slightly unique position in that although their wages were only slightly better than factory workers, they viewed their positions as superior—because their environment was clean and their positions required more education and English fluency. On the surface, their work life seemed better than the harsh conditions of factories, but they were subject to extreme regimentation, monitoring, continuous repetition, and a general speedup, which may account for the eagerness with which they unionized. Many were ardent suffragists as well. Thus telephone operators were a core group of young women who were challenging the economic and legal discrimination they faced, and this spirit influenced many Signal Corps operators' worldview.[66]

Taken together, the work and life experiences of the Signal Corps women suggest the spirit of a "new woman." This spirit of independence undoubtedly shaped women's desire to serve in the Signal Corps. As was the case with other women who went abroad, eagerness for adventure and foreign travel played an important part as well. Patriotism was also a factor. Mary Snow noted: "We are the happiest women in the world for we were allowed to come to France to do our part in winning the war." Patriotic motives may have been even more intense for native French-speaking women, who presumably had a particular affinity for France or Belgium. Oleda Joure-Christides, for example, recalled in an oral history: "War propaganda, especially that of accusing the Germans of massacring innocent Belgian civilians, coupled with Kaiser William's ambitions to Germanize Europe and President Woodrow Wilson's pronouncements to make the world safe for democracy, had fired my imagination and thinking. Being of French descent, I felt some personal and patriotic interest in the conflict." She later noted that after she saw the casualties of war, she became more doubtful about the possibility of saving the world for democracy.[67]

The work was demanding, with the same type of oversight and discipline experienced at domestic switchboards. The women were subjected to a scientific management approach, also known as Taylorism, after Frederick Taylor, whereby their productivity and speed were closely monitored and personal conversations were prohibited. Yet the operators rarely protested and instead took pride in their accuracy and speed, with one operator explaining, "The girls are always early at their work and their greatest pleasure in life is to give connections accurately and quickly." What made their work so satisfying was the sense of their crucial contribution to the war effort. Berthe Hunt noted, for, example, that it "was most thrilling to sit at that board and feel the importance of it."[68]

To some extent, public commentary on Signal Corps women, similar to that concerning other women abroad, emphasized their femininity. Articles noted their popularity at dances held for them by the YMCA and the YWCA, and others emphasized that they were carefully chaperoned. Authors routinely used the term "Hello Girls," yet significantly, the Signal Corps operators protested to the War Department and insisted upon a more dignified name. Officially they were called "the Woman's Telephone Unit of the American Signal Corps."[69] Yet perhaps because Signal Corps women had such specific training and presumed military rank, public commentary on them did not as frequently use the same language of nurturing women that was so evident in discussions about other women abroad. Observers commented both on their presumed military status and their competence. One newspaper account proclaimed, "In perhaps no other women's corps is there such strict military discipline and such a recognition of the responsibility of being members of a women's organization that is part of the United States army. . . . They are enlisted women just as much as every man in General Pershing's army."[70]

Signal Corps women met with much praise for their competence and bravery, but, like other women abroad, their presence created tensions about the suitability of women participating in war. Susan Zeiger has noted: "Military commanders, unsure of how to integrate women workers into traditionally male areas of endeavor, took a paternalistic approach, treating them as a special and protected category of personnel to be carefully monitored in their work and leisure hours."[71] This was most evident in the AEF decision to ask the YWCA to provide housing and oversight for the operators stationed in Tours and Paris. The YWCA took over two hotels for that purpose. The operators were quite carefully chaperoned and limited in their excursions. Army and navy camps, as well as the docks, were off-limits to them.[72] Although the YWCA secretaries described the Signal Corps operators as extremely competent workers, they also clearly viewed them as vulnerable, especially to sexual danger. The telephone operators for their part understood themselves to be vital parts of the war effort and tended to stress their self-reliance and independence, casting themselves implicitly as new women.

Medical Women

Medical women who worked abroad during the war were in a unique position. Like Hello Girls, their skills made them valuable overseas, despite resistance to women near the front. But they were distinctive because their rising professionalization made many of them more acutely conscious of the sex discrimination they repeatedly encountered. More so than any other group of American women abroad, they collectively understood themselves to be challenging the barriers that constrained women's occupational opportunities.

By the outbreak of World War I in Europe, female physicians had experienced growth in numbers and in expanding professional organizations. Some women doctors, deeply enmeshed in the reform tradition of social work, concentrated on public health medicine geared toward women and children and did not seek equality with male physicians. Yet others, already steeled from a history of combating male resistance to their entrance into the profession, viewed the war as an ideal time to demonstrate their competence and equality. Physicians were often suffragists as well, and this too heightened their sense of war service as a vehicle for advancing their claim to both full citizenship and medical expertise. Organizations supported by an array of women's groups, including the Medical Women's National Association, sought to achieve military rank on par with male physicians but were disappointed at every turn.[73]

Three other options were open. The U.S. military employed physicians as "contract surgeons," who worked without benefit of rank, authority, or status, and many female doctors hoped that signing up for these jobs might be an entering wedge toward achieving their goal of military rank. Fifty-five women signed on as contract surgeons, most of them working at bases in the United States. Only seven were assigned abroad.[74] Here, too, they were quickly disillusioned. They were often treated dismissively, and because many were not trained surgeons, they found themselves relegated to nursing work. Other women adamantly refused the idea of contract work and turned instead to voluntary associations, like the Red Cross. Augusta Williams, whose work abroad was underwritten by Wellesley College, was one of approximately seventy-six women doctors who went abroad with these groups. Although Williams at first felt underutilized, she eventually was assigned to a military hospital, where she served as an anesthetist, noting that this role allowed the male doctors to concentrate on surgery and the nurses to focus on their nursing.[75] More typically, American women doctors treated civilians, as was the case with Ethel Lyon, a Texas suffragist and head of Galveston's Woman's Health Protective Association. Lyon, one of sixteen "stars" in the suffrage flag, served at Chalons, about fifteen miles from the front, in a maternity hospital.[76]

A final option was the all-female medical units, created primarily to serve the needs of French women and children. The Women's Overseas Hospitals (WOH), established in 1917, received sponsorship from the NAWSA to develop women medical units. A second group with the same aims, as well as the expectation of serving military purposes, was the American Women's Hospitals (AWH), a creation of the Medical Women's National Association.

The backdrop for the creation of these units was both the intransigence of the American military in accepting women doctors and the extensive attention given the plight of French women and children. Dr. Esther Pohl Lovejoy, an Oregon physician and prominent suffragist, took the lead in publicizing their dilemma. Sponsored in part by the WCND, as well as the American Red Cross and the AFFW, Lovejoy sailed to Europe in September 1917. There she visited a noted Parisian settlement house already working with poor women, especially single mothers, whose lives were further disrupted by war. She investigated refugee areas as well and was particularly distressed at the sexual abuse and violence women and their children had been subjected to. As she summed it up, "Warfare is much worse for women than for men. Men have the right of death and they die fighting gloriously for their ideals. But women must live and be confiscated with the goods and the chattels."[77]

Both the WOH and the AWH dispatched medical units to France, but neither quite met expectations. The WOH consisted of "gynecologists, general surgeons, obstetricians, a radiologist, bacteriologist, dentist, pharmacist, 21 nurses, 20 nurses' assistants, chauffeurs, laboratory assistants [and] a bookkeeper" and had planned on establishing a hospital in a refugee center. But on arrival, in March 1918, the German offensive in the Somme had started and the French asked them to serve in French military hospitals. About half of the group did so, while the other fulfilled the original purpose of establishing a center for refugee medical care. The women who worked in the military hospital stressed the importance of demonstrating equality with male doctors in serving "men fresh from the trenches." Yet, as historian Kimberly Jensen notes, with less experience in battle medicine, the women doctors had less responsibility and were working under the direction of French male doctors, not as their equals. Nor "were they operating a military unit on their own in which they could set priorities for the medical care for women."[78]

The AWH, in contrast, kept its unit together under female leadership. It had planned to establish a mixed hospital that would serve both soldiers and civilian women and children. The Armistice came before they could implement their plan for tending to soldiers, but they did on occasion answer French calls for temporary work in military hospitals, without compromising their autonomy. While the AWH had not been able to advance its goal of demonstrating medical equality with male doctors, it was successful in serving French women and children. In addition to treating hundreds of patients in their facility at a chateau in Luzancy, it also established a house call visiting system and clinics in nearby villages. After the war, under Lovejoy's direction, the AWH continued its work, shifting its focus to other war-torn regions, such as Armenia and Greece.

Like women physicians, nurses were also in the midst of advancing professionalization in the prewar years. Beginning in the 1870s, nursing-training programs for white women multiplied and a new style of nurses sought to distinguish themselves from the popular association of nursing with servants and suspect sexual behavior. Despite her intimate exposure to the body, and especially the male body, the trained nurse, through both her skill and her gentility, could become a respected practitioner. By the early twentieth century, nursing had become a respectable career for middle-class white women, although professional leaders continued to battle sexism from male doctors and administrators and to attempt to institute more control over nurse training and employment. They also restricted access to the profession by excluding African American women. While many nurses worked as "private care" nurses, from 1910 to 1920 opportunities expanded, not only in hospitals but also in public health nursing, a field prompted by Progressive Era social reforms, especially those associated with settlement houses. Nurses' engagement with progressive reform, along with their ongoing battle with the male medical establishment for appropriate professional recognition, led many nurses, like other career women, to be suffrage supporters, understanding it as a means for "professional advancement and autonomy as well."[79]

White nurses' professional advancement well situated them for a role at the front in World War I. During the Spanish American War (1898), 1,200 contract nurses had served military personnel in Cuba and in camps at home, and in 1901 Congress had created the Army Nurse Corps. Its first head, Jane Delano, was also director of the Red Cross Nursing Service, which was designated as its reserve force. The bulk of nurses who saw overseas duty did so through the Red Cross or the U.S. Army. As Chapter 1 noted, African American nurses were excluded from service abroad until after the war. During the war, 10,000 white nurses served with the military abroad and another 10,000 were stationed in the United States.[80] The relationship between the Red Cross and the military was a complex one. Red Cross nurses who served in military hospitals were, for all practical purposes, the same as those officially in the army or navy. None of the women were accorded rank within the military hierarchy, and thus they were denied the authority, status, and benefits that came with rank.[81]

The issue of rank was a controversial one. In contrast to the experience of female doctors, the concept of female nurses ministering to soldiers abroad met with relatively little resistance, because the need for skilled medical workers was so great and because of the perception that women were "natural" caretakers of the body. Yet women nurses, like doctors, faced extensive discrimination, and the most obvious discrimination came with the refusal of the military to accord them rank. In repeatedly requesting rank, nursing leaders sought recognition of nurses' contributions and of their professionalism. They also sought to protect nurses from arbitrary rules and workplace hostility, including sexual harassment. Nurses also complained that without a clear rank within the military hierarchy, head nurses were limited in their ability to command the nurses under their charge, primarily because male officers could countermand their orders and procedures. Many suffragists, recognizing that the issue highlighted the way in which women were denied full citizenship rights, joined the campaign for rank. In a *New York Times* letter to the editor, Harriot Stanton Blatch, who headed up the Committee to Secure Rank for Nurses, praised nurses' skill and efficiency and concluded that "if Uncle Sam knew his skillful and devoted nurses were being discriminated against and shabbily treated he would quickly set the matter right." The efforts met with little success. After the war, Congress equivocated and in 1920 created the concept of "relative rank," which gave nurses a commission and the right to wear military insignia but denied them the corresponding salary or clear status in the military hierarchy, a compromise that was not changed until 1944 during World War II.[82]

While the popular press often portrayed nurses as heroic patriots, more generally they presented military nurses in a sentimental, romanticized fashion, as either maternal or virginal. These images, however, did not forestall widespread rumors of nurses' sexual impropriety, innuendoes for which there was no basis. Despite being subject to sexual harassment by male officers, nurses apparently behaved with discretion, in part perhaps because they were often subject to strict rules about fraternizing with officers and enlisted men. The rumors can be chalked up to the phenomenon flowing from historic association of nursing with prostitution, but also undoubtedly were tied to nurses' power and independence.[83]

For nurses, the real challenge was the work itself. While canteen workers were occasionally pressed into emergency aid for wounded soldiers, nurses coped with the butchery of war on a constant basis. Like male medicos, they had to learn not to show their horror at the extent of injuries they witnessed and to relentlessly persevere in addressing the needs of their patients. Nursing venues varied, with some stationed at convalescent hospitals and others on special hospital trains or at base hospitals. Small units of medical teams that included nurses also served quite near the front in casualty-clearing stations. With the exception of those stationed at convalescent facilities, most nurses experienced some version of the dramatic spurts of wounded called "the rush." Fierce combat produced hundreds of wounded in a short amount of time, and medical staff worked feverishly, often for forty-eight hours straight with little rest. The rush, as Zeiger argues, was much like the soldiers' "going over the top" and gave nurses a close sense of identity with the battle itself.

Nurses' accounts, far more than those from other women abroad who had less exposure to war's human cost, conveyed a sense of the devastation of war. Gertrude Bowling, a nurse at a field hospital, described the desolation at Château-Thierry when her group arrived just a week after the German evacuation but while the battle still raged. The dead were still unburied, there was filth everywhere, and everything was in ruins. They established their hospital in a damaged building: "Through our paneless windows and the ragged shell holes in our wall, the flare from the big guns and their boom kept us awake." The next day their work began in earnest. "You forgot many things you have been taught. You only remembered to roll up your sleeves and dig in. It was work, eat, sleep, work. One stretch of duty was the same as the next. You forgot the days of the week; you thought only of how many you could keep from dying."[84]

Repeatedly, accounts of nurses near the front stressed the hard work and perilous circumstances. Nurse Julia Stimson said the nurses under her charge were "doing such surgical work as they never in their wildest days dreamed of, but all the time unafraid and unconcerned with the whistling, banging shells exploding around them. Oh, they are fine! One need never tell me that women can't do as much, stand as much, and be as brave as men." And clearly, the women themselves were proud of their grit and accomplishment. Helen C. Bulovsky, a Wisconsin nurse, remembered that after the strain of first duty at the front, "we lost our frail dispositions and developed into husky gypsies who were ready to move in short notice by way of ambulance, truck, or boxcar. Our food and water was limited. We carried mess kits, canteens, gas masks and helmets. I dare say experience taught us to be artful dodgers when it came to shrapnel celebrations at night."[85]

Thus, although nurses experienced ill health from exhaustion, cold, disease, and the strain of coping with the wounded and dying, overwhelmingly they reported a positive sense of service and accomplishment. Victoria Christensen insisted to a reporter that "nursing is [as] important as the fighting, and it must be done. . . . Wonderful is the only way in which the work the women are doing over there can be described." And she concluded that their service would have long-term implications, noting that their work would "be even more brilliant before the war is over."[86] Christensen was probably over-optimistic in her predictions for long-term professional progress as a result of war service, but she was right in assessing the highly valued status of military nursing. As Zeiger sums it up, "For women who enlisted to gain a place within the military, secure public legitimacy, and attain status on a par with men through their work, nursing came closer to fulfilling their goals than did any other form of service open to women in 1917."[87]

WAR REPORTERS

Journalists who covered the war and/or the Russian Revolution were distinctive among women who went abroad because they did not wrap their motives in the mantle of patriotic zeal or service to soldiers and refugees. Instead, their goals were career based, and they clearly sought to demonstrate their own and more generally women's capabilities as professionals. By 1914, American women had made significant inroads into journalism; many wrote for women's magazines from the "feminine angle" or covered social news events, but some were carving out a reputation for "hard" news, and as such many female reporters were eager to obtain press passes to cover the dramatic events of a world at war.

It is not clear how many women negotiated the affiliation with a magazine or newspaper that would allow them to secure a passport and the necessary permissions to travel during wartime. Many reporters were already in Europe, and, like Alice Rohe, a United Press correspondent in Rome, they stayed to continue their reporting when war broke out.[88] In general, securing a commission to cover the war proved difficult, and those women who found editors willing to send them abroad met with adamant military resistance to women covering warfare and the front. Most magazines and newspapers expected their women journalists to report on human-interest stories that would appeal to their women readers. Gertrude Atherton, for example, sent stories back in 1916 on the war work of French and American women engaged in nursing and refugee work; and Jessica Logier Payne, working for the *Brooklyn Eagle,* detailed the activities of British women working at traditional male jobs. Eunice Tietjens, an established poet and author, represented the *Chicago Daily News,* which asked her to cover sentimental stories such as one "about what became of all the socks knitted by the women at home." She rarely did, explaining, "I never was really good at the strictly women's stories I was supposed to write."[89] Though Tietjens managed to get to the front on several occasions, for the most part she, like other women reporters, covered mostly human-interest stories, not the hard news on the war itself.

Most interesting were the women who circumvented the restrictions that kept them from reporting the war. Mary Roberts Rinehart, a highly popular novelist, secured a commission from the *Saturday Evening Post* in 1914 and once in Europe headed to Belgium, where she wrangled accreditation through the Belgian Red Cross. She got close to the fighting and incurred the resentment of male reporters when she was permitted to be among the first group of reporters to visit "No Man's Land" at the trenches. Later, she reported from France, even securing an interview with General Ferdinand Foch. Her experiences were dramatic: "One month I was inspecting an anti-aircraft battery. . . . Again I would be in dressing stations, and for the third time I found myself one day in Ypres, still under fire." Despite her triumph, the experience had unnerved Rinehart, and she determined to return to more feminine endeavors in war, "undertaking such womanly tasks as surveying conditions in French hospitals and, at the behest of the United States government, writing stories to tell families how their sons were trained into soldiers."[90]

Rheta Childe Dorr, a well-known writer and suffragist, who arrived in France in 1918 representing two New York newspapers, also circumvented the restrictions placed on women and what she called "my old sex handicap." To her amazement, the American military "refused point blank to recognize me as a war correspondent, refused even to give me a pass north of Paris." She coped by securing employment as a lecturer with the YMCA, which accommodated her by sending her to speak in places where her reporting took her. Like Rinehart, she got close to the war as well as the troops and eagerly reported on American successes, a reflection of her decidedly pro-Allies, anti-German sentiments. Despite her avowed feminism, Dorr's reporting reflected a strong maternalism, and her book published during the war, *A Soldier's Mother in France*, a reference to her own son's military service, was specifically written for soldiers' mothers.[91] Although Dorr seemingly accepted this feminized version of war reporting, her sensitivity to sex discrimination in the newspaper industry peppers her autobiography, *A Woman of 50*.

Most women wrote from France or England, but a few reported from Germany. Most notable was Madeleine Z. Doty. Both her pacifism and her feminism informed her reporting. Doty had attended the 1915 International Peace Conference, where European and American women sought to halt the war. At its conclusion, she traveled to Germany where she investigated conditions there, paying particular attention to the struggles of the poor and especially of working women, whom she portrayed as victims of war. Her pacifism aroused suspicion in Germany, and she feared arrest, but she eventually made her way to France, where she wrote and served briefly as a nurse. She ended her trip in Great Britain marching with suffragists. She published numerous articles in books and newspapers and then came out with a book about her observations, *Short Rations, An American Woman in Germany* (1918). The success of that book was short-lived because Americans quickly came to view it as too sympathetic to Germany, but its initial reception led *Good Housekeeping* to commission her for a round-the-world trip to report on the conditions of women, a project that Doty told her readers she hoped would further international understanding among women and the promotion of peace.[92]

Doty's reporting agenda was very clear, and we can similarly see the way in which other reporters' specific worldviews shaped their understanding of the events they covered, especially the four women—Doty, Rheta Childe Dorr, Bessie Beatty, and Louise Bryant—who reported on the Russian Revolution, which began in March 1917. The revolution, dramatic for its own sake, was integral to news overage of World War I, because of the pressing question as to whether the new regime would stay in the war or make a separate peace with Germany. Unlike on the Western Front, women reporters had remarkably free access to covering the war and revolution news in Russia.

All four women were suffragists and self-described feminists who embodied the ferment of prewar American urban women caught up in a self-conscious expression of modern womanhood. Doty, a Smith College graduate, was a well-respected attorney and social worker with a major book on prison reform, which she had researched by going undercover as a prisoner herself. She was part of a radical New York Greenwich Village community and in 1919 would enter an unconventional "50–50" marriage, designed to give each partner independence, with Roger Baldwin, who was jailed for refusing the draft and who would later cofound the American Civil Liberties Union. Louise Bryant, a left-wing writer associated with the radical magazine the *Masses*, was part of a literary and artistic group also centered in New York and, though married to fellow radical John Reed, had an open affair with playwright Eugene O'Neill. Bessie Beatty, a reporter for the *San Francisco Bulletin*, wrote a guide for California women voters after they won the franchise in 1911. Well known on the West Coast for her reporting on labor issues, she attracted particular attention for sympathetic coverage of the impact of

Figure 9. Reporter Bessie Beatty with Russian soldiers. Courtesy of Occidental College Special Collections and College Archives.

closing the city's red-light district on the prostitutes themselves and went on to help the women organize a prostitutes' union. Like Beatty, Rheta Childe Dorr made a name for herself covering labor news. She became a proponent of working-class women and children and a leading prosuffrage journalist.[93]

All four were boundary-crossing women, and their zeal to make the arduous journey to Russia and to witness, firsthand, history in the making reflected their self-consciously modern and independent spirits, as well as their eagerness to make names for themselves as writers and reporters. Although Bryant as a socialist was the most politically radical, Beatty, Dorr, and Doty had long histories of social justice concerns and thus were attracted to the notion of the Russian Revolution being the harbinger of the emergence of a democratic regime. Each wrote newspaper and magazine articles, with Beatty particularly prolific, as the *San Francisco Bulletin* ran weekly letters from her with editorial comments that emphasized the drama of a woman reporting from a tumultuous and dangerous place. The image in figure 9 was one of several photographs that illustrated Beatty's book, *The Red Heart of Russia,* and it conveys a sense of Beatty's adventurous spirit. All four women published articles as events unfolded and produced books about the revolution immediately upon their return to the United States.

They witnessed a dramatically tumultuous time as the revolutionaries fought among themselves, with the Bolsheviks ultimately coming to power in November 1917. The chaotic conditions meant that intrepid male and female reporters had unusual opportunities to report the extraordinary events, such as the storming of the Winter Palace in Petrograd that unfolded as the Bolsheviks solidified their power. Beatty not only wrote about her experiences, but she also became a news subject herself. The Associated Press reported her presence at a confrontation between Bolshevik troops and supporters of Aleksandr Kerensky in the telephone exchange in Petrograd, where she helped tend wounded Kerensky troops and encouraged panicked women telephone operators. "Brave Bessie Beatty, American Newspaper Girl, a Heroine in Petrograd," the storyline read.[94] Not surprisingly, Beatty later said, "I had been alive at a great moment and I knew it was great."

All four women reporters sought and obtained interviews with key leaders and wrote knowledgeably about the complicated forces determining the disposition of power and the decision of the Bolsheviks in March 1918 to withdraw from the war, making a separate peace with Germany. Beatty became friendly with Leon Trotsky and was talking to Vladimir Lenin during an assassination attempt. All four were particularly interested in meeting with Russian women, with radical Louise Bryant lionizing the Bolshevik women, while the more politically conservative Dorr reported sympathetically on the hardships faced by the aristocratic women associated with Czar Nicholas.

Not surprisingly, the reporters showed particular interest in Russian women soldiers. In an era when women were crossing boundaries, these soldiers represented the most dramatic example of challenges to stereotypical sex roles and the most emphatic claim to the implications of full citizenship. From the beginning of the war, a number of Russian women had fought side by side with men against the Germans, but in June 1917, the Revolutionary Provisional Government created distinct combat units of women. Probably as many as 4,000 women served in eleven units throughout Russia, but the Americans had firsthand knowledge of only a few of these and especially of the first one, a so-called Battalion of Death, which was established by Botchkareva, a peasant woman soldier who was dismayed by male desertions and argued that an all-woman unit could serve to rally troops by either inspiring them or shaming them. Although patriotic nationalism—"to die for Mother Russia"—undoubtedly influenced women to volunteer, historian Melissa Stockdale argues that even as the revolutionary government enfranchised women, the sense of equal citizenship may also have played a part: "Thousands of women interpreted this equality to mean that women could and should assume the citizen's right to bear arms."[95]

Dorr and Beatty actually traveled with them for several days (neither reported the other's presence in their accounts), sharing their rough lodgings and food and watching them prepare for battle, only leaving their company shortly before the women went to the front. Beatty described a composite female soldier and her own closeness to the front: "I met her first in Petrograd when she was a raw recruit with a kerchief or a nurse's coif or a Parisian hat upon her head. I watched her change her woman skirts for the blouse and breeches of a soldier's uniform and saw her long braids and her soft curls fall beneath the barber's scissors. I stood by while she learned to stand and march, to salute, to load, to aim and to fire. When she was a full-fledged soldier ready to pit her strength and her courage against Prussian bomb and bayonet, I went to the front and shared her hard plank bed by night and her soup and kasha by day."[96]

The four Americans all admired these women's bravery but took different lessons from their example. Madeleine Doty, a committed pacifist, was clearly troubled by women bearing arms and argued that women were creators, not slayers. "To abuse the body is to abuse the child of the future, and women live for the future. . . . They must be warriors of the spirit, not slayers of the body."[97] Bessie Beatty explicitly rejected this essentialist view of women. She argued that the Battalion of Death countered the antisuffrage argument that because women could not bear arms they could not vote, that it countered the feminist view that women did not need to bear arms because they bore soldiers, and, finally, "against the fervid faith of the Pacifist—that 'women, who will pay such a terrible price to give life will never be able to take it away'—she was preparing to drive her saddest and bitterest blow. Destiny, in short, was about to bring confusion upon the tidy pigeonholes in which we keep our firm convictions ready for all emergencies." Dorr similarly believed that the Russian women soldiers demonstrated women's essential equality. She described herself as a "feminist finding in these women the realization of a theory stubbornly adhered to, that women are not a class, governed by limited impulses and emotions. They belong to the race."[98]

Both Dorr and Bryant viewed Russian women soldiers through their own particular political lens. Dorr, a fervent anti-German, prowar advocate, criticized the cowardice of Russian men, who were allegedly responsible for the women's decision to take up arms, and in particular noted the equal danger these women faced from their own comrades, detailing the ways in which the unit she traveled with was harassed by men, even to the point of stationing an armed guard in their barracks to ward off Russian soldiers "looking for the girls." Appalled by the Bolshevik regime and critical of its decision to withdraw from the war, she reported on the Botchkareva unit as part of the defense of the Winter Palace and claimed that the Bolsheviks had killed and/or raped the women as they conquered the palace. Bryant, an adamant apologist for the Bolsheviks, countered this argument by tracking down surviving women, who refuted the claim, and Bryant was almost certainly correct.

The four reporters helped to make the Battalion of Death familiar to Americans, a process heightened by Botchkareva's tour of the United States. The battalion became yet another example of the way in which women defied traditional expectations in the war era.[99] Beatty, Bryant, Dorr, and Doty themselves were even more potent evidence. As they covered the Russian Revolution, they inevitably presented themselves as independent, resourceful, and brave. As a reviewer of their books commented, "The sheer physical endurance represented by these volumes, quite apart from the courage involved, seem amazing in a woman."[100]

THE MEANING OF WOMEN'S WAR SERVICE

During the summer of 1918, Red Cross office worker Charlotte Bannon wrote a series of letters home in which she repeatedly commented on the vitality of life in wartime Paris. "We are really living here," she exclaimed in one letter, and elaborated: "And we race on through the weeks—eager to live it all up to the hilt. Everyone over here feels a sort of desperation at times about it,—that we are going to live it all to the depths, and we sort of close our eyes to what will come après la guerre. We often think of the normal quiet life back at home and wonder what you'll think of us when we all come back. We shall never be the same again."[101] Ironically, it was Bannon who had complained that her desk job was too boring. Clearly even an administrator could find the war experience exhilarating. Beyond the unusually articulate Bannon, assessing the impact of war service on the diverse American women who worked abroad is difficult. Although their sense of adventure has been emphasized here, certainly women who served abroad took the war and their duties seriously. Nurses wrote movingly of the soldiers they tended, both those who lived and those who died. The fierce protectiveness of many YMCA canteeners toward "their" men also revealed an understanding of the high human costs of war. But letters and memoirs tended to be surprisingly upbeat in tone, especially compared to their European counterparts. Government censorship during the war, as well as self-censorship, may have been a factor that shaped their accounts. Self-dramatization, too, may have played a part. Moreover, Americans' experience of the war was much shorter and less brutal than that of Europeans and may explain to some extent Americans' stress on adventure and even self-realization. What is absolutely clear is that American women abroad found excitement in the pace and challenge in their work, or their nearness to the front. Whatever hardships they may have encountered or whatever devastation they witnessed, they reveled in the sense of being part of such an important drama on the world stage.

Others sought even more thrills beyond their assigned tasks. Elsie Janis, a vaudeville star who entertained the troops, often under fire, which she found "pepped" her performance up, not only wrangled a trip to the front but was permitted to fire a big gun, an experience she described as "thrilling as I have never thrilled before. " She came away "very proud" and pleased to hear that "I was the only woman who had fired regular hundred and fifty-five power hate into Germany."[102] Marion Watts, a YWCA official, reported excitedly that she had even ridden in a motorcycle sidecar and that "there is nothing that we have not done or tried to do." A YMCA worker whose letters were published anonymously was clearly a sheltered young woman before her war experience, who constantly reassured her parents about her safety and the appropriate behavior of the soldiers she served. Yet she too evinced a clear zest for adventure and recounted her excitement when a pilot took her up for an airplane ride: "Oh! It was great! There was not the slightest suggestion of fear; just a tremendous exhilaration. Never in my life have I so enjoyed anything. All the time I was up I wanted to shout and sing. . . . Such is the sensation of irresistible power imparted by the machine."[103]

War-related excitement was often accompanied as well by the delight in living in a foreign country. In many ways, these women were tourists, enjoying a beautiful country with compelling scenery, charming villages, and stunning cities. This aspect of war service appeared in the letters of soldiers as well, men who, remarkably, found time to appreciate the very "foreignness" of France, which, despite the disfigurement of trench warfare, retained much of its beauty and a semblance of everyday life outside the zone of battle. Some women who served abroad were already experienced travelers, but even they delighted in discovering quaint villages, purchasing small antiques to bring home, and enjoying French cuisine. Paris-detailed women especially enjoyed being able to live in that city, which, despite food and coal shortages and frightening bombing raids, still charmed. Elizabeth Cabot Putnam's letters sparkled with their descriptions of picnics, daytrips, and elegant meals, and she reported, "One nice thing about this job is that I have to cross the Champs Elysees, about midway between Etoile and Concorde, every morning, when the sun (if any) shines directly on the Arc de Triomphe, and the chestnut trees are all russet-colored and the avenues are full of blueness — it is really worth while."[104] Molly Dewson described the area near Aix-les-Bains as "beautiful here beyond words."[105] Signal Corps operator Louise Barbour, who had previously been in Paris, was nonetheless enthralled with the usual tourist sites along the Champs-Élysée, remarking in a letter to her mother, "O Boy! Ain't it a grand and glorious feeling."[106]

For other women, travel was new. Telephone operator Merle Egan recalled in an oral history account: "Travel to Europe was a luxury. Few of us, with minimum incomes, expected to make such a trip. There were no planes to take us there, most ships two weeks or more to cross the Atlantic." Noting that the "United States was an isolated country," she explained that Americans cared very little about the rest of the world "before the war broke out." Elsie Mead, a YMCA official, wrote home, "In all my life nothing has ever compared with the experience of the last three days. — This beautiful France, I don't wonder the French die willingly to save it."[107]

The romance of travel often means romantic love, but there is little hard evidence as to whether or not women abroad commonly formed romantic liaisons. Certainly many women, especially those in Paris, described dinners and theater dates with men, but rarely with any commentary on the men themselves. Organized dances in which women who were associated with most of the agencies were more or less required to attend were a common occurrence, but these were often viewed as burdens — exhausting rounds of dancing with dozens of different men — rather than opportunities for pleasure. The Smith Relief Unit women, who seem to have operated fairly autonomously, enjoyed numerous social gatherings with English and French officers, which either they or the men hosted. And for them, some romance may have flourished. One Smith woman married a man she met while at Grécourt.

In contrast, Signal Corps operators, nurses, and YMCA canteen workers were subject to much chaperoning and oversight, which may have limited their courtship possibilities somewhat, as would the highly demanding nature of their work. After the Armistice, when YMCA women continued to serve abroad in canteens for another year, YMCA officials were concerned that standards were slipping, at least for a small proportion of women. Mrs. Mead, head of the Women's Bureau of the YMCA, issued a letter to all women workers reminding them that they were to wear their regulation uniforms in public at all times and that they were not to smoke or drink in public places or dine with officers in the field. The latter restriction was apparently prompted by enlisted men's resentment that YMCA women were spending "too much time with their friends among the officers," thus giving the impression that "they have come to France for their own amusement, and not because they wished to serve their country."[108]

Their experiences abroad might have offered women opportunities for more freedom with the opposite sex, but far more important was another type of freedom: the sense of independence that living and working abroad offered. Certainly many women had already had opportunities to live away from their families, yet letters and memoirs pulse with a sense of accomplishment in moving about the country, attending to business, or taking leaves. Despite the much-talked-about chaperoning of phone operators, they often traveled alone to their posts. Reporter Sterling Heilig quoted the captain in charge of Signal Corps women as saying that "they can be counted on. . . . We say to a young lady: 'Go to Paris.' She packs her baggage and we take her to the station, and she goes up to Paris by herself. She travels about France where she is sent, without making conditions or objections or observations. Our Signal Corps girls give no trouble, but go on time and take care of themselves."[109] Edith K. O. Clark, a Wyoming school administrator who went to France to work for the YMCA after the Armistice, not only thrilled at being in France but prided herself on her independence, noting in a letter home about her time in Paris: "Work during the day. . . . Home alone on the metro at 10pm—feeling very smart and independent."[110]

The most dramatic example of independent travel came from the round-the-world trips of reporters Bessie Beatty and Madeleine Doty. Beatty's newspaper, the *San Francisco Bulletin*, sponsored Beatty's trip, while Doty journeyed separately under the auspices of *Good Housekeeping*. Both journals made much of the women's adventuresome journeys through Asia and then to Russia on the Siberian Express, with the story of their traveling, for the most part alone and in dangerous and exotic settings, news in itself. In her published articles for the *Bulletin*, Beatty emphasized the chaos in foreign train stations, especially in revolutionary Russia, but minimized the danger, noting that English-speaking men gallantly came to her rescue on a number of occasions when she found herself stranded.

Doty, in contrast, highlighted one episode that dramatized the danger of a woman traveling alone en route to Russia. When she was already undressed and in her train compartment in bed, the door burst open. A Russian

Cossack, leering at her, began undressing, clearly enjoying her discomfort, and climbed into the upper berth. Doty got dressed under the covers, then left the compartment, spending the night in the corridor. The next day, she sought out two American men, who found her a private place to sleep. Despite her discomfiture, Doty concluded, "Life had got down to the elementals. There was no room for conventions, and I had better stay at home if I was so particular. I swallowed hard and tried to adjust myself to new conditions."

What is most interesting about this account is the way in which *Good Housekeeping* presented it. A full-page illustration by the noted artist James Montgomery Flagg portrayed the threatening Cossack looming over Doty, pictured as a beautiful woman, hair down around her shoulders, with bedcovers drawn up over her body (fig. 10). *Good Housekeeping*'s image may have stressed Doty's vulnerability, but her account, and especially her decision to "adjust," suggests the self-conscious way in which Doty recognized that in order to bring home the story, to do her work, she had to cross boundaries that defied traditional notions of female respectability, and that she willingly did so. Some of Doty's breathless account about her female sense of propriety may have been a bit disingenuous. As a prison reformer and journalist, Doty had already gone undercover to investigate a woman's prison, hardly a genteel occupation.[111] Although Doty and Beatty were unusual cases, other women shared their sense of transgressing expectations about women's behavior. Traveling alone in dangerous places, negotiating transportation in wartime, solving problems their work presented, coping with stress or, in the case of nurses, the trauma of wounded soldiers, women abroad found frequent opportunities to take satisfaction in their competence. War had not created their independent spirit but rather had given them a vehicle for its expression.

Whether this independence was deepened by serving in the war and subsequently shaped their lives is the kind of question historians simply can't answer for such a large and diverse number of women. Yet one story is suggestive and well worth detailing, even though it cannot be viewed as representative. Dorothy Ainsworth graduated from Smith College in 1916. In an oral history she recounted: "Most of us, when I graduated from College, had no idea of a profession. I supposed many people thought they would marry sometime, but they did not feel they had to get out and do something. Most felt the need to go back and be with their families who had been kind enough to send them to college. . . . I wasn't very articulate about this, but I had some such feelings. Therefore I went home to work."[112]

Figure 10. *Good Housekeeping*'s rendition of Madeleine Z. Doty on the Siberian Express. *Good Housekeeping* 66 (June 1918): 43.

Home was Moline, Illinois, and there Ainsworth lived with her family, taught Sunday school, worked at a community center, and, though she had no formal training, taught physical education classes at the Moline high school. Ainsworth had been too young to go to France with the original Smith Relief Unit in 1917, but in spring 1919, she was selected for the unit's postwar reconstruction work and felt it was a "golden opportunity," as she still had not decided what she wanted to do with herself and had no "particular future ambitions." Ainsworth thrived in the work in France and, when she returned to the United States, had apparently found her professional bearings. She received a Ph.D. from Columbia University Teachers College and spent most of her career as a professor and later director of Smith College's Physical Education Department. Fittingly, she was noted internationally as well. She cofounded an international association for women and girls in sport.[113]

Ainsworth found her calling, but what about other women? The creation of the Overseas Service League in 1921 indicated that many wanted to hold on to the sense of purpose and camaraderie that their time abroad had sparked. The Overseas Service League emerged out of clubs formed in various cities and by 1922 claimed 2,000 members. Journalist Frederic J. Haskin reported, "Overseas women, back from huts and canteens, have not been content to settle down to the old routine of work and play. The thrill of being in contact with a world war is not easily forgotten." The new organization hoped to offer a sense of larger, patriotic purpose that would allow the women "to maintain the ties of comradeship born of" their war service and to assist men and women veterans who had been wounded in the war.[114]

Local groups took on a variety of projects, including creating servicemen's reading rooms and employment bureaus and visiting injured veterans in institutions. At least among the national leadership, women in the league tended to echo the nationalistic sentiments of the American Legion (a male veterans' organization that apparently admitted some women who had served abroad) and in particular promoted the idea of universal male military training.

If Overseas Service League women focused on maintaining a link to military service, other women who had served abroad took up the prewar emphasis on women's rights and women's suffrage. In a postwar article, "You Went to France: Now What Did It Do to You?," Anne Warwick insisted that war service had proved women's equality, noting that women had become "superwomen" and that "we cannot go back—we won't! . . . We want to hang on like grim death to these new selves we have acquired; and by means of which we have found that life is not dull, but gloriously inspiring." Warwick suggested that women could support the League of Nations or address problems in "her own America, with its immediate call for reconstruction and home-service work of all sorts—better housing conditions, better sanitation, better education in the science of living generally." Similarly, an article, "Women and the Future National Welfare," quoted Martha Cook, who after the war took up community service work: "There is so much that ought to be done in the way of national welfare and so very many ways in which women can help. I think the war has greatly changed women—at least every woman who took an active part in it." Cook particularly stressed the importance of women using the ballot.[115] Still other women were active in the postwar peace movement, with Madeleine Doty, for example, continuing her prewar pacifism through a lifetime commitment to the Women's International League for Peace and Freedom. Addie Hunton not only participated in this organization, but she also engaged with Pan-African organizations, reflecting a new militancy her war years had engendered.

Some women's longer view of the war also reflected the disillusionment we associate with the Lost Generation of American writers who wrote cynically about the American idealism that had justified the war and bitterly about its devastating human cost. The American public may have been less disenchanted with the war than popular memory suggests, a point taken up in the Epilogue. Yet we do have evidence of women's critical stance toward World War I.[116] Particularly compelling is Mary Lee's 1929 prize-winning novel, *It's a Great War,* which offered an evocative critique of the war that stemmed from Lee's overseas experience as well as her disillusionment on return to the United States.

Lee, a Massachusetts-born Radcliffe College graduate, traced the fictional war experiences of Anne Wentworth, who worked variously as a stenographer for the Red Cross and the American Air Service in Paris and as a YMCA canteen worker, jobs that Lee herself had done. Anne, like real women who served abroad, was a competent new woman who enjoyed her independence and the adventures war offered her. Yet Lee consistently tried to deromanticize the war and the role of women in it. She emphasized bureaucratic bungles, military officiousness, and the sheer drudgery and boredom that faced the soldiers and civilian men and women who served behind the lines. Offering a largely sympathetic portrayal of the doughboys themselves, as well as most nurses and YMCA women secretaries, Lee cast male YMCA workers largely as provincials who were far less competent than the female canteeners. And, in contrast to the popular pronouncements about women's moral influence on soldiers, Lee presented a more jaundiced view. Two of her subsidiary female characters — a secretary and a nurse — had sexual affairs, and a major male character in the book, Anne's future brother-in-law — conducted a serious affair with a French woman. In addition, Lee pulled no punches when it came to revealing the high incidence of sexually transmitted disease among soldiers.

If Americans abroad did not hold to the high moral standards supposedly revered in mainstream culture, nor did the United States — according to Lee — maintain the political idealism that had led the nation to war in the first place. Lee's account of war's aftermath is the most compelling aspect of the book. At war's end, Anne remains in Europe to work with the YMCA in Germany, staffing canteens for American soldiers in the now-occupied region. Lee details vast demoralization, including drunkenness and sexual debauchery, and Anne herself is the recipient of sexual attentions from a vile American colonel. As her character leaves for home, she is outraged to discover that the YMCA has arranged for luxurious first-class passage home for men, while the women are crowded in uncomfortable second-class compartments.

More profound is Anne's disillusionment about the war's larger meaning. She's appalled by the crass commercialism of Americans at home and by the mindless Red Scare that vilified workers and rewarded corporate America. As she says to her parents when she lands in New York and sees everyone bustling about, "Why, these people don't know there's been a war, do they?"[117] Like many Americans returning from the war, she feels adrift and incapable of finding meaningful work after the intensity of her YMCA job working with soldiers. Even more demoralizing was the failure of the League of Nations and President Warren G. Harding's call for a return to "normalcy," which Anne described as "'normalcy,' creeping about one . . . glassing one in . . . keeping the air out . . . making one smug, provincial."[118]

Lee insisted that her stories were true and that they reflected either her own experiences or those of friends. The novel received much attention when it shared a Best War Novel prize awarded by the *American Legion Monthly* and Houghton Mifflin. Some members of the prize committee as well as others were outspokenly critical of her account. Her exposé about sexual promiscuity and disease among soldiers, as well as her unflattering portrayal of YMCA men, came in for particular criticism, which she refuted in speech and print with detailed references to official government documents.[119] But while she had her critics for her unflattering view of war behind the lines, reviews and personal letters to her indicate that Lee had captured the experience well. Mrs. James S. Brown Jr. of Pasadena, California, exclaimed, "The book to me is almost like personal war experiences and shall be handed down thru my family as 'the only true war story I have ever read.'" Katharine Gay similarly wrote to express her delight that "at least one woman with the A.E.F. has the ability and the guts to paint a picture that will inevitably be distorted by every romantic novelist in the next fifty years who writes a World War novel with welfare workers in it."[120] Writing ten years after the war ended, Lee's correspondents suggest that they shared her critique of more romantic visions of war and women's role in it. But they also convey a still deeply felt connection to their war experiences and a desire to have their contributions appreciated and accurately documented.

The story of women abroad that this chapter documents is a multifaceted one that eludes easy generalizations. Unquestionably, women played an important role in U.S. war mobilization and civilian relief abroad. As was the case with women's home-front mobilization, their work overseas suggests the changing nature of warfare itself, with World War I marking a point at which civilian populations became integral parts of war and women in particular began to staff the ancillary posts that organize, transport, and care for troops. Women's work abroad also clearly reflects the broader history of early twentieth-century American women's education, social reform, and professional development, a history that shaped the thousands of women who eagerly sought meaningful wartime jobs in Europe. More so than in other types of war work, we can draw upon these women's own words in memoirs, newspapers, and letters to tell their stories. That so many women preserved their letters or wrote memoirs is in itself revealing of their understanding that their experiences were novel ones for women of their era. And their words evoke their extraordinary sense of excitement about participating in the drama of war—from their canteen work with enlisted men, to their experience of bombs in Paris, to the relentless efforts to "see the front," to their sense of satisfaction, as one women put it, of being part of "the whole machine." Not all women abroad were young, not all were self-consciously feminists or "modern," yet most embodied the "new" woman's sense of independence, competence, and agency. And, as we will see in Chapter 5, media attention usually glamorized the women who went abroad.

Yet as we examine these women's experiences, we see, too, a counternarrative in the resistance they encountered and the persistence of conventional ideas about women's proper roles. Doctors, nurses, telephone operators, reporters, all faced discrimination from the military. More generally, cultural assumptions that made it feasible for many women to go "over there" envisioned women's roles as maternal reformers, such as the Smith relief workers, or chaste guardians of sexual morality, such as the YWCA canteen workers. As was the case with other ways in which women challenged the boundaries that restricted them, women's war service abroad both exposed the limits to their opportunities and heralded the new woman of the twentieth century.

FOUR

The Second Line of Defense

Women Workers and War

> For every American man in khaki there is an American girl in industry. At the time the American Army numbered 1,500,000 there were 1,500,000 girls at work in war industries, working on shells, munitions of other kinds, all kinds of machine processes or airplane motor parts, painting camouflage, doing machine work on Government trucks and working in the chemicals that are used to make ammunition. . . . In shop after shop, as you look down the long rows of flying belts and clanking, buzzing machines, you see fair heads bent over big drills, grinding their way through fat pieces of steel, or a pretty brown mass of hair showing under a machinist's cap with its long black visor.
>
> *Elizabeth Porter Wyckoff, 1918*

"WOMEN OF NATION ARE READY TO DON OVERALLS AND REPLACE MEN IN VARIOUS OCCUPATIONS," screamed a headline in the *Grand Rapids (Michigan) Press* on May 9, 1917. The enthusiastic reporter breathlessly proclaimed that as the men left for war, "women will start work as elevator operators, elevated, subway and street car conductors, machine shop experts, ticket agents, motion picture mechanics and distributors, telegraphers, railway car cleaners, office clerks, bell 'boys,' chauffeurs, automobile mechanics, shoemakers, bank clerks, farm hands, railway checkers and callers, waiters in exclusive cafes, train dispatchers, gatemen and theater musicians."[1] While it is true that during World War I women temporarily broke down the rigid distinctions between men's and women's work, for all the hype and excitement, the war did not permanently alter gender or racial segregation in the labor market.

This chapter sets the stage for examining women's war employment by outlining the prewar contours of their wage labor. The rigidity of these patterns is what made the war years seem so dramatic to contemporaries. The African American Great Migration brought black women to the cities of the North and the South, which offered expanded opportunities beyond the kitchen and the farm. Many white working-class women tackled jobs once assumed to be men's prerogative and in doing so found better pay and often more interesting work. The most enduring result of World War I, however, was the expansion of feminized jobs in the professional and clerical fields. That such "women's work" marked the war's impact suggests that in the long run there were built-in limits to possibilities for women to challenge sex segregation and, in the case of black women, racial segregation. Even as women broke barriers, traditional expectations on the part of male employers and workers, as well as women reformers and government administrators, who mobilized to protect women war workers, constrained opportunities both during and after the war. Not surprisingly, the Armistice in November 1918 brought much disappointment. As one woman reformer dramatically exclaimed, "During the war they called us heroines—but they throw us on the scrap-heap now."[2]

PREWAR WORK

Women's participation in paid labor had steadily increased since the Civil War as America's industrialization created an enormous demand for labor, much of it filled by immigrants and their children. Statistically, the expansion of women's paid work in the pre–World War I era is striking. In 1890, 18.2 percent of American adult women worked, and by 1910, that percentage had grown to 24.8. The 1920 census, however, reported that the percentage had actually gone down, to 23.9 percent (although contemporary experts thought this figure a reflection of changed census enumeration rules, and that in all likelihood there was a slight increase from 1910 to 1920). The real growth spurt, nonetheless, was before the war, and World War I did not stimulate a significant expansion of the female workforce, a phenomenon contemporary experts recognized when they explained that while women took on novel and highly visible jobs during the war, these women had already been in the workforce and left less desirable jobs for the new opportunities war created.[3]

A Segmented Labor Market

Fundamental to understanding the short-term impact of World War I on the contours of women's work is the segmented nature of the labor market, which was divided hierarchically by sex, race, and ethnicity. As women entered the workforce in increasing numbers in the late nineteenth century, they did so in jobs understood to be "women's work." In the early twentieth century, 90 percent of all women white-collar workers were concentrated in such jobs as office workers, telephone operators, teachers, sales clerks, and nurses. Factory employment divided along gender lines as well, with women clustered in lower-skilled jobs. Although cultural rationales for feminized job categories played a role in this phenomenon, with female nurses and teachers seemingly "natural" nurturers and domestic servants expanding on women's expected roles as housekeepers, the sex-segregated labor market, which was accompanied by lower wages and status for women's jobs, benefited employers hoping to keep wages low and male workers bent on maintaining exclusive access to higher-skilled and better-paid labor.

Fused with this hierarchical system was the way in which race, ethnicity, and marital status constricted women's work opportunities. European immigrant daughters dominated factory work, while white native daughters filled clerical jobs and for the most part dominated the professions. Most white working women in this era were young and single, divorced, or widowed. African American wives were eight times more likely than their white counterparts to be in the paid labor force, primarily because of the low incomes of their husbands and in part because African Americans, unlike many immigrant groups, hoped to keep their children in school and sent their mothers to the workforce instead.[4]

While most women were disadvantaged workers, sex and racial discrimination had its greatest impact on African American women. African American women had high rates of participation in the workforce (in 1910, 34.7 percent of black women worked, as opposed to 17.1 percent of native white and 24.6 percent of foreign-born white).[5] Few black women (or black men, for that matter) had access to relatively higher-paying factory jobs, although some found work in cotton mills, food-processing plants, and tobacco plants. In 1910, 42.4 percent of black women workers were domestics, and another 52.2 percent were farm laborers. Only 1.5 percent of all black working women had professions. A small group of educated black women did find professional work as teachers, nurses, and social workers, but, as we have seen, they met with constant discrimination and generally labored in segregated contexts. Clerical work was limited to the small number of black-owned enterprises.[6]

Other women of color in this era—Mexican Americans in the West and Southwest and Chinese and Japanese Americans in the West—were not a large component of the American population, and we have little record of their prewar work lives. The defining issue for Mexican Americans was the beginning of their massive migration, which started in 1910, as the Mexican Revolution wreaked havoc in that country, and continued through the 1920s. Yet we know that, like African Americans, their options were limited, with some engaged in the food-processing industry, in farm labor, and in domestic service. Asian American women found similar employment and also worked in family-owned small businesses.[7]

White women's options were better but still limited. Among immigrant families, married women rarely worked outside the home for wages, but they contributed to the family income through taking in boarders and through piecework for manufacturing concerns, especially the garment industry. Older married immigrant women often worked as domestics. Although single immigrant women also worked as domestic laborers, increasingly factory work attracted young ethnic European women, who overwhelmingly turned to unskilled or semiskilled factory jobs, mostly in textiles, garments, and shoes, characterized by low wages, seasonal unemployment, long hours, and unsafe conditions. Factory work could be harsh and exploitative, but these young women found sociability with their female peers in the workplace, and for male companionship many turned to the new urban amusements of dance halls and amusement parks, which stood in sharp contrast to the discipline of the factory and the restraint of their crowded homes.[8]

Given their youth and their own assumptions about leaving the workforce when they married, as well as male union's hostility, not surprisingly factory workers did not turn to unions to bargain collectively for better work lives. In the garment workers' "uprising of the women," as well as in a handful of other notable strikes, women workers in the prewar years clearly demonstrated that they were not only capable of being organized, but also could be militant in defense of their rights. The powerful American Federation of Labor (AFL) generally did not support women's unionization efforts, but the Women's Trade Union League (WTUL) assisted garment workers, as well as those in a few other industries, including telephone operators. Elite women who sought to assist working women in helping themselves through unions and educational programs organized the WTUL in 1903.[9] Despite WTUL efforts and some successes in unionization, most industrial women workers had few avenues for improving their wages or working conditions.

Pink- and White-Collar Work

In the early twentieth century, women expanded into clerical and sales work and into what we now call pink-collar work—especially telephone operators, which had become an almost exclusively female position.[10] White-collar office and sales work was primarily the arena of native-born white middle-class and aspiring middle-class women, for whom such jobs offered new options for "respectable" employment. Sales work had expanded because of the growth of department stores, entities that catered to the burgeoning consumer culture of the urban middle class. The demand for clerical workers (including typists, bookkeepers, file clerks, office machine operators, and timekeepers) accompanied American corporate and business development in the late nineteenth century. The work demanded literacy, and since more women finished high school than men in this period, they furnished a ready labor supply. By the 1880s, as demand for cheaper office labor increased, the invention of the typewriter had further spurred women's employment, and 40 percent of stenographers and typists were women. That number would rise in 1890 to 75 percent. Clerical work paid better than most jobs available to women and offered a clean environment and shorter hours. Yet wages were not sufficient for independence, and most women worked to contribute to the family wages.[11]

White native-born women also dominated the small cadre of professional women in the prewar era. Most college-educated women opted for teaching, which was increasingly feminized. In 1910, they constituted almost 80 percent of the profession.[12] But, as we have seen, the early twentieth century also saw more women pursuing social work, law, library jobs, and medicine. Female doctors and lawyers were nonetheless still rarities. In 1910, women made up only 1 percent of the nation's lawyers and 6 percent of its doctors. By contrast, women constituted 93 percent of trained nurses, 52 percent of social workers, and 79 percent of librarians.[13] In 1910, the percentage of African American workers employed as teachers was a mere 2.4 percent, and the census data did not enumerate any other professional work for black women.[14]

Thus, in all aspects of prewar women's work, racial, ethnic and gender hierarchies shaped women's opportunities in the labor market. As we have seen in Chapter 2, concerns about the hardships working women endured led maternalist social reformers to mount successful campaigns for wage and hour "protective" legislation. However valuable these laws may have been to working women, they also reinforced ideas about physical difference and, indeed, weakness and thus limited opportunities to find equality in the workplace, an approach that shaped reformers' response to women's work in World War I as well.

OVERVIEW: WORLD WAR I AND WOMEN'S WORK

This backdrop of powerful ideological and economic forces that channeled women into low-status jobs made the wartime change in women's opportunities appear all the more dramatic. With immigration cut off, men drafted into the army, and production demands skyrocketing, women's labor became a hot commodity. A similar process occurred in other combatant nations, a testament to the centrality of civilians to modern total warfare. German women were least likely to take on war jobs, but British and French women had high visibility, especially in munitions work. In the United States, newspapers continually ran ads for "Women Wanted," and magazines carried articles detailing the types of jobs available and contact details for applications.[15] In 1918, the U.S. Employment Bureau created a women's section to funnel women into crucial industries. Describing the new service her agency provided, Alice Field Newkirk was enthusiastic, noting that "the day of the dependent woman has passed," and that now Uncle Sam has taken on the task "of finding the right job for every able-bodied woman who is free to work."[16]

During the war, most women continued to work in jobs associated with female labor: textiles, food processing and canneries, boot making, tobacco plants, laundries, and clerical work. But significant numbers found work traditionally limited to men. And they not only filled men's jobs but also wore clothing associated with men—uniforms or overalls—a phenomenon much commented upon and illustrated, as Chapter 5 analyzes. Uniformed women served as streetcar conductors and elevator operators. In overalls or "woman-alls," they worked for the munitions industry and railroads and often performed heavy physical labor. And they entered industries largely closed to them previously: steel, iron, chemicals, and the metal trades. Some women found employment in fairly skilled work—they might read gauges as quality inspectors or operate cranes and other machinery.[17] For the most part, however, employers did not offer women sufficient training for highly skilled work, both because of time constraints and because of resistance to women as skilled laborers. Significantly the U.S. Employment Service did not offer classes for women, although it did for men. Local WCNDs and agencies like the YWCA, by contrast, often provided low-cost courses in telegraphy, accounting, and clerical work, as did business schools. Training for women personnel managers also expanded during the war, a reflection of the need for hiring and overseeing an enlarged female workforce, and itself a significant result of the war's effect on women's labor.[18]

For all its promise, war work posed difficulties as well. In addition to dealing with pervasive male hostility, women found that war jobs often made arduous demands in terms of hours and conditions. Few safeguards were in place in factories that used dangerous chemicals, and the munitions industry could be particularly hazardous. Even when "equal pay" provisions were in place, women often earned less than men working the same job. And women and men workers alike found that high inflation eroded much of their increased pay. Some women workers could turn to a number of resources in negotiating improved conditions. Defense workers could take their concerns to new government agencies. The National War Labor Board was created to mediate between workers and employers, and the Women's Branch of the Ordnance Department of the U.S. Army and the Women's Section of the United States Railway Administration were designed to promote efficiency and fair treatment among women working in defense-related industries and the railways. As discussed below, however, government intervention provided women mixed success in improving their work lives.

Women also turned to labor unions, again with varied results. Primarily because of the intercession of government agencies in labor disputes that threatened war production, a variety of federal agencies, often staffed by progressive reformers, mediated industrial conflicts and in general supported labor's right to organize and to bargain collectively for higher wages and better hours. Between the possibility of federal assistance and a tight labor market, unions exploded, growing from 2.8 million members in 1916 to 4 million in 1919. Women were part of this process, especially in areas where they already demonstrated union success—telephones, textiles, garment trade, and shoemaking. In 1910, only 1.5 percent (or 76,748) of women workers were unionized; by 1920, that figure was 6.6 percent (396,900). Although male unionists were often hostile, the threat of employers using women to break strikes or lower wages led some unions to include women. This varied by locality, but women did join unions formerly unavailable to them, especially in meatpacking and the machine trades and for streetcar conductors and railway clerks. African American women were far less likely than white ones to find unions welcoming. As a result, black women reformers in Washington, D.C., founded the Women Wage-Earners Association, which helped a number of women in various cities working in laundries, as domestics, and in tobacco factories to agitate for better conditions, although with limited success.[19]

An impressive group of women organizers struggled to bring women, who were generally unaccustomed to union procedures and often uninterested in long-term agendas because they viewed their work as temporary, into what was commonly called the fight for industrial democracy. Elizabeth Curry, a boot and shoe worker organizer whom the WTUL sent to organize munitions workers, attempted to rally them, explaining, "No self-respecting woman is willing to be used by an avaricious employer as a means of lowering the wage of her brother workers, much less of forcing them out of their jobs. She will not permit herself to be used to break unions or debase living conditions in her community."[20]

Although some women did eagerly engage in union activism and strikes, their gains were limited. In Bridgeport, Connecticut, even before the United States entered the war, munitions workers there achieved the eight-hour day from reluctant employers, successful in part because male workers joined with them. Women working in the railways found some success in the struggle for equal pay, but telephone operators, despite their militancy, the cooperation of male unionists, and their willingness to strike, had few successes in achieving better wages and conditions. Not only were the telephone companies resistant, but the federal agency that took over the nation's telephone service as part of the war emergency in late 1918 was headed by Postmaster General Albert Burleson, who was adamantly hostile to unions and offered telephone operators little hope for positive federal intervention. The war years may have spurred more organization among women workers and some governmental intervention, but they offered relatively little meaningful or lasting power for women workers.[21]

But there were compensations beyond better jobs and better pay. All told, an estimated 1.5 to 2 million women held jobs deemed connected to the war effort. Women munitions makers might take special pride in the novelty of their labor and its direct link to serving the front line "over there," but women in more conventional work—sewing uniforms or canning food for the military—could also understand their work as serving their own needs while fulfilling their patriotic duty. Yet even as women enjoyed better opportunities in war work, they faced significant challenges, in particular the persistence of sex-segregated labor. Moreover, the hierarchy of race and ethnicity continued to be powerful factors in determining job opportunities, with white women continuing to dominate higher status blue-collar and clerical work as well as the professions. But more so than in the past, black women found more opportunities, although their labor was likely to be the most physically demanding.

AFRICAN AMERICAN WOMEN AND THE GREAT MIGRATION

While the experiences of African American women will be discussed in other sections of this chapter, the unique impact of the war on black migration and women's opportunities calls for a separate account. African Americans began what is now called the Great Migration as early as 1910, spurred by a boll weevil infestation that crippled the southern cotton economy. But the outbreak of war in Europe in 1914 turned a trickle of migrants into a torrent. An estimated 500,000 African Americans left the South for northern and midwestern cities between 1910 and 1920, eager to take advantage of the enormous demand for labor that war production and the halt to immigration created. African Americans congregated in such cities as Chicago, New York, Pittsburgh, and Detroit. Rural migrants also went to southern cities. After a long history of being denied factory work, now African American men and to some extent women could find work in mostly unskilled or semiskilled manufacturing jobs.

The "pull" of opportunity was a significant factor, but so too was "push." Institutionalized racism translated into poor quality segregated schools, disenfranchisement, and impoverishment. Southern whites kept blacks in their place through intimidation and violence, including lynchings and rapes. Although women maintained a "culture of dissemblance"—the term historian Darlene Clark Hine uses for their reluctance to discuss pervasive sexual assault—escape from sexual violence was another reason women joined the migratory stream.[22]

War brought a new "push" factor. The federal draft law included a provision requiring that men "work or fight," and many states passed their own work or fight laws, which permitted local draft boards to induct unemployed men into the army. Although the laws were not supposed to apply to women, in many southern localities black women were forced to take paid labor as domestics, whether or not they wanted or needed to work.[23] In Bainbridge, Georgia, for example, the city council required black women not at work to take paid jobs and followed up by sending an officer "around to the homes of the colored people and summoned the wives of the colored men to appear before the city council." They were fined $15 for their failure to work. The council ordered that "all black women, 'including married women whose only duties were of [in] their homes,' to accept work outside the home." In other places, they were jailed or threatened with violence.

Resentment about federal benefits paid to black wives of soldiers further fueled efforts to control black women's labor in the South. The War Risk Insurance Act followed Progressive Era maternal reformers' concerns for the family and in particular their anxieties about mothers working. Wives and other dependents of soldiers (other than officers) would receive mandatory allotments drawn from their husband's pay as well as a minimum of $15 per month ($275 in contemporary dollars) allowance from the government. Thus a wife with no children would receive $30 a month, with additional funds for children. Soldiers could request exemption from mandatory allotments if they could prove their wives were undeserving on the basis of infidelity or child neglect. Historian K. Walter Hickel has argued that the provisions of the act on the one hand reinforced notions of female dependence and subordination in the family. On the other hand, federal allotments paid directly to wives gave them new financial resources and power. While the allotments benefited many working-class women, they had particular meaning for African American women, especially those in the South. Resentment over modest federal allotments to dependents of servicemen being paid to black families ran high, especially if it encouraged a black woman to leave the paid labor force. This pervasive practice of intimidating black southern women galvanized the NAACP in the South and led to some successful resistance, but anger over the white efforts to control black labor also stimulated black migration.[24]

Women constituted about half of the wartime migration, traveling alone or with families. Southern blacks followed a chain migration pattern similar to immigrants, following a pioneer who went north first, to make contacts and earn money to finance the family's relocation. Often whole communities or church groups moved together, making the migration process itself less traumatic than it might have been. Letters to the black newspaper the *Chicago Defender* vibrate with men's and women's eagerness to secure good jobs in the North. One woman describing herself as a "willen workin woman" wrote, "I hope that you will healp me as I want to get out of this land of sufring. I no there is som thing that I can do here. . . . I don't know just whah but I hope the Lord will find a place."[25]

For women, work in the North was often the same as in the South: domestic labor was still the most common job for a black women, but at better

Figure 11. African American women weighing wire coils. National Archives, RG 86G-5L-1.

pay, earning perhaps twice as much as they might in a southern city.[26] As the need for industrial workers escalated during the war, factories north and south eventually began to hire black women. A Labor Department Survey of 150 plants found 12,000 black women working in manufacturing fields previously closed to them.[27] They labored in meatpacking plants, glass companies, foundries, cigar manufacture, railroad yards, commercial laundries, munitions plants, and the garment industry. Figure 11, one of the Women's Bureau's carefully posed photographs of women in defense works, shows two African American women weighing wire coils, while a third records the weight. The one on the left wears the bloomer-style pants typical of war-era dress for industrial women workers. This tidy picture was hardly typical of the dirty and strenuous jobs usually assigned to black women in defense plants. However, compared to domestic and agricultural work, the pay in these jobs was significantly better. Yet relatively few black women found such employment, as resistance to hiring African Americans remained high.[28]

In 1918, the YWCA, the WTUL, the National Consumers League, the New York Urban League, and other institutions formed a committee to survey black working women's conditions in the New York City area. A white investigator conducted extensive interviews with employers, while an African American woman contacted 175 black workers. They found that black women in industry were generally unmarried, southern, and former domestic workers, who now worked primarily in unskilled jobs. The investigators characterized conditions as "bad," especially noting that African American women were discriminated against through segregation and differential pay.[29]

Thus, even if they secured factory work, African American women were given the hardest and dirtiest jobs and they generally worked in segregated facilities, a reflection of white women's resistance to sharing the workplace and status with black women. Mary Roberts Smith, writing in 1918, explained, "Wherever tried[,] these women have made a good showing, and when given a fair chance have proved themselves just as efficient as the white workers." Despite segregated work, lunch, and waiting rooms, she continued, they have "accepted the places offered them, so anxious were they for employment, and for a chance to show their fitness for the place."[30]

Although the WTUL in Chicago, working with African American labor organizer Irene Sappington Groines, did make an effort to bring black women into a meatpacking union, for the most part African American women were excluded from unions, and indeed their labor was often used to undermine striking workers.[31] Nonetheless, black women did try to organize to improve their conditions. The Women Wage-Earners Association helped organize some women to fight for better wages and conditions, and in Pittsburgh, 1,000 black women met at the Rodman Street Baptist Church to form the Negro Industrial Labor Union of America. They called for wages of $3 daily, a nine-hour day, and carfare to their places of employment. Similar activities among domestic workers emerged in a number of cities, most notably Houston, Little Rock, and Atlanta.

While sex segregation and racial segregation eroded somewhat during the war, race continued to circumscribe black women's options. As Helen B. Irvin, a Women's Bureau special agent, wrote at the end of the war, the black woman "has been accepted, in the main, as an experiment; her admittance to a given occupation or plant has been conditioned upon no other workers being available, and her continuance hinged upon the same. She was usually given the least desirable jobs."[32] The limits to African American women's prospects nonetheless did not negate the enthusiasm they had for new jobs, especially those related to defense, a sentiment white women shared as well.

GOVERNMENT AGENCIES AND VOLUNTARY ASSOCIATIONS: PROMOTING AND PROTECTING WOMEN WORKERS

We know as much as we do about World War I–era working women because both governmental agencies and voluntary associations created reams of documents and published articles detailing their investigations into women's work. Often these reports allow us to hear women's voices, relatively unmediated, but for the most part reformers' and administrators' own assumptions about women's proper work life predominated. These assumptions form an important part of our story about the factors that both encouraged and restrained women's opportunities. Even as they trumpeted working women's contributions to defense and called for their equal treatment, they reinforced the sense that women's physical limitations made them inherently unequal as workers. This ambivalence would persist through the war years and beyond.

"Maintenance of Standards"

The "women's dominion of reform," analyzed in Chapter 2, was deeply engaged in safeguarding working women during the war, with its approach closely following prewar concerns to maintain/establish legislation regulating their hours, night work, and wages. Because the war brought women into new jobs and production pressure, reformers and social workers were particularly concerned about health issues. They repeatedly cited the British example, in which men and women early in the war worked to the breaking point, with absenteeism, poor work, and accidents rampant, leading the British government to establish regulations regarding hours and conditions.[33] They worried, too, that employers would exploit women by using them to bring down wages, and thus they clamored for "equal pay for equal work" so that women would not undercut the male wage structure, a reflection—at least initially—of fears for the working-class family as much as for individual women workers. These concerns led to a strong commitment to what was popularly called "maintenance of standards," which generally included no night work, rest periods throughout the day, one day off in seven, limits on heavy lifting and hazardous work, an eight-hour day, and equal pay for equal work.[34]

Initial leadership for promoting these standards devolved on the Council of National Defense's subcommittee of Women in Industry, headed by Mary Anderson, a well-known labor organizer who had been with the boot and shoemakers union before taking up a fulltime job with the WTUL. AFL president Samuel Gompers, who headed the Council of National Defense Advisory Committee on Labor, had created the committee after much pressure from women's groups, including the WTUL and the National Consumers League. Anderson's committee had little meaningful power, but she relied upon the extensive network of women's organizations and the WCND in the states to establish a voice for working women's concerns within the federal government.[35] The committee commissioned or drew upon investigations throughout the states, usually depending upon volunteer work of women's groups associated with state WCNDs, to report on working women's conditions and wages and in particular to note whether state laws were being violated by war industries. Stressing the value of publicity, Anderson urged them to keep the issue before the public in their respective states.[36] In addition to WCND and the Women in Industry Committee efforts to investigate and protect women war workers, a variety of women's voluntary associations, including the YWCA, the WTUL, and the female-dominated National Consumers League all supported maintaining prewar standards/legislation for women's labor, a theme they invoked constantly.

As we have seen in Chapter 2, the YWCA showed contradictory impulses in its desire to assist women workers. It wanted both to protect them because of their physical weakness and to encourage their equal treatment as valuable workers. Similar ambiguities over protecting and promoting emerged in the WTUL. Although the original emphasis of the WTUL had been helping women to organize into unions, by World War I, it had expanded its focus significantly, with achieving suffrage and bringing working-class women into the movement becoming major goals. Equally important, the WTUL became increasingly focused on protective legislation, in part out of frustration with male unions and, especially, the AFL's resistance to organizing women in unions, and in part out of disappointment over the difficulty in convincing women themselves of the value of unionization.

During the war, WTUL units in the various cities continued organizing work, most notably assisting drives for unions of maids, waitresses, telephone operators, and cigar makers.[37] Their efforts in Washington, D.C., helped the 4,000 women working in the printing and engraving bureau of the Treasury Department to join the National Federation of Federal Employees and the Plate Printers' Union. The WTUL collaborated with other women reformers in Washington, D.C., especially Representative Jeannette Rankin, in vigorously lobbying Congress to adhere to an eight-hour day for hard-pressed employees turning out liberty bonds and other war-related government issues. Particularly noting the role of Rankin, the WTUL journal *Life and Labor* reported that "what was done in this fight was done by women, and it was a woman congressman who, alone of all the government officials who might have done so, took up the case of the wage earning woman."[38] The organization was less successful in helping the women to obtain significant raises comparable to those afforded male bureau workers, but the WTUL emphatically used the example of these workers to rail against the inequality of wages paid to women in comparison to men.[39]

The WTUL's support of unionization for women in Chicago's vast meatpacking industry also proved successful, and it highlights the theme of equal pay, a concept that the war brought into sharp focus. Here, the WTUL took advantage of a reinvigorated union drive among men over horrific conditions for workers and their families to send out WTUL agents among women to encourage them to join the effort. Galvanized by the organizing drive, the WTUL helped to bring 1,500 Polish American women into the Amalgamated Meatcutters and Butchers Workmen of North America and even had some success in reaching African American women, although here white prejudice limited its efforts. The WTUL was also active when the union brought a successful challenge to a federal mediation commission in early 1918. Agnes Nestor, president of the Chicago WTUL, testified, demanding "in the name of justice that women doing the same class of work as men be paid the same wage."[40]

That mediation, as the WTUL's bulletin *Women's Work and War* reported, included an insightful discussion by industrial labor expert Frank P. Walsh about the issue of equal wages. In arguing before the federal commission, Walsh insisted that women doing comparable work to men deserved the same pay. Walsh explained that small differences between the tasks assigned men and women generally justified unequal pay and called instead for a determination of classes of labor that would bring more equity to women's paychecks. The mediator agreed, and equal pay for equal work or what we would now call "comparable worth" formed part of the settlement, which also provided all workers with an eight-hour day and increased wages.[41] Despite the agreement, it is difficult to know if significant improvements in women's wages resulted, as throughout the war many companies avoided compliance.[42]

The March 1918 *Women's Work and War* continued to engage with the issue. And although the argument that low pay for women would undercut male workers' wages continued to be a theme, the WTUL vigorously insisted on women's equal pay as a right they had earned. Echoing a theme it raised repeatedly, the bulletin noted that there "seems to be a very general public belief that the woman worker is a carefree individual who lives at home with her family and is partially supported by them," a point that articles in the bulletin constantly refuted with detailed statistical evidence.[43] One article summed up the inequity and inconsistency by first remarking that in the midst of a war for democracy the government should apply democratic principles to women. "There is no justice in the family wage for men and the individual wage for women," it continued. "The bachelor's pay is not reduced because he has no family to support, and anyone who has studied the wage-earning family knows that it is the daughter who assumes the responsibility of household expenses three times out of five."[44]

The WTUL's support for wage equality coexisted, however, with a strong commitment to protective legislation that presumed women's difference based on physical strength and reproductivity, the ideas at the center of maternalist protective reforms. Agnes Nestor explained early in the war, for example, that new jobs opened to women could be dangerous. "The question is faced of how seriously the long hours of labor under present day industrial conditions, with women speed up, standing in certain trades and running heavy machines, will affect the future of the race."[45] Night work by mothers was a particularly alarming trend. Concern over long hours led the WTUL to call unsuccessfully for a "blanket law as to hours for women in industry which relieve us of making the fight for decent hours every time the industrial field widens for women."[46]

The WTUL in New York City was particularly active during the war, and its efforts to sustain restrictions on hours and night work met with some success. The WTUL claimed victory in defeating state legislation that would permit exemptions for longer hours and in passing legislation that prevented women under twenty-one from serving as messengers. And after the war, in March 1919, it finally achieved another goal. The Lockwood-Caulfield Act extended hour limitations to women streetcar employees. As a result, 1,500 women lost their jobs. This caused a rift within the WTUL because many working women members resented "society women" interfering in working women's lives. As Margaret Hinchey, a working-class league member, explained, "I stand for the right of working women to kick themselves when and where they want work 8 or 9 hours day or night just the same as men[;] they have no club over them why should we?"[47] Tensions over the issue of protective legislation would persist within the WTUL after the war, as the organization definitively moved from its earlier focus on unionization to the maternalism embodied in the protective legislation approach.

Defense Workers and Government Women

In 1917, early in the war, the Russell Sage Foundation conducted an extensive survey of women munitions workers in Bridgeport, Connecticut, addressing the nature of their work, hours, and wages, as well as details about their home lives. The report noted that although women's wages in munitions plants were higher than for other factory work, they still lagged behind men's, and that the eight-hour day was more theoretical than actual. Amy Hewes, the author of the survey, paid particular attention to the lack of rest periods and the resulting fatigue. Few women enjoyed much respite from the speed and pressure of work. "The girls certainly earn every cent they get," one woman reported. "We have to work every minute without any letting up at all."[48]

Pressured by women reformers about these issues and worried as well about defense industry productivity, in January 1918 the federal government created the Woman's Branch of the Industrial Section of the Ordnance Department (hereafter Women's Ordnance Committee), U.S. Army. This unprecedented engagement of the federal government in the issues that animated maternalist social reformers mandated federal oversight of the conditions of women working on government contracts with the Ordnance Department. That department was responsible for "supplying the army with cannon, rifles, cartridges, shrapnel, high explosives, and many other forms of ammunition, and also with many other articles of equipment needed by the soldier in the field, including helmets, leather belts and harness for horses in the artillery."[49] Women's jobs included assembling cartridges and inspecting them, welding, and some machine operation, especially drilling machines and punch presses (fig. 12).[50]

Mary van Kleeck accepted the appointment to head the Women's Ordnance Committee. A member of the Women in Industry Committee, van Kleeck had also acted as a consultant for the Ordnance Department. Well

Figure 12. Women employed in Liberty Motors munition factory, Detroit. National Archives, 165-WW-592-A44.

before the war, she had established an impressive record as an industrial social scientist. From a middle-class background, van Kleeck went to Smith College where she focused on economics and industrial justice. She eventually went to work for the Russell Sage Foundation, running its industrial surveys. Although she focused specifically on women and children, her broader agenda was improving the lives of the working class as a whole, a goal reinforced by her profoundly spiritual commitment to the Social Gospel.

Van Kleeck asked Mary Anderson to join her, and the two of them began an ambitious program to investigate women working under Ordnance Department contracts. They sought to pursue the agenda of "maintenance of standards," including equal pay for women, but also worked to facilitate more efficient production for the war effort. By war's end, van Kleeck's committee had established eleven offices throughout the country to coordinate with ordnance manufacturers. Van Kleeck had a staunch commitment to Scientific Management, the system pioneered by industrial engineer Frederick Winslow Taylor, which was gathering new converts in the drive for efficient production. Although Scientific Management often meant that corporations assessed individual job tasks to extract the most possible work from their employers, van Kleeck understood Scientific Management as a system for fostering better employee/employer relations and promoting more worker power within the plant.[51] To this end, the teams of inspectors van Kleeck and Anderson sent out assessed the jobs women were asked to perform and suggested modifications to suit their strength and skill levels.[52]

Van Kleeck's investigators routinely faced resistance from male workers and managers. They often had to negotiate with employers to extract better treatment for women. In the case of Bethlehem Steel, for example, which employed around 1,000 women, van Kleeck agreed to the company's request for an exemption from night work restrictions in exchange for more attention to women's needs for facilities for rest and improved transportation to and from work. More impressively, later Bethlehem Steel was convinced to institute the eight-hour day for all employees. The Women's Ordnance Committee had mixed success in negotiating equal wages, in part because of deskilling, which allowed employers to claim that women did not do the same work as men, in part because it had limited power to enforce decisions.[53]

To further attend to the special problems of working women, van Kleeck's committee also put female personnel directors in all government arsenals. This in itself proved a notable development of the war years. The expansion in numbers of women workers and the pressure from reformers and social workers to ensure women's health led to the demand for professional personnel workers. The committee, working with the YWCA, even set up a course for training these women personnel specialists—"employment managers, welfare workers, factory inspectors, and trained investigators of industrial conditions"—at Mount Holyoke College. In June 1918, the War Industries Board widened the effort by creating a program at the University of Rochester to train women for personnel work and planned others at major universities in the nation. As a government press release explained, "Most of the approved methods of dealing equitably with the working force have been devised or brought to notice by the new type of industrial specialist—the employment manager."[54] The innovation of female specialists undoubtedly served working women well, but it also reinscribed the notion of women workers as "different" and having special needs.

The railroad industry, which the federal government controlled from

December 1917 to March 1920, created a federal committee to oversee women workers as well. When the war began, railroad traffic quickly became snarled, undermining the nation's ability to mobilize. As a result, the Wilson administration created the Railroad Administration, which took over operations, including labor management, from the companies. The railroads had been resistant to unions, but under federal control, unions flourished and wages increased dramatically. As more women became employed, the Railroad Administration established the Women's Service Section (WSS), in August 1918, under the direction of Pauline Goldmark, who had previously worked with the National Consumers League. Goldmark's office of around ten workers tackled questions of wages, hours, discrimination, health and safety, and sexual harassment. With one exception of a trade union woman, Goldmark's inspectors were college-educated women, many of whom were well connected to the women's dominion of reform, having served in a wide range of organizations, like the Children's Bureau and the National Consumers League. Because the federal government took over the railroads during the war, the WSS may have been able to exercise more power than van Kleeck's committee, which worked mostly with private defense contractors.

Like the Women's Ordnance Committee, the WSS focused on "maintenance of standards" to protect women workers. It also worried about the potential for sexual immorality in the new work environment. Alert to both sexual harassment and improper behavior among young working-class women, the WSS's notion of protection, like that of the YWCA, included anxieties about sexual freedom and license among working-class women. In addition to this focus on protection, shared by both committees, Goldmark, more so than van Kleeck, saw her group as an advocate for women railway workers in the face of sex discrimination and, to some extent, racial discrimination. These interventions, discussed in greater detail below, reveal that like other women reformers and administrators of the war era, WSS agents vacillated between the desire to protect women and the desire to secure their equality in the workplace.[55]

Meanwhile, in summer 1918, continued lobbying for attention to women's labor led to yet another federal agency, the Women in Industry Service, with van Kleeck at its head and Mary Anderson as her assistant.[56] Women reformers were jubilant. The WTUL reported that it was "a dream come true for an army of earnest women who for the last six years have worked steadily toward" its establishment. They understood, an article in *Women's Work and War* explained, that "equal opportunity for women in the industry fight could never come until some assistance were given to the equalizing process."[57] Despite this enthusiasm, the new labor bureau came late in the war and had relatively little impact on war workers. Van Kleeck focused on bringing together women leaders, especially union organizers, to hammer out a set of labor standards for women that all could agree on, with the goal that the Labor Department would endorse these and encourage the various states to act upon the recommendations. In keeping with her previous work, van Kleeck also commissioned a number of investigations, including one on hazardous conditions in chemical plants at Niagara Falls, New York. In addition, reflecting the increased role of African American women in urban employment, van Kleeck took the unprecedented step of appointing Helen Irvin, a black woman, as a special assistant to address "economic problems affecting Negro women wage-earners." Irvin's educational and occupational background was similar to the white women van Kleeck worked with—she had pursued graduate work in economics and psychology, taught Domestic Science at Howard University, and served with the Food Administration and the Red Cross. Van Kleeck put her to work surveying plants in the upper South and the Midwest, which employed more than 16,000 African American women in total.[58]

As van Kleeck sought to shape the new agency, she supported protective legislation for women, particularly because women's lack of access to unions gave them little power in protecting themselves in the workplace. Like other women reformers of the time, she believed that women's reproductive functions were important and that jobs known to be damaging, such as any that brought workers into contact with lead, should be prohibited for women. But for the most part, van Kleeck insisted upon women's opportunities to have skilled and satisfying work. She thought the real problem was not women's labor, but all labor. "The great task now," van Kleeck wrote, "is not to set apart women from industry, but to apply the medical and engineering knowledge of the country to making all work safe and healthful for the men and women who are producing for the Nation's needs."[59]

The Women in Industry Service became the U.S. Department of Labor's Women's Bureau in 1920, with Mary Anderson at its head. Until well after World War II, the bureau continued to promote protective legislation and "special treatment" for women, while at the same time hoping to promote their equal treatment in the workplace. Women reformers' and administrators' embrace of the rhetoric of protective legislation can hardly be blamed for the limited gains women workers achieved through their World War I labor. Yet the repeated emphasis on dangers to women's physical health and reproductivity so evident in the war years helped to maintain a cultural norm that viewed women workers as temporary and subordinate and made it more difficult to challenge the significant resistance male workers and employers offered women who dared to break down the barriers of sex-segregated labor.

OPPORTUNITIES AND OPPOSITION: WOMEN RAILROAD WORKERS, CONDUCTORS, AND CLERKS

In May 1917, when war mobilization was just beginning, the *San Francisco Chronicle* published a striking photo of nine "Women Railway Workers" employed by the Baltimore and Ohio Railroad. The caption explained that the four wearing overalls were in the car and locomotive repair shop. The others, it noted, "fill the positions of oil house superintendent, blacksmith's helper, yard cleaner, clerk in the shop office, and assorter of small supplies and scrap material."[60] This type of reporting on railroad women typified the early war years, and like many other popular representations of women at work, was misleading. Certainly the railroads hired women in significant numbers, but relatively few did hard manual labor or skilled work during the war and its immediate aftermath. At the height of women's employment in October 1918, as many as 72 percent of the over 100,000 women workers performed clerical work. Yet because women breached the all-male culture of railroad work in the war, observers were correct in thinking that there was dramatic potential for them to make inroads into the sex-segregated workplace. Their opportunities, as well as the limits, beautifully illustrate the paradoxical nature of women's work in World War I.

Working for the Railroads: Women, Men, and Government Agents

Railway work during the war produced modest improvements in sex segregation. But as WSS reports repeatedly indicated, these were met with much opposition. The railway managers resisted paying women wages equal to men's, and although managers recognized the necessity of using women's labor, they generally lamented it, viewing women as a temporary expediency who, in one manager's words, "are not desired."[61] Not only did conventional attitudes about women's proper work role persist, but also the racial hierarchy that characterized work prove to be intractable.

African Americans and older married immigrant women found employment in the harshest and lowest-status jobs of cleaners and common laborers. Before the war, railroads had hired women primarily as cleaners for the interiors of passenger railway cars. An extension of domestic work

Figure 13. Crew of women track walkers and cleaners on the Erie Railroad. National Archives, 165-WW-595-D22.

associated with women, cleaning jobs did not challenge the gender order on the roads. Labor shortages during the war meant that this opportunity for black and foreign-born women expanded (approximately 5,600 women were cleaners during the war). Newly hired women cleaners came to the railroads from work as domestics in homes or public places, attracted by war wages that were at times close to twice their prewar rates. In most cases, the work teams were segregated so that black women did not work on the same cars as whites, and in the South no white women were employed as cleaners. In addition, black women often earned less than white women. In Elmira, New York, Mary McMahon, a white woman, earned $56 per month, in contrast to Myrtle Jackson, a black woman who had worked for the station since 1913, who received $50 a month for more hours than McMahon.[62]

Less numerous than cleaners were black and immigrant women who performed manual labor in the yards, picking up scraps, weighing as much as twenty-five pounds, and moving heavy equipment with hand trucks. Figure 13, a photograph of grimy mature track walkers, is in stark contrast to the images of young neatly uniformed workers that appeared in newspapers and magazines during the war.[63] A WSS inspector described typical activity for such women: "As the cars are repaired, they pick up the small iron pieces, such as old bolts, nuts, etc., and rake up accumulated trash, wood, paper, and the like. The latter they gather together in piles and burn. The small iron pieces are put on a wheelbarrow and taken to the scrap heap. All heavy pieces of iron are left and later picked up by boys."[64] Although the jobs were attractive to women because of the relatively high pay, the WSS, in keeping with concerns about women's health, worried that such labor was too demanding for women and in September 1919 decreed an end to their employment. Despite their protests, hundreds of women lost their jobs and the lucrative salaries that came with them.

A 1918 report from WSS inspector Helen Ross on black women truckers in Kansas City, Missouri, poignantly reveals their disappointment. Ross revealed that most of the women, whom she described as "very quiet, orderly and businesslike, and most eager to please," had been domestics or laundry workers before coming to the railroads and that they much preferred railway jobs. Pearl Jones, a young woman with three years of high school, spoke at length to the meaning of these new jobs for herself and other black women. "All the colored women like this work and want to keep it," she explained, contrasting it with the poorer wages paid domestics. She concluded, "Of course we should like easier work than this if it were opened to us, but this pays well and is no harder than other work open to us. With three dollars a day, we can buy bonds to take care of us in our old age, we can dress decently and not be tempted to find our living on the streets. . . . Please don't take this work away from us."[65]

As Jones indicated, black women's opportunities were severely limited, and they did not have access to the handful of skilled and semiskilled jobs available to women during the war. Nor did many white women obtain these better jobs, though some became "helpers" in machine shops and others found employment in the highly visible towers as "block operators," who controlled the trains at depots to keep them from running into each other. Higher-status jobs, they also were usually limited to white, non-immigrant, single women. The work required climbing into the towers and shifting controls, sometimes heavy ones. These women worked in isolation, a factor that worried WSS inspectors concerned for their safety, especially because their shifts often overlapped with those of men. Clearly, however, many women enjoyed these jobs. Reporting on Mrs. Margaret Downing in Pennsylvania, a WSS agent commented, "She is very enthusiastic over her present work, liking especially the freedom from work outside the fixed hours, and the friendly human contact with passing trainmen and other operators over the telephone." Even more eloquently, Trenton operator Annie Wolfsberg exclaimed, "I just loved my work—every time I see a train go by it seems as if I just couldn't bear not belonging to the railroad."[66]

But inspectors also found women hard-pressed by the circumstances of block operations. In Kansas, women working for the Santa Fe railroads in remote locations endured isolated lives housed in boxcars, with primitive toilet and washing facilities. In Light, Kansas, two sisters worked together and, out of concern for their safety, arranged their schedule so that they were never alone, a system they also shared with a third young woman at the yard. Yet the women seemed satisfied with their competence: "There's lots to learn that the Rule book does not say anything about," commented one woman. And, as the inspector noted, "the operator interviewed is pretty and neat and most businesslike in their attitude toward her work. She began this work last March; before this, she had been waiting on tables at her mother's restaurant since she was ten years old. Her mother is now in the station at Vanora as a block operator." Nonetheless, both sisters hoped to find work at a "station where there is more work and more society." These compelling narratives of block operators' experiences suggest the pleasure they took in their competence in handling a responsible job, but also indicate hardships that were made bearable by both familial bonds and the allure of high wages such difficult jobs commanded.

Although the press paid a great deal of attention to women performing such unconventional labor, the vast majority of railroad women worked in clerical capacities, and since clerical work was already feminized, on the surface their employment in a wide variety of low-level white-collar jobs seems unremarkable. Their profile followed typical clerical work as well: they were white, native-born, with some education, and usually young and single. But the railroad world had largely excluded women from white-collar jobs, even as the tasks themselves became more routinized. For male clerks, whose work was becoming less skilled and less an avenue for upward mobility, the invasion of their workplace by young women particularly rankled. Historian Janet Davidson argues, "Women's entrance into railroad work thus functioned as a visible marker of a more generalized set of changes in clerks' work opportunities."[67]

Whatever their position in the railroad industry, women sought out the WSS with complaints about a variety of issues, and most of their cases make it clear that whatever the attraction of railway jobs, men often treated women as interlopers. WSS inspectors sought to ensure that women worked in a safe environment, that laws limiting their hours and night work were honored, and that women, both black and white, were paid the same rate as men. Their reports reveal a great deal about the nature of women's work as well as the agents' efforts to counter male resistance to the new employees. In an inspection of African American car cleaners for the Baltimore and Ohio Railroad in October 16, 1918, for example, Florence Clark discovered that the white supervisor, Mary J. Davis, received the same pay as the women she was in charge of, a situation the manager justified by saying she did not do everything that male supervisors did. Yet Clark concluded that the manager "was not at all fair-minded and could not be relied upon to see that justice be done in this case."[68]

Much of the WSS inspection work involved questions of pay, hours, and classification, but agents were also concerned about the physical work environment, especially toilets and facilities for changing and washing. Almost every report offered a description of these areas, which were usually substandard. The issues involved questions of sanitation, but also ones about creating safe environments separate from men, as a means of protecting women's modesty and forestalling opportunities for sexual improprieties. The complaint from a group of clerks in the Illinois Central Railroad reveals how these issues elided with women's understanding that they were unwelcome in the railroad world. They explained that they wished to "protest against the inhuman and brutal treatment we are receiving from our boss, . . . who denies us the privacy of our dressing room by peeping in the door and keeping time on us while we are in there." They continued, "We hope you will send an inspector here to see that we are treated with respect and that we are permitted to cover the lower windows so that we are not humiliated by people looking at us from a platform on the lower floor."[69]

For African American women, the question of toilets presented a different kind of humiliation. As historian Robin Dearmon Muhammad has demonstrated, African American women seized upon the presence of WSS agents to agitate for better conditions. Although they protested unequal wages, they also drew attention to the harsh and degrading working environment. "Toilets," Muhammad notes, "were among the most prominent physical markers of class and racial privileges in the railroads." Dressing and lunchroom facilities, as well as toilets, were segregated, and black women's facilities were unpleasant at best. In one yard in Minnesota, for example, African American car cleaners were required to use a "colored" privy perched over the Mississippi River while the one white woman clerk, Mrs. Place, had access to a flush toilet. Black women protested to the WSS, and in what was a rare success, the agent convinced the railroad supervisor to make the flush toilet available to the black women as well, whereupon Mrs. Place said she would not use it. Mrs. Place's response was typical, not just in the railroads but throughout sectors where white and black women worked in the same facilities. White women's insistence on separate facilities, steeped in a sense that black women's bodies were unclean, helped to maintain a racial hierarchy that kept them elevated above the low status associated with their work. The WSS agitated for improved facilities for both white and black women and had some success in convincing managers to improve those designated for white women, but they did not significantly change the circumstances of most black workers.[70]

Another important category of WSS inspections turned on women's and men's alleged improper sexual behavior. The worrisome conduct ran the gamut from flirtatious language to consensual affairs, from revealing clothing to what we would now call sexual harassment. The reports reveal the agents' own conflicted attitudes about working-class women's sexuality (discussed in Chapter 2), as well as differing notions among working men and women about what constituted respectable behavior. As well, they speak to anxiety about the presence of women in a formerly all-male work environment.

Men's complaints about women's immoral conduct were in keeping with patterns of resistance to their employment. Men working for the Pennsylvania Railroad, for example, often accused block tower workers, as a group, of being of dubious respectability. The ostensible evidence, that block operators were in isolated towers, a potential site for both danger and pleasure, and that on occasion men whose shifts followed them might stay there until transportation was available, deflected attention from what was really at issue: women constituted a disruptive force. As one manager explained, the draft had forced him to hire women whom he believed were "irresponsible and inclined to deteriorate morally."[71]

And it was not just men who lamented the potential for the operators' sexual misbehavior. Annie Geary, an experienced operator, complained that the trainmen are "rough and that many of them will go as far as they are allowed in familiarity with the women operators, but her experience has been that no girl who makes it known that she does not wish advances need have any trouble. She never hears of the men forcing their attentions where it is not wanted." Continuing in this vein, that it was the young women who were to blame for any sexual misconduct, Geary insisted, "Every restaurant waitress in Ridgeway had applied [for work]. Many of those who at first came to work in simple serge or gingham dresses are now wearing silk and Georgette waists utterly unsuitable to their positions." Moreover, she felt that they were too focused on the thrill of railroad life: "When not on duty they are forever using their passes to run back and forth on the road."[72] Geary's comments reveal significant anxieties about young women workers, whose style and personal behavior ignored a more conservative notion of working-class women's deportment that emphasized respectability and subordination. In the formerly male club of the railroads, women posed a threat to jobs and to work culture, which the focus on sexual misbehavior sometimes obscured.

It is difficult to estimate the extent of sexual liaisons, consensual or otherwise. Many incidents turned on sexual harassment. Unwanted sexual advances on the job had long plagued many working women, who had few avenues for seeking redress. In taking women's complaints seriously, the short-lived WSS took unprecedented interest in the issue, which was not just about sex, but also about power relations. Given that employees only recently have had legal and procedural recourses in the face of such harassment, it is not surprising that the WSS apparently had mixed success in resolving women's complaints. Although part of the issue was ascertaining the facts surrounding complaints, inspectors also had to deal with their own ambivalent feelings about working-class women's sexual behavior as well as male employers' and employees' hostility to WSS's interventions.

Florence Clark had to mediate a case brought by Esther Garlin, who complained about the persistent unwanted attention of her coworker, Ed Stair, who was apparently notorious for trying to "embarrass us women by trying to sit in our laps," and specifically about an episode in which he "goosed" (pinched) her on the thigh. Complicating the issue, Garlin and four other women had been forced to resign over incidents in which they goosed each other. Clark's assessment was that the women had been treated unfairly because they were forced to quit over behavior that was not grounds for the dismissal of men and of other women in the office. Yet Clark also disapproved of women who were known to goose each other as lacking in decorum, and moreover, she acknowledged, "some of the women may have been guilty of immoral conduct." Although Clark was clearly critical of the young women's behavior, she also tried to insist on a single standard for men and women, a pattern that characterized most agents' response to reports of sexual impropriety. She successfully pressured the railroad company to fire three men who had harassed female coworkers.[73]

Cases involving sexual harassment often produced a wide-ranging narrative of work grievances experienced by women. In January 1920, Mayme Hayes, a Cincinnati clerk with thirteen years of experience, filed a complaint with the WSS over the sexual misconduct of at least two men in her office. But Hayes's dissatisfaction had multiple roots. The records include a copy of an official complaint she had filed with the railroad in December 1918, in which she argued that she had not been given an account of her (unnamed) discipline in accordance with established grievance procedures. Hayes expanded on her dissatisfaction, by telling Mr. D. E. Driscoll, auditor for Freight and Station Accounts, "You certainly are aware of the fact that I have received no consideration whatsoever in this office and I want to know is it due to stupidity on my part or because I wear skirts." The crux of her complaint was that, after twelve years, she had received only one promotion (when the government took over the railroads) and earned only $95 a month, a salary that was only $7.50 more than apprentices. At the same time, less-experienced men earned more.

There is no indication of how this earlier complaint was resolved, but it provides context for the vigor with which Hayes later pursued her complaint about sexual impropriety.[74] In a series of interviews and letters for the new complaint, Hayes indicated that women clerks were routinely sexually harassed and that women who were willing to put up with it received better treatment from bosses. Hayes focused primarily on the activities of George Patterson and Ed Dill, two married men, whom she claimed "are ruining the discipline of the office by their unprincipled actions and deeds. They have a hobby of hugging the girls in the office and if one falls for them their life is pleasant and agreeable and those that do not fall for them are burdened with work and knocked and antagonized and their life made miserable." Hayes offered lurid details of these men's sexually aggressive behavior with other women, but she also recounted that Patterson had fondled her breast as she passed by him. "[He] deliberately insulted me, the first time in all my 20 years in the R.R. office any man ever dared to insult me, but he did and I don't know what kept me from slaying him in his tracks." She felt obliged to resign: "I could not sit by and be a real woman and see these low principles things going on around that office day after day and no one interfering."

Inspector Clark interviewed a number of people to try to get to the bottom of the story. At least one woman canceled her appointment because she was "too frightened." While one woman was noncommittal and uncooperative, others, including one male clerk, tended to agree with Hayes about the three men's dubious behavior. No record is available as to how Clark handled the sexual harassment complaint, but a letter from Pauline Goldmark to Hayes, on February 27, 1920, thanked Hayes for her work and explained that "the matter is being dealt with by the Administration and I very much hope that substantial improvements may be secured as a result of our work." Goldmark further explained that because the WSS was closing soon, they would not be able to follow up their report with a future investigation.[75]

In another case involving black cleaners in Pennsylvania Station in New York City, commentary by inspector Edith R. Hall suggests that the sexual harassment issue was especially difficult to resolve when black women were the complainants. Hall confirmed that she believed the women's claim that Mr. Small, an African American who was the gang leader for car cleaners, made improper advances to them. An interviewee, Margaret Harrington, explained, "When you first go in he is very nice and lets you do as he likes, whether it is right or wrong. Then he makes advances, and when these are rejected he becomes spiteful and mean. He made improper advances to her and has been mean every since." And, in the case of a number of women who were dismissed, Hall further thought it was because of the meanness of Small, not inadequate work.[76] Hall doubted that much would come of her report. She regretted that she had not been able to interview any white men, "for I think I could have learned much from them, not only of Mr. Small's behavior, but of the women's conduct as well, and the general attitude of the management toward the negro women." She continued that these interviews would likely have strengthened the charge against Small, suggesting her recognition that the word of black women alone would be given little credence by management. Hall was undoubtedly correct. Despite the clear statements to him about his subordinate's unfair treatment and sexual misconduct, General Superintendent R. V. Massey's response to Hall's report was not encouraging. Massey wrote that he had spoken with both Small and his boss, Mr. Ackerman, about "the necessity for treating the colored women with the respect which is due them, and will have the matter followed up closely to see that this [is] done." But the tone of the letter as well as the lack of any disciplinary action suggested to both Hall and Goldmark that there was little reason to think that any of the men would take the issue seriously. Even if Hall and Goldmark failed in forcing any disciplinary action against Small, the incident is nonetheless remarkable in indicating that relatively powerless black women like Margaret Harrington had an avenue for complaint about sexual harassment.[77]

The WSS's short history reveals the maternalist notion that woman workers needed protection, most evidently in the decision to prohibit women from doing heavy manual labor, regardless of their wishes. But the treatment of women by railway men, so painstakingly recorded by Goldmark's staff, makes it clear that the biggest obstacle to women's railroad job opportunities during the war was male resistance to encroachment on their turf. While some of this hostility emerged in managers' decisions as to classification and wages, it also appeared in controversies over facilities like toilets. Sexual harassment on the job, too, was a way of exerting male power and devaluing women as competent workers.

Conductorets and Women's Occupational Freedom

The power of male hostility was equally important in the experiences of another group of women who breached the barriers to take men's jobs: streetcar conductors. Women conductors, or "conductorets," as they were often called, are particularly interesting because they were so highly visible and their presence was especially contested. Before the war, women found city railway employment only in low-status jobs as cleaners or ticket takers. By January 1918, over a dozen city electric railway companies had begun training and hiring white women as conductors on interurban trolleys and streetcars. In many cities, these new conductors were related to male employees of the trolley system, a status that helped defuse tension between male and female workers, in part because it reassured men that women would be willing to leave their positions at war's end. But a significant number of new conductors were self-supporting working women or those with dependents. They needed to work, and the higher wages were compelling, as was the relative attractiveness of streetcar work as compared to domestic labor, laundry work, factory work, and other unskilled or semiskilled jobs traditionally available to women. As journalist Frederic J. Haskin exclaimed in a syndicated column, "Each day the employment offices in cities where the conductorette is in vogue are besieged by swarms of the sex ranging in age from seventeen to sixty."[78]

News accounts, often illustrated, stressed their spiffy uniforms of neatly tailored jackets and skirts, with matching hat, but also happily quoted companies' assessment of their necessity and competence. In a cheery article entitled "Good Morning, Miss Conductoret!" the *Cleveland Plain Dealer* exulted that "there is no doubt that women will be found equal to the task." The writer, however, could not resist adding a jocular "p.s." warning men not "to flirt with the conductoret. She might punch you instead of the transfer."[79] Despite praise for their abilities, company representatives often reiterated that the measures were temporary and that they did not challenge women's essential femininity. But the key reason offered for employing women in such novel positions was national service: their use was a vital war measure, and customers should recognize "that the women are doing a patriotic duty."[80]

Despite employers' praise for their new employees, maternalist reformers expressed concern about the possible effects of such work on women's health and morals and were openly suspicious of employers who aimed to exploit them. A survey of New York and Brooklyn women conductors for the U.S. Bureau of Labor Statistics in May 1918 compiled detailed statistics on working conditions and concluded that the hours required were excessive and that night work was potentially dangerous. The physical strain of standing for long hours and enduring harsh weather was particularly harmful for women's health. The study concluded, "It is practically impossible to make the conditions of street railway employment even tolerably endurable to woman employees. . . . The operation of street cars is one of the last occupations into which women should be lured and forced."[81]

The report was quickly challenged. Two women doctors, one of whom consulted for one of the New York companies as a medical inspector, insisted that the work was in many cases less harmful than the jobs women had previously held as waitresses, laundresses, and factory workers and that, moreover, the women she interviewed seemed in excellent health and eager to pursue their work.[82] One conductoret explained that her new job was "so much better than anything I ever did. The wages are good, it's outdoor work, and a million times easier than washing. . . . Laundry work . . . means new bosses every day and often unpleasant matters come up. Here no one bothers us if we attend to our jobs."[83]

Shortly after the controversial report, the New York grand jury also investigated the conditions of women conductors and reported that moral conditions were "shocking," and that not only were young girls of fifteen and sixteen being hired, but that prostitutes and drug addicts were among the new conductors on the rosters. The grand jury called for state legislation to protect women in the railway industry. Josephine Goldmark, then still at the National Consumers League, concurred. She approvingly noted that the Wisconsin Industrial Commission "has recognized the extra-hazardous nature of the employment from the point of view of morals, and made a far stricter ruling than applies to factories." In Wisconsin, women conductors could not work at night or more than eight hours a day.[84] Despite reformers' concerns, except for Wisconsin, no legislation or rulings explicitly barred women from conducting until after the war.

The more serious threat to women's access to these new jobs was male resistance. Streetcar companies often turned to women because of growing union militancy among male railway workers, who were demanding recognition and higher wages. In Montgomery, Alabama, for example, as a strike threatened to paralyze the city as well as war mobilization efforts, the streetcar company refused to negotiate and publicly began to discuss using women conductors as strike replacements, reporting that applications were "pouring" in.[85] Although the national leadership of the Amalgamated Association of Street, Electric Railway, and Motor Coach Employees of America early on was adamant against hiring women, dramatic labor shortages led in September 1918 to their permitting women, but it did so with a series of rules that limited their opportunities for advancement.

In August 1918, the tension over women conductors boiled over in Cleveland, where the local union (which refused admission to women and black men) threatened to strike if women were not removed from their jobs. The Cleveland Street Railway Company had insisted that the rationale for hiring women was a shortage of male workers, with company president John Stanley noting, "We must and will employ women to run the street cars of Cleveland. It is a dire necessity of war and absolutely the only solution to the problem of the shortage of men."[86] The men challenged this interpretation, insisting that it was a ploy to undercut male employment, and their union refused to allow men to train the women.[87] The following month, when the number of women conductors had grown to 200, the union threatened a strike that would take out 2,500 men and lodged a complaint with the Department of Labor, which sent out two investigators. The investigators decided to adjudicate based on the narrow issue of whether or not there was a labor shortage, and after an investigation, which did not consult with the women conductors themselves, determined that no labor shortage existed and that women should be discharged from their positions as conductors, as of November 1, 1918.[88]

Here the story takes a fascinating twist. The outraged conductorets wanted their jobs back. Under the leadership of Rose Moriarty, a well-known local suffragist and professional woman, and Laura Prince, a former waitress active in the Cleveland Waitresses' Union who had "been working as a conductor to help support her two children during the absence of her soldier husband," they staged a mass meeting, the tone of which was "militant," according to the *Plain Dealer*. The speakers included not just the conductors but also "leaders in the suffrage party and of the Cleveland Federation of Women's Clubs." Moriarty called for "a fair and square deal for women in industry" and was met with "tumultuous approval."[89] Prince insisted, "The men don't want women as competitors for jobs. We applied for admission to their union and they wouldn't have us. And we didn't go on this conductoret job just for a lark, or even as a war-winning necessity. We went because we can handle the job as well as men and because we need the money." In an argument often made in defense of their jobs, Prince insisted that these women were primary wage earners: "Of the 160 conductorets employed," she said, "over 100 supported dependents by their earnings. They are as much breadwinners for a family as men could be."[90]

Following the meeting, the women organized their own union, the Association of Women Street Railway Employees, and gathered 35,000 passenger signatures to bolster their case. They argued that their dismissal violated "the right of women to labor and remain employed when hired while performing satisfactory service" and permitted men to have a monopoly on certain jobs that women were qualified to hold. They further claimed that it violated the government's call "for women to fill non-essential jobs so that men could be released for essential jobs and the draft."[91]

The union next hired attorney Florence Allen (who would later become a noted Ohio judge), who engineered the assistance of the national WTUL, and with its help the women brought the case before the National War Labor Board. The NWLB, created in April 1918, sought to defuse labor unrest by mediating between employers and their workers, a historic first for the federal government. For the most part, the NWLB proved sympathetic to unions and worker complaints. After the war, however, Mary van Kleeck criticized the NWLB for its limited interest in protecting working women's rights. In their argument before the NWLB, the conductorets rejected the issue of labor shortages and framed the issue as one of discrimination, terming the question "an amazing infringement of fundamental rights."[92] By the time the NWLB met, the war had ended, and the Cleveland men's union was in the midst of a three-day strike over the issue of women's employment. The board upheld the initial call for the women's dismissal, claiming that with the war emergency over, their positions could be filled with competent men. In a sop to the women, it encouraged the railway company to find them jobs within the firm—traditional women's jobs such as car cleaner and ticket taker, clearly rejecting the women's claims for freedom in choosing occupations.

In response, the women petitioned for yet another hearing and secured the services of noted labor lawyer Frank Walsh. The WTUL, the Women in Industry Service agency, and Anna Howard Shaw of NAWSA joined the effort, and in the second hearing, held March 14, 1919, the NWLB reversed itself and held in the women's favor, deciding that Cleveland should rehire them.

The decision was based primarily on procedural grounds, thus avoiding the broader question of women's right to work. Moriarty and her group were jubilant. "Wasn't it a great victory?" Moriarty asked Walsh. But the joy soon fizzled. The men's union refused to honor the NWLB's decision and again threatened a strike if women were hired. Although the company might have preferred to keep women in the mix, the threatened strike was too disruptive, and thus the company, too, ignored the NWLB's decision, and women conductors lost their toehold in the new job opportunity.

Men did not resist women conductors everywhere, but the Cleveland case dramatically demonstrates the tenuous nature of women's access to jobs viewed as men's prerogatives. Van Kleeck said of the Cleveland controversy that it was "impossible to exaggerate the importance of this case to American women. No more critical issue in labor problems is before the country at this moment than to give women freedom to choose their occupation."[93] She may have been right, but the upshot of the conductorets' campaign for that freedom was a disappointing failure.

WOMEN ON THE LAND

At first blush, the "farmerettes" of the Woman's Land Army (WLA) and similar groups charged with alleviating a severe farm labor shortage fit the profile of the women who challenged sex segregation in the urban workforce. These young women donned overalls, handled heavy machinery, and performed strenuous manual labor. And like other women who crossed gendered work barriers, they received extensive media coverage. Yet their story was significantly different although equally telling about the limits placed on women's work opportunities during the war. Although some farmerettes (a term they embraced) were urban working-class women employed in seasonal industries who sought jobs in their off-seasons, the majority were either college women or teachers. The income earned may have been a factor in their decision, but most women seemed to have been attracted to the challenge, as well as the opportunity to do their patriotic bit. Few expected the experience to be more than temporary war service.

The idea of organizing young women for farm labor originated with the British. Slow to recognize the need to tap female labor, despite ardent women advocates, a food crisis ultimately led to the British government creating the Woman's Land Service in 1917. The notion that the United States would need to do the same arose in the women's preparedness movement, discussed in Chapter 1. The League for Women's National Service, joined by a professional society, the Women's National Farm and Garden Association, established the New York City Woman's Land Service Gardens and Training Camp in April 1918. Once the United States entered the war, enthusiasm for women taking on farm labor as war service accelerated. NAWSA created an agricultural committee, and in a number of states the WCND began promoting farming as a key vehicle for demonstrating women's contribution to victory. As the *Woman's Journal* put it, "All over America today suffragists are leading a back-to-the-land movement in response to the nation's call for greater production of foodstuffs," and in familiar rhetoric that equated women's service to soldiering, the magazine exclaimed, "They have put their hand to the plow and are not turning back. The woman with a hoe is easily discernible just back of the man with the gun."[94]

Some feminists who viewed the war as an opportunity to demonstrate women's capabilities had a broader vision. Harriot Stanton Blatch, for example, criticized the WCND's eager support for Hooverism and the relentless demand that women conserve food. In *Mobilizing Woman-Power,* she argued, "Instead of just conserving, women should be producing, becoming soldiers of the soil, not just the garbage pail."[95] Anne Higginson Spicer, in an article for the WTUL's *Life and Labor* entitled "Hoeing Uncle Sam's Row: The Woman's Land Army in the Making," clearly emphasized the patriotic component of the WLA, but she also insisted that "they are also being provided with a means of livelihood which is dignified, healthful and increasingly useful. Women who do not wish to do much actual farming when the war is over, may still be equipped to serve as farm managers, directors of estates and private gardens, or even to be teachers in agricultural schools. The vistas opening out seem to be endless."[96]

The enthusiasm of women's groups—preparedness advocates, suffragists, social reformers, and clubwomen—led to several farm programs. In New York City, the Mayor's Committee of Women on National Defense established an agriculture committee, headed by Virginia Gildersleeve, dean of Barnard College, which aimed to promote neighborhood gardens in the city and to identify and train women to work on farms. By summer 1917, it had established eleven "units," agricultural camps where women lived communally and went out to work locally by contract. Its most successful endeavor, a camp in Bedford, New York, recruited 141 women (38 of whom were "working women") for the 1917 season, and after much resistance from local farmers, made good. By midsummer, they could not keep up with the demand from farmers.[97] At the same time, East Coast women's colleges began promoting women as farm laborers. Vassar College fed the campus on the food produced on its own farm, run and operated by students and faculty. Beginning in the summer of 1917, Bryn Mawr and Mount Holyoke women also worked on college farms.

Organizers had hoped that the success of the various farm experiments would prompt the Wilson administration to create something along the lines of the British Woman's Land Service, but the federal government proved indifferent, even hostile. In response, farm enthusiasts created the Woman's Land Army of America in December 1917. Although colleges, the YWCA, and local groups put women into the fields during the war, the WLA became the public face of women agricultural workers during World War I. A voluntary organization that depended upon fund-raising from wealthy donors, the WLA built upon networks of clubwomen and reformers and developed an impressive publicity arm that touted the value of women farm laborers in the nation's service. By the fall of 1918, 15,000 women were serving in the WLA, which had established branches in forty states, twenty-three of which could be considered truly active. The most successful states included New York, California, Massachusetts, Pennsylvania, Illinois, New Jersey, Connecticut, and Maryland.[98]

At the center of the WLA's plan was the "unit" idea, originally devised by the New York mayor's committee. As Virginia Gildersleeve wrote in the *New Republic*, describing the original unit plan, "The essence of the unit plan is that the women workers live in a community, under a captain or supervisor, with a system of cooperative housekeeping, and go out from this centre in squads to work on neighboring farms or estates. This relieves the farmer's wife of the burden of feeding the extra laborers; and though you cannot persuade women to go and help cook in the farmer's kitchen you can, oddly enough—or perhaps naturally enough secure women who will go as a 'dietitian' or cook with one of these units, to be a member of the community in full and important standing, in charge of the catering and cooking."[99] The plan not only ensured that wives would not have extra burdens, but also removed the possibility of tension over sharing living space with attractive young women. And for the farmerettes, the unit plan minimized the possibilities for sexual harassment and in many cases gave them more comfortable quarters than they might have had in rough farmhouses.

A further innovation of the WLA was the insistence that women farmers keep to the same hours recommended for industrial workers—eight-hour days—and that they receive the same wages that male agricultural laborers would, which usually translated into $15 a month. The WLA had much in common with the women reform groups analyzed in Chapter 2. Creating their own agenda, which was not only separate but also in this case clearly unwelcomed by the government, they carved out a platform for women's war contributions that challenged conventional notions about women's proper place.[100]

The problems the WLA and other farmerettes groups faced reveal how pervasive were the notions of women's proper role. Many farmers, indeed, initially refused farmerettes, and said that they would welcome women to aid in farmhouses but not in the fields. This was the U.S. Department of Agriculture's view as well. A USDA pamphlet urged city women to volunteer to aid farmwives, arguing that "they would contribute to the worlds food supply as surely as if they ran tractors or hoed vegetables."[101] A press release in March 1918 indicated that only in dire emergency would women be needed as farm laborers, and in that case, it offered a scenario that completely excluded the WLA, suggesting instead that the Agriculture Department's county agent system could be the vehicle for organizing women's farmwork.[102]

Not surprisingly, southern states did not embrace the WLA. African American women worked in the fields in the South, and placing white women in similar work would challenge a fundamental aspect of racial hierarchy that kept black women subordinate, a phenomenon the WLA ignored in its broader discussion of the role of women on the land. Exceptions included northern Maryland, where the *Baltimore Sun* noted that the women would be "guarded in everyway possible," presumably from association with black farmworkers.[103] Despite reservations about using women, Maryland farmers there were enthusiastic. One wrote, "They hoed and thinned corn, hoed beans, tomatoes and gardens, picked tomatoes, helped make hay and helped thresh—yes, actually helped thresh. . . . They deserve credit and praise for their hard work."[104] Georgia's use of the WLA was limited to a few units picking cotton in Augusta. WLA leader Clara Mathewson promised Georgians that the women would "be adequately chaperoned and not allowed to work until exhausted or overheated." The WLA also assured Augustans that the WLA would not interfere with "industrial conditions" by calling upon "the college women, the Girl Scouts, the young society girls, the Camp Fire Girls, and any other girls out of employment."[105] Unlike other WLA units, in Augusta the women stayed at home, not in camps, and were transported to the fields. Newspaper coverage was enthusiastic, listing the young women by name and framing the project as a contest, with Grace Strauss picking the most, twenty pounds of cotton, on their first effort.[106]

Although the WLA apparently made inroads only in Augusta, other Georgia cities did report that white women worked in the fields. A severe labor shortage, in part because African Americans sought work elsewhere, brought higher wages, enough so that the *Macon Telegraph* headlined one report, "White Women Go to Cotton Fields: High Price Paid Cotton Pickers Attract Whole Families and Big Money Being Made." At the same time, elite women in Georgia were encouraged to go into the fields out of patriotic necessity. In Macon, 100 women from Methodist Columbia College picked cotton, and more remarkably, in Columbia, members of the United Daughters of the Confederacy joined the labor force to meet the cotton harvest crisis.[107]

Southern newspapers framed the presence of white women in the fields as highly unusual, but it should be noted that throughout the nation many white women worked on family farms and, in the crunch of wartime labor shortages, may well have performed unaccustomed labor in the fields. Certainly, farmwives worked hard. They raised poultry and kept gardens, carried water and coal, cooked, cleaned, and laundered for their families and for field hands, and for the most part did so without the technological conveniences that urban women were starting to enjoy.[108] In some cases, women operated farms themselves, either because of absentee husbands off at war or because they were independent.[109]

WLA organizers claimed that working-class women formed part of their units and that the nature of the work had a democratizing effect. But, for the most part, farmerettes were educated women. The Connecticut WLA for example, listed 65 percent college-linked women (a category that included teachers); another 20 percent were described as professional; and 15 percent were listed as "miscellaneous."[110] These women clearly saw farming as a novel way to earn some income while doing their patriotic bit. One woman associated with a YWCA farm unit in Peekskill, New York, enthused that "it isn't for ourselves alone, or even for the farmers, that we are doing this, it's for the good old U.S.A." She continued, "We are soldiers now and even though we are not in the trenches, facing the deadly rain of shells, we are in the trenches made of corn hills or potato rows, and we are fighting against the weed and potato bug invaders, which, in their own way, prove as deadly as the Huns."[111] News coverage agreed with this interpretation, stressing that farmerettes offered examples of "college girl patriotism," and predictably paid as much attention to their clothing (khaki jodhpurs or overalls with a wide-brimmed hat) as to the nature of their work.[112]

Despite the emphasis on the WLA as a form of patriotic war service, when the Armistice came, in November 1918, WLA leaders quickly shifted gears to suggest that the organization might well be a permanent one, offering solutions to persistent seasonal farm labor needs. Shortly before war's end, the federal government finally endorsed the WLA and created a hybrid organization, controlled by the Labor Department's U.S. Employment Service but with active participation by the voluntary association run by women. The WLA would continue to recruit and train women, but the government would make decisions about wages, hours, and accommodations. The Labor Department finalized the plan in December 1918. Frustrated by their loss of power, WLA leaders were nonetheless optimistic about the future and argued that the end of the war did not alleviate the need for farmerettes. A looming food crisis in devastated Europe meant that American agricultural production must still operate at high capacity. Much like the maternal reformers analyzed in Chapter 2, WLA leaders had enjoyed the sense of meaningful civic contributions during wartime and hoped to maintain an alliance with the state in years to come.

My mid-1919, the WLA had collapsed. Congress defunded the U.S. Employment Service, thus eliminating the federal government's engagement with the WLA. Private contributions to the WLA had dried up with war's end. In the states where the WLA had been strong, leaders had kept the organization afloat and found both eager women recruits and farmers willing to use them, but they lacked funds for training and establishing camp units. The WLA disbanded in December 1920. Although the WLA could take pride in its accomplishments, it had not permanently transformed ideas about white women's role in agriculture.

CLERICAL WORKERS

In July 1917, advice columnist Beatrice Fairfax asked women if they were proving their patriotism. She disparaged women who aspired to be nurses or farmers, arguing that most were not qualified "physically or temperamentally" for either. "Farming is not a matter of cute little overalls," she warned. Instead she pointed out that women should focus on training for "such positions as telephone operators, file clerks, bookkeepers, secretaries, and all the routine office 'jobs.'" This, she argued, "is how they can do their bit. Train at once for office positions which will not require great physical force, arduous efforts to strange fields or long and dangerous journeys to foreign shores."[113]

Between 1910 and 1920, the number of women clerical workers tripled while the increase in women workers over all increased by 16 percent. Clerical jobs accounted for the largest number of women workers in 1920 (25.6 percent), and the feminization of office work proceeded. In 1900, 29.3 percent of clerical staff were women; in 1910, the figure was 37.6 percent; in 1920, the figure was 49.2 percent.[114] The most notable incursion into the clerical field was bookkeeping, facilitated by the widening use of office equipment, such as calculators, adding machines, and key punch machines, all of which were viewed as supporting routine mechanical processes and thus suitable for women. The need for more record keeping by institutions because of the newly instituted federal income tax in 1914 added to companies' need for staff. The war undoubtedly stimulated the demand for clerical work by calling for increased production, administration of government contracts, and the need for more office workers in city, state, and federal governments. By war's end, the use of women clerks had spread throughout the economy, in retail, banking, insurance, and civil service, as well as in manufacturing.

Although not as fascinating or photoworthy as women donning overalls or uniforms to take on men's work in factories, on farms, on streetcars, or on railroads, the media covered the clerical phenomenon as well, especially in small towns and cities where women who took over traditional male office work made the news. In Grand Forks, North Dakota, the *Daily Herald* reported that "banks, stores, business houses generally and railroad offices are constantly" hiring the "fairer sex," and that they are "filling the bill."[115] The *Duluth News-Tribune* informed its readers that the sixty-five banks in Duluth and Minneapolis–St. Paul had doubled their use of women clerks.[116] Aberdeen, South Dakota, saw women appear in offices throughout the city: "Girls and women nowadays are seen everywhere—in stores, shops, banks, auto companies, railway stations, grocery's, newspaper offices, etc."[117]

Newspapers heavily publicized the government's urgent needs for 10,000 new clerks in the summer of 1917 and reported that civil service examinations were being held weekly in over 400 cities. Many articles provided listings of the types of jobs and salaries available and specifically urged women to apply.[118] In May 1918, the *Tucson Daily Citizen* headlined with "More Women Are Needed for the War." In addition to describing openings for "stenographers, typists, bookkeepers, other clerks and a score or more of classifications which require training in some special or technical line, statisticians, operators or various kinds of calculating, addressing and duplication machines, proof readers, law clerks, welfare executive secretaries, draftsmen of a dozen kinds, telegraph and telephone operators, trained nurses, chemists, physicists, library assistants, inspectors of under garments, finger-print classifiers, and many others," it reported the Civil Service Commission's argument that "as men are called to the colors, women must take their places and keep the machinery behind the armed forces moving at the maximum of efficiency."[119]

The call for women clerks represented a sea change in the federal offices in Washington, D.C. Although federal law did not establish sex segregation in the civil service, administrators created procedures that sex-typed jobs and limited women's opportunities dramatically. As many as 60 percent of civil service jobs excluded women, who were particularly limited in professional and technical opportunities.[120] As recently as January 1917, civil service women had sent a letter to congressional members from suffrage states, complaining that women were barred from taking exams for which they were qualified. They further reported that women's starting salaries as clerks were $720 ($2,015 in contemporary dollars) a year, while men's were $900, and that even as stenographers, men received jobs while women were ignored, noting in this case that since September 1916, only 4 of 212 clerical appointments had gone to women. The writers asked, "Will you not in behalf of the women of your State, call upon the president and the heads of the executive departments to require that women be admitted and promoted in the federal civil service upon the same terms as men?"[121]

The war changed opportunities for entry-level positions dramatically, with at least 100,000 new jobs created; and in June 1918, Secretary of War Newton Baker announced that women would be given precedence in hiring for clerical work. Civil service lists, however, continued to specify men for some employment, such as scientific assistant, meat inspector, and accountant supervisor. But women were urged to apply for positions such as agricultural specialists, draftsmen, and photographic negative cutters.[122] Equal pay continued to be an issue, however, a point Carrie Catt of NAWSA brought up when she complained to the secretaries of state, war, navy, and commerce that women's and men's salaries as clerks were significantly unequal.[123] The high demand for clerical workers ultimately led to increased wages for all clerks of $1,000–1,200 per year and apparently some attention to the concept of equal pay for equal work. Overall, about 75 percent of new hires in Washington, D.C., during the war were women.[124]

Business colleges and individuals seized on the possibilities. Want ad columns offered tutoring for the exams to young women, and business colleges promised wonderful opportunities. In Kansas, the Lawrence Business College celebrated "Days of Opportunity for Women" and explained that "stenography is an entering wedge and appeals to women of refinement and ability who have attained some of the best positions the business world has to offer." It featured photographs of young women who had left Kansas for Washington, D.C., and noted that Miss Beulah Woodard and her sister Juletta were now in the nation's capitol., "doing their best to help win the war."[125] Although much of the work must have involved deadly routine, the diary of Josephine Lehman, a young woman from a small town in Michigan, fairly sizzles with the excitement of being in wartime Washington, D.C. And while part of her enthusiasm stemmed from the whirl of social activity occasioned by sailors and soldiers stationed nearby, Lehman, a competent woman who quickly became a private secretary in the War Department, enjoyed the hubbub of engagement in important military work. "I have just finished typing a long report," she wrote. "Our office is a continual uproar. Two dozen typewriters are going at the same time, forty-seven people are yelling over the different telephones to places from New York to Chicago, men are shouting at each other across the room, and workers are rushing back and forth until I can't hear myself think. This is the life."[126]

These new positions were almost exclusively for white women. By 1913, much of the federal bureaucracy in Washington, D.C., had been segregated, with offices, toilets, and cafeterias separated by race, a process reinforced by the requirement in 1914 that applicants send photographs with their applications. Part of the argument made by Wilson administration officials was that white women should not be forced to work with African Americans. While black men and women continued to work for the government (about 5,000 black women worked in Washington, D.C., offices during the war), their opportunities were circumscribed and the circumstances often humiliating. In August 1918, the *Washington Bee* had witheringly compared the war for democracy with the circumstance in federal offices—"separate toilets are maintained for cultured, refined and intelligent and efficient colored employees, just as if they were lepers."[127] That same month it railed against the wholesale rejection of black applicants for new jobs. It told the story of a black woman applicant who had passed her civil service exams and was called to Washington, D.C., for a conference about her proposed job. After the time and expense involved in travel, she was denied the position, and then, upon returning home, she learned that the War Trade Bureau would hire her. But once again in Washington, D.C., "on discovering she was colored, she suffered the embarrassment, the injustice, of being sent from room to room to receive the cruel advice of division chiefs that they WOULD NOT take her because she was colored."[128]

Black women were largely excluded from another opportunity to serve the government in a clerical capacity. Both the U.S. Navy and the U.S. Marine Corps addressed severe labor shortages by inducting women into the military to work primarily in office jobs. With the exception of fourteen women who discreetly enlisted in the navy through the efforts of a black civil service man in charge of mustering women for the navy, women inducted into it and the Marines were white and middle class. The origins of female military service began with Secretary of the Navy Josephus Daniels, whose wife was a well-known suffragist. He dramatically broke with military tradition when he decided in March 1917 that no regulations prevented women from joining the navy. Perhaps because the need for clerical staff was so pressing, Daniels's plan created relatively little controversy, although the Marine Corps, similarly pressed for stateside labor, did not begin to recruit women until August 1918.

When the U.S. Navy and later the Marine Corps advertised for enlistees, the response was overwhelming. In New York City, on one day alone, 2,000 women appeared to sign up for the Marines. Applicants faced interviews and shorthand and stenographic tests.[129] The physical exam proved particularly challenging, because military officials insisted that women be treated like men, which included stripping down in the company of other women and being examined by a male physician. Later a female nurse was included to offer women a greater patina of respectability for this daunting hurdle.

Military recruits ranged from elite women like Sydney and Lucy Burleson, daughters of the postmaster general, to experienced stenographers and young women with little useful training. The Marine Corps, which only recruited for four months, ultimately enlisted just over 300 women, while the U.S. Navy inducted a little over 11,000 in the course of the war. Navy yeomen (F) and Marine Corps reservists (F)—the military resisted the more popular terms of Yeomanette or Marinette as undignified—signed up in part for patriotic reasons. One woman reported, "We had the idea that every time we hit a letter on the typewriter we were driving another nail in the Kaiser's coffin." Others were attracted by adventure. As one woman enthused to another, "They might send us anywhere, even to Paris!"[130] Only a handful of women went abroad. Most worked stateside, many of them in Washington, D.C. Women also joined because the military paid well and equitably. Daniels, perhaps reflecting the influence of his wife, insisted, "A woman who works as well as a man ought to receive the same pay." The starting salary for yeoman first class was $30 but could increase significantly with promotions and was supplemented by a daily subsistence payment of $1.25 and later $1.50. Moreover, unlike nurses and Signal Corps women, who served as civilians overseas, naval and marine inductees received the same benefits as men, including veterans' rights.[131]

Most military women worked in some sort of office capacity, but a few drove trucks, assembled munitions, or did propaganda work. Both the U.S.

Figure 14. "Tell That to the Marines!" Marine Corps women pasting recruitment posters. National Archives, 165-WW-598-A4.

Navy and the Marines actively publicized women's service as a recruiting tool for men. They appeared in recruitment offices and in countless photographs. Figure 14, for example, features women Marines, neatly uniformed and proudly posing as they go about their work of pasting Marine enlistment posters on the wall behind them. Although enlisted women were never issued arms, many learned to drill in military fashion, and they were often featured in parades. The propaganda role of one young Los Angeles woman, Florence Tongate, was unique. The day she enrolled, she met artist Howard

Chandler Christy in the Los Angeles navy recruitment office, who asked her to pose for him in a navy uniform. The resulting poster, featuring a somewhat seductive Tongate rigged out in saucy naval cap, teasing, "Gee I Wish I Were a Man. I'd Join the Navy," became an iconic World War I–era poster.[132]

As the war came to a close, Daniels conducted a survey to see if yeomen (F) would wish to continue working for the navy as civilians through the civil service and found that the majority were eager to do so. They had enlisted for four-year terms, but when the war ended, Congress decreed that they be discharged. The process took a while, but by March 1920 all women had left the navy and the Marines, and they would not be invited back to the U.S. military until World War II created another labor shortage crisis.

Whether they had worked for the military, the civil service, railroads, or other concerns, clerical workers did not disappear into the woodwork after war's end. More so than any other category of women's employment, opportunities in clerical work had expanded during the war and would continue to grow in the postwar era when the corporate expansion of the 1920s fueled still more need for white-collar office workers, jobs that increasingly became the purview of young middle-class white women.

Even before the war ended, commentators questioned whether women workers would be willing to return to their prewar circumstances. Columnist Dorothy Dix was gleeful at the prospect of women's new power, writing in August 1918 that "there are millions of other women who have been engaged in piddling women's work where they received only starving wages. They have found out, since the war began, that they can do men's work and earn men's salaries. Are they going to be willing to give up the lathe and the big jobs they now have and retire once more to the kitchen and wash tub, and the dollar a day envelope?" She thought not and suggested that the change could affect marriages as well: "Will any one be able to shoo these women back into the home to haggle with husband over pennies when the war is over? The woman who has once known the joy of her own pocketbook is like the tiger who has tasted 'blood.'"[133]

Less enthusiastically, a few months after the war ended, a headline in the *Fort Wayne Sentinel* proclaimed "WOMEN WAR WORKERS CLING TO THEIR JOBS: Ladies Who Donned Jumpers to Let Men Go Fight for Liberty Do Not Fancy Return to Soft Life—Better Pay and Greater Independence Lures That Hold Them; Few Will Yield Places to Men without Contest." Reporting on a UPI story, the newspaper noted the determination of women workers to stay in their jobs, as well as the AFL's insistence that they return to their former work. According to the account, women "of their own accord, will drift back to what is generally classed as women's work, largely because of the hostile feeling of the men."[134]

As the UPI story recognized, many employers and male workers quickly called for a return to prewar conditions. Women in the munitions industry were first to be laid off. Changes in the railroads came more slowly, as the WSS persisted into 1920 and sought to protect women in the period of transition. The records of the WSS reveal a few letters in which men complained bitterly about women being kept on in the railroads after the Armistice. They encapsulate the hostility to women's encroachment in the all-male environment. In February 1919, one anonymous man wrote to a superintendent on the Pennsylvania Railroad: "Our men came first before the war, why not now? Women help ought to be entirely taken off the railroads, it is no place for the finest of women."[135] Although WSS agents succeeded in restoring the jobs of some women who had been fired from the railroads in violation of seniority rules, eventually women were pushed out of jobs deemed to be men's. The situation was made worse because most of the unions refused to support women in their complaints. Overall, 20,000 women left railway jobs in 1919. Those that remained were in "women's" jobs—doing cleaning or clerical work.[136]

Although it is difficult to be precise about statistics, for most white women, the pattern of the railroads characterized other industries as well. Many women kept their jobs—as unskilled and semiskilled factory operatives or clerks—but lost positions in those deemed to be "men's jobs." For African American women, the discrimination experienced during the war persisted in its aftermath. Although domestic labor jobs declined for all women between 1910 and 1920, for black women the percentage actually increased, from 42.4 percent to 50.3 percent of working black women. In 1920, the majority of black women (89.2 percent) worked as farm laborers or in domestic service jobs. And wages dropped as well. In Washington, D.C., servants earned $10 a week during the war, but afterward they took in $7. As to factory jobs, black women had been the last hired and would be the first fired. One black observer bitterly commented, "The history of the experiences of colored women in the present war should make fair-minded Americans blush with shame. They have been universally the last to be employed. They were the marginal workers of industry all through the war. They have been given, with few exceptions, the most undesirable and lowest paid work, and now that the war is over they are the first to be released."[137] Nevertheless, while African American women lost many of the gains they had made in access to factory work, some of the progress they made in finding employment in industries formerly closed to them, such as the garment trade and chemical industries, persisted and offered black women, especially those who had migrated north, slightly more opportunities to better their circumstances.[138]

As women who had so happily donned conductoret uniforms or learned a metalworking skill sought more conventional blue-collar women's work, white middle-class women's options expanded in the postwar era. The number of women employed in office work tripled between 1910 and 1920 and represented the largest sector of employed women (25.6 percent). At the same time, the feminization of the clerical field proceeded. Women had represented 37.4 percent of office workers in 1910, but in 1920, that number was 49.6 percent.[139] Professional women, too, saw their numbers increase, with a half million more women listed as professional in 1920 than in 1910 (from 9.1 percent to 11.9 percent of working women). Wartime needs encouraged the growth of social work, nursing, and personnel management positions, but teaching continued to be the dominant professional job for women. Though women slightly increased their representation in such fields as medicine and law, women professionals were overwhelmingly in feminized lines of work.[140]

Professional and clerical work, like other jobs women pursued in the postwar era, were primarily "women's jobs." In the 1920s, job classifications had shifted somewhat, and the war undoubtedly stimulated these shifts. But the gender and racial hierarchy of prewar years persisted with only small modifications, and this would continue in the postwar decades. As historian Alice Kessler-Harris said of the 1920s, "Women were invited into the workforce and again invited not to expect too much of it."[141]

What meaning can we assign to this short period of time in which women stormed the barriers of sex- and race-segregated labor and yet seemed to have relatively little to show for it? Although the media often glamorized women at work at men's jobs, it is worthwhile to note that, for many, the work was arduous and for African American women often accompanied by the humiliations of racial discrimination. And even women with more pleasant work might face sexual harassment, male hostility, and the stress of long hours and crowded living conditions. But whatever the reality of their work experiences, even women in the least glamorous war jobs had hoped to keep them because they were so much better than the usual options of women's work. A railway common laborer, for example, bitter at being laid off, explained, "We never took a soldier's place, a soldier would not do the work we did . . . such as sweeping, picking up waste and paper and hauling steel shavings."[142]

Beyond the undeniable lure of better wages, women found satisfaction in their new jobs. Some for patriotic reasons—doing their bit gave meaning to ordinary labor—and some for the consumption and leisure pleasures better salaries bought them. Josephine Lehman, civil service secretary, for example, had a good time. She loved her work, but she also loved living in the excitement of wartime Washington, D.C., writing in her diary, "Some thrilling thing is going on all the time and the city is full of soldiers, sailors aviators, etc. A dozen or more were at the dance, from privates to lieutenants and Marines." After seeing the low-cut and glamorous gowns of other women, she vowed, "After I have some new glad rags I am going to have some large pictures taken to astonish the native Ionians [her home town] by the general absentness of the upper part of my gown."[143] Equally important, the higher wages of wartime work could bring a degree of independence. Amy Hewes, in her study of munitions women, reported that most of the workers were young and single and living at home. Even though half of the women gave their paychecks to their families, Hewes observed that "the dependence of many of the families upon the women workers gave them an important position in directing family life. Even young girls, on account of their earning capacity, had a controlling hand in making family plans."[144]

In the decades after the war, women's increasing participation in the workforce would continue unabated, as would the sex- and racially segmented labor market. A few women could look to unions to mediate the conditions of their work, but the Red Scare that enveloped the United States between 1919 and 1921 eviscerated the American labor movement, which would not revive until the 1930s. Despite growing hostility to reform activism in the 1920s, on the state level, reformers kept much protective legislation in place for women workers, which persisted in both protecting and constraining them. The Women's Bureau continued to be an investigatory agency, working closely with voluntary associations. It actively resisted a proposed equal rights amendment that helped fracture the women's movement of the prewar era out of fear that it would undermine protective laws. Women would once again break down sex and race segregation in World War II, as the iconic Rosie the Riveter shows us, and even more so than in World War I, they made significant contributions to the mobilization necessary for a global modern war. But in that war, as well, women were only moderately successful in permanently securing women's access to higher pay and more skilled labor. It was not until the 1960s that a new feminist movement and an enlarged women's labor union presence, armed with the 1964 Civil Rights Act, would help women challenge the concept of sex-segregated labor and find more (though far from complete) equality in the workplace.

FIVE

Visual Representations of Women in Popular Culture

"Imposing Red Cross Parade Opens Duluth's Eyes to Scope of Woman's Part in World War I."

Caption for news photograph featuring uniformed Red Cross workers in Duluth's May 1918 parade

Although few Americans experienced the suffering, sacrifice, or drama of World War I at first hand, they had constant reminders that the United States was a nation at war. Government agencies, voluntary associations, and the media bombarded the public with accounts of battles at the front and civilian service and defense work on the home front. And, befitting a time when newspapers and magazines had already developed inexpensive photographic reproduction processes and movies were making the transition from short films tailored to working-class audiences to feature films with broad appeal, many of the reminders of war were visual. Public spaces and streets were awash in colorful propaganda posters, adopted from a late nineteenth-century revolution in commercial art. These images created a striking and powerful impact for Americans who experienced a war fought thousands of miles away. And considering them now, they illuminate not just the ways in which the media represented women but also a gendered interpretation of the role of citizens in defending the nation.

This chapter focuses on the rich archive of visual material portraying American women during World War I. We have photographic archives of the experiences of African American women, and these photos appeared occasionally in black newspapers and journals, but they almost never appeared in the mainstream media.[1] Representations of traditional white womanhood, however, were quite evident in the war years. They conveyed the notion of vulnerable women needing the protection of masculine men in times of war. Yet these images competed with those that featured youthful modern women, who, while feminine, were also depicted as independent and resourceful. They appear in photographs of workplace scenes where women are shown in the act of doing what was once considered men's work or in military-style uniforms marching in patriotic parades. In films, they spurred men to enlist and foiled the plots of enemy agents by extraordinary feats of physical daring and courage. Their agency offers a striking contrast to the notion of women as objects in need of masculine protection. In keeping with women activists' arguments, they supported the idea of women as a second line of national defense.

The competing visual interpretations of women's role in war helps us to understand the opportunities new women enjoyed during the war, as well as their limits. That conventional notions of womanhood persisted suggests the continuing power of expectations about women's traditional roles in the family. The attention given to "modern" women's war service and heroic activism on the one hand offered dramatic evidence of boundary-crossing women. But on the other hand, the media's fascination with the novelty of women at war undoubtedly led it to exaggerate the degree to which American women challenged gender conventions. The ubiquitous images of the new woman illuminate why many observers believed—inaccurately—that the war would prove transformative in reshaping women's lives.

CONTINUITY AND CHANGE IN PHOTOGRAPHS AND POSTERS

In our age of Instagram and selfies, it is hard to imagine a time when the proliferation of mass-distributed imagery was relatively new. Although magazines and newspapers contained some illustrations throughout the nineteenth century, it was not until the 1890s that technology revolutionized the print media.[2] The "half-tone" method, which breaks images into a pattern of dots, simplified and cheapened the process of inserting images into the pages of newspapers and magazines, thus permitting them to be lavishly illustrated with black and white photographs instead of artists' renditions. At the same time, more portable cameras further stimulated the meteoric rise of photojournalism. These cheaper illustrated newspapers and magazines significantly expanded the audience for print media. Technological developments had lowered costs, but so, too, had the turn to extensive advertising, which in turn introduced still further images for public consumption.

A measure of the importance of photojournalism in particular is the 1911 data for New York City's fourteen daily newspapers: they averaged 900 pictures per week. While consumers and readers may have enjoyed the phenomenon, many critics were alarmed. In a 1911 op-ed entitled "Over Illustration," a *Harper's Weekly* writer complained, "We can't see the ideas for the illustrations. Our world is simply flooded with them. They lurk in almost every form of printed matter."[3]

Harper's Weekly was right. Images, especially photographs, also appeared in the immensely popular fad of postcards and stereopticon sets, which were slides that gave a three-dimensional effect. Firms emerged that distributed photographs nationally in the same way that news services operated. Equally important, the burgeoning advertising industry was intimately tied to the production and distribution of images. Businesses turned to posters to sell products and advertise entertainments such as circuses and vaudeville shows. A visual revolution was thus already under way by World War I.[4]

Women, of course, figured prominently in these images. During World War I, their representation in propaganda posters and in illustrations in the print media constituted a powerful way of recording and interpreting American women's role in the war. Although the National Archives contain a treasure trove of images of women for this era, the analysis here focuses on those that were made public in the war years themselves.[5]

Traditional Womanhood and War Images

This chapter emphasizes representations of "new" white women, but public attention also focused on women's war contributions by emphasizing traditional female virtues associated with their domestic duties. Maternal rhetoric suffused accounts of the activities of volunteer workers, none more so than the Red Cross. The Red Cross poster "The Greatest Mother in the World" was ubiquitous, appearing in over 60,000 shop windows in 600 cities and in more than 1,200 print publications. The image, with its oversized nurse cradling a diminutive wounded soldier in a pose that resembled the Pietà, certainly conveyed a sense of power as the huge female figure dwarfs the enfeebled male. Yet that power is derived not from the nurse's size but from her ability to nurture. The poster's message evoked maternal, even spiritual, care.[6]

Government-issued posters similarly reinforced maternalist rhetoric, encouraging women to participate in war activities such as knitting or food conservation that closely related to their domestic roles. Posters depicted women in the Women's Land Army as cheerful harvesters in a sunny field, not agricultural laborers performing hard manual labor. Food conservation posters featured charming housewives in their kitchens. A Liberty Loan poster urging women to "Help America's Sons Win the War" depicted a white-haired motherly woman, arms outstretched in a beseeching manner. Although some European nations' posters featured munitions workers and their contribution to the war effort, for the most part U.S. government–issued posters failed to represent the claim of women activists who insisted that women war workers were the second line of defense.[7]

Like government propaganda, commercial media usually portrayed women in traditional roles. Poignant depictions of soldiers leaving their womenfolk behind as they went off to war illustrated a popular motif. Covers for sheet music, for instance for "America: Here's My Boy" or "So Long Mother," featured sentimental renderings of mother-son love, with white-haired mothers wearing old-fashioned dresses, sadly but willingly bidding good-bye. Romantic pictures of soldiers and their sweethearts were equally compelling and emphasized that war is men's work. Typical of the soldier and the woman he left behind was an *American Magazine* cover, which featured an embrace (fig. 15). The small star-embossed flag she holds conveys her patriotism. Readers would know that she would hang that star in the window to symbolize her man at the front. The cover was not tied to a story in the issue; it stood alone to convey its message of women bravely sending their men to war.[8]

The perception of men's duty to protect women saw its most extreme version in U.S. propaganda posters that presented the enemy as vile rapists. One, for the Fourth Liberty Loan, stated starkly, "Remember Belgium" (fig. 16). The image—in shadowed profile—features a rifle-carrying soldier, wearing the distinctive pointed German helmet, who drags a young woman behind him. In the background stands a dimly sketched city engulfed in flames. A different approach, adopted by the Associated Motion Picture Advertisers to promote enlistment, proclaims, "It's Up to You" (fig. 17). The image is of a sober-faced Uncle Sam, arm outstretched, pointing to the viewer. Kneeling in front him, head bowed, is an iconic "Lady Liberty." Both U.S. and European propaganda posters frequently used female figures as abstract icons representing the nation and its war aims. Most commonly, these allegorical figures appear as masculinized women warriors, who, in Pearl James's words, embodied "a nation's power, despite women's lack of power within it." American posters, however, often featured a more modern, even sexy, Lady Liberty, a reflection of the influence of commercial commodification of women's

Figure 15. The woman he leaves behind. *American Magazine*, July 1918.

bodies already under way in American advertising. Here she is dressed in white and draped with the red and white stripes of the flag. Her white body, drawn with erotic overtones, reinforces the notion of sexual menace suggested by the poster's subtitle, "Protect the Nation's Honor—Enlist Now."[9]

This visual merging of a woman's virtue with national honor signaled the way in which wartime representations of sexual violation symbolized

Figure 16. "Remember Belgium" poster. Library of Congress, Prints and Photographs Division, LC-USCZC4-4441.

Figure 17. "It's Up to You: Protect the Nation's Honor" poster. Library of Congress, Prints & Photographs Division, WWI Posters, LC-USZC4-1960.

the threat to both patriarchal and national power. This sexualized menace of conquest was even more overt in the poster "Destroy the Mad Brute," originally produced in Britain. The U.S. version features a vicious-looking gorilla, wearing the German helmet and wielding a club emblazoned with the word "Kultur," as he strides up a beach labeled "America" (fig. 18). In his arms is a struggling bare-breasted nubile white woman. In small letters, the poster warns, "If this war is not brought to a finish in Europe, it will be on the shores of the United States." This haunting image reflects even more than the artist's depiction of the Germans as beasts. Its power derives in part from the pervasive American convention of depicting racial others as apelike hulks. It specifically enjoins popular stereotypes of racial others—both blacks and immigrants—as threats to pure white womanhood, and by extension, to the nation itself.[10] For contemporaries, such posters were meant to evoke the tales of brutal killings of children and rapes of women that were the subject of extensive Allied propaganda, in both Europe and the United States. Although the propaganda was undoubtedly exaggerated, wartime rapes did indeed take place, reflecting the way in which rape often becomes an expression of conquest and revenge in the context of war.[11] In this presentation of women as objects to be saved by heroic men, propaganda posters thus offered a compelling rationale for American engagement in the Great War.

Boundary-Crossing New Women

Alongside images that emphasized the need for men to protect their women and those that depicted maternal or feminine women doing their part for the war in ways that did not challenge gender norms, alternative representations competed with the more conventional ones. In particular, coverage in newspapers and magazines of women's war efforts seized upon the way in which women were breaking new ground. As Anne Emerson reported in the 1918 *Forum* article, "Today SHE is everywhere; a Salvation lassie, serving coffee and doughnuts *on the firing line*; in the Red Cross Emergency Hospital *at the front*; in the munitions factory *at home*; filling the gaps in man-made industry everywhere. . . . She is omnipresent."[12] Written descriptions like Emerson's conveyed compelling word pictures of these new activities, but even more so, photographs and drawings offered compelling black and white evidence of women's war opportunities. This type of reporting emphasized women's competence at new jobs, but also played up the novelty, particularly in its descriptions of the clothes women wore as they made their contributions to the war effort.

Figure 18. “Destroy This Mad Brute” poster. Library of Congress, Prints & Photographs Division, WWI Posters, LC-DIG-ds-03216.

Print media gave extensive coverage to white women workers who took jobs formerly assumed to be men's, especially those specifically tied to defense industries. Having closely followed the story of British female munitions workers, by summer 1917 American newspapers were reporting on the call for women munitions workers in the United States. In early 1918, they began to run illustrated articles, such as "4,000 Women Making Munitions for Uncle Sam," in which author Sophie Irene Loeb reported on women in the "largest ordnance factory in the United States." Impressed with their accomplishments and also recognizing that the fundamental shift at stake was not *new* women workers but new opportunities to employ skills many women had already practiced, she enthused, "Truly, sewing machines and typewriters have been put in the shade in the realm of mechanism where woman may prove her worth. It has become as easy for women to arrange tools, speed the lathes, test and adjust electric devices in fuses as it once was to change the needles on the sewing machines or put in a ribbon on the typewriter." Her point was reinforced by the accompanying photograph, which featured a large factory room with dozens of women intently occupied at their tasks.[13]

Following this theme, the *Philadelphia Inquirer* featured an illustration of seven powder workers in a New Jersey munitions plant (fig. 19). The women, arms around each other and looking boldly into the camera, are dressed in identical overalls with simple caps. Their smiles are bright and suggest sheer delight, if not in their work, then in having their pictures taken. Their uniforms demarcated a sense of shared identity that set them apart from other workers and women in the home. The very nature of a group photograph like this, moreover, reinforced a sense of common purpose among the women as much-touted munitions workers. The accompanying article offered details of the 300 women, noting that they came from a variety of backgrounds, but that all were white, as the factory observed a color line. Most had mill or other factory work experience and thus quickly adjusted to the new jobs. "The girls employed here . . . have shown that they are not afraid of their jobs as powder makers, but go to their work with the same coolness as the men."[14]

Extensive publicity also attended women's appearance in the railroad industry, and the overall thrust was again not only to emphasize the novelty, but also to illustrate women's competency at their new jobs. The *Colorado Gazette-Telegraph* reported on a New York story, in which the operating chief of the New York Central Railroad observed that women have "taken up railroad work eagerly and energetically." While he did not feel women should do heavy labor, he believed that "there was nothing about railroad work requir-

Figure 19. Munitions workers, New Jersey, 1918. *Philadelphia Inquirer*, January 20, 1918.

ing skill or accuracy which women cannot do."[15] Images that accompanied this type of article featured strong-looking women, usually wearing overalls and often posed dramatically next to railway engines, thus underlining the heavily industrial and presumed masculine nature of their work.

Articles and the images that accompanied them stressed not only the

Figure 20. Hollywood "Women Fill the War Breaches."
Motion Picture Magazine, October 1918.

novelty of women's work but also that they were wearing the same kinds of clothes as men as they labored in "factories, munitions plants, railways yards and wharves."[16] Although some authors were clearly disconcerted at this evidence for women usurping male roles, others insisted that women retained their femininity despite their apparel. At times, the portrayal minimized the threat to established gender order. An article, "The Win-the-War Girl: Art's New Inspiration," offered three artists' renditions of uniformed women appearing coolly confident and capable. But a fourth drawing featured illustrator J. V. Early's "Munitions Girl." Dressed in pants that hugged her body, she sits somewhat seductively against a workbench, with a huge phallic-looking shell standing on the table next to her. She is demure and feminine, with her head facing away from the camera, and from the shell.[17]

The movie industry often played women in men's clothing for laughs, which lessened the perceived threat. *Motion Picture Magazine* in October 1918 offered "Women Fill the War Breaches," a two-page spread of dramatically posed photographs of glamorous movie stars dressed as men (fig. 20). Dorothy Dalton, wearing what appears to be a military uniform and standing on a platform that makes her taller than her listeners, pointedly gives orders to a group of men. Mary Pickford is posed as an artist, palette in hand. In contrast to the images in which movie stars retain their femininity despite their clothing is the center picture, whose caption reads, "Dress-Suits Are Passed along to the Girls — Now That Men Wear Uniforms."[18] Here the stars not only dress like men but pose like them as well. The slicked-back hair, too, suggests masculine attributes. The image hints at lesbianism or at least "unnatural" mannishness and is notable for its rarity. Perhaps because of the patriotic nature of women's wartime work, few images or authors challenged their femininity. Taken as a whole, "Women Fill the War Breaches" was clearly meant as a humorous and even mocking commentary on women's new war work.

For the most part, illustrations of women workers' masculine attire were realistic drawings or photographs of real women who worked. A photograph of nine New York City women, dressed in conductors' uniforms, featured a group of smiling and confident women.[19] The *Rock Valley (Iowa) Bee* offered a photograph of a pants-wearing munitions worker standing at a formidable-looking machine and explained that women workers at the Frankford Arsenal had designed the outfit that the U.S. government adopted for "use of women workers in government munitions plants."[20] Posters issued by women's organizations also featured women in uniform or masculine clothing. Figure 21, "For Every Fighter a Woman Worker," produced by the YWCA, is notable among World War I propaganda posters. In keeping with YWCA literature that praised women factory workers' vital contributions to defense, this image emphasizes female strength and solidarity, underlined by the long line of marching women, which stretches far into the distance. Significantly, the women are dressed in masculine-styled clothing and wear caps or have short hair. As Pearl James has noted, the bottom of the YWCA triangle emphasizes the largest figure, who carries a sledgehammer and wears pants. The graphic style itself reinforces the modern message of these women's labor.[21]

The attention to women's working clothing underscores the novelty of women taking on what were formerly men's jobs. Before the war, a working woman's costume usually consisted of a blouse and simple dark skirt. This would persist in the war years for most, although skirt lengths shortened to just above the ankle. The women whose new jobs required pants, overalls, or skirted uniforms broke dramatically with convention. Their masculinized clothes signaled the way in which they were taking on male jobs. And women who wore uniforms, especially conductors, elevator operators, and the like were notable in that their apparel was linked to the idea of a military uniform. The uniforms not only suggested that women were moving across workplace boundaries, but also symbolized that women's work was also part of their

Figure 21. "For Every Fighter a Woman Worker": The Second Line of Defense poster. Library of Congress, Prints & Photographs Division, WWI Posters, LC-USZC4-1419.

service to their nation in time of war. Women's employment choices may have been determined by the financial reward, but war-related employment was generally portrayed as serving the nation in times of need, and thus was an expression of citizenship. Images of the overalled or uniformed worker signaled the boundary-crossing "new woman."[22]

Women who served overseas or volunteered at home for government or quasi-governmental agencies also received extensive visual publicity that both promoted a sense of a "new" woman and celebrated her patriotic contributions. Here, too, whether they were in voluntary associations like the YWCA or in government positions as nurses or Signal Corps operators, their uniforms were central to their representation. And, indeed, uniformed women were so familiar that fashions of the era reflected a military style, with tailored jackets and coats, slim skirts, and buttons and braids as trim. The uniforms' novelty may have been startling to some observers, but for the women who wore them they were appealing symbols of their war service.[23]

Women who served abroad were in a special category: they faced danger, in both the Atlantic crossing and the war zone itself. Firsthand accounts, offered by the women themselves or on-the-spot reporters, proliferated in newspapers and magazines, many of them illustrated. The themes varied, from sentimental depictions of nurturing nurses or YMCA canteen workers serving soldiers as reminders of home, to highly skilled professional nurses or indomitable telephone Hello Girls. Nurses received an extraordinary amount of attention. In an article in the *Independent*, Henry Noble McCracken suggested why, noting, "Next to being in battle, staunching the wounds of men who have just been carried off the fields is the most direct form of participation in war. That is why so many women 'want to go to France.'"[24] Newspaper articles stressed the adventures nurses experienced. The *Cleveland Plain Dealer* ran a series, "Experiences of a Nurse at the Front," written by Emily Harris Dodd, a volunteer nurse with the Sixth French Army. Dodd emphasized the danger and her "thrilling adventures" but also noted the hard physical labor and the "horror" of the wounds she treated. The article's illustrations, however, contradicted her own narrative. The accompanying photograph of the young and attractive Dodd was demure, and the artists' sketches of her stories, in keeping with popular magazine conventions of illustrations featuring beautiful women, depicted glamorous nurses tending to the wounded. One account that spoke directly to that disjuncture was the report by Julia Stimson, chief nurse of the Red Cross in France. Like Dodd, she emphasized the nurses' bravery, telling of a grueling experience in which twenty nurses at the front had to work in virtual darkness after a harrowing raid had cut power. Stimson offered a bit of sardonic commentary. "When the chief nurse saw them the next morning with their faces and dresses covered with dust from their trip, with towels pinned across the front of their cloth dresses, she could not help thinking that some of the illustrators of modern magazines might change their opinion of war nurses if they could see this group."[25]

The media also lauded other uniformed women at the front for their brave service. Frederic J. Haskin reported on Salvation Army canteen workers: "In their costume [of khaki uniform, a tin hat, and a gingham apron], with gas mask convenient, they are ready to meet shrapnel, mud, and a roaring hot kitchen fire while they prepared doughnuts and coffee for our men at the front."[26] The Signal Corps women telephone operators were noted for their efficiency and also for their courage. A YWCA poster made the point visually (fig. 22) by portraying the operator, in her neat uniform, competently at work at her switchboard. Most compelling, however, is the backdrop of a teeming scene of uniformed men in battle. She, like the men, is clearly at the "the front," a message her military uniform underscored.

Less romantic and dramatic but nonetheless ubiquitous was the press representation of women as loyal citizens on the home front, and here too women earned praise as exemplary citizens. Publicity for women's civil defense work (Red Cross work on the home front, food conservation, fundraising, and so on) was extensive, in part because women activists in the WCND and other organizations actively pursued publicity as a record of their achievements. To some extent, this desire for recognition was linked to the suffrage campaign's insistence that women's war service had earned them full citizenship. While some of media coverage emphasized women's contributions in traditional ways, others offered a more activist sense of women's patriotic work.

As was the case with wage-earning women, the media gave the uniforms of overseas war workers and those at home extensive attention. At times, their outfits were the subject of the reporting. Praising the new look, an article in *Touchstone* repeatedly stressed uniforms' practicality but also emphasized the pride that women took in wearing them, noting, "Never has a diamond coronet been worn with greater pride than the metal insignia 'U.S.' at the collar of a woman war worker."[27] The *Touchstone* article was amply illustrated, as was the *Independent*'s 1918 News-Pictorial essay, "Our Women Over There," which offered six illustrations of uniforms, including Red Cross and U.S. Army nurses, a YWCA canteen worker, and a Signal Corps operator.[28]

Red Cross volunteer uniforms were perhaps the most widely seen war-

Figure 22. A Signal Corps operator in France. Library of Congress, Prints & Photographs Division, WWI Posters, 598-c.

time uniforms. Women wore the white dress with the Red Cross emblazoned on the front as they made bandages, ran canteens, or met troops trains to pass out coffee, doughnuts, and cigarettes. Because the Red Cross was the most diverse in its membership, these uniforms were also worn by ethnic and racial minorities. Wartime photos of African American women in these uniforms occasionally appeared in black publications such as *Half-Century* or the *Chicago Defender* but were not printed in the mainstream media. Immigrant and black women frequently marched in urban patriotic parades wearing their Red Cross uniforms, however, so their war service did have some visual representation before the broader American public.

The press was particularly fascinated with the nattily attired Motor Corps established by both the Red Cross and the League for Women's National Service. Drivers often furnished their own cars and needed to be adept not only at driving but also at basic repairs. Their jobs were to transport organization officials, run errands, and serve a variety of civil defense needs. Well before the war, elite women drove cars. Juvenile book series for young girls even featured teenaged girls traveling across the country in their own automobiles, illustrating the freedom and independence that driving offered. The woman at the wheel symbolized the new woman and the way in which she was infiltrating the masculine sphere before the war. But the notion of women as *professional* drivers was nonetheless novel.

Images of Motor Corps women in their spiffy uniforms, some in breeches, others in skirted outfits, abounded. A typical photograph, appearing in the *Baltimore Sun*, portrayed one woman saluting and a group of Motor Corps women lined up in military formation as they were being drilled by a male officer, thus reinforcing their assumed soldierly identity. The accompanying text emphasized that the clothing was not a "fad" but rather "real uniforms" that indicate "just what line of endeavor the wearer is following in 'doing her bit' for her country in the place of men called to the colors."[29] Another striking article, "'Hello Girls' Ready to Go to France; 'Goodbye Girls' Hope to Follow Soon," provided a large photograph of uniformed Signal Corps workers ready to embark for France, but the more arresting image was of three uniformed Motor Corps of America members, aiming pistols toward the viewer as they practice target shooting. The commentary pointed out that these women, too, hoped "to be sailing to France before long. . . . They have perfected themselves in the methods of driving trucks and ambulance and are now becoming expert revolver shots."[30] Figure 23, which appeared in the *New York Herald*, reveals the striking picture these uniformed

Figure 23. Motor Corps of America women take aim. National Archives, 165-WW-598-C05.

and armed women presented. By toting guns *and* driving, the uniformed Motor Corps represented obvious challenges to male prerogative.[31]

The activities of women as wage earners, overseas participants, and home-front volunteers received their clearest expression of both citizenship and the boundary-crossing new woman in the newspaper and magazine coverage of parades, such as the Liberty Bond Parades or the Red Cross ones. These, too, emphasized the uniformed woman. Just a few years before the war, it was considered radical for women to march in public. The suffrage movement began its parades in 1910, taking to the streets in a forceful challenge to notions of respectability. This bold occupation of public spaces was an important demonstration of women's legitimacy as political actors, but it was a contested one, so it is particularly significant that women played such a visible part in these patriotic demonstrations.[32] Probably few of these women who paraded in wartime would have viewed themselves as suffragists or "modern," yet they engaged dramatically in a civic ritual that would have been largely closed to them in the past, unless they appeared dressed as "Lady Liberty" in a float. Now, newspapers described women's parade participation in glowing terms that emphasized the theme of service and reinforced the sense of women as a second line in the nation's defense.

Women in Red Cross parades rated extensive publicity. Much of the coverage included striking photographs or compelling detailed descriptions of the marching women's appearance. In Cleveland, a week before its 1917 parade, the *Cleveland Plain Dealer* announced that "natty mannish motor service uniforms for Red Cross women workers" had been ordered for twenty Cleveland women.[33] The *Los Angeles Times* devoted a full page, complete with illustrations, to that city's enormous May 1918 parade, which attracted 10,000 marchers. Most of the marchers were women, and the *Los Angeles Times* described the march as a "Seven Mile Tribute to Women's Work in War." The paper exulted, "Never in Los Angeles has there been a parade where its womanhood took such a conspicuous part." The *Times* also reported that the Mexican Society's float featured seven Red Cross nurses and that African American women also marched, forty-five of whom were associated with the Phyllis Wheatley branch of the Santa Monica Red Cross and others who were affiliated with the African Methodist Episcopal Church. Class interests were recognized as well, with men and women who marched from the "Van Nuys Building" auxiliary carrying a banner that read, "We work all day and give our evenings. Can't you Give an Hour."[34] Repeatedly, newspapers marveled at the sheer number of women who took to the streets to demonstrate their service to the Red Cross and their loyalty to the nation, describing their uniforms in detail and praising their demeanor.

Liberty Loan parades were the other major opportunity for patriotic women to march, and here, too, women, especially those in uniforms, captured the public imagination. Figure 24, of YWCA women participating in an October 1918 Liberty Loan parade, shows women dressed in typical tailored uniforms and marching in sharp formation. Proudly carrying the YWCA banner, they symbolize the way in which women war workers served through their various associations. In Philadelphia, the *Philadelphia Inquirer* enthusiastically reported on the 5,000 women, representing a wide variety of groups, who were required to "wear the uniforms of their respective organizations," as they marched in a Liberty Pageant in September 1918 for the Fourth Liberty Loan Drive. Newspapers reports thus teemed with women's participation in patriotic parades and pageants, some of which were organized and peopled exclusively by women and often included descriptions of white working women and African American women who marched.[35]

Not all coverage celebrated women's participation in the same way that the *Philadelphia Inquirer* did. Some reporting emphasized the presence of Gold Star Mothers, which cast women's war participation in a maternal light. De-

Figure 24. YWCA women on parade, October 1918. In front are Blanche Geary and Henrietta Roelofs. Courtesy of YWCA of the USA Records, Sophia Smith Collection, Smith College, Northampton, Mass.

spite the novelty of women in parades, other reporters described them in conventional and highly feminine terms. The *Macon Weekly Telegraph*, for example, did not offer photographs of parading women. Instead the reporter offered a somewhat florid description of their visual impact. He or she described the Red Cross women in a Liberty Loan parade as "vestal virgins" and "Florence Nightingales" and referred to the Canteen Service members as a "bit of heavenly blue in their bright new uniforms and caps." As for the farmerettes, they were "charming and demure under broad-brimmed straw bonnets, with their checked gingham aprons."[36]

This type of commentary was the exception, but it serves as a reminder that the reporting for women's war work was often ambivalent. Many observers interpreted women's war contributions as extensions of maternal, nurturing qualities. And the general tenor of enthusiasm that accompanied so much of the reporting discussed here did not necessarily reflect a broad public enthusiasm for the "new woman" or accurately describe most American women's war activities. Moreover, the images of boundary-crossing women and the commentary that accompanied them often minimized the challenge they represented by emphasizing these transgressive women's inherent femininity. Also, their transgressions were generally legitimized in the context of a national crisis that literally required women to step outside convention. But if this ambivalence provides a clue to the obstacles women faced in carving out a larger sphere of activity, these images, as well as the compelling written descriptions of women's war work, nonetheless help us to understand why so many contemporaries thought that the war would usher in dramatic changes in women's status. The coverage of wage-earning women, overseas workers, and at-home volunteers, especially in photographs, offered a powerful vision of white women inhabiting space that was previously thought to be exclusively male. If not all women donned male attire or mannish uniforms or took to the streets to join male citizens in parading for the national cause, many did. And their actions garnered extensive publicity that offered the American public a strikingly visual sense that the "new woman" so often debated in the years before the war had seized the war as an opportunity for challenging gender conventions in the name of patriotism.

WOMEN IN WAR FILMS: OBJECTS OF RESCUE AND AGENTS OF PATRIOTISM

The American public encountered a barrage of images and descriptions of boundary-crossing women during the war years. Film, too, was another significant source of representations of new women. Most films produced from 1914 to 1918 did not depict the war, as the industry continued to rely on films that featured dramas, adventure stories, comedies, and romance, as well as serialized short movies that mostly targeted working-class audiences. In the months following the U.S. entrance into the conflict, studios expanded their repertoire to capitalize on the nation's patriotic sprit. Although not subject to formal federal censorship, movie producers turned out films that glorified war and valorized heroes.

Romantic or dramatic films that incorporated women formed a subset of the war genre. Few films of the era are extant, and the number dealing with women and war that is available is fewer than ten feature-length films and two multi-part serials, one of them fragmentary. Fortunately, there are other ways of accessing film content. Trade and fan magazines, newspaper reviews, and a few scripts reveal plot synopses, and, in some cases, illustrated "storyizations" offered the film in textual form as a short story and provided film still photographs. Equally valuable are publicity materials (posters, advertisements, and photographs) and movie stills, which provide some sense of the visual vocabulary of the films themselves. Despite the limitations, then, it is possible to explore the major ways in which filmmakers portrayed women in the context of World War I. Plot summaries allow us to glimpse the messages conveyed to audiences as they watched the moving images. Overtly patriotic, these films often explored the ways in which women served as inspiration for valiant male soldiers. But many also suggested that women, too, could be active in defending their country. Reflecting the public ambivalence about the modern woman and hinting at the limits to her liberation, movies that featured a conventional ideal of genteel womanhood coexisted with adventuresome new women.[37]

Just as we must use caution in assessing how the public responded to propaganda posters and photographic imagery for women's participation in war work, so too must we exercise care in judging audience response to film portrayals of women. But we do know that women were a crucial component of film audiences as early as the nickelodeon period, when short films attracted primarily a working-class clientele. Film going offered working women entertainment, "cheap amusements," that could be the site of freedom from the constraints of work and family. Moreover, this early film viewing could have provided women a degree of agency. Film scholar Miriam Hansen notes, for example, that women were unexpectedly interested in viewing the popular *The Corbett-Fitzsimmons Fight* (1897), a 100-minute long film of a heavyweight championship match. She argues that the film offered them the unique opportunity of turning a "female gaze" on partially nude male bodies.[38]

If the female audience for *The Corbett-Fitzsimmons Fight* was accidental, not so for later films. By the teens, studios consciously marketed movies to women. Working-class women made up the audience for serials featuring derring-do heroines. At the same time, a new development, the emergence of the full-length feature film characterized by a sustained narrative and more sophisticated cinematography, also prompted filmmakers to seek out female viewers, in part because they saw women's presence as adding respectability and legitimacy to the fledging business.[39] Many of these "classical" silent films featured romance as well as showcasing fashionable clothes. The war films discussed here, many of which were advertised explicitly as having "no battle scenes" or representing "the personal side of war," were clearly designed with women spectators in mind.

What women or general audiences took away from these films could be quite variable, shaped not only by their own inclinations but also by the contradictory images in the films themselves. Arguably the most provocative, war-created, new woman—the overalled or uniform-wearing defense worker—was virtually absent from the war genre, and indeed working women were largely invisible in these films. And although these wartime films often portrayed modern, independent resourceful women, few were unambiguous in the messages they seemingly imparted. This ambiguity in itself hints at the limited impact World War I would have on American women's challenges to conventional expectations. By way of introduction, an analysis of one of these films, *Joan the Woman*, can set the stage for the complicated rendering of women in war films.

Joan the Woman, a Cecil B. DeMille film written by Jeannie MacPherson, a pioneer woman scriptwriter, was filmed in 1916 and screened in the months before the United States entered the war. It was critically well reviewed but failed to become the box office smash anticipated. For his choice of subject, DeMille may have been swayed by the extraordinary popularity of the Joan of Arc story in progressive-era America. Her image appeared in a range of venues—from masquerade costumes to monumental sculptures, such as Anna Vaughn Hyatt's 1915 *Joan of Arc* on a New York square at 93rd and Riverside Drive.[40]

DeMille was interested in both box office success and filming a spectacular epic, and thus his motivations were not in the same propagandistic vein as most "preparedness" plots that centered on stimulating U.S. military buildup.[41] Nonetheless, he portrayed the contemporary crisis of France in highly sympathetic terms and offered a vision of Joan of Arc that privileged the state over personal needs. The film starred Geraldine Farrar, a celebrated opera star. Critics at the time and subsequently have suggested that Farrar was miscast for the role of a young village maiden. A mature and hefty woman, she did not look the part usually associated with the Joan legend. In the scenes where Joan, following the visionary voices she hears, dons her armor and fights valiantly for France, however, Farrar's Joan makes a magnificent visual impression. She displays a commanding presence, complete with phallic sword bearing. DeMille followed the legend closely in terms of the heresy trial, highlighting the way in which the clerics tortured her to force her to recant her story of the voices she hears and, significantly, to eschew wearing men's clothes. Joan briefly recants but at the end returns to her male garb and is ultimately burned at the stake in a highly dramatic finale.

This portion of the film reveals not only a woman who saved France, but also a woman determined to follow her own counsel, no matter what the cost, but DeMille and McPherson introduced a second plot line that featured a love interest for Joan. Early in the film, before she has had her vision, Joan rescues an English nobleman, who has been part of an invading army. They fall in love, and the scenes are highly sentimental and in soft focus, including a prolonged sequence of a "she loves me, she loves me not" daisy-plucking episode. In the course of the film, Joan, now the armored warrior, rescues him once more. They have a romantic exchange, yet Joan insists that she has room in her heart only for France. Freed from captivity, he goes his way. Yet later, when she is captured by his troops, he betrays her, and the capture eventually leads to her return to the hands of the clerics, who try her for heresy. Guilt stricken, he tries to rescue her but fails. As she walks to her execution, he hands her a crudely made cross as she goes bravely to her death.[42]

The film offered contradictory messages about Joan. In one, she is a commanding warrior who, after all, "saves France." In the other, Joan's strength is undercut. Robin Blaetz sums up the implications of this added story succinctly. She argues that DeMille's Joan gave up "her boyfriend for her country. Although Joan still acts nobly by sacrificing herself, her virtue is strictly personal. The restoration of the traditional gender hierarchy that comes with her death is her ultimate act of patriotism."[43] Blaetz's argument about the overall effect of the combined narratives is convincing to modern and feminist ears, yet it is difficult to judge the audience response, and contemporaries apparently viewed the film in strikingly different ways. One feminist reviewer praised *Joan the Woman* for promoting the "respect for the power and hearts of womankind who can rise to the highest pinnacle of success without the aid of men." Apparently more common was the view of the *New York American*, which claimed that the film presented "the quivering heart" of woman.[44] Unique in some respects, in its contradictory images of its main character, *Joan the Woman* has much in common with other popular wartime films. Women in these films were both vulnerable victims and brave heroines, and sometimes both. Even those films that emphasized a "new woman" tempered that vision with an emphasis on femininity and romance, a linkage also evident in prewar popular culture.[45]

The contested nature of acceptable roles for women emerged most spectacularly in a small group of films produced after the war in Europe began, in the period when the United States debated neutrality and preparedness. As we have seen, women played an important role in the national debate because they were among the most outspoken pacifists in the anti-preparedness movement. And because so many women suffragists were pacifists and members of the Women's International League for Peace and Freedom, middle-class white women's resistance to the United States entering World War I had particularly high visibility. Not surprising, given this association, in both "preparedness" and "peace" films women figured prominently.

The female argument against war that emphasized maternalism emerged in two major films. *Civilization*, directed by Thomas H. Ince, still extant, was a major 1915 film that received extensive publicity and apparently was quite popular.[46] The plot features the efforts to convince the King of Wredpryd to end a devastating war. It was strongly religious in tone, with an extended scene featuring Jesus as the Prince of Peace. Women's motivations are tied closely to religion, but even more emphatically to their maternal role. As one woman exclaims when soldiers are trying to conscript her son: "You cannot take him. He belongs to me." This point is further borne out in a striking publicity poster for the film that features two soldiers in the background, with a young woman in the foreground seemingly fleeing in desperation as she clasps a baby to her breast. Central to the plot is a group of women who have "an unseen army of peace," with the cross as their symbol. Eventually, this army marches en masse on the royal palace. They prayerfully beseech the king to end the war. The queen, moved by the sight, tells the king, "The mothers of men plead for the war to end." The war ends shortly thereafter, and the final scenes are of tearful families happily uniting.

A different twist on the maternal theme appeared in *War Brides*. *Motion Picture News* reported that the film, starring famed actress Alla Nazimova, "dwells on the suffering of war's women." The plot of the now-lost film centers on a king who in the midst of war decrees that any man who is recruited to war may "take for his bride any young woman he may choose." The husband of the heroine, aptly named Joan, presumably invoking Joan of Arc, has died in battle, leaving her pregnant. She disapproves of the marriage arrangement of the king, exclaiming, "We women have a duty—yes. But it is not to the King. It is to ourselves and more important, still—to our children." The *Fort Worth Star-Telegram* reported the dialogue as Joan insisting that if women are fit to bear men for an army, "we are fit to have a voice in the fate of the men we bear. If we can bring forth men for the nation, we can sit with you in your councils" to decide for peace or war.[47]

Joan's maternalism clearly takes a feminist cast. She proclaims women's right to have a say in the affairs of state on equal terms with men. Already having shown her activism by leading factory workers in a strike, Joan now vows to organize women and bring their power to bear upon the nation's leaders. "Without women's help, there can be no more wars," she exclaims, and insists that the women tell the king "that wars must cease, or we will refuse to give the country another generation of soldiers." In effect, Joan calls for a sex strike, a la Lysistrata. Joan is jailed (and miscarries) but escapes with the help of a female jailer and organizes a group of women to present a demand to the king to stop the war. At the end of the film, she gives a dramatic speech, and having delivered her message, kills herself.[48] The *Boston Journal*, which called the film "stupendous," vividly offered a verbal description of the "overwhelming" final scene as "hundreds upon hundreds of mothers with infants in their arms blocking the highways and swarming around the royal car of their king, bearing aloft on upstretched hands the body of Nazimova, the war bride who killed herself rather than be the mother of a child who would ultimately share the battlefield death of her husband."[49] While strikingly different in portraying women's militancy (in *Civilization*, they pray; in *War Brides*, a militant Joan rabble-rouses), both turn on women's maternal function as central to their identity and their stance toward war and were in keeping with the way in which many women pacifists articulated their antiwar stance.[50]

The flip side of these peace films were preparedness films that called the nation to arms, and these too gave women significant roles. *The Fall of a Nation*, produced in 1916 by Thomas Dixon, the author of the book *Clansman*, which became the infamous *Birth of a Nation*, centered in part on the danger that suffragists and pacifists posed to the nation as war loomed on the horizon.[51] Suffragist Virginia Holland is convinced that votes for women will end war. The expansion of women's suffrage has resulted in Congress voting to disarm the country, which is then invaded by a generic European nation, assisted by America's immigrant population. The nation falls, as one city after another is conquered.

Ironically, although the film blamed womanhood gone awry for America's plight, women also become its salvation. The film is lost, but, according to one reviewer, Virginia Holland "professes loyalty to the new regime" and agrees to organize American women in the "Imperial Legion of Honor." But Holland has seen the error of her former ideology and instead secretly establishes "the oath-bound order of the Daughters of Jael. She swears a million girls and women to the destruction of the foreign usurpers" (fig. 25).[52] In his novel, Dixon offered a striking description of these women: "They were taught in secret two things—to keep their lithe young bodies hard and sun-tanned and learn to wield a steel knife whose blade was eight inches long, slender and keen."[53] Film stills, while lacking the almost pornographic quality of Dixon's description, nonetheless show a large contingent of masterful-looking women, dressed in uniforms with pants, sitting astride horses as they march in a triumphal parade.[54]

Dixon's representation was clearly a complex one. As pacifists and suffragists, women endangered the nation. Yet, as the Daughters of Jael, they are also its salvation. His incorporation of a female army may have been for the

Figure 25. The Daughters of Jael. Film still from *The Fall of a Nation*. Courtesy of the Museum of Modern Art, Department of Film Special Collections, New York, N.Y.

spectacle. A number of reviewers noted that the Daughters of Jael bore striking resemblance to the Clan of Dixon's earlier work, and he may well have been building upon his success with a dramatic secret army in this film. One vividly described the women's army "as dashing and as courageous as were the Ku Klux Klan."[55] Equally possible, his purpose may have been to deny that women were inherently "pacifists." Whatever his intent, Dixon's representation of women clearly suggests that women's roles, especially as to suffrage and peace, were highly contested ones.

Another major and hugely successful preparedness film treated women far more conventionally. *Moving Picture World* approvingly described the *Battle Cry of Peace* (1915) as being as "personal as an alarm of fire."[56] Produced by J. Stuart Blackton, one of the most vociferous preparedness advocates, it presents the nation as being undermined by pacifists who promote disarmament.[57] The fiancée of the hero, who supports preparedness, is the daughter of a millionaire and ardent pacifist. The major point of the plot is that as a result of disarmament, an unnamed European enemy, whose uniforms clearly suggest the Germans, invades New York. The mother and daughter of one key family die in the invasion, while the wife and daughters of the millionaire pacifist are captured. Figure 26 dramatically depicts the lecherous enemy soldiers as they lay violent hands on the adult daughter and her mother while the

Figure 26. A depraved enemy attacks women and children. Film still from *The Battle Cry of Peace*. Courtesy of the Academy of Motion Picture Arts and Sciences.

younger sister looks on in shock. Realizing that her daughters will be raped, the mother shoots and kills them and then goes insane with grief. Another still from the film, which appeared in movie magazines, reveals the horrific results. The shocked mother sits cradling one dead daughter while the other lies motionless beside her. In the background, a gang of the vicious enemies looms threateningly. As one approving reviewer put it, the film showed the way in which the enemy "makes a laughing stock of the honor of American women."[58] The message was clear. If the nation fails to arm, its women will be subject to rape, and the social order will crumble.

Once the United States entered the war, this theme of rape became even more present in cinematic stories featuring women and, as posters like the "Remember Belgium" poster suggest, pervaded propaganda as well. These representations of German atrocities took on heightened meaning in the context of prewar American cultural anxieties about racial and ethnic others, on the one hand, and untamed and threatening female sexuality on the other. A look at prewar films that teemed with sexuality help to set the context for war films' attention to sexual assault. One popular genre featured the vamp, most notably in the films of Theda Bara, who debuted in *A Fool There Was* in 1915. Vamps were typically dark haired, vaguely ethnic, and exotic. Often garbed in revealing clothes, they brimmed with sexual power. In their quest to exploit and ruin weak men, they embodied the period's fascination with and fear of female sexual danger. Although films portrayed vamps in a negative light, Bara herself was popular with women fans. According to her, "Women are my greatest fans because they see in my vampire the impersonal vengeance of all their unavenged wrongs. . . . They have lacked either the courage or will power to address their grievances." Bara's popularity hints at what alarmed conservative Americans: the fascination with female sexuality associated with the new and modern woman who threatened to overturn the social order.[59]

If one extreme of the treatment of sexual danger in the prewar years was the vamp, at the other end of the spectrum were films about rape and sexual assault of innocent, virginal women. Nineteenth-century theatrical melodramas had generally featured helpless, virtuous young women at risk from mercenary villains.[60] By the early twentieth century, the threats embodied in melodrama and other popular cultural forms became more explicitly sexual and suggest the heightened concern over the changing sexual behavior of women. This anxiety was particularly notable in the outpouring of films, plays, novels, and articles about the so-called white slavery menace. In the period from roughly 1907 to 1915, purity reformers became convinced that white rural women were being kidnapped, raped, and forced into urban prostitution rings, usually at the hands of immigrant males. Prostitution was indeed real, especially affecting immigrant women. But the white slavery story was largely overblown, and the moral panic that ensued spoke less to the reality of the victims of prostitution rings and more to the interlocking fears about urban America teeming with immigrants and changing patterns of women's work and sexuality that seemed to be threatening the social order. White slavery tales, evident in lurid films such as *Inside the White Slave Traffic* (1913), may have offered audiences, both male and female, a degree of sexual titillation. Certainly reformers worried that such films offered young women unsavory details of brothel life. But the tone of these films primarily served to reinforce Victorian notions of female purity, which denied the threat of women's sexual and personal agency and portrayed them instead as hapless victims of a modernizing America.[61]

Another significant prewar drama of rape and social disorder, which would have been particularly relevant to World War I audiences, was the 1915 *Birth of a Nation*. Based on Dixon's *The Clansman*, the film also reflected the racist perspective of director D. W. Griffith, as well as his obsessive focus on the salvation of pure and delicate white womanhood.[62] The film featured two threatened rapes. In one, Elsie Stoneman (played by Lillian Gish), the daughter of white northern liberal Austin Stoneman, finds herself trapped by the mulatto Silas Lynch, who insists upon a forced marriage. The father threatens to engineer his daughter's death rather than "see her in your arms," he tells Lynch. This ultimate sacrifice of his daughter proves unnecessary, as the Klan arrives to save the day.[63] The second threatened rape ends more tragically. A white woman, pursued by a freedman, jumps off a cliff to her death rather than be subjected to a fate understood to be literally worse than death. The centrality of rape in *Birth of a Nation* is not ultimately about the threatened women themselves, but rather about the way in which white patriarchal power is challenged by the newly freed southern blacks. For there to be a redeemed and unified nation, "a birth of a nation," blacks must be subordinated, white male patriarchy confirmed, and social order, including the purity of white womanhood, restored.

The Progressive Era's representation of rape in popular culture, especially in the white slavery plots and in the viciously racist plots of films like *Birth of a Nation,* helps to explain the receptivity to the rape motif in World War I–era films. Audiences would have been well conditioned to interpret the theme of sexual assault against white women at the hands of an ethnic "other" in the context of both white male and national honor. Moreover, the films' presentation of these victimized women would reinscribe the desirability of Victorian notions of female sexual passivity and purity.

Depiction of or allusion to German atrocities that ranged from rape to murder was omnipresent in war-themed movies. In the 1918 film *The Heart of Humanity,* a German officer tries to rape a Red Cross nurse while he simultaneously throws a baby out the window to its death. *To Hell with the Kaiser* (1918), directed by George Irving and written by well-known screenwriter June Mathias, featured a complicated plot that centered on the rape of an American woman, Ruth Moore, by the German crown prince. Advertising stills indicate that the film portrayed at least the threat of the violence on screen, with one image showing a grim-faced Mother Superior trying to shield a group of terrified young women, another showing the Mother Superior's body sprawled on the floor, and yet another featuring the German prince as he seizes the young woman of his choice.[64] D. W. Griffith's *The Great Love* (1918) also included the theme of rape by emphasizing that what happened in Belgium prompted the hero's decision to enlist. The plot, as "storyized" in *Motion Picture Magazine,* began with Jim Young's horror over the news of the Belgian atrocities. "It smote Jim Young straight in the pit of his stomach. . . . Babies were being stabbed straight in their trusting eyes. Girls were being hurled against grim knowledge that it rent their inviolate flesh." And, moreover, Jim envisioned the "slender prettiness" of his "best girl . . . crushed against the vile, desecrating body of a Hun."[65]

Griffith made the point even more emphatically in the extant 1918 *Hearts of the World*, which centers on a small village in France where two young Americans, Marie and Douglas, fall in love. Their wedding plans, however, are disrupted by the coming of war and the young man's decision to fight for France. The film repeatedly details the "Hun's" degradation of the villagers. The couple's mothers both die because of German brutality, and drunken Germans sexually assault the young women of the village. Marie is reduced to slave labor in a potato field, and the image of the villainous German Von Strohm standing over a terrified Marie as he lifts a whip to strike her appeared on one of the film's publicity posters. Even more alarmingly, Von Strohm manhandles Marie. According to *Photoplay*'s description, "He cornered her by the locked door, chuckling, muttering vile words in German, running a lascivious hand over her arm and shoulders, as he held her close" (fig. 27).[66]

The denouement comes when Marie escapes to the attic, where she also finds Douglas. As they await their inevitable capture, they pledge their marriage vows and Marie extracts from Douglas his pledge that he will shoot her himself if the Germans come in, thus saving her from an ignominious fate. As the Germans approach, Douglas places his pistol to her breast, but mercifully they are rescued when a secondary comedic character, Henriette, a spunky, un-genteel young woman, saves them by lobbing a grenade at the Germans as they advance up the steps. Significantly, Lillian Gish, who played Marie in *Hearts of the World*, also starred in Griffith's *Birth of a Nation*, where she played Elsie, the woman whose father was prepared to kill her rather than see her in the arms of the mulatto. The similarities in the two films certainly reflected Griffith's own worldview, and *Hearts of the World*, like *Birth of a Nation*, was a resounding success with reviewers and audiences. In neither film was his depiction of the indelible stain of rape and its implications outside the conventions of American popular culture.

But if nineteenth- and early twentieth-century theatergoers and film viewers were familiar with the rape/assault plot, especially in the context of a racial or ethnic "other," the war did add an extra layer of meaning by having the rape symbolize a key aspect of what was popularly defined as at stake in the war: brutality against women and the disruption of the family. The notion of the war as a threat to the family was central to how propaganda portrayed war aims for the Americans, the French, and the British. Nicoletta F. Gullace, commenting on the power of the Rape of Belgium in defining war aims in Britain, argues, "A vision of the brutalization of women and children domes-

Figure 27. A fate worse than death. Film still from *Hearts of the World*. Courtesy of the Academy of Motion Pictures Arts and Sciences.

ticated the meaning of British foreign policy and privileged a set of familial and sexual concerns within the stated military policy of the liberal state."[67] The same was true in the United States.

Film plots reiterated the common belief that for American men support for the war and obligation to the state, especially military service, equated with protection for their families. For women, these images could produce empathy with Belgian and French women, and historian Kimberly Jensen suggests that American women's concerns about violence against European women encouraged volunteer service abroad. These depictions could also lead them to believe that they too had a crucial stake in making sure the war did not come to America.[68] The imagined threat to women and the family, then, became a particularly powerful tool for demanding sacrifice from all citizens. We cannot assume American women's response to these images—they could and did interpret the threatened danger in various ways. But whatever its reception, the message of Hollywood's rape imagery not only supported and indeed defined Allied war aims, but also served as a vehicle for reinforcing very traditional notions of women's dependency and vulnerability.

If wartime film and propaganda stressed the strength of private, familial obligations, it also explored the dangerous side of familial love and, specifically, maternal love. In 1915, when the preparedness film *Battle Cry of Peace* premiered in New York City, producer J. Stuart Blackton noted his "abhorrence of the song that set forth 'I didn't raise my boy to be a soldier.'"[69] This popular 1915 antiwar song was a focal point for preparedness advocates' critique of women pacifists in the prewar and war years. Government propaganda specifically sought to promote a vision of sacrificing mothers and wives while demonizing women pacifists, suggesting, in Susan Zeiger's words, that "women held an inappropriate power which they would try to wield for nefarious purposes."[70]

This motif emerges in what Zeiger calls "enlistment" dramas. She identified about a dozen such films, but there were probably more. In the 1916 *If His Country Calls* (a partial print is still extant), a mother drugs her son with a medication that affects his heartbeat to keep him from enlisting. Believing himself to be seriously ill, he releases his fiancée from their engagement, and she marries another. He becomes an alcoholic, and the mother is racked with guilt. Happily, she wakes to learn it was all a dream and encourages her boy to enlist. The tellingly titled *The Man Who Was Afraid* (1917) explained in an intertitle that the son had been "stripped of his right to aggressive young manhood by an overzealous mother," who tried to use influence peddling to keep him out of the military.

The theme of female power and its implications for war continues with the 1918 film *Her Boy,* which features a mother who alters her son David's birth certificate to make him ineligible for service. According to *Photoplay,* the mother is a "strange study in affection and unscrupulousness."[71] No print

Figure 28. A mother lies to protect her son. Film still from *Her Boy*. Courtesy of the Academy of Motion Pictures Arts and Sciences.

exists of the film, but the stills are highly revealing. One is set in the recruiting office, with the mother the central figure (fig. 28). Unsmiling, she leans over a desk to face two men, presumably draft officials. All of the young men in the room, including her son directly behind her, are riveted on the conversation. Only one other woman, the boy's sweetheart, Virginia Gordon, is present. In a second still, in the same room, the mother is absent (fig. 29). A smiling recruiting official is handing David a piece of paper. Front and center are Virginia and David shaking hands over the recruiting desk. He looks resolute; she looks proud and confident. A third still shows David, now in uniform, in what appears to be a bedroom in his home. He stands between his seated mother on one side and Virginia on the other. The two women look at each other intently, but he looks out into the distance. On the two women's laps is an enormous American flag. What is striking about the stills, besides the secondary drama of what appears to be a struggle between the two women for the man's affection, is the appearance of Virginia. She is the all-American girl, whose image evokes modern young womanhood.

As *Her Boy* alludes to, in these slacker films, young women become the vehicle for restoring men's patriotism and manhood. The portrayal of young

Figure 29. The modern young woman and the former slacker. Film still from *Her Boy*. Courtesy of the Academy of Motion Pictures Arts and Sciences.

and older women in these films is intriguing. If mothers are portrayed as "unscrupulous" and neurotic, they are also presented as overly protective. The films seem not just a critique of mothers who obstruct their sons' enlistment, but of sentimental motherhood itself. These films, then, suggest a rejection of nineteenth-century notions of motherhood, which will become more pronounced after the war. In contrast, the young women in these films are not just young, they are "modern." They shame the men through a critique of their manhood, and they are themselves clear patriots who are eager to serve their country. In fact, they bear striking resemblance to the "new woman" wage earners and war workers analyzed in previous chapters. While portrayed in conventionally feminine terms, and often as needing rescue, these women are nonetheless engaged in activist roles, and at least in some instances, they express regret about their gender limiting their ability to serve. In *Over There* (1917), the heroine goes to France to become a Red Cross nurse, and advertising stills feature her in a Red Cross uniform. The young woman in *Draft 258* (1917) takes to the hustings as a patriotic orator. Public speaking in support of the war showed women moving beyond conventional roles as citizens. In the past, it was the exception for a woman to speak out on politics in public to mixed audiences. In the years before the war, suffrage leaders were the most well-known public speakers, and their public performances were highly controversial. But the war changed things. In the service of patriotism, women crossed physical boundaries that had formerly constrained "respectable" women. Wartime films reflected this transformation.[72]

This boundary crossing, as well as hints of the "modern" young woman, is also evident in a final World War I film genre—one involving plucky, adventuresome women. In numerous war films, young women face danger and show bravery and resourcefulness. And, in many cases, they wear men's clothes for at least a part of the film. They have similarities with the modern women in the slacker films, yet in this case, they are the ones who directly take on the enemy, usually a spy ring, and rout them through physical and mental prowess.

The heroic woman was not new to film in the war era. In the teens, serial films primarily targeted working-class young women and featured heroines who acted in unconventional ways by courting and escaping danger and by showing pluck and derring-do. The serials had extensive ties-ins to print media, with the stories generally appearing weekly in newspapers or magazines, where audience interest was stimulated by contests and souvenirs. The engagement of these female spectators and their devotion to the serial-queen heroines offer a superb example of the symbiotic relationship between producers and audience, with filmmakers seemingly eager to give young women what they wanted on the screen: independent women reveling in exciting experiences.[73]

As many scholars argue, serial queens were not always portrayed as unambiguously independent. In most serials, the heroine initially eschews marriage, sometimes explicitly for freedom, but the plot usually ends in matrimony. Scenes often included depiction of "female distress, helplessness, and abject terror."[74] Most serials, moreover, began with the death of a male parent or guardian, suggesting that the heroine's liberation became possible only through family tragedy. But, as in the most famous prewar serial, *The Perils of Pauline* (1914), the heroine, despite her bravery, almost always required rescue by the devoted hero.[75]

A number of very popular serials, however, featured far less vulnerable heroines who routinely rescued themselves by their own resourcefulness. The extremely successful *Hazards of Helen* (1914–17), for example, ran to over a hundred episodes in which Helen, who is technically a telegraph operator, finds occasion to save runaway trains (usually by running on top of them in breathtaking fashion) and thwart villains with extraordinary regularity. She frequently appears in overalls and often wields a pistol. Romance, and an emphasis on Helen's sexual attractiveness, is only a subtheme to her adventure and her autonomy.[76] Equally important was the genre's representation of emancipated women who challenged the domestic ideology that so restricted their sex.[77]

The ways in which serials present women dressed in male clothing does not seem to be cross-dressing per se. The women do not don masculine apparel as disguise or masquerade. Nor do they attempt to hide their femininity. Rather, their adoption of uniforms or pants meets the needs of their various adventures. That said, even if women are not technically cross-dressing, they are certainly engaged in gender-bending. Serials featuring women in men's clothing undoubtedly sought to signal that these women were crossing boundaries in their search for adventure and expressions of bravery.

Several serials were tied explicitly to the war. And like prewar serials, they suggested the constraint placed on adventurous young women as well as serving as examples of independent self-reliance. *Pearl of the Army*, filmed in 1916 but shown through 1917, starred the most well-known serial queen, Pearl White of *The Perils of Pauline*. Not many details are known about the episodes. A reviewer approvingly described the character as an American "Joan of Arc," and numerous scenes portrayed Pearl as powerful.[78] One, for example, showed Pearl dressed in a male military uniform training a pistol on a villain. Pathé, the distributor of the series, mounted an extensive publicity campaign for the serial. A photograph of Pearl White posing with illustrator Howard Chandler Christy, along with the war poster he created using her as a model, appeared on front pages in newspapers. The poster asks, "Did you think *I'd* Stay at home? Gosh!!" The poster features a beautiful young woman dressed in a male military uniform.[79] The real Pearl, standing next to the poster, is less sensual but clearly feminine. Yet both the poster and the photograph of Pearl White next to it reinforce conventional femininity. They contrast strikingly with the movie still that shows Pearl with pistol drawn, thus suggesting the ambiguous messages contained in *Pearl of the Army*.

The only completely extant serial for this period, *Wolves of Kultur* (1917), was a classic cliff-hanger, with the heroine, Alice Grayson (played by Leah Baird), and the hero, Robert Moore (Charles Hutchinson), facing death numerous times in each twenty-minute episode. The serial begins with Alice discovering that her uncle has been killed by agents of a foreign power (thinly disguised Germans) in order to steal his invention for a torpedo. Alice, now free of familial restraints, swears revenge for her uncle and plots with her beau, Robert, to regain the device. Plucky and determined, Alice constantly performs daunting athletic feats. The camera records her scaling down buildings and jumping off a moving boat and swimming to safety. In these scenes, her dress is disheveled and her hair cascades down her shoulders, a striking contrast to the fashionably dressed and elegantly coiffured Alice as she appears when she is not in danger. Although she fights furiously against her attackers, including one intent on raping her, rarely does Alice effect her own rescue without the help of Robert, and throughout the serial their romantic attachment flourishes.

The conclusion of the serial, however, gives Alice the ultimate triumph over the enemies. It is she who stops the spies from blowing up an American ship by bashing the torpedo operator over the head with a huge rock. Alice then escapes from a cave in which she was trapped, surprises another agent, and then takes his rifle. She arrives just in the nick of time to shoot and kill a man attacking Robert. Later, with the mastermind spies dead and their minions arrested, Alice receives a letter from the government praising her service to the country. As was typical in most serials, *Wolves of Kultur* ended with the heroine marrying. The serial thus offered the athletic and brave escapades of a feminine woman who has power and transcends the boundaries of her sex, but ultimately contained that power in a conventional romantic ending.

Pathé's popular fifteen-part wartime serial, *Patria,* produced by International, a company owned by media mogul William Randolph Hearst, portrayed a powerful woman less ambivalently. Patria Channing, while very feminine, usually accomplished her own rescues. First screened in early 1917, *Patria* starred Irene Castle, who, with her husband, Vernon, was an internationally famous dancer, whom the ads described variously as the "most well-known" and "best-dressed" woman in America. Patria, an heiress described by her guardian as a "woman of common sense, intelligence and fortitude, without loss of womanliness," discovers upon attaining her majority that she now controls the Channing Secret Defense Fund, consisting of $1 million and set up by her patriotic ancestors to be used in case of national emergencies. But the enemies of America, an unholy alliance of Japanese and Mexicans, steal the fortune and plot their invasion of the country. The rest of the series is a deadly contest between Patria and her secret agent, Warren Parr, on the one hand, and Japanese and Mexican villains on the other.[80]

The serial is important historically for Hearst's propaganda efforts and for its racist portrayals of the Mexicans and the Japanese, but it is also significant in its presentation of the new woman, Patria Channing. Most of the film series itself is lost, but like other serials of the time, *Patria* was serialized every week in the newspapers. Absent the film, we miss the thrilling drama and the glamor of Castle's portrayal.[81] But text and still images are nonetheless highly revealing of what *Patria* conveyed to the audience. Billed as the "first society serial of romance and preparedness," advertisements and reviewers' comments featured the fabulously wealthy Patria's gorgeous clothing, including an elegantly tailored skirted military uniform. Figure 30, an advertisement showing Castle standing alone in full military garb, with her arms outstretched and her body leaning forward, conveys something of the feminine power the serial sought to convey. The intent was clearly to target a wider audience than the working-class women who were the assumed audience of serials like *Pauline* and *The Hazards of Helen*.[82] But in other ways, *Patria*'s plot and devices seem quite similar. Week after week, Patria and Parr face one horrific threat after another, and Patria proves herself to be a crack shot, an ace pilot, and a fearless defender of herself and others. One reviewer's breathless comment is worth reprinting at length. In this case, the reviewer is actually discussing Castle herself, assuming that she performed all of her own stunts, an assumption common to the depiction of female stars of serials:

> In "Patria" she is thrown from the back of a galloping horse, she dives headlong from the deck of an ocean going steamship and swims to a motor boat into which she climbs unassisted, she is thrown from the upper deck of a Sound steamer and in the water divests herself of her superfluous clothing; she climbs the mast of a burning ship with the flames licking the shrouds and falls with the mast into the water far below, she plunges over a waterfall into the whirlpool, she races her motor against a railroad car loaded with dynamite; she flies an aeroplane; she operates a machine gun and does many other things that make you gasp. But never for a moment does she lose her dainty graceful, feminine charm.[83]

The emphasis on Castle's and, by extension, Patria's, femininity is pervasive in the serialized version of the plot as well as in reviews and advertisements. One ad, featuring Patria in a uniform, described her as a "womanly woman" and the film as "full of grace and charm which makes our women the envied of the world. 'Patria' is wholly American." This commentary beautifully illustrates scholar Martha Banta's argument about the way in which American women "types" had become tied up so closely with American identity.[84] And in this instance, the American type is the "new woman," who manages to maintain her femininity while being confident and independent.

Figure 30. Irene Castle as "Patria." *Moving Picture World,* March 31, 1917.
Courtesy of the Media History Digital Library.

Patria Channing is all of that. On occasion, she requires rescue from her fiancé, but equally often she rescues herself and sometimes him. In the final episode, when the Mexicans and the Japanese invade the United States at the border, Parr, whom Patria had put in charge of her army, is wounded, and Patria takes "into her own hands the command which she had resigned to his." Needless to say, the invasion is repelled, and the series ends with the couple committing themselves to each other and to the "service of their country."[85]

Although the makers of *Patria* clearly aimed at depicting strong American womanhood, the serial did offer some scenes of sexual danger. In two instances, a Japanese man and then a Mexican man seek to kiss Patria, and in both cases, she brings out a pistol and handily fends them off. Once, it appears that the head Japanese spy would force her to marry his Mexican henchman, but in this case she is rescued by her fiancé. These are minor bits of the action but notable because the offenders are men of color and thus merge perfectly with the trend in popular culture of the sexual menace of racial "others" and reinforce the symbol of Patria as the young white "new woman."

Spy and detective plots featuring adventuresome women also appeared in numerous feature films of the war era and seemed to take their cue from the serial queens in featuring fearless women who face down villains. None of these films is extant, but plot summaries and reviews suggest depictions of resolute women who tangle with the enemy in a number of hair-raising adventures. Yet these plots at times took a comedic form that suggested ambivalence about the strong woman motif. *Her Country First*, based on a short story by popular author Mary Roberts Rinehart, definitely sends mixed messages about female bravado. Dorothy Grant wants to help the war effort and decides to train her friends in a Girls Aviation Corps. But much of this part of the film is played for laughs. She is presented as self-dramatizing, immature, and slightly comical. She seems more interested in the outfits for her corps than the seriousness of her effort. Dressed in a male uniform, posed Napoleon-like, she is surrounded by her corps of uniformed young women, all sprawled on the ground and looking more like chorines than soldiers. They are clearly discomfited by their leader. One still has the dialogue printed on it: "Napoleon looked like me." Figure 31 clearly indicates that she is not to be taken seriously. She is not a threat to masculine power.[86]

As a number of scholars have noted, gender-bending dressing used for comedic effect often serves to reinscribe gender differences. Thus, in the famous war posters by Christy featuring saucy young women in uniform, such

Figure 31. "Napoleon Looked Like Me." Film still from *Her Country First*. Courtesy of the Academy of Motion Pictures Arts and Sciences.

as the recruitment poster that has the nubile young woman exclaim, "Gee!! I Wish I were *A MAN. I'd Join the Navy*," the effect was to emphasize her femininity and sexuality. Martha Banta claims that this sort of poster had its origin in vaudeville and in the "pert and sexy girls of the theater world" who "often appeared in male uniforms."[87] Thus, not surprisingly, the movie industry's depiction of women in male uniforms usually drew from the same tradition of enhancing femininity and sexuality through the appearance of women dressed in male clothing.

The ambiguous message of the gender-bending woman also emerged in an important war feature film, *Johanna Enlists* (1918), which starred Mary Pickford, who was already a major star in the teens. Beloved for her blond curls and her winsome performance, she invariably played young girls, not women. In this and other war-related films, she took on a more mature persona. *Johanna Enlists* (1918) features a homely girl stuck on a farm, bored with the tedium of rural life and farm chores and frustrated with the strictness of her parents, all of which is portrayed in comedic form. Johanna's boredom evaporates when a military unit camps on her father's land and she becomes interested in attracting a beau. She transforms herself physically so that she becomes a lovely young woman, and eventually she attracts a handsome army officer who becomes her fiancé. The plot thickens when Johanna steals a small soldier's uniform and attempts to decamp with the army. At least initially, Johanna is cross-dressing as a deliberate disguise. Although she is discovered, the commander agrees that she might become a mascot. The film ends with Johanna, still dressed in the uniform, riding off with her fiancé and his army unit atop a cannon wagon.[88]

The film is interesting on several counts, including of course the cross-dressing, which seems to suggest Johanna's frustration with her limited sphere on the farm—or perhaps as a woman. But such outfits as worn by Pickford were never meant to signal conventional masculine traits of strength associated with a military uniform. In figure 32, a still from the film, the diminutive Pickford, with the trademark curls cascading down under the severe military hat, exudes feminine charm. She transgresses boundaries, but her liberation is constrained by her femininity and her romantic desire. The film is also significant because it was closely tied to Pickford's real life persona: she was definitely a modern woman, especially in her war activities. She had "adopted" the 143rd Field Artillery unit in California, and indeed "her" troops were the extras in the movie. At the end of the film, she is shown dressed in a skirted uniform with the real-life commander of the unit as she offers a military salute to the audience. This connection to the military and war effort was a significant part of Pickford's public image during the war. She appeared with both Charlie Chaplin and Douglas Fairbanks, as well as alone, to sell war bonds, and like the modern young women in the "slacker" movies, she offered rousing orations, encouraging men to enlist and women to urge their menfolk to the colors. Thus, when the young women in slacker films made recruitment speeches, their real-life model may have been another actress. Pickford's appearances for the war attracted thousands of spectators, and she became the most well-known female supporter of the war effort.

There is no reason to think that Pickford's patriotic activism was merely a publicity ploy, but certainly her studio made the most of her war effort when publicizing her pictures. Several of the posters for *The Little American* (released in 1917, before the United States entered the war) transform Pickford into an icon of America, proudly carrying the Stars and Stripes. The image in figure 33 so perfectly captures the conventions of the genre that it could easily have served as an American propaganda poster. Given the similarity to the usual iconic depiction of Lady Liberty, Pickford and America become one. The quintessential American woman, known as America's Sweet-

Figure 32. Mary Pickford in *Johanna Enlists*. Courtesy of Joseph Yranski.

Figure 33. Mary Pickford as "The Little American." Courtesy of the Academy of Motion Pictures Arts and Sciences.

heart (a term first appearing around the time of this film), symbolizes what soldiers are fighting for—but as the poster suggests, in this film, she herself, like other heroines, is not a passive recipient of that protection.[89]

The Little American is a fascinating production. Here Pickford plays an adult woman, less girlish than the Johanna figure. Correspondence between director Cecil B. DeMille and producer Jesse Lasky reveals that Lasky specifically wanted Pickford to represent "the spirit of the American Girl in War Times." Indeed the working title for the film was "The American Girl," a telling choice that emphasized the notion of an iconic American young woman representing the spirit of the nation.[90] Interestingly, Lasky also urged that Pickford "portray a girl in the sort of role that the feminists in the country are now interested in—the kind of girl that dominates, for instance, Great Britain in War time—the kind of girl who jumps in and does a man's work when men are at the front."[91] Although this is not quite what Pickford's character does, she is nonetheless remarkably competent and confident. Before the war, Angela Moore has two suitors, one French (Jules) and one German (Karl). Both go off to fight for their respective countries, and, shortly thereafter, Angela, a neutral American, sails to Europe to help her aunt in Belgium. A German U-boat torpedoes the ship, and the disaster scene on the ship is specifically designed to evoke the *Lusitania* disaster. In the rescue boat, we get the first hint of Angela's spunkiness: she shakes her fist at the submarine commanders and, waving the United States flag, exclaims: "You've fired on American women and children."[92]

By the time she reaches the chateau, her aunt has died and the Germans are fast approaching. Angela, now effectively without family, must take charge. Her initial goal is to protect her women servants. She bundles them off to the attic and then faces alone the marauding Germans who take over her villa. They are brutes who threaten her. Then a new soldier appears who, of course, is her former beau, Karl, and in the dark he almost rapes her. Once they recognize each other, she chastises him for having become part of the military machine, and together they hear the off-screen scream of a servant. She says to Karl, "If there's a spark of manhood left in you, go and save those young women." Karl fails her here, but later, after she's been harassed herself and when we see the distraught raped servant with her torn dress, Karl finally breaks down and he and Angela weep together. An image of the aftermath of that rape, with Mary comforting her young despairing servant, was featured in one of the posters advertising the movie, indicating the centrality of the rape motif in war films. Figure 34 stands in stark contrast to figure 33, as the heroic Lady Liberty figure gives way to a relatively demure woman comfort-

Figure 34. "Silent Sufferers," in *The Little American*. Courtesy of the Academy of Motion Pictures Arts and Sciences.

ing her servant. While the colors in figure 34 are in bold red, white, and blue, those in figure 33 are soft pastels. The war message, too, is subsumed to the drama of "the silent sufferers."[93]

Through a complex set of developments, Mary bravely spies for the French. As was the case of young women in "slacker" films, through her own moral courage and decency she redeems Karl, who tries to keep her from getting caught. Both end up arrested, and they face a firing squad. They are saved by the arrival of the French army, and a bomb wipes out the Germans and almost kills Karl. Significantly, Angela rescues him, half-dead, from the rubble. The film ends with Karl in a POW camp, while Angela feeds him through the barbed wire. She learns that, because of her service to France, Karl will be released to her care, and they both sail off to America, presumably to marry.

Pickford's heroine stands resolute in her determination to do what is right. Angela emerges as an independent, resourceful woman who thinks nothing of going to Belgium alone in the midst of war. When she becomes entangled in the war, she is resourceful and brave in saving both herself and the man she loves. The plucky heroine, especially as portrayed by glamorous actresses like Pickford and Irene Castle, signaled challenges to conventional notions about women's essentially passive role in war. The radical potential of this challenge, however, was constrained by the emphasis on femininity and the predictable happy ending of love and marriage. Moreover, the persistent motif of sexual danger remained a potent reminder of women's vulnerability in the face of a vile enemy. Films, then, hint at a provocative new woman enjoying new freedoms and independence, but they ultimately reflect the limits of wartime opportunities for significant change in women's roles.[94]

Hollywood's interest in portraying this type of adventuresome new woman largely disappeared in the postwar years, a disinterest startlingly evident in the 1919 comedy *Oh, You Women*. Written by John Emerson and Anita Loos, the film mocks women's wartime assumption of power and independence. Or, as one reviewer put it, it was a "good-natured satire upon upholders of the feministic doctrine who carry their zeal for the cause to absurd lengths."[95] The film takes place in a small town in which women, led by two ardent women's rights advocates, Aurora and her daughter Lotta, take over when the men go to war. They invade the mayoral office and the workplace as well. And they do so wearing men's suits, responding to Aurora's insistence that it was time for "women to discard hampering feminine clothing." She called for dress reform with the slogan, "Pants Will Win the War. Wear Them."[96] The fun begins when the men return from soldiering to discover that the women will not give up their jobs, a problem that one reviewer noted was a serious one and one in which many "folks are deeply interested."[97] The men regain control only after one of them shows motion pictures featuring the town men cavorting with French women "over there." The women of the town capitulate to the threat that their menfolk will bring French women to America, and the genders assume their proper roles. The moral, according to one reviewer, was that it was appropriate for women to take war jobs, but not to keep them, and moreover, "While it is all very well for women to take their proper place in the world's affairs, let them—for the love of heaven—still remain *women* and not become *freaks*!"[98]

In the postwar decade, Hollywood may have turned its back on the brave and independent woman, but it also ceased to feature prominently the D.W. Griffith image of pure womanhood. The new women of the 1920s that Hollywood celebrated clearly owed something to the serial queens and daring women of World War I feature films. The flapper film featured young white women, who also crossed boundaries that had restricted women's proper behavior. They danced exuberantly, smoked and drank, wore revealing clothing, and sought erotic experiences. And, although many 1920s heroines were elite women able to engage in an expensive milieu of nightclubs and glamorous clothes, films also featured working women, usually clerical office workers, who also wanted to participate in the world of urban consumer goods and amusements. They were often liberated women, but unlike the new women of World War I patriotic films, whose activism had political connotations, this was a liberation channeled solely into the personal world of romance, family, and consumption.

In World War I print and film media, conventional images of women, especially those that featured their sexual vulnerability, coexisted with more modern representations. Women as objects to be protected and women themselves as defenders of the nation offered two different messages about the role of women in war. The juxtaposition of these two interpretations suggests the way in which the era was suffused with tensions about the changing roles of American women. Clearly, the media recognized—and provocatively pictured—the potential for dramatic change in women's lives. Working women challenged men's prerogatives, never more obviously that when they donned overalls and uniforms. Parading women, who took their patriotism to the streets, also suggested that many women were eager to move beyond the constraints of home and family to a larger arena. Many film heroines were resourceful, independent, and brave. American audiences were relentlessly exposed to women who challenged conventions—in work, in clothing, in freedom of movement, in the occupation of physical space. So much so that many were convinced the war had produced dramatic change.

But although these representations hinted at possibilities for female agency and power, they exaggerated the degree of change the war engendered. The persistence in visual popular culture of traditional notions about women's proper roles signaled how very contested the new woman was. Despite the need for women in defense industries, government propaganda portrayed white women's war contributions primarily as extensions of maternal and domestic duties. Wartime films might feature women fighting the nation's enemies, but the ubiquitous motif of female sexual vulnerability reinforced Victorian notions of chaste womanhood that masked profound anxieties about changing sexual mores. Popular culture, then, brings into sharp visual focus a central theme of this book. Many women embraced the possibilities World War I provided to carve out greater opportunities in the workplace and in political life. This was true of African American women as well as white women, although mainstream popular culture ignored them. Yet, for all the sense of change, the status quo persisted for the most part. Above all, deeply entrenched cultural assumptions about women's maternal and domestic roles limited World War I's transformative promise for a modern American woman.

Epilogue

> Labor officials doubt that women will stay in some fields of men's work permanently, such as street car conductors, baggage workers and shop workers. They believe the women of their own accord will drift back to what is generally classed as women's work, largely because of the hostile feeling of the men.
>
> *Kansas City Star*, February 26, 1919

Unresolved in the war years, the debate over the new woman continued to resonate in the 1920s. Some of the themes echoed earlier anxieties. Conservatives worried about radical women, and these included not just firebrands like Emma Goldman but also liberal reformers like Jane Addams. In the context of the antiradical Red Scare, maternalist social welfare legislation and peace activism became synonymous with Bolshevik-influenced anti-Americanism. Conservatives similarly feared what newly enfranchised women would do with the vote, an issue particularly alarming the southern white men and women who resisted black women's efforts to register to vote. Anxiety focused, too, on women in the workforce, even though few of the wartime challenges to male economic prerogatives persisted. The most consistent lightning rod for gender anxiety, however, was the flapper. Smoking, drinking, dancing to jazz, wearing makeup and provocative clothing, the iconic flapper embodied new social freedoms, especially an overt sexuality that profoundly challenged traditional notions of women's role in the family.

The contested new woman of the 1920s offers a clue to the limits to change that resulted from World War I. However much some women staked a claim to political, social, and economic equality during the war and in the 1920s, they faced deeply rooted ideas about women's primary role in the home as a talisman of social order. Both continuity and change, with modern and traditional notions of womanhood coexisting uneasily, mark the postwar decade. But if the war did not cause significant changes, it nonetheless served as a marker, a symbolic beginning for ushering in yet another version of the new woman.[1]

Situating the new woman in the 1920s requires deconstructing enduring stereotypes about the era. In popular memory, that decade is known as the "roaring twenties," a period characterized by a booming economy, rampant consumerism, and a retreat from the idealism of progressive reform and the "war to end all wars." In this vision, flappers, jazz, bootlegged gin, and sex embodied the era. As F. Scott Fitzgerald summed it up, the 1920s represented the "world's most expensive orgy." But the story of the decade is far more complex. After all, it began with a repressive Red Scare and a series of brutal race riots in twenty cities. Moreover, the type of culture wars we are so familiar with now first came to national attention in the 1920s. On one side of the divide, old-stock Americans sought to restore their political and cultural dominance as well as traditional values. They railed against secularism, evolution, jazz, the new woman, immigrants, and lax enforcement of the Prohibition amendment. Hostility to racial and ethnic pluralism led to stringent immigration restrictions, and a resurgent Ku Klux Klan targeted blacks, immigrants, Jews, Catholics, and, at times, violators of sexual mores. In opposition, black and ethnic Americans insisted upon their claims to American identity and called for cultural pluralism. Self-professed modernists, in revolt against what they called the "village" mentality, embraced secularism, the new woman, technological change, and modern culture generally. Anxieties about the new woman and her threat to social order helped fuel the culture wars, which also exposed profound differences among activist women.[2]

WOMEN AND POLITICS IN THE 1920S

"Carry On," screamed the new masthead for the bulletin of Michigan's WCND on November 23, 1918, twelve days after the Armistice. Arguing that the nation had to stand up to the ideals for which it had fought, editor Caroline Bartlett Crane insisted their organization needed to continue in peacetime to promote social reforms such as Americanization, protective legislation for women and children, and enforcement of Prohibition. Crane ended with a telling point. Referring to the state's passage of woman suffrage a few weeks before, which had removed "every political disability . . . from our path," she concluded that Michigan women had learned "to think and feel and hope and work together." She asked, "Have we not boundless opportunity and incentive to 'carry on,' to help build the world anew?"[3] Similar sentiments appeared across the nation. Expressing joy at war's end, women progressive activists were eager to keep their state WCND committees alive and repurposed (the national organization had merged with the men's committee), as well as to use other organizations like the YWCA to promote national reconstruction. Implicit in these calls to action was the assumption that the war had allowed women to prove themselves through their patriotic service. They had earned the right to influence public policy. War did not create the suffrage movement or women's reform agenda, but it did accelerate the Nineteenth Amendment's adoption. Moreover, it contributed to activist women's postwar determination to exercise their political voice. This determination persisted into the 1920s and was evident among both black women and white women. The white women included maternalist reformers and former suffragists, but conservative women also labored to influence politics and public policy.[4]

African American Women and Political Activism

For black men and women, the war had raised expectations—through both the hope of rewards for patriotic service and the promise that the Great Migration to the urban North seemed to hold. Disillusionment over continued discrimination and violence, made even worse during 1919 when race riots ignited over twenty cities, led race leaders to call for a "new negro" who would insist upon racial justice and racial pride. The militant new negro, much celebrated in the black press, was held up as a masculinized ideal. The cultural movement of the Harlem Renaissance, the black nationalist focus of Marcus Garvey's Universal Negro Improvement Association (UNIA), and the civil rights activism of the NAACP placed men at the forefront of the drive for racial justice and respect, thus creating a dilemma for black women leaders. Despite its activism in the war years, in the postwar era the National Association of Colored Women (NACW) focused primarily on racial uplift through local reforms and community building, thus leaving the field open for the NAACP to be the preeminent leader in civil rights agitation.

Nonetheless, black women, too, sought to be part of the postwar campaign for racial justice. Their efforts were channeled through organizations other than the NACW, however. Black women in the YWCA pressed for more equality within that organization and, moreover, sought to create interracial alliances among working-class women.[5] Continuing their wartime commitment to fighting racial violence, black women, including especially Mary Talbert, founded the Anti-Lynching Crusaders as part of the NAACP in 1922 to lobby and raise funds for the Dyer Anti-Lynching Bill. They were not successful, but their approach to lobbying Congress for national legislation continued to be an important part of black civil rights activism. At the same time, a number of black women expanded their interests to the international racial arena, a development in part inspired by the war. They became involved in the Pan-African movement, which men nonetheless dominated. In an effort to carve out a space for their internationalism in 1922, they created the International Council of Women of the Darker Races of the World, which focused on a range of countries, including Nigeria, Haiti, and Puerto Rico.[6] Addie Hunton, Mary Church Terrell, Nannie Burroughs, and Margaret Murray Washington, the widow of Booker T. Washington, were founding members of this small group determined to promote knowledge about people of color around the world and to encourage "women in their local communities to learn more about international issues and hence see their day-to-day struggles in a larger global context."[7] Wartime leaders such as Alice Dunbar-Nelson, Hunton, and Terrell also played a highly visible role in the reconfiguration of the Woman's Peace Party into the Women's International League for Peace and Freedom, bringing to it an analysis of the relationships among war, peace, colonialism, and racial oppression.

Black women were also central to Garvey's UNIA. The organization attracted working-class, and to a lesser extent middle-class, blacks with its ideology of racial pride and militant separatism. Garvey rejected the NAACP's focus on assimilation and its challenges to disenfranchisement and segregation. He called for African Americans to build their own economic and political basis for power, including the plan to construct a strong nation in Africa that might empower blacks everywhere. Garvey's rhetoric emphasized masculine strength and feminine dependence. But, according to historian Deborah Gray White, black women in the UNIA took up the cause of black women's importance to the drive for racial uplift from the declining NACW. Despite Garvey's masculinized rhetoric, some black women in the organization challenged his perception of a subordinate role for women, none more so than his second wife, Amy Jacques Garvey. In her column in the UNIA newspaper, *Negro World*, she insisted, "We serve notice on our men that Negro women will demand equal opportunity to fill any position in the Universal Negro Improvement Association or anywhere else without discrimination because of sex."[8] Many women were important local leaders in the organization, and a few took on national roles as well.

Because of their separatism, Garveyites paid little attention to using the vote to effect change. But many African American women hoped to influence party politics. They anticipated that suffrage would allow them to address issues such as Jim Crow, lynching, male disenfranchisement, the sexual abuse of black women, and economic discrimination, goals that underlined their view that the elevation of black women was inseparable from racial progress. Although they were not successful in getting assistance from white women's groups in challenging women's disenfranchisement in the South, black women created suffrage clubs throughout the South to educate black women on the process of registering to vote. Determined southern resistance made this a difficult process with modest success, but black women's political activism was impressive nonetheless.[9]

Black women had one advantage over white women in politics: they were all concentrated in a single party. The white South was identified with the Democratic Party and, moreover, for African Americans, the Republicans were still viewed as the party of Abraham Lincoln. In the states outside the South, women organized "Republican Clubs" to support the candidates of the party that they viewed as sympathetic to black issues. And in 1924 they created the National League of Republican Colored Women, with the slogan, "We are in politics to stay and we shall be a stay in politics."[10] Initially the Republican Party was attentive to black women leaders, inviting them to its first national conference of women leaders, where the league president, Nannie Burroughs, spoke. African American women also obtained some patronage appointments to political offices outside the South. But while the Republicans offered symbolic nods to black voters, by the end of the decade black women were increasingly disenchanted with the Republicans' failure to address the issues of primary concern to them.[11] Thus despite their efforts and enthusiasm, African American women were not able to exercise much power within the political parties. In the 1920s, they gained experience in grassroots organizing and lobbying but saw few tangible results.

White Women's Rights Activists and Progressive Reformers

White women reformers and former suffragists entered the new decade with optimism about their newly enlarged public responsibilities. As they sought to expand their political influence, they debated among themselves as to how, and whether, they should act within the Democratic and Republican parties.

Because suffragists had claimed that women were unsullied by the corruption of political parties, many now had grave reservations about working within the established party system. Indeed, the League of Women Voters (1920), the successor organization of NAWSA, was established as a nonpartisan group that urged women's active citizenship rather than the support of a particular political party or specific candidates. Some former suffragists followed Alice Paul's lead into the National Woman's Party (NWP), which became a single-issue organization that after 1923 focused exclusively on an equal rights amendment to build on the success of constitutional enfranchisement. Others attempted to exert influence within the Republican and Democratic parties. While many progressive women reformers had long been connected to the reformist wing of the Republican Party, some now began to support the Democrats, attracted by the urban liberalism that was emerging in the party in New York State.[12]

In 1920, both Democrats and Republicans recognized women's issues in their platforms, presumably taking women at their word that they would use their combined votes as a powerful political tool. And they opened up places within the organizational structure of their parties for female members, although the positions granted were marginal in terms of power or influence. Women became officeholders as well. Only a handful were elected to the House of Representatives (a high of seven in 1928), and none were elected to the Senate, but hundreds served at the state level in legislatures and executive positions earmarked as women's jobs, such as secretary of education and secretary of state. Women were more successful in local government, in part because many of these positions were nonpartisan and thus seemingly more in keeping with ideas that women should operate "above politics." Despite these inroads, female officeholders generally operated within the context of prevailing assumptions that women should keep to women's issues, or to "municipal housekeeping," the same assumption that limited their ability to wield much power within their political parties. As the *New York Times* magazine *Current History* summed it up, "Where there is dignity of office but little else, or where there is routine work, little glory, and low pay, men prove willing to admit women to an equal share in the spoils of office."[13]

Although one focus of these women's energies centered specifically on breaking down the barriers to their participation in politics, equally important was the determination to marshal their new political clout to effect social justice reforms. The hope to use WCND committees for peacetime purposes was not realized—they were disbanded relatively quickly. But in the 1920s, women continued what they had begun in the Progressive Era and continued during the war: a "dominion of reform" of interlocking groups of women who lobbied for mothers' pensions for impoverished dependent women, education and industrial reform, wage and hour laws for working women, a wide range of child health programs on the state level, as well as a broad extension of women's legal rights.[14]

The lobbying efforts of these women underline the importance of women activists in pioneering twentieth-century interest group politics.[15] Progressive-era women activists had worked largely at the state level, but this changed in the 1920s. An astute recognition of the growing importance of national associations' lobbying efforts in Washington, D.C., led fourteen white women's organizations to form the Women's Joint Congressional Committee, with the goal of promoting federal legislation backed by the member organizations. War experiences working with government agencies may have provided some of the catalyst for this national focus, but the passage of the suffrage amendment in 1920 was pivotal. Armed with the sense that they could claim to represent "the woman's vote," national leaders mobilized women's groups throughout the country as they passionately advocated for the Child Labor Amendment—after the Supreme Court invalidated a second national child labor law in 1921. Although that effort ultimately failed, the women's lobby saw an early success in the federal Sheppard-Towner Act of 1921, which gave matching federal funds to states to provide health care and other services for mothers and children.

Women's groups also lobbied in behalf of disarmament and the peace movement. The interwar years peace movement, particularly the efforts of the Women's International League for Peace and Freedom (WILPF), was closely linked to the prewar era and revealed the same divergent attitudes about women's pacifism. Some women portrayed their movement as particularly meaningful to women because they were the mothers of sons at risk in wartime. Others talked about the peace movement in less essentialist terms and cast peace as a human rights issue and not necessarily a gendered one. The persistence of the essentialist ideas, however, suggests the power of conventional notions about women's maternal qualities that had shaped many Progressive Era women activists. The concept of peace as a women's issue led other organizations, such as the League of Women Voters, the Women's Trade Union League, and the General Federation of Women's Clubs, to join with the WILPF in a coordinated drive to put pressure on President Warren Harding to support disarmament. Their lobbying was a decisive factor in the convening of the Washington Conference on the Limitation of Armament in 1922, although women were disappointed that more was not accomplished.

Later in the decade, it was again women's groups, especially the WILPF, that led the way in securing U.S. support for the Kellogg-Briand Peace Pact of 1928, which embodied isolationist sentiments to renounce war "as an instrument of national policy."[16]

Yet, as was the case with their entry into partisan politics, these women activists had limited success in lobbying. Although many states had passed laws extending women's legal rights and implementing social reforms, by the end of the decade progress had slowed. Reformers were particularly discouraged by the failure of the effort to get a child labor amendment through Congress. Indeed, most national legislation supported by women lobbyists was unsuccessful. Congress successively cut the Sheppard-Towner Act's appropriations and finally ended the program in 1929. By decade's end, many women activists were frustrated because while both political parties seemed eager to woo the woman's vote by making rhetorical appeals to women's role as homemaker, they paid significantly less attention to the specific reforms demanded by the "women's lobby."[17]

Moreover, the women's rights movement itself was in shambles, with white women divided among themselves as to tactics and goals. Ironically, the problems hindering a sustained feminist movement to some extent grew out of the success of the suffrage battle. Before national suffrage was achieved, a great many women—equally excluded from this basic right of citizenship—could come under the same umbrella of "votes for women." Once the Nineteenth Amendment was ratified, the lines that divided women—class, race, age, and ideology—became more significant. By gaining the individual right they had so vigorously sought, they laid the groundwork for the fracturing of female communities. As one activist ruefully put it in 1923, "The American woman's movement, and her interest in great moral and social questions, is splintered into a hundred fragments under as many warring leaders."[18]

This fragmentation was particularly evident in the tensions between social reformers and the NWP. NAWSA's anger over the NWP's White House pickets during the war had already driven a profound wedge into the suffrage movement. In the 1920s, a new issue—a ferocious debate over the NWP's proposed Equal Rights Amendment (ERA)—would deepen the divide. The amendment simply stated, "Men and women shall have equal rights throughout the United States and every place subject to its jurisdiction." Under the leadership of Alice Paul, the NWP focused so exclusively on the ERA as a means of achieving political and economic equality that the newly coined term "feminism" soon came to refer exclusively to its specific agenda. Women interested in broader social reform, especially the sex-specific labor laws that they had worked so hard to achieve for working women and to sustain during the war, were alarmed at this "blanket amendment," which they feared would undermine labor protections for women.

Another serious issue that hampered women's efforts in behalf of reform was the white racism and indifference that limited black and white women activists' ability to work together. In the face of southern resistance to black women's voter registration, African American women, through the NACW, assisted by the NAACP, fought back. They assembled evidence on behalf of the Tinkham bill, designed to reduce congressional representation of states that restricted women's suffrage. When this tactic failed, black women approached white women's organizations to elicit some support for enforcing the Nineteenth Amendment. But neither the League of Women Voters nor the NWP was willing to support the anti-disenfranchisement efforts of black women voters in the South.

The Red Scare and Conservative Politics

While the difficulties all women reformers faced arose in part from women's disunity, the underlying problem was the decade's political climate. Despite activist women's enthusiasm, the American public was increasingly less engaged in political issues. Observers in the 1920s, citing declining voter participation during the decade (roughly half of those eligible voted), assumed that women's nonvoting accounted for the decline. With only sparse data of voting by sex available, many historians have echoed this assumption. More recent studies, however, maintain that women's participation in elections varied significantly by location and by election. Women in states that had only recently enfranchised them seem to have been less likely to vote than those living in states like California where they had longer experience with the electoral process. What is most interesting is that men's voting decreased in this period as well, following a long-standing trend of declining engagement in partisan politics. Jane Addams ruefully commented in 1924 that the question should not be, "Is woman suffrage failing," but rather, "Is suffrage failing."[19] That both men and women were not voting in large numbers points to a political climate of disaffected or disinterested citizenry; and it is this broader context of American politics, not women's failures as voters, that offers the most compelling explanation for the difficulties women reformers faced.[20]

A related problem was a conservative political climate hostile to reform that made it impossible to sustain the prewar enthusiasm for progressive measures. On the national scene, the Republicans, now largely divested of their progressive elements, dominated the White House and Congress, and, reflecting in part the party's ties to corporate business interests, resisted efforts to expand federal regulatory powers or raise taxes to pay for social welfare legislation. The Prohibition amendment, ratified in 1919, further increased many Americans' wariness of intrusive social reforms. Prohibition met with vigorous opposition, especially among urban cosmopolitans and ethnic and working-class Americans. Many resented and circumvented the law, and others worried that the ineffectual effort to control alcohol consumption had fostered contempt for the law. That women reformers were so closely associated with the controversial amendment surely fueled hostility to the social reforms women activists promoted in the 1920s. Finally, the widening prosperity of the period may well have influenced many Americans to turn toward new consumer and leisure pleasures and away from political engagement and concern for the nation's poor.

Perhaps most damaging to reform and especially women's part in it was the "Red Scare" of 1919 to 1921. Prompted initially by American fear of the Russian Revolution of 1917 and the revolutionary ambitions of the fledgling Communist Party in the United States to topple this nation's government, Americans succumbed to a hysteria in which wild-eyed Bolsheviks seemed to be lurking around every corner. The Red Scare quickly expanded to target a wide range of people and associations deemed "un-American," and it led to the deportation of "suspicious" immigrants, the suppression of the labor movement, and massive violations of civil liberties. The deportation of Emma Goldman, discussed in Chapter 1, was part of the Red Scare. It also helped to fuel the growth of the second Ku Klux Klan, which promised to promote 100 percent Americanism. Finally, the Red Scare contributed to the passage of the restrictive immigration laws of the 1920s and in addition became a weapon for opponents of reform legislation, who could now argue that efforts to increase government's role in regulating the economy or protecting workers and the poor would lead America down the same path as Russia.

Conservative Women's Activism

Many individuals and groups jumped on the Red Scare bandwagon, and self-proclaimed patriotic organizations played an important role. Preeminent among the opponents of reform were right-wing women's organizations. Ideological divisions among activist women had emerged clearly in the war era, as pacifists and preparedness advocates squared off over the

United States joining the combatants. By the 1920s, this divide proved even more corrosive. The Woman Patriots, a small but vocal group that had originated in the antisuffrage movement, vehemently opposed social reform in the 1920s as being the forerunner of Bolshevism. The DAR, initially interested in women's social reform efforts, had by mid-decade also taken up the antiradical mantra. The DAR became closely associated with the Woman's Auxiliary of the American Legion (WAAL), an organization open to women relatives of servicemen and servicewomen. Antiradical women came together in 1925 to create the Women's Patriotic Conference on National Defense, which they viewed as a counter to both the Women's Joint Congressional Committee and the WILPF. Women in an auxiliary of the all-male Ku Klux Klan supported some reforms like Prohibition, but, like other right-wing women's groups, they were suspicious of the liberal goals of the white women's lobby and hostile to black women's demands for equal citizenship.

Red Scare hysteria, especially that promoted by women, particularly focused on a number of progressive women's groups. Right-wing women's organizations and activism in the 1920s not only reflects their own interest in finding political voice, but also starkly reveals that, despite the suffragists' vision of universal womanhood, in fact women were profoundly divided. Opponents claimed, for example, that the Women's Joint Congressional Committee and the Women's International League for Peace and Freedom were spreading Bolshevism in the United States and seeking to undermine the nation's military preparedness. Jane Addams in particular came in for forceful criticism. But conservative groups tended to conflate liberal maternal reformers, feminists who challenged the patriarchal family, peace activists, and NWP members into a vague category of "feminists" who threatened the social order.

Resistance to expanded government to promote social reforms fueled part of the anxiety. But fears that American feminists sought to spread notions of free love and the state's "nationalization" of women, which conservatives claimed were imported from Bolshevism, made up a key part of the anti-"feminist" rhetoric. Women's groups were particularly attuned to the threat Bolsheviks and their presumed American women allies posed to the family. Lurid tales of rapes and murders of upper-class Russian women and of the Bolshevik regime "nationalizing" women and creating a "Bureau of Free Love" that made women available to all men had particular resonance for women's groups. Echoing the wartime anxiety about German rapes and assaults on innocent women, for example, DAR leader Grace Brosseau warned a DAR convention that members must protect "the lovely young girlhood of America," by resisting un-American forces.[21] This vocabulary, invoking almost Victorian notions of female vulnerability, speaks to larger anxieties about challenges to the gender order the new women seemingly represented. The Bolshevik threat was not merely external, but internal, and thus all the more alarming.

VALORIZING SOLDIERS AND THEIR MOTHERS

Patriotic groups' efforts to reinscribe traditional gender roles also appeared in the ways in which they sought to shape public memory about World War I. In the interwar years, Americans disagreed profoundly about World War I's meaning. Many, including, most famously, the writers of the Lost Generation, saw the war as a tragic mistake, emblematic of a corrupt civilization. As we have seen, pacifist organizations flourished. Rejecting war, they sought to promote not just peace but international understanding. Other Americans were perhaps less focused on geopolitical aspects of war and instead merely weary of the fevered pitch of the war climate. Assailed by propaganda posters, four-minute men and three-minute women orators, calls for food conservation, Liberty Loan subscriptions, and Red Cross donations, they may have had their fill of the unrelenting demand for sacrifice and service—much of it by women—that the war engendered.

Yet many Americans viewed the war as representing strength in the international arena. They may have been disappointed in the peacemaking process and the persistence of business as usual among the European powers, but they insisted upon remembering the war itself and America's role in it as noble. So while antiwar sentiment grew steadily in the postwar decade, conservative politicians and groups, especially the American Legion veterans' organization and its female auxiliary, eagerly sought to keep the memory of war alive.[22] And they did so in ways that reinforced a traditional gender order. As they promoted the war's positive legacy, they focused primarily on the male soldier's valor. Despite many women's wartime efforts to broaden the definition of patriotic wartime citizenship to include noncombatant women who served the state in other, but nonetheless vital, ways, these contributions were largely forgotten.[23]

A partial exception to this was the Women's Overseas Service League (WOSL) (see Chapter 3). Throughout the interwar years, WOSL leaders continued to insist upon equal benefit rights for military women. Their lobbying efforts registered a few successes. They convinced the Veterans Bureau, for example, to open two hospitals for enlisted women veterans. They also sought to convince Congress to extend veterans' privileges to civilians who had served abroad — canteen workers, Signal Corps operators, and clerical staff. Mildred Taubles, WOSL president, told a radio audience in 1930 of the 22,000 women who had served abroad in a range of capacities. She explained that they "braved the dangers of the submarine and the air raid and stood the same chance of disease" as men, yet received no hospitalization benefits. The WOSL's vision of women's war contributions was a narrow one that privileged only those women who had gone to Europe.[24]

Other women's groups similarly reinforced this privileging of male patriotism. The WAAL, like its male counterpart, the American Legion, sought to honor veterans while promoting patriotism and military preparedness. In doing so, the organization valorized male soldiers and celebrated conventional notions of women's role in the home. The WAAL particularly concentrated on aid to veterans and their families. Mrs. O. D. Oliphant, for example, told a Springfield, Illinois, audience of the work of the WAAL in 1925. She said that its members did not seek leadership roles and explained that "woman's work in rehabilitating the service man is that kind of work for which woman is best fitted, the ministering care in the hospital, the tender visitation in the hospital, and the welfare work among the families of disabled men."[25] This conventional focus on women's nurturing roles was given an added resonance in 1922 when the WAAL organized a well-publicized ceremony at the recently created Tomb of the Unknown Soldier in Washington, D.C. The ceremony's purpose was to honor the mother of that soldier. Speeches by women included that of Mrs. George Gordon Seibold, whose pilot son died in the war. Speaking of the Unknown Soldier, she said, "God gave him to some mother and that mother gave him with her most cherished hopes."[26]

Other organizations, especially the American War Mothers and the American Gold Star Mothers, joined with the WAAL in promoting this valorization of the soldier's mother. During the war itself, community parade organizers usually featured such mothers, but their glorification was muted somewhat. The WCND called for bereaved women to forgo the traditional wearing of black for mourning, arguing that it emphasized loss more than patriotic sacrifice, and President Woodrow Wilson agreed. Thus, men who lost loved sons wore armbands with a gold star, and women placed similar stars in their windows to symbolize their fallen soldiers. With war's end, groups like the WAAL began to emphasize women's primary role in war as bereaved mothers. The American War Mothers (AWM), started in 1917, and the American Gold Star Mothers, founded in 1928, as well as a few other similar organizations, made honoring such women their focal point. In yet another example of the way in which women's associations became so skilled at lobbying, these groups campaigned to have Congress recognize their loss in official ways. In 1925, Congress gave the AWM a charter. The nation's formal recognition of the organization, its legislative chairperson, Margaret N. McCluer, argued, would "let our allied countries see that our America realized what its women did and has made this recognition of their sacrifices."[27]

Throughout the 1920s, the major focus of these two organizations was to convince Congress to authorize and fund Gold Star Mothers' pilgrimages to visit their sons' graves in France. The U.S. government gave families the choice of repatriation of bodies to their homes or burial in American cemeteries in France. Most opted for the former, but about 30,000 interments were abroad. The all-white relatively elite women in the Gold Star Mothers argued that facilitating women's ability to visit these graves honored the soldiers sacrificed to the altar of country. But more, the pilgrimages honored the women who had given their sons. At its extreme, the women's rhetoric credited mothers with the victory. Mathilda A. Burling, for example, exclaimed, "It was our flesh and blood that enriched the foreign soil. After all it was the mothers who had won the war."[28]

Congress finally authorized the trips in 1929. Only women were eligible for this government largesse. Men, presumably, grieved less. And the focus was overwhelmingly on mothers. Widows might be included in a pilgrimage, but only if they had not remarried. An estimated 6,693 women took advantage of the program between 1930 and 1933. Of these, only a handful—97—were African Americans. In the first sailing, 23 black women dropped out when they learned that the trip would be segregated, and, furthermore, that black women would be assigned to inferior accommodations, a circumstance that provoked protest from both the NACW and the NAACP, to no avail. Just as black soldiers had been denied combat roles, the government chose to reinforce racial hierarchy in this program to honor war mothers. The trips were all the more remarkable because they took place in some of the worst years of the Great Depression, including the period when the Bonus Army of former World War I soldiers faced brutal treatment in Washington, D.C., where they encamped to demand an early payment of their war pensions. 1929 was also the year that Congress defunded the Sheppard-Towner Act for maternal and child health. Historian Jo Ann Plant calls the arguments of reformers for such social legislation "progressive motherhood," which she contrasts with the Gold Star Mothers' "patriotic motherhood." At least in terms of politics, patriotic motherhood had more clout in the late 1920s.[29]

Although "patriotic mothers" and "progressive mothers" tended to disagree over key issues such as the peace movement and social welfare legislation, many of them shared a common assumption about women's maternal natures. This similarity in itself, stressing as it did women's differences from men, offers telling evidence about the limits those women who sought political equality with men faced. Shared assumptions aside, women activists in the 1920s pursued profoundly different directions. Black women created and sustained organizational efforts that would give them more political influence in the 1930s and beyond. Although the reform agenda of progressive white women's groups stalled at the nation's capital—in part because of the efforts of right-wing women's organizations—it is impressive that women activists accomplished as much as they did on the local and state levels. In the process, they helped to keep the reform spirit alive, if not well, and served as a crucial bridge to the social welfare reforms of the 1930s introduced by President Franklin D. Roosevelt's New Deal. At the same time, in the short term, right-wing women contributed to the conservative climate that would limit social reform and fuel anxieties about "new women." In the long term, they laid the foundations for what would shape women's roles in twentieth-century right-wing conservatism.[30] Although their war experiences contributed to women's activism, the suffrage amendment was the defining factor in shaping women's politics in the 1920s. Many women may have been disappointed that their war service did not result in extensive political power in the postwar decade. But women and their organizations did develop tactics and skills that would shape American women's political activism for the rest of the twentieth century.

WOMEN AND WORK IN THE POSTWAR ERA

In his popular history, *Only Yesterday* (1931), Frederick Lewis Allen exclaimed that after the war, women had "poured out of schools and colleges into all manners of occupations." This presumed financial independence, Allen continued, had led to "the slackening of husbandly and parental authority." The upshot was a moral revolution that encouraged both divorce and women's "headlong pursuit of freedom." It is true that, in part because of the expansion of white-collar jobs, working women became more publicly visible in the 1920s. And women's participation rate steadily rose in the early twentieth century, increasing from 20.6 percent in 1910 to 25.3 percent in 1930. Allen's sense of a dramatic postwar change in the nature of women's economic opportunities and independence, however, was far off the mark.

First, the race segmentation that characterized women's labor in the prewar years persisted into the 1920s and beyond. African American women's opportunities in factories contracted significantly at war's end, and domestic and farm labor continued to be their most likely form of employment. Mexican American women, whose migration dramatically increased during the postwar decade, also clustered in these low-status jobs, although some young women found work in food processing and garment factories. The same was true of Asian American women. Women of color might find clerical jobs within their own racial or ethnic communities, but rarely would white offices employ them, although black women maintained their precarious place in government civil service work. Thus race continued to be the defining factor in economic opportunity, and the promise implicit in war work quickly eroded.

Second, the sex-segregated labor market, so evident in the prewar era, returned to limit women's job opportunities after the war. In the 1920s, 86 percent of women clustered in ten occupations, in jobs in which they made less money and had lower status and lower levels of skills than men. Industrial labor, primarily in unskilled and semiskilled positions, continued to be dominated by immigrant daughters, although they increasingly found opportunities in clerical work. The expansion of clerical work (19 percent of employed women were clerks at the end of the decade) may have made work more respectable for middle-class daughters as it offered a clean environment and required at least a high school education. Professional careers also offered middle-class women enhanced opportunities. The percentage of women with professional jobs was still small, but it rose from 9 percent in 1910 to 14 percent in 1930. Most professionals were white women, though African Americans found limited opportunities. The war stimulated new fields for women, especially in social work and as personnel managers. But in the final analysis, professional work, like other categories, tended to be in sex-segregated, "feminized fields," like nursing, teaching, and social work.

Perhaps the most startling aspect of women's paid work in the 1920s was the increase in married women's employment. In 1900, 15 percent of working women had been married, but by 1930, that number had climbed to 29 percent. For the most part, they worked in agriculture, manufacturing, retail trade, and domestic and personal service, in poorly paid and low-status work. Given the cultural imperatives of married women's domestic responsibilities, it is likely that most who took on jobs did so out of necessity. Nonetheless, the question of working wives sparked a lively debate. The attention was out of proportion, given the actual number of wives working, and clearly indicated that the issue struck a sensitive nerve in the American public.

Most pundits were negative. Typical was marriage expert Ernest Groves, who in 1925 declared, "When the woman herself earns and her maintenance is not entirely at her husband's will, diminishing masculine authority necessarily follows."[31] Even women's colleges expressed ambivalence. On the one hand, Smith College created the Institute to Coordinate Women's Interests, which experimented with cooperative facilities such as nurseries and kitchens to devise means of simplifying housework and child care so that wives could take on at least part-time work. On the other hand, Vassar in 1924 set up a School of Euthenics to channel "education for women along the lines of their chief interests and responsibilities, motherhood and the home." Focusing primarily on educated, privileged women, the debate expressed hostility to wives who worked out of a sense of personal fulfillment rather than from dire need. Historian Nancy Cott has pointed out that wives who pursued such an individualistic course were labeled "the enemies of society."[32]

Even observers seemingly supportive of working wives were ambivalent about the issue. Maternalist reformers were highly sympathetic to the working-class wife when they believed she worked out of necessity, yet they regarded her as unfortunate. The Women's Bureau and the Women's Trade Union League, for example, recognized the legitimacy of working-class wives' work. But their insistence that these wives worked because of an absent husband, or one unable to earn sufficient income, made it clear that they did not consider wives' work desirable or normal. These reformers might campaign for improved conditions for working women, but ideally an income provided by a male wage adequate for a family's support would solve the dilemma by taking wives out of the workplace altogether. These embedded notions about working wives go a long way toward explaining why women's economic opportunities were so constricted. The war emergency opened the door to challenging sex segregation, which had the potential to offer women significant advances, but that potential bore little fruit. Contemporary observer Constance Green summed up the situation pithily: "The brief interlude . . . which some enthusiasts heralded as launching a new era for women in industry . . . came and went with astonishingly little permanent effect upon women's opportunities."

But if women could not expect much from work, that did not mean that the experience had no impact on them. Although wage labor had its limitations, working for wages could enhance women's sense of autonomy and individual identity. Working, even at less than satisfying jobs, may have offered opportunities to challenge patriarchal authority in the home. And even if young women's wages were rarely sufficient for economic independence, it did give them opportunities to participate in the burgeoning consumer culture of the era. In particular, their earning power may have allowed them to carve out more social freedoms as they participated in the heterosexual culture of dating and urban amusements. As was the case with political developments, in the 1920s, working women did not realize the promises that seemed implicit in wartime jobs, but many could use work as a means to a degree of independence and access to the pleasures of the modern consumer culture.

FLAPPERS, SEXUALITY, AND WOMEN'S FREEDOM

This association of consumption, leisure, and social freedom found full expression in the iconic flapper. To contemporaries, as well as in popular memory, one of the most compelling aspects of the "new woman" was this youthful, frivolous creature. She smoked, she drank, she wore makeup and provocative clothing. Seemingly, she lived in a feverish whirl of jazz dancing and reckless fun. And in keeping with the movies' fascination with sexualized romances, she channeled novelist Elinor Glyn's "The It Girl," with "it" referring to sex appeal. Although the affluent and ebullient flapper bore little resemblance to most women and their experiences, the flapper style in clothing and dancing crossed race, class, and ethnic lines and spoke to a broad desire for more freedom in women's lives.

This freedom included sexual expression. The sexual revolution embodied in this new woman can be overstated. Certainly, in the 1920s, many young women publicly engaged in far more erotic play, termed "petting," and were more likely to have premarital intercourse than preceding generations. Yet the double standard still persisted, and most women felt the need to find the balance between sexual fun and a poor reputation that might damage their marriage chances. Although some African American women might idolize the era's black jazz and blues singers, like Bessie Smith, who conveyed a powerful sexuality, others, especially middle-class women, continued to harbor concerns about invidious stereotypes concerning their respectability. Too, some immigrant groups, especially recent ones like Mexican Americans, tried to exercise tight control over their children's social lives. Even as young women's sexual experimentation fueled both titillation and anxiety, a cultural shift in expectations about married women's sexuality also contributed to contemporaries' sense of a more erotic sexual terrain for the new woman. Historians see in the 1920s an emerging "affectionate family," with more equality between husbands and wives and an assumption that sexual passion for both men and women was vital to a happy marriage.[33]

The links between these changes in sexual and personal behavior and women's experiences in World War I are tenuous. But as we have seen, paid war work and war service offered women opportunities to challenge barriers that restricted them. Fashion styles led to less ornate and restrictive clothing. Young women engaged in unprecedented physical mobility as they served abroad or moved away from home to find war jobs. Women marched in parades, and some picketed the White House. The "plucky" women of the movies no longer appeared just in serials for working-class women but became part of feature films as well. As many real women did in the war years, movie heroines exuded a sense of adventure and independence. A subtle shift occurred—evident especially in visual media—that suggested more personal freedom for women. But the sexual component of 1920s new women cannot be attributed primarily to the war. Certainly, social reformers were worried that "the lure of the khaki" would lead to promiscuity, and there is some evidence that wartime conditions promoted the practice of "treating," which would transform courtship patterns in the postwar decade.[34]

But for the most part, the roots of change can instead be traced to the prewar era. Feminists and sex radicals associated with the bohemian culture of Greenwich Village who called for sexual liberation for men and women had influence beyond their small numbers as they wrote books, plays, and magazine articles. Working-class women's reworking of courtship patterns in the anonymity of urban amusements too exerted cultural influence on the broader society. The media popularized the ideas of sexologists like Havelock Ellis and psychologists like Sigmund Freud to disseminate the notions that women had sexual drives and that "repression was bad" for both men and women. Also important was the spread of birth control among the middle classes. Margaret Sanger largely abandoned her focus on working-class women and allied with the medical establishment to legitimize the distribution of the diaphragm through doctors, thus radically transforming the ability of prosperous women to control their fertility and separate sex from reproduction. And 1920s popular culture, movies especially, glamorized the sexualized women, even if film plots punished promiscuity and channeled eroticism into heterosexual marriage. If, in the teens, women's sexual agency in films was associated primarily with dangerous vamps like Theda Bara, now it became the hallmark of attractive, marriageable young women.

CONCLUSION

Historians of American women have long recognized that the conventional periodization of U.S. history that posits World War I as a fundamental turning point limits our understanding of the dramatic changes shaping early twentieth-century women's experiences. For women, war did not create a sharp break with the past. Rather, the war era provides a remarkably fine lens for examining the changes that began to unfold in the early 1900s and would continue to develop in the postwar decade. The modern quality of World War I, requiring, as it did, extensive civilian mobilization in voluntary associations and defense industries, intersected with well-organized women's movements and ongoing changes in the nature of women's work. This confluence allowed diverse groups of women—radicals, conservatives, pacifists, suffragists, and reformers—to seize the opportunity to influence American policy and politics. Suffragists, reformers, and black civil rights activists especially hoped that patriotic war service would give them a political voice, and they used that voice repeatedly to claim their rights as citizens. At the same time, labor shortages offered women unprecedented opportunities to break down the restrictive barriers of the sex- and racially segmented labor market. Although these jobs primarily benefited working-class women already in the workplace, the war also stimulated white-collar opportunities for the middle class, options that would continue to attract more women in the postwar years.

Women not only challenged barriers in the job market during the war. They also crossed boundaries that had defined "respectable behavior." Working-class women donned overalls when they took on jobs formerly the prerogative of men. Women marched in patriotic parades in unison and in uniform to express their patriotism and stake claims to citizenship. Public protests such as the National Woman's Party picketing of the White House and African American women's participation in the silent march that drew attention to the East St. Louis riots are further examples of the ways in which women's occupation of public space symbolized their rejection of ladylike norms. Women who went abroad as nurses, welfare workers, reporters, or Signal Corps telephone operators found meaningful work in the nation's cause, and as they did so, they satisfied a thirst for adventure, a desire to be part of the "big show" of war that signaled their independent spirit.

Popular culture—especially visual media—widely publicized women's various boundary crossings. Pictures of uniformed Motor Corps drivers, overalled munitions workers, heroic nurses near the front, and volunteers who represented a range of war workers filling the streets in patriotic parades made a powerful statement about the possibilities the war crisis had opened up. War films sent a mixed message, with one major motif the vulnerable maiden at risk of rape by the brutal Hun. Yet the more modern woman evident in serials like *Patria* and in heroines like Mary Pickford's "Little American" signaled a more independent and less conventional woman.

But for all the attention given to war's possibility for offering women more equality, opportunity, and political influence, the war's promise for women fell short. Certainly individual women—especially those who served abroad—might have found their war experiences transformative. But for women as a group, the war did not lead to political power or economic equality. Although specific circumstances of the 1920s help to explain these limits, we can also point to the ambiguous legacy of the war years. The racial and ideological differences so evident during the war that divided activist women came to the fore sharply in the postwar era and limited their ability to turn suffrage into power. Equally important were the forces aligned against women's claims to more equality. During the war, as we have seen, workers, employers, politicians, and antisuffragists combined to resist women's efforts to break down the barriers that constrained them. African American women faced the added challenges of discrimination and segregation. And even maternal reformers who sought improvements in women's work lives reinforced women's subordinate status in the workforce by insisting upon the need for protective legislation to safeguard the future mothers of the nation. In the 1920s, these limits persisted, especially the assumption of women's primary role in the home. And, indeed, the debate over the new woman and the threat she posed to the social order gained added traction in the 1920s as Americans grappled with changes that were transforming the nation into a modern pluralistic society. In this political, ideological, and cultural context, the new woman was far from "liberated" or equal, and this was particularly true for poor women and women of color.

Yet, between 1900 and 1930, real changes took place. As was so clearly evident in World War I, women were breaking down barriers, challenging boundaries that constrained them. In their workforce participation, in their political organizing and lobbying, and in their search for more freedom and independence in their personal lives, they ushered in new notions of womanhood. But again, as the war and its aftermath made clear, these changes were contested. The unfulfilled promises of World War I reveal the powerful limits to women's achieving equality, constraints that would continue to shape women's lives and the struggle for equal rights and opportunities for the next century and beyond.

Notes

Abbreviations Used in the Notes

ARC	American National Red Cross, Record Group 200, National Archives, College Park, Maryland
Bannon Papers	Charlotte Bannon Papers, Sophia Smith Collection, Smith College, Northampton, Massachusetts
Barbour Papers	Louise Barbour Papers, 1917–39, Schlesinger Library, Radcliffe Institute, Harvard University, Cambridge, Massachusetts
Children's Bureau Records	Records of the Children's Bureau, Record Group 102, National Archives, College Park, Maryland
Dewson Papers	Molly Dewson Papers, 1893–1962, Series II: 20–27, Schlesinger Library, Radcliffe Institute, Harvard University, Cambridge, Massachusetts
FMC Collection	Friday Morning Club Collection, Huntington Library, San Marino, California
Hunt Collection	Myron Hunt Collection, Huntington Library, San Marino, California
Lee Papers	Mary Lee Papers, Schlesinger Library, Radcliffe Institute, Harvard University, Cambridge, Massachusetts
NAACP Papers	National Association for the Advancement of Colored People Papers, Library of Congress, Washington, D.C.
Radcliffe in France	Radcliffe College in France: Scrapbooks, 1917–20, vol. 1, Schlesinger Library, Radcliffe Institute, Harvard University, Cambridge, Massachusetts
Stedman Papers	Edith Gratia Stedman Papers, 1833–1978, Schlesinger Library, Radcliffe Institute, Harvard University, Cambridge, Massachusetts

Van Kleeck Papers	Mary van Kleeck Papers, Sophia Smith Collection, Smith College, Northampton, Massachusetts
War History Committee Records	War History Committee Records, Seaver Center for Western Research, Natural History Museum, Los Angeles County
WCND Records	Records of the Council of National Defense Committee on Women's Defense Work, Record Group 62, National Archives, College Park, Maryland
Women's Bureau Records	Records of the Women's Bureau, Record Group 86, National Archives, College Park, Maryland
Women's Committee Records	State Council of Defense, Women's Committee Records, Seaver Center for Western History Research, Natural History Museum, Los Angeles County
WSS Records	Records of the Women's Service Section, Records of the U.S. Railroad Administration, Record Group 14, National Archives, College Park, Maryland
WWI Manuscripts	World War I Manuscript Collection, Seaver Center for Western History Research, Natural History Museum, Los Angeles County
YMCA of the USA Records	Young Men's Christian Association of the USA Records, Kautz Family YMCA Archives, University of Minnesota Libraries, Minneapolis, Minnesota
YWCA of LA Collection	Young Women's Christian Association of Los Angeles Collection, 1894–1979, Special Collections and Archives, California State University, Northridge, California
YWCA of the USA Records	Young Women's Christian Association of the USA Records, 1860–1920, Sophia Smith Collection, Smith College, Northampton, Massachusetts

Introduction

1. Young Women's Christian Association War Work Program of the Industrial Committee, typescript of conference proceedings, September 10, 1918, Chicago, box 702, folder 4, p. 9, YWCA of the USA Records.

2. Key works on American women and World War I are Zeiger, *In Uncle Sam's Service*; Schneider and Schneider, *Into the Breach*; Steinson, *American Women's Activism*; Nikki Brown, *Private Politics and Public Voices*; Greenwald, *Women, War, and Work*; Carrie Brown, *Rosie's Mom*; Brownell, "The Women's Committees"; and Gavin, *American Women in World War I*. See also Kingsbury, *For Home and Country*.

3. On World War I nationalism, see Capozzola, *Uncle Sam Wants You*; Kennedy, *Disloyal Mothers and Scurrilous Citizens*; Kennedy, *Over Here*; Schaffer, *America in the Great War*; and Zieger, *America's Great War*.

4. Anne Emerson, "Who's She in War Work," *Forum* 59 (June 1918): 745.

5. Grayzel, *Women's Identities at War*; Grayzel, *Women and the First World War*;

Kuhlman, *Reconstructing Patriarchy after the Great War*; Gullace, *The Blood of Our Sons*. The classic account of the failure of war to improve women's status is Higonnet and Higonnet, "The Double Helix," 31–47.

6. For an overview on working women in this era, see Kessler-Harris, *Out to Work*, 46–216; Tentler, *Wage-Earning Women*; Blackwelder, *Now Hiring*, 11–35; Peiss, *Cheap Amusements*; Meyerowitz, *Women Adrift*; and Jacqueline Jones, *Labor of Love, Labor of Sorrow*, 79–151.

7. On women and progressive reform, see Ladd-Taylor, *Mother-Work*; Linda Gordon, *Pitied but Not Entitled*; Wikander, Kessler-Harris, and Lewis, *Protecting Women*; Muncy, *Creating a Female Dominion*; and Neverdon-Morton, *Afro-American Women of the South*.

8. Ladd-Taylor, *Mother-Work*, 3–11; Baker, "The Domestication of Politics"; Koven and Michel, *Mothers of a New World*.

9. Ford, *Iron-Jawed Angels*, 18–31.

10. Lumsden, "Beauty and the Beasts," 595.

11. Cott, *The Grounding of Modern Feminism*, 56–57.

12. Stansell, *American Moderns*, 90. For feminism, see also Cott, *The Grounding of Modern Feminism*; Schwarz, *Radical Feminists of Heterodoxy*; Susan Glenn, *Female Spectacle*; and Trimberger, *Intimate Warriors*.

13. Proctor, *Civilians in a World at War*, 1–12. On women's mobilization for war, in the United States and elsewhere, see Kingsbury, *For Home and Country*, chap. 3.

Chapter 1

1. Anna Howard Shaw, "What Women Ask for War Service," *Ladies' Home Journal*, March 1918, 30.

2. Other organizations included the Emergency Peace Federation, the Fellowship of Reconciliation, the People's Council, and the Union for Democratic Control. Witt, "Crystal Eastman," 724.

3. Marchand, *The American Peace Movement*, xiv. For an excellent overview of women in the peace movement that emphasizes the international context, see Patterson, *The Search for a Negotiated Peace*.

4. Alonso, *Peace as a Women's Issue*, 61.

5. Addams, "The Working Woman and the Ballot," *Woman's Home Companion*, April 1908, quoted in Marchand, *The American Peace Movement*, 201. The argument in this paragraph is drawn from Marchand's chapter "The Maternal Instinct."

6. Kennedy, "Declaring War on War."

7. Alonso, *Peace as a Women's Issue*, 52, 56–84. On Addams, see Victoria Bissell Brown, *Education of Jane Addams*; and Elshtain, *Jane Addams*.

8. Quoted in Steinson, *American Women's Activism*, 35.

9. Wald directed the Henry Street Settlement and was also a member of the AUAM; Grace Abbott directed the Immigration Protective League; Breckinridge was a professor of social work; Alice Hamilton worked for the U.S. Department of Labor; and Balch had founded a settlement house and went on to become an influential professor of economics at Wellesley College. Sullivan, "Social Work's Legacy of Peace," 516.

10. *Report of the International Congress of Women*, quoted in Degen, *The History of the Woman's Peace Party*, 84.

11. Degen, *The History of the Woman's Peace Party*, 84.

12. Sullivan, "Social Work's Legacy of Peace," 516–17; Alonso, *Peace as a Women's Issue*, 69.

13. Witt, "Crystal Eastman," 734.

14. Steinson, *American Women's Activism*, 127.

15. Marchand, *The American Peace Movement*, 243–45. The AUAM even had some success in tempering nationalist fervor during a crisis with Mexico in 1916. Initial reports of a clash between American and Mexican troops in Carrizal in 1916 had painted the Mexicans as aggressors, but the AUAM accurately reported that the United States had made the first move.

16. Steinson, *American Women's Activism*, 137.

17. Zeiger, "The Schoolhouse vs. the Armory," 154, 160, 163. Although the militant leaders of the ASPL tended to be young, Blake, born in 1853, was older.

18. *New York Tribune*, August 22, 1915, as quoted in Steinson, *American Women's Activism*, 181.

19. Steinson, *American Women's Activism*, 185–204.

20. "This Summer It Will Be the Girl Rookies," *Portland Oregonian*, April 2, 1916, section 6, p. 1; Hubbard, "The Soldier Girls of the National Service School," 519.

21. Steinson, *American Women's Activism*, 283.

22. Smith, *Jeannette Rankin*, 102, 111.

23. Brownell, "The Women's Committees," 63.

24. Joan M. Jensen, *The Price of Vigilance*, 169.

25. Zeiger, "She Didn't Raise Her Boy to Be a Slacker," 7–39.

26. "Pacifist Suffers from Beating and Offers Reward for Attackers," *Bisbee Daily Review*, October 30, 1917, p. 1; "Women Make Use of Tar and Feathers," *Twin Falls News*, April 13, 1918, p. 1; Two Negro Women Are Tarred and Feathered by Vicksburg Committee," *Augusta Chronicle*, July 25, 1918, p. 2.

27. Morgan, *Women and Patriotism*, 111.

28. "Showed Up Disloyalty," *Fort Wayne Sentinel*, November 23, 1917, p. 7.

29. Kennedy, *Over Here*, 62.

30. "Cleveland Women as Spy Hunters," *Logansport Pharos-Tribune*, June 28, 1918, p. 1, reported that two women employed by the Cleveland APL had uncovered a German spy. In Cincinnati, Elise Howland ran the offices of the APL. "Helping Uncle Sam," *Cincinnati Enquirer*, August 3, 1918, p. 12. "Raiders Take Women from Five N.O. Houses," *New Orleans Item*, May 14, 1918, p. 3.

31. Capozzola, *Uncle Sam Wants You*, 114.

32. "Disloyal Teachers Will Lose Their Certificates," *Idaho Statesman*, March 21, 1918, p. 7; "Teacher Refuses to Honor Flag," *Oakland Tribune*, July 21, 1917, p. 11; "Teacher Refuses Oath of Loyalty," *Portland Oregonian*, April 15, 1918, p. 4.

33. The original title of the organization was the New York Bureau of Legal First Aid. Early, *A World without War*, 49; see also Early, "Feminism, Peace, and Civil Liberties."

34. Early, *A World without War*, 26. Eventually, the War Risk Insurance program, established by the government and by the Red Cross, addressed these kinds of problems.

35. Ibid., 107–10.

36. This discussion relies on Kennedy, *Disloyal Mothers and Scurrilous Citizens*. On the links among birth control, feminism, and radicalism, see Linda Gordon, *Woman's Body, Woman's Rights*, 183–242.

37. Other women indicted for sedition included Mari Equi, Mollie Steimer, Louise Olivereau, and Leona Warneson Moore.

38. Kennedy, *Disloyal Mothers and Scurrilous Citizens*, 41.

39. See ibid.; and "Anarchists Still in Tombs," *New York Times*, June 18, 1917, p. 5.

40. "Berkman Queries Stir Judge's Ire," *Trenton Evening Times*, June 29, 1917, p. 11.

41. Goldman believed herself to be a citizen, but the man she had married to obtain her papers, Jacob Kershaw, had been stripped of his citizenship in 1909. Because federal law maintained that a woman's citizenship followed that of her husband, the government declared Goldman eligible for deportation. Kennedy, *Disloyal Mothers and Scurrilous Citizens*, 52.

42. "Arraign Rose Stokes," *Kansas City Star*, April 23, 1918, p. 1.

43. Kennedy, *Disloyal Mothers and Scurrilous Citizens*, 61–62; "Mrs. Rose Pastor Stokes Convicted of Disloyalty," *New York Times*, May 24, 1918, p. 1.

44. For the assessment of Stokes as a radical woman, see Kennedy, *Disloyal Mothers and Scurrilous Citizens*, 54–68; and Zipser and Zipser, *Fire and Grace*, 160–98.

45. Kennedy, *Disloyal Mothers and Scurrilous Citizens*, 18–27.

46. Sannes, "Queen of the Lecture Platform," 16.

47. Krieger, "Queen of the Bolsheviks," 67.

48. Kennedy, *Disloyal Mothers and Scurrilous Citizens*, 74–76.

49. Cott, *The Grounding of Modern Feminism*, 56–57.

50. On black women's suffrage activism, see Salem, *To Better Our World*, 125–30; and Terborg-Penn, *African American Women in the Struggle for the Vote*, 93–106.

51. Unsel, "Woman's Hour," 278. Works on the suffrage movement include Lunardini, *From Equal Suffrage*; Ford, *Iron-Jawed Angels*; DuBois, *Harriot Stanton Blatch*; and Scott and Scott, *One Half the People*.

52. Lunardini, *From Equal Suffrage*, 103.

53. Dodd, "Parades, Pickets," 360–61.

54. Lunardini, *From Equal Suffrage*, 110.

55. "Is Suffrage Work War Work?" *Woman Citizen* 22 (April 27, 1918): 425.

56. Unsel, "Woman's Hour," 312.

57. "Suffragists Protect Women Workers," *Lexington Herald*, May 21, 1917, p. 10.

58. "Suffrage Service Flag Now Has Twenty-Three Stars," *Woman Citizen* 3 (October 18, 1918): 414.

59. *Woman Citizen* 3 (November 9, 1918): 485. On the perception of citizenship being linked to military service, see Kerber, *No Constitutional Right to Be Ladies*, 243–46.

60. Clara Ueland, "While We Wage War," *Woman Citizen* 1 (October 17, 1917): 413; Carrie Chapman Catt, "War Messages to the American People," *Woman Citizen* 3 (June 22, 1918): 74–75.

61. Lunardini, *From Equal Suffrage*, 115.

62. "Suffrage Sign Causes a Riot at White House," *Denver Post*, June 20, 1917, p. 4; "They Deserve Rebuke," *Baltimore Sun*, June 22, 1917, p. 6.

63. Lunardini, *From Equal Suffrage*, 125. On the importance of the example of the perceived gains of Russian women to the American suffrage movement, see Mickenberg, "Suffragettes and Soviets."

64. Source: http://www.loc.gov/resource/mnwp.160030.

65. Ford, *Iron-Jawed Angels*, 172, 137.

66. Fowler, *Carrie Catt: Feminist Politician*, 216.

67. "The Men of America on Trial," *Woman Citizen* 1 (September 1, 1917): 253.

68. Dodd, "Parades, Pickets," 406–7.

69. "Miss Maud Younger and Mrs. Howard Gould to Speak on Suffrage," *Gulfport Daily Herald*, October 20, 1917, p. 5; "Noted Suffragist Here to Arrange for Great Rally," *New Orleans Times-Picayune*, October 18, 1917, p. 11.

70. "The Prison Notes of Rose Winslow," *Suffragist* 5 (December 1, 1917): 6.

71. "Letter Smuggled from Jail Gives 'Picket's' Story," *Macon Telegraph*, November 4, 1917, p. 10.

72. Lunardini, *From Equal Suffrage*, 135–36.

73. Ibid., 145.

74. Dodd, "Parades, Pickets," 420.

75. By 1920, Michigan, Oklahoma, and South Dakota had been added to the list. Unsel, "Woman's Hour," 269.

76. Dodd, "Parades, Pickets," 425. See also Unsel, "Woman's Hour," 318; and Lunardini, *From Equal Suffrage*, 138.

77. Nikki Brown, "Your Patriotism Is of the Purest Quality," 107.

78. White, *Too Heavy a Load*, 85.

79. Dunbar-Nelson, "Mine Eyes Have Seen," *Crisis* 15 (April 1918): 271–75; Plastas, "A Band of Noble Women," 100–102.

80. "Civic League Urges Support of U.S. in War," *Afro-American*, February 22, 1918, p. 2.

81. Both Randolph and Owen were arrested for their war criticism and charged under the Espionage Act, although they were not convicted. Federal agents recruited African Americans to report on friends and colleagues. Hallie E. Queen, for example, was responsible for an investigation of Nannie Burroughs. Kornweibel, *Investigate Everything*, 227–37.

82. Nikki Brown, "Your Patriotism Is of the Purest Quality," 8.

83. As quoted in Nikki Brown, *Private Politics and Public Voices*, 9–10.

84. Browder, "Working Out Their Economic Problems Together," 245.

85. On *Half-Century Magazine*, see Rooks, *Ladies' Pages*, 65–84. Rooks (p. 80) notes that a brief article accompanying the cover explicitly acknowledged that the caption meant to convey the notion of "Made in America," by stating that African Americans were "the only loyal element having no hyphenate affiliations and sympathies—the only element displaying at all times, despite the most bitter discouragements and the most utter handicaps, an unswerving loyalty to the colors that give them so little consideration and protection in their national life." Jennifer D. Keene analyzes the small group of propaganda posters targeting African Americans during the war, which includes a few images featuring women. Keene, "Images of Racial Pride."

86. "Negro Women Urged to Help," *Daily News*, November 11, 1918, p. 6.

87. "Margaret Black's Corner: Doing Your Bit," *Afro-American*, April 26, 1918, p. 7.

88. As quoted in Lentz-Smith, *Freedom Struggles*, 37.

89. Kathryn M. Johnson, "The Negro and the World War," *Half-Century* (June 1917): 13.

90. Keene, "A Comparative Study of White and Black American Soldiers."

91. Lewenson, *Taking Charge*, 101.

92. "Is the Line Drawn Yet?" *Appeal*, June 22, 1918, p. 2; "Negro Red Cross Nurses and Over Seas Service," *Savannah Tribune*, June 8, 1918, p. 4.

93. "Negro Red Cross Nurses," *Savannah Tribune*, August 3, 1918, p. 4; Lewenson, *Taking Charge*, 113–14.

94. Rudwick, *Race Riot*; Ellis, *Race, War, and Surveillance*, chap. 1.

95. Kathryn M. Johnson, "East St. Louis," *Half-Century* 3 (August 1918): 8; "Women's Column," *Afro-American*, August 4, 1917, p. 3.

96. *New York Age*, August 2, 1917, clipping, box 432, NAACP Papers; "Women at Prayer in Washington," *Afro-American*, July 14, 1917, p. 1.

97. "Colored Women to Gather at 5 O'clock Monday for Prayer," *Winston-Salem Journal*, August 19, 1917, p. 3; "Lynch Horrors Poison Nation," *Cleveland Gazette*, August 25, 1917, p. 1; "Miss Nannie H. Burroughs," *Washington Bee*, August 11, 1917, p. 1. The *Washington Bee* reported that Burroughs complained, "A few of 'your' would be leaders, rushed in at the last minute to have it appear that they had worked. Father, forgive our spineless friends who seek the lime light and the newspaper and are satisfied."

98. Schechter, *Ida B. Wells-Barnett and American Reform*, 152.

99. "Thousands March in Silent Protests," *Chicago Defender*, August 4, 1917, p. 1; *Afro-American*, October 27, 1917, p. 4; *Afro-American*, June 21, 1918.

100. Clipping, box 432, NAACP Papers.

101. Madam Walker Family Archives; Bundles, *On Her Own Ground*, 208–9.

102. Lentz-Smith, *Freedom Struggles*, 63.

103. As quoted in ibid., 74.

104. "Federation of Women's Clubs Elects Officers," *Chicago Defender*, September 1, 1917, p. 7.

105. Carlotta Bass, "Lynching Must Be Stopped," *California Eagle*, October 6, 1917, p. 1.

106. Quoted in Kornweibel, *Investigate Everything*, 171.

107. Ibid., 172. The comments of another black woman, Lillian Smith, of Iowa, were never published because the newspaper she sent them to, the *Pueblo Chieftain*, turned them over to the U.S. attorney in Iowa. Smith had justified the soldiers' action as retribution for the endemic violence African Americans faced. Lenz-Smith, *Freedom Struggles*, 78.

108. "Negro Rioters 'Martyrs,' Says Mrs. Barnett," *Chicago Daily Tribune*, December 23, 1917, p. 7; Schechter, *Ida B. Wells-Barnett and American Reform*, 157; Kornweibel, *Investigate Everything*, 52.

109. "Negro Women Hold Humiliation Service," *Savannah Tribune*, June 8, 1918, p. 1. On the powerful use of Turner's lynching in later protests against racial violence, including those of black women artists, see Armstrong, *Mary Turner and the Memory of Lynching*.

110. "Negro Women Hold Humiliation Service," *Savannah Tribune*, June 8, 1918, p. 1.

Chapter 2

1. Some material in this chapter appeared in Dumenil, "Women's Reform Organizations and Wartime Mobilization in World War I–Era Los Angeles," reprinted with permission and copyright 2011, Society for Historians of the Gilded Age and Progressive Era.

2. For war and soldiers, see Keegan, *The Face of Battle*; and Fussell, *The Boys' Crusade*. The role of voluntarism in World War I mobilization among other combatants appears in Darrow, *French Women and the First World War*, chap. 3; Grayzel, *Women and the First World War*, chap. 3; Grayzel, *Women's Identities at War*, chap. 6; Higonnet and Jenson, *Behind the Lines*; Proctor, *Civilians in a World at War*; and Horne, *State, Society, and Mobilization in Europe*. For a comparative discussion of war mobilization, see Rodgers, *Atlantic Crossings*, 267–317. On the importance of voluntary associations in the United States during the war, begin with Breen, *Uncle Sam at Home*. See also Capozzola, *Uncle Sam Wants You*; Cuff, "The Cooperative Impulse and War"; and Capozzola, "The Only Badge Needed Is Your Patriotic Fervor."

3. On the Creel committee, see Vaughn, *Holding Fast the Inner Lines*.

4. Key secondary sources for the WCND are Brownell, "The Women's Committees"; Breen, *Uncle Sam at Home*; and Steinson, *American Women's Activism*. For a contemporary account, see Blair, *The Woman's Committee*.

5. For a valuable discussion of women's volunteer efforts and class in Great Britain, see Summers, "Public Functions." On the Civil War, see Scott, *Natural Allies*, 58–77; and Attie, *Patriotic Toil*.

6. Blair, *The Woman's Committee*, 74–88.

7. The difficulties facing the Woman's Committee of the Council of National Defense were immense and included conflicts in Washington, D.C., with the Council of National Defense and tensions at the state level between male and female committees. In addition, both nationally and in many communities, there were conflicts between women's groups over responsibilities and activities that created duplication of efforts and ill-feeling. Suffrage and antisuffrage sentiment also troubled the national WCND, which was dominated by suffrage women but included women lukewarm or hostile to suffrage. See Breen, *Uncle Sam at Home*, 115–36; and Steinson, *American Women's Activism*, 307–28. The best account of the WCND is Unsel, "Woman's Hour." For an excellent firsthand account of the WCND, see Blair, *The Woman's Committee*.

8. Brownell, "The Women's Committees," offers an extensive analysis of the tensions concerning WCND activities. See especially chap. 4.

9. "War Activities of the Woman's Committee, Los Angeles City Unit of the Council of National Defense," 4, 10. For the most comprehensive discussion of Los Angeles clubwomen in this period, see Christman, "The Best Laid Plans," 41–89.

10. *Annual Report of the War Activities of the Woman's Committee of the Los Angeles City Unit*, 3. See *Catholic Women's Club Bulletin "United War-Work Number"* 1 (November 1918). Scattered material on Jewish women's war work may be found in the local Jewish newspaper. See, for example, *B'nai B'rith Messenger*, May 3, 1918, p. 19; ibid., October 19, 1917, p. 44; and ibid., October 4, 1918, p. 25. Scant references appear on black women's war work in the city's African American newspaper, the *California Eagle*. On racial and

ethnic barriers in white women's clubs, see Raftery, "Los Angeles Clubwomen and Progressive Reform"; and Davis, "An Era and Generation of Civic Engagement."

11. Blair, *The Woman's Committee*, 25. A number of studies explore Los Angeles's Progressive Era women's clubs. See Raftery, "Los Angeles Clubwomen and Progressive Reform"; Christman, "The Best Laid Plans"; and Davis, "An Era and Generation of Civil Engagement."

12. *Examiner*, April 27, 1918, news clipping, album 5, p. 14, FMC Collection; *B'Nai B'rith Messenger*, October 11, 1918, p. 5. On the dynamics of leadership in voluntary associations, see Dumenil, *Freemasonry and American Culture*, passim and 148.

13. "Women's Work, Women's Clubs," *Los Angeles Times*, June 19, 1917, sec. 2, p. 3.

14. Brownell, "The Women's Committees," 17.

15. Although the Navy League hoped to survey women willing to do volunteer work, in May 1917 it offered its cooperation with the WCND and announced that it had reached over 2,000,000 women thus far and could enroll that number in forty states for the WCND's registration drive. "Women to Unify Work for Nation," *Indianapolis Star*, May 20, 1917, 4.

16. Brownell, "The Women's Committees," 68–72. For more on the iconography of war, see Chapter 5.

17. "What the Government Expects of Women to Help End War," *New Orleans Times-Picayune*, October 17, 1917, p. 13; Breen, "Southern Women in the War," 262.

18. Damico, "The Rush to the Colors"; "September 10th Is Named Second Day for Registration," *Montgomery Advertiser*, August 25, 1917, p. 3. On the link between the suffrage campaign and the registration drive, see Unsel, "Woman's Hour," 297–300.

19. "Women Flock to War Aid," *Kansas City Star*, July 29, 1917, p. 1.

20. "Military Air about Women's Registration," *Belleville News Democrat*, November 11, 1917, p. 1; "Will Enroll Ohio Women in War Aid," *Cleveland Plain Dealer*, May 5, 1917, p. 5; "20,000 Wyoming Women Arranging to Go to Registration Places Tomorrow," *Cleveland Plain Dealer*, July 16, 1917, p. 11.

21. Brownell, "The Women's Committees," 169–70.

22. "Patriotism Shown in All Precincts," *New Orleans Times-Picayune*, October 18, 1917, p. 14.

23. Ladd-Taylor, *Mother-Work*, 3–11; Baker, "The Domestication of Politics"; Koven and Michel, *Mothers of a New World*; Muncy, *Creating a Female Dominion*.

24. Gullett, "Women Progressives and the Politics of Americanization."

25. "National Society, Daughters of the American Revolution," *Montgomery Advertiser*, December 2, 1917, p. 22.

26. Brownell, "The Women's Committees," 119–20, 133–34.

27. "The Department of Americanization," box 18, Women's Committee Records; "Report of the Women's State Council of Defense of California, from June 1, 1917, to January 1, 1919" (n.d.), 42, box 956, WCND Records.

28. "The Department of Americanization," box 18, Women's Committee Records.

29. "Report, Women's Committee of the State Council of Defense of California from June 1, 1917, to January 1, 1919," 111. See Kennedy, *Disloyal Mothers and Scurrilous Citizens*, 14–15. For more on California women and Americanization, see Van Nuys, *Americanizing*

the West, 33–69; and Gullett, "Women Progressives and the Politics of Americanization." Unsel, in "Woman's Hour," 300–303, argues that WCND Americanization activities also echoed the suffrage movement's interest in countering perceived resistance to suffrage on the part of immigrant communities.

30. Lehrer, *Origins of Protective Labor Legislation*.

31. Kessler-Harris, *Out to Work*, 188.

32. "Committee on Women in Industry of the Advisory Commission of the Council of National Defense"; Blackwell, "The Battle Line—From France to Factory," *Woman's Journal* 22 (1918): 436; "Report of the Committee on Industrial Standards of the Committee on Women in Industry," typescript, September 6, 1917, box 63, van Kleeck Papers.

33. These included Illinois, Rhode Island, New York, Wisconsin, Massachusetts, and Michigan. Brownell, "The Women's Committees," 34.

34. "War Opens New Fields of Work for Women," *Chicago Tribune*, October 14, 1917, VII, p. 5.

35. "Publicity Posters and Exhibition Panels Are Essential to the Success of Your Children's Year Campaign," box 2, WWI Manuscripts.

36. Peixotto, "The Children's Year," 260. For further descriptions of Children's Year, see Rude, "The Children's Year Campaign," 346–51; and Unsel, "Woman's Hour," 258–63.

37. "Suggestions for State or Local Communities," undated typescript, p. 3, Central File 1914–20, box 141, Children's Bureau Records. For a summary of Children's Year activities, see Rude, "The Children's Year Campaign."

38. "County Council of Defense for Los Angeles County, September 27, 1918," doc 1363 H, box 83, Correspondence, Los Angeles County Board of Supervisors, Los Angeles County Archives; "Saving the Babies as War Winning Measure," *Los Angeles Times*, September 1, 1918, section 2, p. 3; "Report of the Women's Committee of the State Council of Defense of California from June 1, 1917, to January 1, 1919," 107.

39. Peixotto, "The Children's Year," 257. For the prewar backdrop of the Children's Bureau's cooperation with women's clubs and organizations, see also Lindenmeyer, *A Right to Childhood*, 71–74; and Muncy, *Creating a Female Dominion*, 38–65.

40. Westbrook, "Fighting for the American Family," 198. See also Lipsitz, "Dilemmas of Beset Nationhood." For the importance of the family metaphor in British propaganda, see Gullace, "Sexual Violence and Family Honor." For World War I posters, see James, *Picture This*; Rawls, *Wake Up, America*; and Shover, "Roles and Images of Women."

41. For other examples of the ways in which women countered the masculine definition of citizenship during wartime, see Kerber, *No Constitutional Right to Be Ladies*, 221–302; and Kimberly Jensen, *Mobilizing Minerva*, 36–59. Jensen provides a fascinating discussion of women who organized home defense groups and literally took up arms in defense of their communities.

42. On the way in which the continued importance of the theme of motherhood narrowly channeled their efforts, see Kennedy, *Disloyal Mothers and Scurrilous Citizens*, 1–17; and Higonnet and Higonnet, "The Double Helix," 31–50.

43. For a brief account of the YWCA, see Scott, *Natural Allies*, 104–10. Robertson's *Christian Sisterhood*, 45–70, offers a chapter on the YWCA during World War I. In addition to describing the organization's war activities, the chapter analyzes the way in

which the war emergency enabled black women to circumvent local resistance to African American YWCA branches in many areas.

44. "For 'United America' Division for Foreign Born Women, War Work Council of the Y.W.C.A. [1918]," box 709, YWCA of the USA Records; *California State Conference Social Agencies Bulletin* 2 (September 1918): 43; "Report of Miss Crawford, Associate Executive, Division on Work for Foreign-Born Women, War Work Council, YWCA, August to October 1918," typescript, file 17, box 70, YWCA of the USA Records.

45. Excerpted from "Report Sent to the National Council of Women," typescript, January 1932, p. 4, file 1, box 702, YWCA of the USA Records.

46. "An Industrial Hostess House," *War Work Bulletin* 36 (August 2, 1918): 1, file 12, box 710, YWCA of the USA Records.

47. Estella T. Weeks, "The Young Women's Christian Association and the Woman Worker," unpublished typescript, New York, 1919, 14–15, box 705, folder 4, YWCA of the USA Records.

48. Ibid., 7, 5.

49. Emily Rosenberg, *Spreading the American Dream*, 104–10. For a general discussion of the campaign against prostitution, see Brandt, *No Magic Bullet*, 52–95; Pivar, "Cleansing the Nation"; Bristow, *Making Men Moral*; Alexander, *The "Girl Problem"*; Odem, *Delinquent Daughters*, 121–27; and Abrams, "Guardians of Virtue." On the theme of "cheap amusements" and charity girls, see Peiss, *Cheap Amusements*; and Clement, *Love for Sale*.

50. For local studies, see Judson, "Leisure Is a Foe to Any Man"; Shah, "Against Their Own Weakness"; and Hickey, "Waging War on 'Loose Living Hotels.'"

51. Bristow, *Making Men Moral*; Reilly, "A Perilous Venture for Democracy"; Keire, *For Business and Pleasure*.

52. Clement, *Love for Sale*, 144–76.

53. "Department of Health and Recreation, National Conference of the Woman's Committee, May 13, 14, 15, 1918," typescript, p. 11, box 531, WCND Records. Odem discusses the comparative harshness of the CTCA programs, as well as the federal funding for reformatories and houses of detention for wayward girls. Odem, *Delinquent Daughters*, 124–26. The punitive treatment meted out by the CTCA led to protest on the part of many women reformers, most notably Maude Miner, who chaired the CTCA's Committee on Protective Work for Girls. Brandt, *No Magic Bullet*, 86.

54. "Report of the Young Women's Christian Association in California for the Year 1917–1918," p. 4. On YWCA activities generally, see copies of the *War Work Bulletin*, for example, Special Number, September 10, 1918, and August 30, 1918.

55. Hopkins, "Conserving Woman Power in War Time," 171.

56. Brandt, *No Magic Bullet*, 71. On the YWCA activity, see *Los Angeles Tribune*, October 12, 1917, news clipping, YWCA News Clippings, 1915–17, box 16-14, YWCA of LA; "What the War Work Council of the Young Women's Christian Association Is Doing" (n.d.), box 4, WWI Manuscripts; and *Los Angeles Times*, August 3, 1917.

57. War Work Council Minutes, typescript, October 22, 1918, p. 2, file 5, box 705, YWCA of the USA Records; "Report of the Young Women's Christian Association in California for the Year 1917–1918," p. 5, box 4, Women's Committee Records; Odem, *Delinquent Daughters*, 24; Clement, *Love for Sale*, 170–76.

58. "Secretaries' Report of Activities of Office for Week of August 1 to 8, 1919," box 1, Women's Committee Records.

59. Elizabeth Putnam Gordon, *Women Torch-Bearers*, 121; Woman's Christian Temperance Union of Indiana, *Forty-fourth Annual Report*, 36.

60. On general accounts of the WCTU, see Pegram, *Battling Demon Rum*; Schiffner, "Continuing to 'Do Everything,'" 132–33; and Tyler, *Where Prayer and Purpose Meet*.

61. On the background of women pacifists in Los Angeles, see Katz, *Dual Commitments*, 493–98.

62. Garbutt, *Victories of Four Decades*, 46, 75, 105, 142. See also "Pacifist and Pickets Condemned by WCTU," *Los Angeles Times*, December 20, 1917, section 2, p. 1.

63. Elizabeth Putnam Gordon, *Women Torch-Bearers*, 118.

64. "Brief Record of the War Service of the Woman's Christian Temperance Union of Southern California" (1919?), typescript, box 5, WWI Manuscripts.

65. Ibid., p. 2; Elizabeth Putnam Gordon, *Women Torch-Bearers*, 4; Garbutt, *Victories of Four Decades*, 142.

66. Zeiger, "She Didn't Raise Her Boy to Be a Slacker."

67. The starting place for black women in World War I is Nikki Brown, *Private Politics and Public Voices*. See also Nikki Brown, "Your Patriotism Is of the Purest Quality."

68. Brownell, "The Women's Committees," 91; Gilmore, *Gender and Jim Crow*, 195–202.

69. "Mrs. Montgomery on Honor Roll," *Chicago Defender*, October 26, 1918, p. 10; "Red Cross Workers Giving Excellent Help," *Chicago Defender*, March 30, 1918, p. 5.

70. Breen, "Black Women and the Great War," 424; Nikki Brown, *Private Politics and Public Voices*, 35. A particular source of resentment was the Red Cross refusal to allow African American nurses to work within its organization. See Chapter 1.

71. Nikki Brown, *Private Politics and Public Voices*, 31.

72. Breen, "Southern Women in the War," 245.

73. Nikki Brown, *Private Politics and Public Voices*, 49–50.

74. Breen, "Black Women and the Great War," 428.

75. Brownell, "The Women's Committees," 89–90; "Report of City Federation of Colored Women's Clubs of Jacksonville, Florida," June 1917, Eartha M. White Collection, Florida Heritage On-Line Collection; Nikki Brown, *Private Politics and Public Voices*, 49–50.

76. Dunbar-Nelson, "Negro Women in War Work."

77. Nikki Brown, "Your Patriotism Is of the Purest Quality," 191.

78. On the YWCA and African American women, see Robertson, *Christian Sisterhood*; and Adrienne Lash Jones, "Struggle among Saints."

79. In the words of Adrienne Lash Jones, "Struggle among Saints," 177, "in spite of its flawed racial policies, the YWCA provided a structure whereby the women of the talented tenth could finally thrive."

80. Mrs. Mary B. Talbert to All State Presidents & Heads of Departments of the N.A.C.W., August 14, 1917, CC file, box 512, WCND Records.

81. Olcott, *The Work of Colored Women*, 15, 25; Dunbar-Nelson, "Negro Women in War Work," 4.

82. Robertson, *Christian Sisterhood*, 54.

83. Olcott, *The Work of Colored Women*, 44.

84. Ibid., 52–53.

85. Ibid., 47, 49, 52–53, 61, 72.

86. Browder, "Working Out Their Economic Problems Together."

87. Olcott, *The Work of Colored Women*, 54–55, 113, 122.

88. Ibid., 119–20, 59, 16.

89. Terrell, as quoted in Nikki Brown, "Your Patriotism Is of the Purest Quality," 61, 228.

90. Terrell, *A Colored Woman in a White World*, 322.

91. Ibid., 327.

92. Kimberly Jensen has detailed the way in which women medical professionals, as well as women organized to bear arms in "home defense" groups, organized to contribute to the war effort and did so in gendered ways that sought to expand women's claims to citizenship and suffrage. Kimberly Jensen, *Mobilizing Minerva*, 36–59.

93. American Red Cross, *The Work of the American Red Cross*, 13.

94. "The Greatest Mother," http://www.ww1propaganda.com/ww1-poster/greatest-mother-world-red-cross-christmas-roll-call-dec-16-23rd.

95. Throughout the United States, there were 70,000 of these canteens, staffed by almost 800 women. See Davison, *The American Red Cross in the Great War*, 39.

96. "Great Pageant Drives Home Message of the Red Cross," *Los Angeles Times*, May 19, 1918, section 2, pp. 1, 7.

97. "Women's Work and Women's Clubs," *Los Angeles Times*, December 16, 1917, section 3, p. 4; *Catholic Woman's Club Bulletin* 1 (November 1918): 13.

98. *Y.W.C.A. Bulletin War Work Council* 3 (September 28, 1917): 1; "American Red Cross Canteeners in the Army of Humanity," *Chicago Defender*, November 2, 1918, p. 1; "History of Japanese War Work in Los Angeles, 1917–1918," typescript, box 11, War History Committee Records.

99. American Red Cross, Pittsburgh Chapter, *American Red Cross: A History of the Activities of the Chapter*, 112–245.

100. Norton, *Liberty's Daughters*, 178–87.

101. Macdonald, *No Idle Hands*, 215.

102. Steinson, *American Women's Activism*, 262. Katherine Anthony, a member of the Woman's Peace Party, who argued that volunteer knitting was misplaced patriotism that usurped jobs from working women, made the comment.

103. "Red Cross Activities," *Los Angeles Times*, November 21, 1917, section 2, p. 8.

104. Virginia Hunt, "Pasadena Chapter Woman's Section of the Navy League of the United States from May 5, 1917, to October 5, 1917," file 20, box 15, Hunt Collection; undated news clipping from the *Pasadena Star News*, file 38, box 15, ibid.

105. Hunt to Mr. Arthur Admun, Secretary, Navy League of the United States, October 31, 1917, file 62, box 15, ibid.

106. "Report of Meeting of Board of Directors of the Army and Navy League [Pasadena, Women's Section]," October 3, 1918, file 34, box 15, ibid.

107. Dulles, *The American Red Cross*, 145, 165; Ruth Walrad, "The History of the American Red Cross," typescript, ARC; Hickel, "War, Region, and Social Welfare."

108. Dulles, *The American Red Cross*, 67; Porter Lee, "Training for the Home Service of the Red Cross," 82–83; Pickett, *The American National Red Cross*, 65; "The First Line Here at Home: What the American Red Cross Is Doing along Its Entire Length," *Ladies' Home Journal*, July 1918, 4.

109. As cited in Kennedy, *Over Here*, 118.

110. "Hoover's Plans Told to Women," *Los Angeles Times*, June 20, 1917, section 1, p. 7; "To the Volunteer Enlistment Sergeant," from Ralph P. Merritt, U.S. Food Conservation Army, California Division, 1917, box 14, Women's Committee Records. Marsha Gordon makes a similar point about the militarized language of food conservation campaigns, in "Onward Kitchen Soldiers." In *For Home and Country*, Celia Malone Kingsbury offers extensive analysis of both government propaganda and media promotion of the food conservation drive. She emphasizes the ways in which food conservation promoted a sense of women's ultimately domestic role in war mobilization. See chap. 1, "Food Will Win the War."

111. Alice H. Wood, Executive Secretary, Woman's Committee, CND, to "state Chairmen," June 15, 1917, box 13, Women's Committee Records.

112. *War Activities of the Women's Committee, Los Angeles City Unit of the Council of National Defense, 1917–1918*; Reports of State and Local Councils, Council of National Defense, Field Division, box 956, WCND Records.

113. California Women's Committee of the Councils of State and National Defense, typescript report, December 17, 1917, box 7, Women's Committee Records.

114. "War Winning Women," *Ladies' Home Journal*, March 1918, 33.

115. As cited in Nikki Brown, "Your Patriotism Is of the Purest Quality," 197.

116. Breen, "Black Women and the Great War," 437.

117. "Readily Sign Food Pledge," *Los Angeles Times*, November 1, 1917, section 1, p. 11; *War Activities of the Women's Committee*, p. 6; Mullendore, *History of the United States Food Administration*, 87.

118. "Americans Urged to Save Wheat," *Wilkes-Barre Record*, January 12, 1918, p. 4. Christopher Capozzola has written about the fine line between voluntarism and coercion, in "The Only Badge Needed Is Your Patriotic Fervor."

119. Brownell, "The Women's Committees," 75–79.

120. Blair, *The Woman's Committee*, 59.

121. Ibid., 35.

122. Mrs. Herbert Cable to Ann Howard Shaw, December 31, 1918, box 13, Women's Committee Records.

Chapter 3

1. Elizabeth Ashe to A.G., May 1, 1918, in Ashe, *Intimate Letters*, 86.

2. The definitive work on American women abroad in World War I is Zeiger, *In Uncle Sam's Service*; see also Cobbs, *The Hello Girls*; Schneider and Schneider, *Into the Breach*; Kimberly Jensen, *Mobilizing Minerva*; and Gavin, *American Women in World War I*.

3. Putnam, *On Duty and Off*, 57.

4. Chuppa-Cornell, "The U.S. Women's Motor Corps in France," 466.

5. Mitchell, "Back of the Front," 36.

6. Solomon, *In the Company of Educated Women*, 115–40. On social work, see Lubove, *The Professional Altruist*, 80–84; Muncy, *Creating a Female Dominion*, 66–92; Kunzel, *Fallen Women*, 36–48; and Leiby, *A History of Social Welfare*, 111–62. "Between 1890 and 1910, the number of professional social workers grew from 1,000 to 30,000, 80 percent of whom were women." Abrams, "Guardians of Virtue," 442. When Stanford University organized its relief group, newspaper reportage emphasized that they were highly trained, well-educated women. In September 1918, the *Vassar Miscellany News* reported in detail on the backgrounds of the eleven women who formed the Vassar Relief Unit. One was a nurse. The rest had social work or teaching experience. Most could also drive a car and were fluent in French. The Barnard unit worked near the former Hindenberg Line; the Vassar women focused on Verdun refugees; and the Wellesley Unit was at Château-Thierry, with a second one at Constantinople. *Vassar Miscellany News* 3 (September 28, 1918): 1–4. On the Wellesley women, see "The Overseas Work of the Wellesley College Relief Units," *Wellesley College Bulletin* (July 1919); and the introduction to Wellesley College's archival holdings at http://www.ourstory.info/library/2-ww1/Wellesley.html.

7. The Wellesley Unit went to France in the summer of 1918, but the women served as a group for only three months before being dispersed to other entities. They re-formed after the war to continue their work in reconstruction.

8. "Editorial," *Smith College Monthly* 52 (October 1918): 49; Dalby, *An Irrepressible Crew*, 10.

9. Clout, *After the Ruins*, 79–84. The project was modeled on the earlier work of Morgan's group in Aisne, which had charge of the reconstruction of over sixty villages. Morgan's committee was the Comité Américain pour la France Dévastée, which was a successor to AFFW.

10. Dalby, *An Irrepressible Crew*, 16.

11. "Keep the Home Fires Burning in the Zone of Ruin," *Cleveland Plain Dealer*, April 28, 1918, p. 44.

12. Gaines, *Ladies of Grécourt*, 54.

13. Dalby, *An Irrepressible Crew*, 38; Committee for Public Information, "War Work of Women in Colleges," 12.

14. Dalby, *An Irrepressible Crew*, 23, 50–51.

15. History 355, Smith College, "Biographical Sketches," courtesy of Jennifer Hall-Witt.

16. "Women Cool under Fire," *Forth Worth Star-Telegram*, April 6, 1918, p. 7.

17. Dalby, *An Irrepressible Crew*, 69.

18. Gaines, *Ladies of Grécourt*, 172.

19. McGuire, "Commercial Philanthropy as Panacea," 29, unpublished article, courtesy of the author. McGuire argues that the shops and distribution of goods were the most crucial part of the reconstruction work. On the Americanizing goal, see Rodgers, *Atlantic Crossings*, 367–71.

20. Kernodle, *The Red Cross Nurse in Action*, 150–88.

21. Irwin, *Making the World Safe*, 97. For a valuable article on Red Cross volunteers, see Nancy O'Brien Wagner's account of Minnesota women, "Red Cross Women in France during World War I," *Minnesota History* 63 (Spring 2002): 25–85.

22. Ware, *Partner and I*, 75.

23. Typescript, "Personnel Bureau of Refugees South Intermediate Zone on August 26, 1918," and correspondence, "Well Billy," March 1, 1918, and "Dear Family," April 7, 1918, Dewson Papers.

24. Ware, *Partner and I*, 80.

25. Ibid., 80.

26. Charlotte Bannon to Dear Mother, June 2, 1918, and Charlotte Bannon to my dear Leona, August 11, 1918, Bannon Papers.

27. For a discussion of ARC workers' expectations that they could help shape France's children's health programs, see Irwin, *Making the World Safe*, 125–35.

28. Elizabeth Ashe to E.E.S., December 1, 1917, in Ashe, *Intimate Letters*, 53; Elizabeth Ashe to A.G., February 2, 1918, in ibid., 62–63. For a further discussion of the Red Cross's work with children in France and Ashe's contribution, see Marian Moser Jones, *The American Red Cross*, 168–70.

29. Elizabeth Ashe to A.G., July 21, 1918, in Ashe, *Intimate Letters*, 111.

30. Kernodle, *The Red Cross Nurse in Action*, 171.

31. Ware, *Partner and I*, 76; Kernodle, *The Red Cross Nurse in Action*, 176–78.

32. "Y.W.C.A. Takes Up Foreign War Work," *Duluth News-Tribune*, September 2, 1917, section 4, p. 4.

33. "War Work," typescript, p. 5, box 702, YWCA of the USA Records.

34. Henrietta Roelofs, "The Military Value of the Association in France," *YWCA Association Monthly* 12 (September 1918): 317; YWCA Forges Ahead on Work in France," *Chicago Daily Tribune*, August 23, 1918, p. 6.

35. Kudlick, "Fighting the Internal and External Enemies," 135–36.

36. "War Work," typescript, p. 5, box 702, YWCA of the USA Records.

37. Schneider and Schneider note that "by war's end, the YWCA estimate, they were serving 2,000 French, British, and American women in France, with eighteen hostess houses for soldiers, American women, and war brides; fifteen Signal Corps houses for 'hello girls'; three Army Service Corps centers, forty-four nurses' clubs; thirty-one *foyers* for Frenchwomen; six recreation centers; five summer camps; a summer conference; an emergency training school; five refuges for port and transport workers; four cemetery huts where they offered lodgings, food, and kindness to visitors to remote cemeteries; and three British/American cooperative undertakings." Schneider and Schneider, *Into the Breach*, 144.

38. Bannan, "Management by Women," 108–14.

39. "YWCA Agents Tell of Work in France," *New York Times*, November 5, 1917, p. 15.

40. "War Work Girls in Paris," *Augusta Chronicle*, September 8, 1918, p. 3.

41. For a discussion of canteen workers, see Zeiger, *In Uncle Sam's Service*, 51–76.

42. Brandt, *No Magic Bullet*, 115; Reilly, "A Perilous Venture for Democracy," 223–55.

43. Douglas, *The Feminization of American Culture*.

44. [American Young Men's Christian Association], *Service with Fighting Men*, 1:258, 2:504–6. On college women's canteen service, see *Intercollegiate Community Service Quarterly* 3 (1918): 9.

45. [American Young Men's Christian Association], *Service with Fighting Men*, 2:142.

46. Frances J. Gulick, "Y Girl," *American Legion Monthly* 8 (February 1930): 24–25.

47. Violet H. Bennet to Mrs. Drexel, undated, Miscellaneous Reports—Women Secretaries, 1918–19, YMCA of the USA Records.

48. Baldwin, *Canteening Overseas*, 76.

49. On the way in which some women did feel sexually threatened, see Zeiger, *In Uncle Sam's Service*, 65.

50. Frances J. Gulick to Dear Family, April 6, 1918, YMCA of the USA Records. Parts of Gulick's letter appeared in newspapers, but this section apparently did not appear in print. See "What an American Woman Does in France," *Denver Post*, October 27, 1918, p. 51, for an edited version of Gulick's letter.

51. Lucy Lester to My dear Miss W, April 22 [1918], YMCA of the USA Records.

52. Baldwin, *Canteening Overseas*, 48; Gulick, "Y Girl"; Noyes, *My A.E.F.*, 6.

53. "Y.M.C.A. in Thick of Fight during St. Mihiel Battle," *Cobb County Times*, October 17, 1918, p. 8; Gavin, *American Women in World War I*, 134–35.

54. Morse, *The Uncensored Letters of a Canteen Girl*, 102; Baldwin, *Canteening Overseas*, 134, 139.

55. Edith Stedman to Dearest Marj, March 10 [1918], and Edith Stedman to Marj, "Good Friday" [1918], box 1, Stedman Papers.

56. Hunton and Johnson, *Two Colored Women*, 6.

57. Ellis, *Race, War, and Surveillance*, 96; Chandler, "That Biting, Stinging Thing"; Chandler, "Addie Hunton."

58. Nikki Brown, "Your Patriotism Is of the Purest Quality," 153, points out that there were 200,000, not 150,000, black troops.

59. Hunton and Johnson, *Two Colored Women*, 16, 80, 20.

60. Ibid.

61. Quoted in Zeiger, *In Uncle Sam's Service*, 78.

62. Grayzel, *Women's Identities at War*, 199–200.

63. "WAACS Relieve 500 American Fighting Men," *Pueblo Chieftain*, August 13, 1918, p. 4; "Paris Jobs Not Open to Girls," *Oregonian*, October 29, 1918, p. 6. On tensions among policy makers as well as an excellent discussion of the bureaucratization of war, see Zeiger, *In Uncle Sam's Service*, 85–103.

64. Christides, "Women Veterans of the Great War." See also Christides's web page, http://www.jungsoul.com/Hello-Girls.html; Frahm, "The Hello Girls"; and Zeiger, *In Uncle Sam's Service*, 3–83.

65. Frahm, "The Hello Girls," 275–84.

66. Zeiger, *In Uncle Sam's Service*, 79; Frahm, "The Hello Girls," 284.

67. "With American Hello Girls in France," *Baltimore American*, September 29, 1918, p. 12; Christides, "Women Veterans of the Great War," 94.

68. Zeiger, *In Uncle Sam's Service*, 98; Schneider and Schneider, *Into the Breach*, 185.

69. See, for example, "Hello Girls Title Passed," *Cleveland Plain Dealer*, September 9, 1918, p. 4.

70. "California Girls in Signal Corps," *Riverside (Calif.) Daily Press*, July 15, 1918, p. 4.

71. Zeiger, *In Uncle Sam's Service*, 78. Frances Barbour, who became the chief operator, noted that the YWCA women did not have authority over the Signal Corps women; the chief operator did. She indicated that the rules were not terribly restrictive, somewhat

like those at a liberal women's college. Typescript, "Introduction" [1937], part of draft for an article for an AT&T publication, Barbour Papers.

72. Schneider and Schneider, *Into the Breach*, 182.

73. Kimberly Jensen, *Mobilizing Minerva*, 77–97; More, "A Certain Restless Ambition."

74. Graf, "With High Hopes," 3.

75. Augusta Williams to Mrs. [Christina] Baker, series of letters, beginning June 5, 1918, Radcliffe in France.

76. "Add a Fourteenth Star to the Suffrage Service Flag," *Woman Citizen* 2 (February 2, 1918): 195.

77. As quoted in Kimberly Jensen, *Mobilizing Minerva*, 102. Lovejoy embarked on a fund-raising speaking tour in which she emphasized German atrocities against women. See, for example, "Columbus Men Shed Tears as Mrs. Esther Lovejoy Tells of Atrocities of German Fiends," *Columbus Ledger*, April 10, 1918, p. 3. For similar reporting, see "Frightful Atrocities upon French Girls, Told by Clubwoman," *New Orleans Item*, May 8, 1918, p. 7; and "American Women Doctors in France," *Lexington Herald*, May 4, 1918, p. 4.

78. Kimberly Jensen, *Mobilizing Minerva*, 107.

79. Lewenson, *Taking Charge*, 68, 217–64; Kimberly Jensen, *Mobilizing Minerva*, 121.

80. Zeiger, *In Uncle Sam's Service*, 108.

81. Kimberly Jensen, *Mobilizing Minerva*, 120.

82. Ibid., 123, 134–41.

83. Zeiger, *In Uncle Sam's Service*, 115.

84. Dock, *History of American Red Cross Nursing*, 661.

85. Stimson, *Finding Themselves*, 134; Bulovsky, "Behind the Trenches," 43.

86. Murphy, "If Only I Shall Have the Right Stuff," 349.

87. Zeiger, *In Uncle Sam's Service*, 105.

88. Schneider and Schneider, *Into the Breach*, 99.

89. Ibid., 207.

90. Ibid., 211.

91. Dorr, *A Woman at Fifty*, 380–85.

92. For an annotated autobiography of Doty, see Rinehart, *One Woman Determined to Make a Difference*.

93. Ishbel Ross, *Ladies of the Press*, 581–83; Bradley, *Women and the Press*, 146–47.

94. "Brave Bessie Beatty," *Baltimore American*, November 14, 1917, p. 2.

95. Stockdale, "My Death for the Motherland Is Happiness," 8.

96. *San Francisco Bulletin*, November 21, 1917.

97. Madeleine Z. Doty, "Women Who Would A-Soldiering Go," *World Outlook* 4 (September 1918): 80.

98. Dorr, *A Woman at Fifty*, 367–68.

99. For a discussion of the way in which American suffragists drew parallels between their struggles and the impact of the Russian Revolution on Russian women, see Mickenberg, "Suffragettes and Soviets."

100. *Chicago Evening Post*, 1918, box 10, Occidental College Special Collections. Cited in Witz, "Reporting on the 'New Woman.'"

101. Charlotte Bannon to My dear Mother, June 2, 1918, Bannon Papers. On American soldiers' perceptions of war, see Kennedy, *Over Here*, 179–90, 212–17.

102. Janis, *The Big Show*, 72–73.

103. *A Red Triangle Girl in France*, 69–70.

104. Putnam, *On Duty and Off*, 94.

105. Molly Dewson to Dear Family, April 7, 1918, Dewson Papers.

106. Louise Barbour to mother, November 24, 1918, Barbour Papers. For soldiers as tourists, see Kennedy, *Over Here*, 206–8.

107. Christides, "Women Veterans of the Great War"; Elsie Mead to Caroline, September 19 [1918], YMCA of the USA Records.

108. Mrs. Mead, Women's Bureau, to Women Workers of the Y.M.C.A., January 13, 1919, YMCA of the USA Records. As to Signal Corps women, Elizabeth Cobbs notes that they did manage to enjoy themselves at social events with the opposite sex and that several marriages resulted from their overseas duty. Cobbs, *The Hello Girls*.

109. "U.S. Army Girls Doing Good Work," *Seattle Times*, November 10, 1918, p. 34.

110. Kilander, "Over There with the YMCA," 7. This contains extracts from the diary of Edith K. O. Clark.

111. Madeleine Z. Doty, "How I Came to Petrograd," *Good Housekeeping*, June 1918, 42–43.

112. Peterson, *Dorothy S. Ainsworth*, 68, 77.

113. We can piece together other stories as well. Of the total of forty-five women in the Smith Relief Unit, we know the career and marriage paths of forty of them. Of these, 65 percent had careers, with nine of them following social work, five becoming educators, and the rest holding a variety of other jobs. Although two of these women were married, most of the married women (35 percent) did not work after marriage. For comparison, from the Smith class of 1911, only 46 percent pursued careers. Unfortunately, we cannot assume that the war experience itself was causal, as the women who went abroad were already at least twenty-five and were perhaps already self-selected as women whose focus was not primarily on marriage and home. Compiled from the Smith College *Alumnae Bulletin*.

114. "The Overseas Women," *Iowa City Press-Citizen*, January 27, 1922, p. 13. See also "Seattle Unit Seeking a Banner," *Seattle Daily Times*, August 21, 1922, p. 8, for accounts of that city's unit of the Service League; and "Service League to Keep Present Chief in Office," *Omaha World Herald*, June 29, 1926, 1.

115. McIvor-Tyndall, "Women and Future National Welfare," 25.

116. American nurse Ellen La Motte, who nursed French soldiers before the United States entered the war, wrote a scathing account of "the human wreckage of the battlefield," subtitling her 1916 book *The Backwash of War*. Besides detailing the grim physical results of battle, she challenged the very concept of military valor and heroism. Her depiction was so disturbing that, once the United States joined the conflict, her book was banned. Tylee, *The Great War and Women's Consciousness*, 94–98.

117. Mary Lee, *It's a Great War*, 520.

118. Ibid., 563.

119. Handwritten notes for lectures include a typescript of the "Surgeon General's Report and stds," Mary Lee to Mr. Stanley U. North, November 1930, box 31, folder 10, Lee Papers. The letter details Raymond B. Fosdick's report to the secretary of war on welfare organizations to back up her critique of YMCA men. Typescript of questions

and answers concerning her claims in the book about the YMCA, sexual disease, and incompetence in the Air Service, Andover, December 15, 1930, box 31, folder 10, Lee Papers.

120. Mrs. James S. Brown, Jr., to Mary Lee, December 28, 1929, box 32, folder 9, Lee Papers; Katharine Gay to Mary Lee, November 11, 1929, box 33, Lee Papers.

Chapter 4

1. "Women of Nation Are Ready to Don Overalls and Replace Men in Various Occupations," *Grand Rapids Press*, May 9, 1917, p. 19.

2. Foner, *Women and the American Labor Movement*, 96. The most significant full-length studies of American women workers in World War I are Greenwald, *Women, War, and Work*; Carrie Brown, *Rosie's Mom*, 69–94; and Davidson, "Women and the Railroad."

3. DuBois and Dumenil, *Through Women's Eyes*, Appendix A-18. Hill, in *Women in Gainful Occupations*, notes that women's agricultural labor was reported inconsistently in the early twentieth-century censuses. A more reliable way of judging changes is to look at figures for women in nonagricultural work. For this group, in 1900, 17.3 percent of American women worked; in 1910, 20.7 percent worked; and in 1920, 21.3 percent of American women worked.

4. The 1900 census data reports that 3.1 percent of native-born white married women, 3 percent of foreign-born, and 26 percent of black women worked. U.S. Bureau of the Census, *Statistics of Women at Work*, 15.

5. U.S. Bureau of the Census, *Thirteenth Census of the United States: 1910 Report on Occupations*, Table 24, p. 67.

6. Amott and Matthaei, *Race, Gender, and Work*, 158; Kessler-Harris, *Out to Work*, 140, 145; Blackwelder, *Now Hiring*, 65.

7. Camarillo, *Chicanos in a Changing Society*, 221; Evelyn Nakano Glenn, "Racial Ethnic Women's Labor," 93–95; Chan, *Asian Americans*.

8. For an overview on working women in this era, see Kessler-Harris, *Out to Work*, 46–216; Tentler, *Wage-Earning Women*; Blackwelder, *Now Hiring*, 11–35; Peiss, *Cheap Amusements*; Meyerowitz, *Women Adrift*; and Jacqueline Jones, *Labor of Love, Labor of Sorrow*, 79–151.

9. On prewar strikes, see Tax, *The Rising of the Women*. On the WTUL, see Dye, *As Equals and as Sisters*; and Payne, *Reform, Labor, and Feminism*. On the uprising of women, see the Introduction.

10. Norwood, *Labor's Flaming Youth*, 91–155.

11. Davies, *Woman's Place Is at the Typewriter*, 55–78. In 1900, 41 percent of women clerical workers were white and native-born of native-born families, 48 percent were native-born with foreign parents, and 11 percent were foreign-born. Less than 1 percent were African American. Weiner, *From Working Girl to Working Mother*, 28; Norwood, *Labor's Flaming Youth*, 91–155; Strom, *Beyond the Typewriter*, 188.

12. Statistical Abstracts of the United States, 1920 (Washington, D.C., 1921), p. 282, Table 192.

13. Solomon, *In the Company of Educated Women*, 127.

14. Hill, *Women in Gainful Occupations*, 117.

15. Grayzel, *Women and the First World War*, 28–35.

16. Newkirk, “Study of a Single Philadelphia Office,” 10.

17. Wolfe and Olson, “War-Time Industrial Employment of Women,” 645.

18. A postwar analysis declared that the war saw a “remarkable apathy with regard to the training of women for industrial life.” See ibid.

19. Foner, *Women and the American Labor Movement*, 65–67; Norwood, *Labor's Flaming Youth*, 156.

20. McCartin, *Labor's Great War*, 112, 143.

21. Foner, *Women and the American Labor Movement*, 80–98.

22. Hine, *Hine Sight*, 37–47.

23. Hunter, *To 'Joy My Freedom*, 228–32.

24. Hickel, “War, Region, and Social Welfare,” 1387–89.

25. Giddings, *When and Where I Enter*, 143. On the Great Migration, see Hunter, *To 'Joy My Freedom*; Grossman, *Land of Hope*; and Marks, *Farewell—We're Good and Gone*.

26. Giddings, *When and Where I Enter*, 141.

27. Greenwald, *Women, War, and Work*, 24. See also Haynes, “Two Million Negro Women at Work,” 64.

28. “Refused Employment in the Charleston Navy,” *Chicago Defender*, May 19, 1917, p. 1; Lau, *Democracy Rising*, 40.

29. “A New Day for the Colored Woman Worker: A Study of Colored Women in Industry in New York City,” microfilm reel 108, YWCA of the USA Records; Olcott, *The Work of Colored Women*, 80.

30. Mary Roberts Smith, “The Negro Woman as an Industrial Factor,” *Life and Labor* 8 (January 1918): 7.

31. Carrie Brown, *Rosie's Mom*, 69–94.

32. U.S. Department of Labor, Division of Negro Economics, *The Negro at Work during the World War and during Reconstruction*, 137.

33. Woollacott, *On Her Their Lives Depend*, 66–70.

34. Alice Stone Blackwell, “The Battle Line—From France to Factory,” *Woman's Journal* 22 (1918): 436. See also “Report of the Committee on Industrial Standards of the Committee on Women in Industry,” typescript, September 6, 1917, box 63, van Kleeck Papers.

35. Carrie Brown, *Rosie's Mom*, 99.

36. *Chicago Tribune*, October 14, 1917.

37. For telephone operators, see “Indorse Strike of Operators,” *Boston Herald*, February 25, 1918, p. 12; and, for cigar workers, “Eighty-Six Employees in Henry T. Offterdinger's Cigar Factory Are Involved,” *Evening Star* (Washington, D.C.), April 30, 1918, p. 13. For waitresses, see “National League Organizes Detroit Committee,” *Life and Labor* 8 (August 1918): 176.

38. “Treasury Workers Get Reduced Work Day,” *Life and Labor* 7 (August 1917): 122.

39. The women obtained a small raise of their minimum wage of forty-five cents a day. “Congress Refuses to Be ‘Coerced’ by Bureau of Engraving Women,” *Life and Labor* 8 (August 1918): 175.

40. Olive M. Sullivan, “The Women's Part in the Stockyards Organization Work,” *Life and Labor* 8 (May 1918): 102.

41. *Women's Work and War* 1 (May 1918): 1–3.

42. After the war, one report on Bridgeport munitions workers, for example, claimed that only 65 percent of the 10,000 women employees received equal pay, despite the government's policy. *Women's Work and War* 1 (December 1918): 2.

43. *Women's Work and War* 1 (March 1918): 1–3.

44. *Women's Work and War* 1 (November 1918): 1.

45. "Hour Laws Still Needed," *Springfield Republican*, July 12, 1917, p. 10.

46. "Women Street Car Conductors," *Life and Labor* 8 (June 1918): 118. A few months later, the WTUL, along with other organizations, urged the Labor Department to completely eliminate night work for women working on government contracts. "Government Calls First Conference of Trade Union Women," *Life and Labor* 8 (November 1918): 239–40.

47. Dye, *As Equals and as Sisters*, 149–50.

48. Hewes, *Women as Munition Makers*; Derickson, "Physiological Science and Scientific Management in the Progressive Era."

49. Greenwald, *Women, War, and Work*, 114.

50. "Work of the Women's Branch of the Industrial Service Section in the Chicago District from April 20, 1918, to December 13, 1918," p. 39, typescript, box 1, Folder "Chicago District," Women's Bureau Records.

51. Alchon, "Mary van Kleeck and Scientific Management," 103.

52. Van Kleeck, "Women in the Munition Industries," 114.

53. Greenwald, *Women, War, and Work*, 73.

54. Report from Industrial Committee to War Work Council, May 17, 1919, typescript, box 706, YWCA of America; Carrie Brown, *Rosie's Mom*, 112; Greenwald, *Women, War, and Work*, 75; *Woman's Journal* 3 (1918): 57.

55. Davidson, "Women and the Railroad," 62–68.

56. "League Member Called to Larger Service," *Life and Labor* 8 (August 1918): 158.

57. *Women's Work and War* 1 (August 1918): 1.

58. *First Annual Report of the Director of the Woman in Industry Service*, Washington, D.C., September 30, 1919, p. 23.

59. Carrie Brown, *Rosie's Mom*, 124.

60. "Women Railway Workers," *San Francisco Chronicle*, May 20, 1917, p. 34.

61. Muhammad, "Separate and Unsanitary," 99.

62. Ibid., 94–98.

63. See Chapter 5.

64. Davidson, "Women and the Railroad," 222.

65. Helen Ross, "Freight House, Kansas City, Mo., Santa Fe, October 17, 1918," box 10, WSS Records.

66. As quoted in Davidson, "Women and the Railroad," 230, 282.

67. As quoted in ibid., 200.

68. Florence E. Clark, "Memoranda: Baltimore, Bailey Yards," October 16, 1918, and Florence E. Clark, "Memoranda: Forewoman, B & O, Baltimore–Locust Point, Car Dept.," October 24, 1918, box 10, WSS Records.

69. Telegram from "The Girls in the Freight Office of the Ills Central Railroad" to Department of Labor, Women's Division, February 15, 1920, box 23, WSS Records.

70. Muhammad, "Separate and Unsanitary," 101.

71. Davidson, "Women and the Railroad," 280.

72. As quoted in ibid., 282.

73. As quoted in ibid., 302–13.

74. Mayme Hayes to Mr. D. E. Driscoll, December 11, 1918, Complaint No. 82, box 22, WSS Records.

75. Complaint No. 82, box 22, WSS Records.

76. Complaint No. 59, box 22, WSS Records.

77. Ibid.

78. "The Conductorette," *Pueblo Chieftain*, July 5, 1918, p. 6.

79. "Good Morning, Miss Conductoret," *Cleveland Plain Dealer*, August 24, 1918, p. 9.

80. As quoted in Triece, "Framing Miss-Conduct," 204.

81. As quoted in ibid., 207. See also "Women Conductors in New York," *Electric Railway Journal* 51 (1918): 1006–10.

82. Benson, "Searching for the Antecedents of Affirmative Action."

83. Quoted in Greenwald, *Women, War, and Work*, 155.

84. Goldmark, "Woman Conductors," 369.

85. "U.S. War Labor Board Takes Hand in Montgomery Traction Strike," *Montgomery Adviser*, August 19, 1918, p. 1.

86. As quoted in Triece, "Framing Miss-Conduct," 204.

87. "Union Men Balk at Conductorets," *Cleveland Plain Dealer*, August 27, 1918, p. 9.

88. *Baltimore American*, September 24, 1918, p. 1.

89. "Car Women Hear Stand Applauded," *Cleveland Plain Dealer*, September 25, 1918, p. 1.

90. "First Labor Clash of Sexes Seen in Cleveland Strike," *Wilkes-Barre Times-Leader*, December 6, 1918, p. 17. Rose Moriarty made a similar point about conductors being bread-earners in a chart she constructed and published in the WTUL's *Life and Labor*, which broke down the women's marital status and number of dependents.

91. Benson, "Searching for the Antecedents of Affirmative Action," 276.

92. "Conductorette Issue Made Nation Wide," *Cleveland Plain Dealer*, December 14, 1918, p. 6.

93. Benson, "Searching for the Antecedents of Affirmative Action," 277.

94. Weiss, *Fruits of Victory*, 33–35. For a comparative perspective, see Gowdy-Wygant, *Cultivating Victory*.

95. Weiss, *Fruits of Victory*, 64.

96. Anne Higginson Spicer, "Hoeing Uncle Sam's Row: The Woman's Land Army in the Making," *Life and Labor* 8 (July 1918): 133.

97. Weiss, *Fruits of Victory*, 49–55.

98. Ibid., 97.

99. Gildersleeve, "Women Farm Workers," 132.

100. Weiss, *Fruits of Victory*, 107.

101. Cited in ibid., 89.

102. "How Women Can Help on the Farms of America," *Trenton Evening Times*, March 18, 1918, p. 12.

103. "To Secure Farmerettes," *Baltimore Sun*, April 4, 1918, p. 14.

104. "Sincere Praise for the Farmerettes," *Baltimore Sun*, September 23, 1918, p. 12.

105. "Augusta Women Form 'Land Army,'" *Augusta Chronicle*, August 25, 1918, p. 27.

106. "Women's Land Army Is Active," *Augusta Chronicle*, August 29, 1918, p. 7.

107. "White Women Go to Cotton Fields," *Macon Telegraph*, September 12, 1917, p. 2; "Girls Will Pick Cotton," *Macon Telegraph*, September 20, 1918, p. 9; "U.D.C. Women Undertake Work of Picking Cotton," *Columbus Ledger*, October 4, 1918, p. 6.

108. Jellison, *Entitled to Power*, 1–32; Neth, *Preserving the Family Farm*, 19–20.

109. "What Farm Women Have Done," *Winston-Salem Journal*, April 7, 1918, p. 6.

110. McLoughlin, "Hoeing Smokes," 39.

111. "For the Land's Sake!" *War Work Bulletin* 35 (July 19, 1918): 3.

112. "These Patriotic Girls Are Raising Crops for Uncle Sam," *Lexington Herald*, May 6, 1918, p. 7.

113. "Are You Doing Your Bit?" *Houston Chronicle*, July 5, 1917, p. 4.

114. Hooks, *Women's Occupations*, 76.

115. "War Conditions Bring New Lines of Work to Women," *Grand Forks Daily Herald*, September 7, 1918, p. 2.

116. In April 1917, 15 percent of bank employees were women, and a year later that figure was over 31 percent. "Employment of Women in Duluth Banks Increasing," *Duluth News-Tribune*, May 2, 1918, p. 3.

117. "Women Take Places of Men Released for War," *Aberdeen Daily News*, July 6, 1918, p. 3.

118. "Civil Service Calls Give Variety of Salaried Jobs," *Duluth News-Tribune*, August 25, 1918, p. 6.

119. "More Women Are Needed for War," *Tucson Daily Citizen*, May 22, 1918, p. 5.

120. Clawson, "Gendered Merit," 241.

121. "Women in Civil Service," *Columbia (S.C.) State*, January 21, 1917, p. 24.

122. "Civil Service Gives Variety of Salaried Jobs," *Duluth News-Tribune*, August 25, 1918, p. 6.

123. "Fight for Equal Pay Is Carried to the Cabinet," *Evening Star*, June 13, 1917, p. 2.

124. Van Riper, *History of the United States Civil Service*, 260. Van Riper argues that, during the war, women constituted about 20 percent of civil service employees, up from 5–10 percent before the war.

125. "Miss Beulah Woodard," *Jeffersonian Gazette*, August 21, 1918, p. 4; "Days of Opportunity for Women," *Topeka Daily Capital*, August 11, 1918, p. 4.

126. Buchholz, *Josephine*, 28.

127. "Where Is the Consistency?" *Washington Bee*, August 24, 1918, p. 4. See also Yellin, *Racism in the Nation's Service*, 136, 140, 178.

128. "Are They German Propagandists?" *Washington Bee*, August 10, 1918, p. 4.

129. Hewitt, *Women Marines in World War I*, 7; Miller, "The Golden Fourteen," 7.

130. Ebbert and Hall, *The First, the Few, the Forgotten*, 18.

131. Godson, *Serving Proudly*, 63; Gavin, *American Women in World War I*, 5.

132. Ebbert and Hall, *The First, the Few, the Forgotten*, 7. For the poster, see http://www.ww1propaganda.com/ww1-poster/gee-i-wish-i-were-man-id-join-navy-be-man-and-do-it-united-states-navy-recruiting-station.

133. "After the War," *Charleston Evening Post*, August 26, 1918, p. 5.

134. "Women War Workers Cling to Their Jobs," *Fort Wayne Sentinel*, February 18, 1919, p. 1.

135. Anonymous letter to Mr. William Elmer, Superintendent, February 1919, box 18, Women's Bureau Records.

136. Carrie Brown, *Rosie's Mom*, 174–76; Greenwald, *Women, War, and Work*, 133–36.

137. Arnesen, *Black Protest and the Great Migration*, xx.

138. Haynes, "Two Million Negro Women at Work"; Blackwelder, *Now Hiring*, 64–65; Hill, *Women in Gainful Occupations*, 36.

139. Hooks, *Women's Occupations*, 75–76.

140. Ibid., 22–23.

141. Kessler-Harris, *Out to Work*, 248.

142. Greenwald, *Women, War, and Work*, 135.

143. Buchholz, *Josephine*, 21–22.

144. Hewes, *Women as Munition Makers*, 65.

Chapter 5

1. *Half-Century* magazine, for example, featured models dressed in Red Cross uniforms on several wartime covers and even represented a black woman as "Lady Liberty" (see Figure 3). For the most part, however, African American periodicals rarely printed photographs of black women active in war work. They did, however, reproduce a handful of posters (most of them privately produced) that featured African Americans in war work. See Keene, "Images of Racial Pride."

2. Neil Harris, "Iconography and Intellectual History," 307.

3. Ibid., 313; Todd, "Photojournalism," 10–11. On newspaper history, see Carlebarch, *American Photojournalism Comes of Age*; and Schudson, *Discovering the New*.

4. Bogart, *Artists, Advertising, and the Borders of Art*, 20–25, 97–106.

5. Shortly after the war, newspapers ran articles noting that the federal Women in Industry Service agency had commissioned photographs of women's wartime work. As one article headlined, "Magnificent Contributions of Feminine Sex Will Be Preserved." "Take Pictures of Women Doing Work for War," *Duluth News-Tribune*, February 9, 1919, p. 4.

6. Knutson offers an insightful analysis of this poster, including commentary from its originator artist, Alonzo Earl Foringer, who wrote that he wanted the image to be "not an ordinary individual nurse doing everyday field service, but a figure of divine mercy and tenderness, large and loving enough to take all the wounded and suffering of the world to heart." Knutson, "Breasts, Brawn, and Selling a War," 191–202. For the quote, see 198–99.

7. On World War I posters, see the essays in James, *Picture This*; Shover, "Roles and Images of Women"; Rawls, *Wake Up America*, n.p.; and Aulich, *War Posters*, 44–129. On the distribution of the Red Cross poster, see U.S. Committee on Public Information, *Government War Advertising*, 14.

8. According to historian Celia Malone Kingsbury, fiction in popular magazines similarly portrayed women in largely conventional terms. See Kingsbury, *For Home and Country*, chap. 2. Pearl James argues that there was much diversity in World

War I propaganda posters and that many suggested "radical possibilities" for women. I would agree that those produced by women's organizations, like the YWCA, did offer new visions of women's possibilities, but most others represented women far more traditionally. James, "Images of Femininity." In a rare, privately produced poster featuring African Americans, a similar message appeared. A mother and her children situated in a cozy living room look reverently at a flag-draped portrait of the man of the household, a soldier in uniform. Such images reinforced an interpretation of war as essentially men's prerogative and framed their military service not just in terms of defending their country, but also of protecting their female dependents. On posters targeted to black Americans, see Keene, "Images of Racial Pride."

9. James, "Images of Femininity," 280.

10. For an analysis of U.S. wartime popular culture representations of Germans as beasts, see Latham, "The Kaiser as the Beast of Berlin"; and Stewart Halsey Ross, *Propaganda for War,* 249–53. Kingsbury addresses the motif in American and Allied popular culture and propaganda; see Kingsbury, *For Home and Country,* chaps. 1 and 3. Nicoletta F. Gullace notes that Allied war posters routinely racialized Germans "as something other, hostile, and non-Western." Gullace, "Barbaric Anti-Modernism," 64.

11. Sexual violence during World War I was undoubtedly underreported, although there is evidence for a high volume of rape by German soldiers. But scholars like Alan Kramer argue, "Rape was probably committed by soldiers in every invasion in the Great War." Quoted in Proctor, *Civilians in a World at War,* 126.

12. Emerson, "Who's She in War Work," 745.

13. "4,000 Women Making Munitions for Uncle Sam," *Fort Wayne Journal Gazette,* March 14, 1918, p. 9.

14. "Girls' Efficient as Powder Workers," *Philadelphia Inquirer,* January 20, 1918, p. 5.

15. "Women Starting Well in Railroad Work," *Colorado Gazette-Telegraph,* August 5, 1917, p. 10.

16. "How She Has Changed in These Trying Days of War," *Cleveland Plain Dealer,* October 28, 1917, p. 77.

17. "The Win-the-War Girl," *Baltimore American,* July 21, 1918, Magazine, p. 3.

18. "Women Fill the War Breaches," *Motion Picture Magazine* (October 1918): 60–61.

19. "New York Women Who Run Broadway Streetcars," *Dallas Morning News,* February 3, 1918, V, p. 6.

20. "For Munitions Workers," *Rock Valley Bee,* April 19, 1918, p. 2.

21. See also "Help Her Carry On," World War I Propaganda Posters, http://www.ww1propaganda.com/world-war-1-posters/women-ww1?page=3; and James, "Images of Femininity," 300–301.

22. On women's uniforms and claims to citizenship, see Vining and Hacker, "From Camp Follower to Lady in Uniform"; and Hacker and Vining, "Cutting a New Pattern." Vining and Hacker note that the National Society of the Colonial Dames of America felt women's uniforms of World War I to be so significant historically that they created a collection for the Smithsonian National Museum, which is currently held by the National Museum of American History. Vining and Hacker, "From Camp Follower to Lady in Uniform," 371.

23. An illustrated article on wartime fashion, entitled "War-Working Woman," offered

suggestions for practical fashions for working women modeled after popular women's uniforms. *Asheville Citizen*, July 14, 1918, p. 21.

24. McCracken, "Girls Who Want to Go to France," 248.

25. "Experiences of a Nurse at the Front," *Cleveland Plain Dealer*, June 2, June 6, June 23, 1918, p. 6; "American Nurses in Raid," *Kansas City Star*, July 20, 1918, p. 6.

26. Frederic J. Haskin, "Salvation Nell in the Trenches," *Lexington Herald*, July 25, 1918, p. 4.

27. "Uniforms Which the American Women Have Adopted for Their War Work," *Touchstone* 4 (October 1918): 63.

28. "Our Women Over There," *Independent* 94 (April 27, 1918): 165.

29. "Her Real Uniforms, 1918 Style," *Baltimore American*, January 6, 1918, Magazine, p. 3. On women and military uniforms in World War I, see Vining and Hacker, "From Camp Follower to Lady in Uniform."

30. "'Hello Girls' Ready to Go to France; 'Goodbye Girls' Hope to Follow Soon," *Lexington Herald*, March 8, 1918, p. 1.

31. "Kaiser Shot All Full of Holes by Squad of Seven Women in City," *New York Herald*, March 7, 1918, II, 7; Romalov, "Modern, Mobile, and Marginal"; Scharff, *Taking the Wheel*; Berger, "Women Drivers!"

32. Martha Banta argues that women in World War I parades did not challenge conventional notions of women's proper place because of the assumption that such public demonstrations were temporary and driven by patriotism, not a demand for "rights." While these parades certainly lacked the militancy of the suffrage parades, I argue that the way in which ordinary women occupied public space during World War I parades did represent a significant departure from notions of respectable women's proper place. Banta, *Imagining American Women*, 571–72. On suffrage parades as spectacle, see Susan Glenn, *Female Spectacle*, 145–48.

33. "Red Cross Women to Have Natty Garb," and "8,000 Women in Red Cross Parade," *Cleveland Plain Dealer*, November 2, 1917, p. 15, and November 11, 1917, VIII, p. 1.

34. "Seven Mile Tribute to Women's Work in War," *Los Angeles Times*, May 19, 1918, II, pp. 1, 7.

35. For women only, see *Philadelphia Inquirer*, April 21, 1918; *Tulsa World*, April 12, 1918; and *Salt Lake Telegram*, April 8, 1918. For the variety of women's participation, see *Wyoming State Tribune–Cheyenne State Leader*, April 6, 1918; *Duluth News-Tribune*, September 29, 1918; *New Orleans Times-Picayune*, September 29, 1918; and *Duluth News-Tribune*, April 10, 1918.

36. "Through Chilling Rain, Women March for Liberty Bonds," *Macon Telegraph*, September 19, 1918, p. 1.

37. Leslie Midkiff DeBauche, in *Reel Patriotism*, closely analyzes the appearance of war-themed films in the era, noting that they constituted a relatively small percentage of productions. She also details the ways in which the industry, including theater operators and film stars, eagerly supported war mobilization in terms of fund-raising, recruitment, and food conservation.

38. Hansen, *Babel and Babylon*, 1–2.

39. On the transformation of the industry, see Lary May, *Screening Out the Past*, 65–66.

40. Blaetz, *Visions of the Maid*, 23–33.

41. In writing to DeMille, Lasky insisted on the importance of spectacle: " I know you are trying to get a good heart story, etc., but public seem to expect spectacle as well, when they pay $1 or more to see a special feature." Usai and Codelli, *The DeMille Legacy*, 361.

42. Robin Blaetz has discovered that the version imported to Europe for French audiences did not have the secondary love story, which was marketed to Americans. Blaetz, *Visions of the Maid*, 56–59.

43. Ibid., 61. For another assessment of the film, see Higashi, *Cecil B. DeMille and American Culture*, 117–41.

44. As quoted in Blaetz, *Visions of the Maid*, 54.

45. On femininity and romance in the context of prewar "new women," see Susan Glenn, *Female Spectacle*, 141–43.

46. Brownlow, *The War, the West, and the Wilderness*, 74–76.

47. "Nazimova's 'War Brides' Chief Feature of New Bill at Majestic," *Fort Worth Star-Telegram*, March 3, 1916, II, p. 30.

48. Jerome Shorey, "War Brides," *Photoplay* 11 (December 1916): 52.

49. "Alla Nazimova in 'War Brides' Is Stupendous," *Boston Journal*, November 21, 1916, p. 5.

50. Note that some reviewers were highly critical. The *Idaho Statesman* called Joan's character "selfish," a woman who had no understanding of patriotism. "War Brides," April 3, 1917, p. 7.

51. Michael Isenberg notes in *A Nation's Peril* "a female pacifist becoming so aroused by the national danger that she led men to the recruiting office." Isenberg, *War on Film*, 100.

52. "Thrilling Story of the Fall of a Nation," *Forth Worth Star-Telegram*, September 3, 1916, p. 8.

53. Shirley, "A Bugle Call to Arms for National Defense," 29.

54. Ibid.

55. "Fall of a Nation," *Morning Star*, November 9, 1916, p. 18.

56. "Battle Cry of Peace," *Moving Picture World* (August 21, 1915): 1514.

57. On Blackton, see Isenberg, *War on Film*, 101–4.

58. "Picture Play a Weapon against Pacifists," *Montgomery Adviser*, March 14, 1916, p. 3.

59. Lary May, *Screening Out the Past*, 106–7; Staiger, *Bad Women*, 155–16; Sara Ross, "Good Little Bad Girls"; Susan Glenn, *Female Spectacle*, 96–125. Ullman, in *Sex Seen*, argues that early twentieth-century short films depicted a surprising degree of female sexual agency.

60. Peter Brook, *The Melodramatic Imagination*, as cited in Singer, *Melodrama and Modernity*, 134–35.

61. Cerabino-Hess, "On Nation and Violation," 120–59; Grittner, *White Slavery*; Stamp, *Movie-Struck Girls*, 41–101. Stamp (p. 100) points out that contemporaries were alarmed that so many women were in the audiences for these white slavery films, viewing this as still further evidence of the dangers that modern urban amusements posed for exposing women to sexual danger. She posits, in contrast to my interpretation, that such female spectatorship potentially empowered women: "Watching white slave narratives unfold on the screen, women were offered the possibility of circumventing prohibitions against

both their physical mobility and their visual license." See also Staiger, *Bad Women*, 116–46.

62. On Griffiths, see Lary May, *Screening Out the Past*, 60–95.

63. Cerabino-Hess, "On Nation and Violation," 260–318; quotes on 296.

64. "To Hell with the Kaiser," *Variety*, July 7, 1918, p. 30; stills from "To Hell with the Kaiser," *Moving Picture World* (July 6, 1918): 16.

65. "'The Great Love,'" *Motion Picture Magazine* (September 1918): 39.

66. "Hearts of the World," *Photoplay* (July 1918): 118. For a more detailed analysis of the plot and the rape motif, see Kingsbury, *For Home and Country*, chap. 5.

67. Gullace, "Sexual Violence and Family Honor," 716. On the French use of the rape motif, see Ruth Harris, "Child of the Barbarian." Harris argues that "individual women victimized by the marauders were thus often transformed into a representation of a feminized nation, *la France civilatrice*, fighting a war of liberation against a plundering, overarmoured brute." On the representation of German atrocities in Europe, see also Grayzel, *Women's Identities at War*. The extent of German rapes and other attacks on civilians continues to be controversial. See Brownmiller, *Against Our Will*, 40–48; and Anderson, "A German Way of War."

68. Kimberly Jensen, *Mobilizing Minerva*, 98–115.

69. "Battle Cry of Peace," *Moving Picture World* (August 21, 1915): 2158.

70. Zeiger, "She Didn't Raise Her Boy to Be a Slacker."

71. "Her Boy," *Photoplay* (April 1918): 111.

72. "Over There," *Moving Picture World* (October 27, 1917): 524; "Metro Pictures Corporation," *Moving Picture World* (December 15, 1917): 1682.

73. Singer, *Melodrama and Modernity*, 232. See also Cooper, "Pearl White and Grace Cunard."

74. Singer, "Female Power," 184.

75. In ibid., Singer makes this point; as does Stamp, in *Movie-Struck Girls*, 125–40; and Mahar, in *Women Filmmakers in Early Hollywood*, 107–8.

76. Enstad, "Dressed for Adventure."

77. Singer, "Female Power," 173. Similar stories featuring adventuresome young women also appeared in books marketed to girls and young women. Celia Malone Kingsbury notes that, despite the heroine's bravery, the message of the books reinforced conventional gender expectations. Kingsbury, *For Home and Country*, chap. 3.

78. "Thrilling Chapter Photoplay Is Woven about Life in the Army," *Duluth News-Tribune*, January 14, 1918, p. 11A.

79. Brownlow, *The War, the West, and the Wilderness*, 107. On the extraordinary publicity gimmicks, see Lahue, *Bound and Gagged*, 126–28.

80. "The Great Romance of Preparedness: *Patria*," *Charlotte Observer*, February 25, 1917, p. 18. *Patria* is a call for preparedness, but it features not Germany as America's potential enemy, but rather Japan (then an ally of Britain), with an assist from Mexico, and as such reflects the long-standing theme of the "yellow peril" in Hearst publications. So viciously were the Japanese portrayed that President Woodrow Wilson himself intervened to insist on censorship, a call that became even more heated when the United States entered the war and allied with Japan. Minor changes were made, which involved the removal of some Japanese flags and changing the major Japanese villain's name to a

Mexican one, but the serial continued to be exhibited through 1917. See Pizzitola, *Hearst over Hollywood*, 153–61.

81. The series ran from February 18 to May 27, 1917.

82. "Mrs. Vernon Castle in Patria," *Fort Worth Star-Telegram*, April 29, 1917, II, p. 4. See also Neal, "Action-Adventure Genre as Hollywood Genre," 64–65.

83. "*Patria* Thrills Don't Bother Mrs. Castle," *Tucson Daily Citizen*, March 21, 1917, II, p. 8. Irene Castle encouraged her public to view Patria Channing's skills as her own, telling one reporter that "any girl who desires to make motion picture acting her profession will find horse-back riding, swimming, golfing, motoring, canoeing, and even aviation, most valuable assets." "Mrs. Vernon Castle Tells of Her Work in the Play *Patria*," *Columbus Daily Enquirer*, February 18, 1917, p. 3.

84. She points out that by the early twentieth century, Americans routinely used an idealized vision of an American "girl," variously the New England Woman, the Beautiful Charmer, or the American Girl as Outdoor Pal, to stand in for the nation's values. She suggests that by 1910 these ideal types had increasingly flowed into a sense of a "New Woman." Always feminine, the ideal New Woman was also strong, athletic, and independent. Banta, *Imagining American Women*.

85. "The Great Romance of Preparedness," *Charlotte Observer*, May 27, 1917, p. 18.

86. In her study of the war spy film *Joan of Platsburgh*, Robin Blaetz also notes the contradictory messages in films that featured adventuresome women yet contained their transgressive quality with an emphasis on femininity and beauty. Blaetz, *Visions of the Maid*, 68–69.

87. Banta, *Imagining American Women*, 572. For the poster, see http://www.ww1propaganda.com/ww1-poster/gee-i-wish-i-were-man-id-join-navy-be-man-and-do-it-united-states-navy-recruiting-station.

88. The last reel of the film is missing, but the script, stills, short-story version, and one reviewer's comment confirm the ending.

89. For more of Pickford's war activities, see DeBauche, *Reel Patriotism*, 68–71; and the Mary Pickford Scrapbooks at the Margaret Herrick Library, Academy of Motion Picture Arts and Sciences, Los Angeles. On Pickford and American identity, see Zdriluk, "When a Canadian Girl Became America's Sweetheart," 61–74.

90. Lasky to DeMille, February 8, 1917, as cited in DeBauche, *Reel Patriotism*, 55.

91. Ibid.

92. For a more detailed analysis of the plot of *The Little American*, see Kingsbury, *For Home and Country*, chap. 5.

93. See, for example, the IMDB website, http://www.imdb.com/title/tt0008188/.

94. For a similar process in musical revues, see Susan Glenn, *Female Spectacle*, 155–87. Glenn notes that "if theater provided the space for assertive self-spectacle *by* women, it also permitted Broadway producers to make spectacle *of* women by presenting them as alluring and nonthreatening objects."

95. "Oh, You Women Remarkably Good," *Exhibitors Trade Review* 5 (May 17, 1918): 1833.

96. "Oh, You Women," *Exhibitors Trade Review* 5 (April 19, 1919): 1469.

97. Oh, You Women Remarkably Good," *Exhibitors Trade Review* 5 (May 17, 1918): 1833.

98. "Oh, You Women," *Exhibitors Trade Review* 5 (April 19, 1919): 1469. For a provocative ad for the movie, see *Motion Picture News*, April 26, 1919, n.p.

Epilogue

1. Historians of European women's postwar experiences have found similar anxiety about the new woman and her threat to gender order. During the war, women in the major combatant nations of Germany, France, and Britain took on new responsibilities in the industrial and agricultural workforce, and their volunteer organizations actively supported the war effort. With the exception of France, most nations that participated in the war gave women at least partial suffrage. But, nonetheless, in the 1920s, European women struggled to exert political influence and saw their economic opportunities constricted. For an insightful analysis of the way in which the French used gender issues to explain war's meaning and impact, see Roberts, *Civilization without Sexes*. See also Grayzel, *Women's Identities at War*; and Grayzel, *Women and the First World War*. The classic account of the failure of war to improve women's status is Higonnet and Higonnet, "The Double Helix."

2. This discussion of the 1920s draws upon Dumenil, *The Modern Temper*.

3. Crane, "Carry On," 1–2.

4. For a detailed assessment of suffragists' expectations about postwar women's activism, see Unser, "Woman's Hour," 375–84.

5. Browder, "Working Out Their Economic Problems Together."

6. White, *Too Heavy a Load*, 135.

7. Rief, "Thinking Locally, Acting Globally," 216. On Hunton specifically, see Chandler, "Addie Hunton."

8. White, *Too Heavy a Load*, 138. She became particularly important in the UNIA after Garvey's imprisonment for mail fraud in 1925–27.

9. Gilmore, *Gender and Jim Crow*, 218–24.

10. Higginbotham, "Clubwomen and Electoral Politics in the 1920s," 144.

11. Nikki Brown, *Private Politics and Public Voices*, 137–60.

12. Some of the material in this section originally appeared in Dumenil, "The New Woman and the Politics of the 1920s."

13. Dorothy Brown, *Setting a Course*, 69. On women and party politics in the 1920s, see Andersen, *After Suffrage*; Harvey, *Votes without Leverage*, 104–35; and Cott, *The Grounding of Modern Feminism*, 53–114.

14. On the maternalist reforms and organized women, see Muncy, *Creating a Female Dominion*; and Lemons, *The Woman Citizen*.

15. Cott, *The Grounding of Modern Feminism*, 97.

16. Jeffreys-Jones, *Changing Differences*, 32–34. For a discussion of the major women's peace organizations of this era, see Alonso, *Peace as a Women's Issue*, 85–124.

17. Harvey, *Votes without Leverage*, 104–35.

18. Dorothy Brown, *Setting a Course*, 50.

19. Cott, *The Grounding of Modern Feminism*, 102.

20. Andersen, *After Suffrage*; Cott, *The Grounding of Modern Feminism*, 104–8, 318–19.

21. Delegard, *Battling Miss Bolsheviki*, 9.

22. On the efforts of the American Legion to promote a heroic memory of war, see Trout, *On the Battlefield of Memory*. Trout (p. 2) notes the extensive efforts on the part of local communities to erect monuments and find other means of commemorating the war. He argues that the popular perception that Americans turned their back on the war in disillusionment is just "one strand in the frayed remembrance discourse of the interwar period."

23. There were a few exceptions to this erasure of women's war experience. Immediately after the war, five YMCA women who had served abroad with the First Division of the AEF were given a place in the division's 1919 victory parade down Pennsylvania Avenue in Washington, D.C. And in 1924, Smith College created a monument to its relief unit: gates modeled after those at Grécourt where the women had served. At the dedication, the college president read the roll of women who had participated. Here the focus was not on celebrating victory in war, but on honoring Smith College women's commitment to international service. "Y.M.C.A. Girls Honored for Courage in France March in Grand Review with First Division," *Evening Star*, September 17, 1919, p. 4; "Grécourt Gates Dedicated at Smith College," *Springfield Republican*, October 19, 1924, pp. 1, 13.

24. Zeiger, *In Uncle Sam's Service*, 172.

25. "Woman's Auxiliary American Legion Hears Address by Mrs. Oliphant," *Daily Illinois State Journal*, April 17, 1925, pp. 1, 16.

26. "War Mothers Pay Tribute to Hero," *Evening Star*, May 15, 1922, p. 10.

27. Kuhlman, *Reconstructing Patriarchy after the Great War*, 168.

28. Budreau, "The Politics of Remembrance," 392. See also Budreau, *Bodies of War*, 192–217.

29. Plant, *Mom*, 207.

30. Nielsen, *Un-American Womanhood*; Ryan, *Red War on the Family*.

31. Dumenil, *The Modern Temper*, 122. On women and work in the 1920s, see Kessler-Harris, *Out to Work*, 217–49; and Blackwelder, *Now Hiring*, 62–95.

32. Cott, *The Grounding of Modern Feminism*, 179–211.

33. On this aspect of the new woman, see Cott, *The Grounding of Modern Feminism*, 143–74; Simmons, *Making Marriage Modern*, 58–177; Stansell, *American Moderns*, 225–310; Fass, *The Damned and the Beautiful*; Elaine Tyler May, *Great Expectations*; D'Emilio and Freedman, *Intimate Matters*; and Mintz and Kellogg, *Domestic Revolutions*.

34. Clement, *Love for Sale*, 146–76. Surveys of sexual behavior vary in their assessment of sexual change in the early twentieth century. Lewis M. Terman, writing in 1938, was rare in trying to determine the impact of war on patterns of virginity before marriage. In his sample, couples who married during the war era were *less* likely to have had sexual intercourse before marriage. Terman, *Psychological Factors in Marital Happiness*, 330.

Bibliography

Manuscripts and Archival Sources

Cambridge, Massachusetts
  Schlesinger Library, Radcliffe Institute
    Louise Barbour Papers
    Molly Dewson Papers, 1893–1962, Series II: 20–27
    Mary Lee Papers
    Edith Gratia Stedman Papers
    Radcliffe College in France: Scrapbooks 1917–20, vol. 1
College Park, Maryland
  National Archives
    American National Red Cross
    Children's Bureau
    Council of National Defense Committee on Women's Defense Work
    Women's Bureau
    Women's Service Section, Records of the U.S. Railroad Administration
Los Angeles, California
  Los Angeles County Board of Supervisors, Los Angeles County Archives
  Margaret Herrick Library, Academy of Motion Picture Arts and Sciences
    Mary Pickford Scrapbooks
  Seaver Center for Western History Research
    State Council of Defense, Women's Committee Records
    War History Committee Records
    World War I Manuscript Collection
Minneapolis, Minnesota
  University of Minnesota Libraries
    Young Men's Christian Association of the USA Records, Kautz Family YMCA Archives
Northampton, Massachusetts
  Sophia Smith Collection, Smith College
    Charlotte Bannon Papers

Mary van Kleeck Papers
YWCA of the USA Records, 1860–1920
Northridge, California
California State University, Northridge, Special Collections and Archives
Young Women's Christian Association of Los Angeles Collection, 1894–1979
San Marino, California
Huntington Library
Friday Morning Club Collection
Myron Hunt Collection
Washington, D.C.
Library of Congress
Moving Image Research Center
National Association for the Advancement of Colored People Papers

Published Primary Sources

American Red Cross. *The Work of the American Red Cross: Report by the War Council.* Washington, D.C.: American Red Cross, 1917.

American Red Cross, Pittsburgh Chapter. *American Red Cross: A History of the Activities of the Chapter from Its Organization to January 1, 1921.* 1922. Google Books.

[American Young Men's Christian Association.] *Service with Fighting Men: An Account of the Work of the American Young Men's Christian Associations in the World War.* New York: Association Press, 1922.

Annual Report of the War Activities of the Woman's Committee of the Los Angeles City Unit of the Council of Defense. [Los Angeles, 1918?] University of California, Los Angeles, Special Collections.

Ashe, Elizabeth. *Intimate Letters from France during America's First Year of War.* San Francisco: Bruce Brough Press, 1918.

Baldwin, Marian. *Canteening Overseas.* New York: Macmillan, 1920.

Blair, Emily Newell. *The Woman's Committee, United States Council of National Defense: An Interpretive Report.* Washington, D.C.: Government Printing Office, 1920.

"Committee on Women in Industry of the Advisory Commission of the Council of National Defense." Pamphlet, December 10, 1917. Committee for Women in Industry Folder, Records of the Women's Bureau, Record Group 86, National Archives.

Crane, Caroline Bartlett. "Carry On." *Carry On* 1 (November 23, 1918): 1–2.

Davison, Henry Pomeroy. *The American Red Cross in the Great War.* New York: Macmillan, 1919.

Dock, Lavinia L. *History of American Red Cross Nursing.* New York: Macmillan, 1922.

Dorr, Rhetta. *A Woman at Fifty.* New York: Funk and Wagnalls, 1924.

Dunbar-Nelson, Alice. "Negro Women in War Work." In Emmett J. Scott, *The American Negro in the World War,* 374–97. Chicago: Homewood Press, 1919.

Gaines, Ruth Louise. *Ladies of Grécourt: The Smith College Relief Unit in the Somme.* New York: E. P. Dutton, 1920, reproduction.

Garbutt, Mary Alderman. *Victories of Four Decades: A History of the Woman's Christian Temperance Union of Southern California, 1893–1924.* Los Angeles: Woman's Christian Temperance Union, 1924.

Gildersleeve, Virginia. "Women Farm Workers." *New Republic* 12 (September 1, 1917): 132–34.
Goldmark, Pauline. "Women Conductors." *Survey* 40 (June 1918): 369–70.
Gordon, Elizabeth Putnam. *Women Torch-Bearers: The Story of the Woman's Christian Temperance Union*. Evanston, Ill., 1924.
Haynes, Elizabeth Ross. "Two Million Negro Women at Work." *Southern Workman* 52 (January 1922): 64–71.
Hewes, Amy. *Women as Munition Makers: A Study of Conditions in Bridgeport, Connecticut.* New York: Russell Sage Foundation, 1917.
Hill, Joseph A. *Women in Gainful Occupations, 1870–1920*. Washington. D.C.: Government Printing Office, 1929.
Hopkins, Mary Alden. "Conserving Woman Power in War Time." *Journal of Home Economics* 10 (1918): 171–73.
Hubbard, Miriam Warren. "The Soldier Girls of the National Service School." *St. Nicholas* 44 (April 1917): 518–20. In *Patriotism and the Flag: Retold from St. Nicholas Magazine*. New York: Century, 1918.
Hunton, Addie W., and Kathryn M. Johnson. *Two Colored Women with the American Expeditionary Forces*. Brooklyn: Brooklyn Eagle Press, 1920.
Janis, Elsie. *The Big Show*. New York: Cosmopolitan Book Corporation, 1919.
La Motte, Ellen. *The Backwash of War: The Human Wreckage of the Battlefield as Witnessed by an American Hospital Nurse*. New York: G. P. Putnam's, 1916.
Lee, Mary. *"It's a Great War."* Boston: Houghton Mifflin, 1929.
Lee, Porter. "Training for the Home Service of the Red Cross." *Annals of the Academy of Political and Social Science* 79 (September 1918): 80–87.
McIvor-Tyndall, Margaret. "Women and Future National Welfare." *National Service with the International Military Digest* 6 (1919): 23–25.
Morse, Katharine. *The Uncensored Letters of a Canteen Girl*. New York: Holt, 1920.
Newkirk, Alice Field. "Study of a Single Philadelphia Office Where 500 Women Daily Find Employment Shows a New Era Has Dawned for Women." *U.S. Employment Service Bulletin* (October 1918): 10.
Noyes, Frances Newbold. *My A.E.F.: A Hail and Farewell*. New York: Frederick A. Stokes, 1920.
Olcott, Jane. *The Work of Colored Women*. New York: Young Women's Christian Association, 1919.
Peixotto, Jessica B. "The Children's Year and the Woman's Committee." *Annals of the American Academy* 79 (September 1918): 257–62.
Pickett, Sarah Elizabeth. *The American National Red Cross: Its Origin, Purposes, and Service*. New York: Century, 1924.
Putnam, Elizabeth Cabot. *On Duty and Off: Letters of Elizabeth Cabot Putnam*. Cambridge: Riverside Press, 1919.
A Red Triangle Girl in France. New York: George H. Doran, 1918.
"Report of the Women's Committee of the State Council of Defense of California from June 1, 1917, to January 1, 1919." Box 956, Record Group 2, National Archives.
Rude, Anna E. "The Children's Year Campaign." *American Journal of Public Health* 9 (May 1919): 346–61.

Stimson, Julia C. *Finding Themselves: The Letters of an American Army Chief Nurse in a British Hospital in France*. New York: Macmillan, 1918.
Terman, Lewis M. *Psychological Factors in Marital Happiness*. New York: McGraw-Hill, 1938.
Terrell, Mary Church. *A Colored Woman in a White World*. Washington, D.C.: Randsdall, 1940.
U.S. Bureau of the Census. *Statistical Abstracts of the United States, 1920*. Washington, D.C.: Government Printing Office, 1921.
———. *Statistics of Women at Work*. Washington, D.C.: Government Printing Office, 1907.
———. *Thirteenth Census of the United States: 1910 Report on Occupations*. http://www2.census.gov/prod2/decennial/documents/36894832v4_TOC.pdf.
U.S. Committee on Public Information. *Government War Advertising: Report of the Division of Advertising, Committee on Public Information*. Washington, D.C.: Committee on Public Information, 1918.
U.S. Department of Labor. Division of Negro Economics. *The Negro at Work during the World War and during Reconstruction*. Washington, D.C.: Government Printing Office, 1921.
Van Kleeck, Mary. "Women in the Munition Industries." *Life and Labor* 8 (June 1918): 114–16.
"War Activities of the Woman's Committee, Los Angeles City Unit of the Council of National Defense." [Los Angeles, 1919?] Box 956, Field Division, Reports of State and Local Councils, Records of the Committee on Women's Defense Work, Record Group 62, National Archives.
Wolfe, A. B., and Helen Olson. "War-Time Industrial Employment of Women in the United States." *Journal of Political Economy* 27 (October 1919): 639–69.
Woman's Christian Temperance Union of Indiana. *Forty-fourth Annual Report*. Anderson, Ind., 1917. Archive.org.

Contemporary Journals

American Legion Monthly
Catholic Women's Club Bulletin (Los Angeles)
Crisis
Electric Railway Journal
Exhibitors' Trade Review
Forum
Good Housekeeping
Half-Century
Independent
Intercollegiate Community Service Quarterly
Ladies' Home Journal
Life and Labor
Motion Picture Magazine
Moving Picture World
Photoplay

Smith College Monthly
Suffragist
Sunset
Touchstone
Vassar Miscellany News
War Work Bulletin (War Work Council of the National Board of the Young Women's Christian Association)
Wellesley College Bulletin
Woman Citizen
Woman's Journal and Suffrage News
Women's Work and War (National Women's Trade Union League)
World Outlook
YWCA Association Monthly

Newspapers

Aberdeen (S.D.) Daily News
Afro-American
Appeal (Saint Paul, Minn.)
Asheville (N.C.) Citizen
Augusta (Ga.) Chronicle
Baltimore American
Baltimore Sun
Belleville (Ill.) News Democrat
Bisbee (Ariz.) Daily Review
B'nai B'rith Messenger
Boston Journal
California Eagle
Charleston Evening Post
Charleston News and Courier
Charlotte Observer
Chicago Daily Tribune
Chicago Defender
Chicago Evening Post
Cincinnati Enquirer
Cleveland Gazette
Cleveland Plain Dealer
Cobb County (Ga.) Times
Colorado Gazette-Telegraph
Columbia (S.C.) State
Columbus (Ga.) Daily Enquirer
Columbus (Ga.) Ledger
Daily Illinois State Journal
Dallas Morning News
Denver Post
Duluth News Tribune
Evening Star (Washington, D.C.)
Evening Star Newark Advocate
Fort Wayne Journal Gazette
Fort Wayne Sentinel
Fort Worth Star-Telegram
Grand Forks Daily Herald
Grand Rapids Press
Greensboro (N.C.) Daily News
Gulfport Daily Herald
Idaho Statesman
Indianapolis Star
Iowa City Press-Citizen
Jeffersonian Gazette (Lawrence, Kans.)
Kansas City Star
Lexington Herald
Logansport (Ind.) Pharos-Tribune
Los Angeles Times
Macon Telegraph
Miami Herald Record
Montgomery Adviser
Newark (Ohio) Advocate
New Orleans Item
New Orleans Times-Picayune
New York Herald
New York Times
Oakland Tribune
Omaha World Herald
Philadelphia Inquirer
Philadelphia Tribune
Portland Oregonian

Pueblo Chieftain (Pueblo, Colo.)
Riverside (Calif.) Daily Press
Rock Valley (Iowa) Bee
Salt Lake Telegram
San Francisco Bulletin
San Francisco Chronicle
Savannah Tribune
Seattle Times
Springfield Republican
Topeka Daily Capital
Trenton Evening Times
Tucson Daily Citizen
Tulsa World
Twin Falls (Idaho) News
Washington Bee
Wilkes-Barre Times-Leader
Winston-Salem Journal
Wyoming State Tribune–Cheyenne State Leader

Web Pages

Internet Movie Database, http://www.imdb.com/title/tt0008188/.

Madam Walker Family Archives, http://madamwalkerfamilyarchives.wordpress.com/2011/08/31/madam-walkers-1917-convention-entrepreneurship-protest-politics/.

Eartha M. White Collection, Florida Heritage Collection, State University Libraries of Florida, http://palmm.digital.flvc.org/islandora/search/eartha%20white?type=edismax&collection=palmm%3Afhp.

World War I Propaganda Posters, http://www.ww1propaganda.com.

Secondary Sources

Abrams, Laura S. "Guardians of Virtue: The Social Reformers and the 'Girl Problem,' 1890–1920." *Social Service Review* 74 (September 2000): 436–52.

Alchon, Guy. "Mary van Kleeck and Scientific Management." In *A Mental Revolution: Scientific Management after Taylor*, edited by Daniel Nelson, 102–29. Columbus: Ohio State University Press, 1992.

Alexander, Ruth M. *The "Girl Problem": Female Sexual Delinquency in New York, 1900–1930*. Ithaca: Cornell University Press, 1995.

Alonso, Harriet Hyman. *Peace as a Women's Issue: A History of the U.S. Movement for World Peace and Women's Rights*. Syracuse: Syracuse University Press, 1993.

Amott, Teresa L., and Julie A. Matthaei. *Race, Gender, and Work: A Multicultural Economic History of Women in the United States*. Boston: South End Press, 1991.

Andersen, Kristi. *After Suffrage: Women in Partisan and Electoral Politics before the New Deal*. Chicago: University of Chicago Press, 1996.

Anderson, Margaret Lavinia. "A German Way of War?" *German History* 22 (2004): 254–58.

Armstrong, Julie Buckner. *Mary Turner and the Memory of Lynching*. Athens: University of Georgia Press, 2011.

Arnesen, Eric. *Black Protest and the Great Migration: A Brief History with Documents*. Boston: Bedford Press, 2003.

Attie, Jeanie. *Patriotic Toil: Northern Women and the American Civil War*. Ithaca: Cornell University Press, 1998.

Aulich, James. *War Posters: Weapons of Mass Communication*. New York: Thames and Hudson, 2007.

Baker, Paula. "The Domestication of Politics: Women and American Political Society, 1780–1920." *American Historical Review* 89 (June 1984): 620–47.

Bannan, Regina. "Management by Women: The First Twenty-five Years of the YWCA National Board, 1906–1931." Ph.D. diss., University of Pennsylvania, 1994.

Banta, Martha. *Imagining American Women: Ideas and Ideals in Cultural History*. New York: Columbia University Press, 1987.

Benson, Ronald. "Searching for the Antecedents of Affirmative Action: The National War Labor Board and the Cleveland Woman Conductors in World War I." *Women's Rights Law Reporter* 5 (1979): 271–82.

Berger, Michael L. "Women Drivers! The Emergence of Folklore and Stereotypic Opinions Concerning Feminine Automotive Behavior." *Women's Studies International Forum* 9 (1986): 257–63.

Blackwelder, Julia Kirk. *Now Hiring: The Feminization of Work in the United States, 1900–1995*. College Station: Texas A&M University Press, 1997.

Blaetz, Robin. *Visions of the Maid: Joan of Arc in American Film and Culture*. Charlottesville: University of Virginia Press, 2001.

Bogart, Michele H. *Artists, Advertising, and the Borders of Art*. Chicago: University of Chicago Press, 1995.

Bradley, Patricia. *Women and the Press: The Struggle for Equality*. Evanston, Ill.: Northwestern University Press, 2005.

Brandt, Allan M. *No Magic Bullet: A Social History of Venereal Disease in the United States since 1880*. New York: Oxford University Press, 1985.

Breen, William J. "Black Women and the Great War: Mobilization and Reform in the South." *Journal of Southern History* 44 (1978): 421–40.

———. "Southern Women in the War: The North Carolina Woman's Committee, 1917–1919." *North Carolina Historical Review* 55 (July 1978): 251–83.

———. *Uncle Sam at Home: Civilian Mobilization, Wartime Federalism, and the Council of National Defense, 1917–1919*. Westport, Conn.: ABC-Clio, 1984.

Bristow, Nancy. *Making Men Moral: Social Engineering during the Great War*. New York: New York University Press, 1997.

Browder, Dorothea. "Working Out Their Economic Problems Together: World War I, Working Women, and Civil Rights in the YWCA." *Journal of the Gilded Age and Progressive Era* 14 (2015): 243–65.

Brown, Carrie. *Rosie's Mom: Forgotten Women Workers of the First World War*. Boston: Northeastern University Press, 2002.

Brown, Dorothy. *Setting a Course: American Women in the 1920s*. Boston: Twayne, 1987.

Brown, Nikki. *Private Politics and Public Voices: Black Women's Activism from World War I to the New Deal*. Bloomington: Indiana University Press, 2006.

———. "'Your Patriotism Is of the Purest Quality': African American Women and World War I." Ph.D. diss., Yale University, 2002.

Brown, Victoria Bissell. *The Education of Jane Addams*. Philadelphia: University of Pennsylvania Press, 2007.

Brownell, Penelope. "The Women's Committees of the First World War: Women in Government, 1917–1919." Ph.D. diss., Brown University, 2002.

Brownlow, Kevin. *The War, the West, and the Wilderness*. New York: Random House, 1979.

Brownmiller, Susan. *Against Our Will: Men, Women, and Rape*. New York: Simon and Schuster, 1975.

Buchholz, Margaret Thomas. *Josephine: From Washington Working Girl to Fisherman's Wife, A Memoir, 1917–1959*. Westcreek, N.J.: Down the Shore Publishing, 2012.
Budreau, Lisa M. *Bodies of War: World War I and the Politics of Commemoration in America, 1919–1933*. New York: New York University Press, 2010.
———. "The Politics of Remembrance: The Gold Star Mothers' Pilgrimage and America's Fading Memory of the Great War." *Journal of Military History* 72 (April 2008): 371–411.
Bulovsky, Helen C. "Behind the Trenches." *Proteus: A Journal of Ideas* 20 (Fall 2003): 39–50.
Bundles, A'Lelia. *On Her Own Ground: The Life and Times of Madam C. J. Walker*. New York: Scribner, 2001.
Camarillo, Albert. *Chicanos in a Changing Society: From Mexican Pueblos to American Barrios in Santa Barbara and Southern California*. Cambridge: Harvard University Press, 1979.
Capozzola, Christopher. "The Only Badge Needed Is Your Patriotic Fervor: Vigilance, Coercion, and the Law in World War I America." *Journal of American History* 88 (2002): 1354–82.
———. *Uncle Sam Wants You: World War I and the Making of the Modern American Citizen*. New York: Oxford University Press, 2008.
Carlebarch, Michael L. *American Photojournalism Comes of Age*. Washington, D.C.: Smithsonian Institution Press, 1997.
Cerabino-Hess, Elizabeth. "On Nation and Violation: Representations of Rape in Popular Theatre and Film of the Progressive Era." Ph.D. diss., New York University, 1977.
Chan, Sucheng. *Asian Americans: An Interpretive History*. Boston: Twayne, 1991.
Chandler, Kerr. "Addie Hunton and the Construction of an African American Female Peace Perspective." *Affilia* 20 (Fall 2005): 270–83.
———. "'That Biting, Stinging Thing Which Ever Shadows Us': African-American Social Workers in France during World War I." *Social Service Review* 69 (September 1995): 498–514.
Christides, Michelle A. "Women Veterans of the Great War." *Minerva* 3 (June 1985): 103–27.
Christman, Anastasia J. "The Best Laid Plans: Women's Clubs and City Planning in Los Angeles, 1890–1930." Ph.D. diss., University of California, Los Angeles, 2000.
Chuppa-Cornell, Kimberly. "The U.S. Women's Motor Corps in France, 1914–1921." *Historian* 56 (August 2007): 465–76.
Clawson, Cathryn. "Gendered Merit: Women and the Merit Concept in Federal Employment, 1864–1944." *American Journal of Legal History* 60 (July 1996): 229–52.
Clement, Elizabeth Alice. *Love for Sale: Courting, Treating, and Prostitution in New York City, 1900–1945*. Chapel Hill: University of North Carolina Press, 2006.
Clout, Hugh. *After the Ruins: Restoring the Countryside of Northern France after the Great War*. Exeter: University of Exeter Press, 1996.
Cobbs, Elizabeth. *The Hello Girls: America's First Women Soldiers*. Cambridge: Harvard University Press, forthcoming.
Cooper, Mark Garrett. "Pearl White and Grace Cunard: The Serial Queen's Volatile

Present." In *Flickers of Desire: Movie Stars of the 1910s*, edited by Jennifer M. Bean, 174–95. New Brunswick: Rutgers University Press, 2011.

Cott, Nancy F. *The Grounding of Modern Feminism*. New Haven: Yale University Press, 1989.

Cuff, Robert D. "The Cooperative Impulse and War: The Origins of the Council of National Defense and Advisory Commission." In *Building the Organizational Society*, edited by Jerry Israel, 233–46. New York: Free Press, 1972.

Dalby, Louise Elliott. *"An Irrepressible Crew": The Smith College Relief Unit*. Northampton, Mass.: Smith College, 1968.

Damico, John K. "The Rush to the Colors: North Louisiana Responds to the Great War, 1917." *Southern Studies* 6 (1995): 25–43.

Darrow, Margaret H. *French Women and the First World War: War Stories of the Home Front*. New York: Bloomsbury Academic, 1990.

Davidson, Janet F. "Women and the Railroad: The Gendering of Work during the First World War Era, 1917–1920." Ph.D. diss., University of Delaware, 1999.

Davies, Margery W. *Woman's Place Is at the Typewriter: Office Work and Office Workers, 1870–1930*. Philadelphia: Temple University Press, 1982.

Davis, Clark. "An Era and Generation of Civic Engagement: The Friday Morning Club in Los Angeles, 1891–1931." *Southern California Quarterly* 84 (Summer 2002): 135–68.

DeBauche, Leslie Midkiff. *Reel Patriotism: The Movie and World War I*. Madison: University of Wisconsin Press, 1997.

Degen, Marie Louise. *The History of the Woman's Peace Party*. Baltimore: Johns Hopkins University Press, 1939.

Delegard, Kirsten Marie. *Battling Miss Bolsheviki: The Origins of Female Conservatism in the United States*. Philadelphia: University of Pennsylvania Press, 2011.

D'Emilio, John D., and Estelle B. Freedman. *Intimate Matters: A History of Sexuality in America*. Chicago: University of Chicago Press, 1988.

Derickson, Alan. "Physiological Science and Scientific Management in the Progressive Era: Frederic S. Lee and the Committee on Industrial Fatigue." *Business History Review* 68 (Winter 1994): 483–514.

Dodd, Lynda G. "Parades, Pickets, and Prison: Alice Paul and the Virtues of Unruly Constitutional Citizenship." *Journal of Law and Politics* 24 (Fall 2008): 339–433.

Douglas, Ann. *The Feminization of American Culture*. New York: Farrar, Straus and Giroux, 1998.

DuBois, Ellen Carol. *Harriot Stanton Blatch and the Winning of Woman Suffrage*. New Haven: Yale University Press, 1997.

DuBois, Ellen Carol, and Lynn Dumenil. *Through Women's Eyes: A History with Documents*, 3rd ed. Boston: Bedford Press, 2014.

Dulles, Foster Rhea. *The American Red Cross: A History*. New York: Harper, 1950.

Dumenil, Lynn. *Freemasonry and American Culture, 1880–1930*. Princeton: Princeton University Press, 1984.

———. *The Modern Temper: American Culture and Society in the 1920s*. New York: Hill and Wang, 1995.

———. "The New Woman and the Politics of the 1920s." *Magazine of History* 21 (July 2007): 22–26.

———. "Women's Reform Organizations and Wartime Mobilization in World War I–Era Los Angeles." *Journal of the Gilded Age and Progressive Era* 10 (April 2011): 213–45.

Dye, Nancy Schrom. *As Equals and as Sisters: Feminism, the Labor Movement, and the Women's Trade Union League of New York*. Columbia: University of Missouri Press, 1980.

Early, Frances H. "Feminism, Peace, and Civil Liberties: Women's Role in the Origins of the World War I Civil Liberties Movement." *Women's Studies* 18 (November 1990): 95–115.

———. *A World without War: How U.S. Feminists and Pacifists Resisted World War I*. Syracuse: Syracuse University Press, 1997.

Ebbert, Jean, and Marie-Beth Hall. *The First, the Few, the Forgotten: Navy and Marine Corps Women in World War I*. Annapolis: Naval Institute Press, 2002.

Ellis, Mark. *Race, War, and Surveillance: African Americans and the United States Government during World War I*. Bloomington: Indiana University Press, 2001.

Elshtain, Jean Bethke. *Jane Addams and the Dream of American Democracy*. New York: Basic Books, 2002.

Enstad, Nan. "Dressed for Adventure: Working Women and Silent Movie Serials in the 1910s." *Feminist Studies* 21 (1995): 67–91.

Fass, Paula. *The Damned and the Beautiful: American Youth in the 1920s*. New York: Oxford University Press, 1977.

Foner, Philip S. *Women and the American Labor Movement: From World War I to the Present*. New York: Free Press, 1980.

Ford, Linda G. *Iron-Jawed Angels: The Suffrage Militancy of the National Woman's Party: 1912–1920*. New York: University Press of America, 1991.

Fowler, Robert Booth. *Carrie Catt: Feminist Politician*. Boston: Northeastern University Press, 1986.

Frahm, Jill. "The Hello Girls: Women Telephone Operators with the American Expeditionary Forces during World War I." *Journal of the Gilded Age and Progressive Era* 3 (July 2004): 271–93.

Fussell, Paul. *The Boys' Crusade: The American Infantry in Northwestern Europe, 1944–1945*. New York: Modern Library, 2003.

Gavin, Lettie. *American Women in World War I: They Also Served*. Niwot: University Press of Colorado, 1997.

Giddings, Paula. *When and Where I Enter: The Impact of Black Women on Race and Sex in America*. New York: Bantam Books, 1984.

Gilmore, Glenda Elizabeth. *Gender and Jim Crow: Women and the Politics of White Supremacy*. Chapel Hill: University of North Carolina Press, 1996.

Glenn, Evelyn Nakano. "Racial Ethnic Women's Labor: The Intersection of Race, Gender, and Class Oppression." *Review of Radical Political Economics* 17 (Fall 1986): 86–108.

Glenn, Susan. *Female Spectacle: The Theatrical Roots of Modern Feminism*. Cambridge: Harvard University Press, 2000.

Godson, Susan H. *Serving Proudly: A History of Women in the U.S. Navy*. Annapolis: Naval Institute Press, 2001.

Gordon, Linda. *Pitied but Not Entitled: Single Mothers and the History of Welfare, 1890–1935*. New York: Free Press, 1994.

———. *Woman's Body, Woman's Rights: Birth Control in America*. New York: Penguin, 1990.

Gordon, Marsha. "Onward Kitchen Soldiers: Mobilizing the Domestic during World War I." *Canadian Reviews of American Studies* 29 (1999): 61–87.

Gowdy-Wygant, Cecilia. *Cultivating Victory: The Women's Land Army and the Victory Garden Movement*. Pittsburgh: University of Pittsburgh Press, 2013.

Graf, Mercedes. "With High Hopes: Women Contract Surgeons in World War I." *Minerva* 20 (July 2002): 16–28.

Grayzel, Susan R. *Women and the First World War*. New York: Routledge, 2002.

———. *Women's Identities at War: Gender, Motherhood, and Politics in Britain and France during the First World War*. Chapel Hill: University of North Carolina Press, 1999.

Greenwald, Maurine Weiner. *Women, War, and Work: The Impact of World War I on Women Workers in the United States*. Westport, Conn.: Greenwood, 1980.

Grittner, Frederick K. *White Slavery: Myth, Ideology, and American Law*. New York: Garland, 1990.

Grossman, James R. *Land of Hope: Chicago, Black Southerners, and the Great Migration*. Chicago: University of Chicago Press, 1989.

Gullace, Nicoletta F. "Barbaric Anti-Modernism: Representations of the 'Hun' in Britain, North America, Australia, and Beyond." In *Picture This: World War I Posters and Visual Culture*, edited by Pearl James, 61–78. Lincoln: University of Nebraska Press, 2009.

———. *"The Blood of Our Sons": Men, Women, and the Renegotiation of British Citizenship during the Great War*. New York: Palgrave Macmillan, 2002.

———. "Sexual Violence and Family Honor: British Propaganda and International Law during the First World War." *American Historical Review* 102 (June 1997): 714–47.

Gullett, Gayle. "Women Progressives and the Politics of Americanization in California, 1915–1920." *Pacific Historical Review* 64 (January 1995): 71–95.

Hacker, Barton C., and Margaret Vining. "Cutting a New Pattern: Uniforms and Women's Mobilization for War, 1854–1919." *Textile History and the Military* 41, supplement (May 2010): 108–43.

Haiken, Elizabeth. "'The Lord Helps Those Who Help Themselves': Black Laundresses in Little Rock, Arkansas, 1917–1921." *Arkansas Historical Quarterly* 49 (Spring 1990): 20–50.

Hansen, Miriam. *Babel and Babylon: Spectatorship in American Silent Film*. Cambridge: Harvard University Press, 1991.

Harris, Neil. "Iconography and Intellectual History: The Halftone Effect." In *New Directions in American Intellectual History*, edited by John Higham and Paul K. Conkin, 196–211. Baltimore: Johns Hopkins University Press, 1979.

Harris, Ruth. "The 'Child of the Barbarian': Rape, Race, and Nationalism in France during the First World War." *Past and Present* 141 (1993): 170–206.

Harvey, Anna L. *Votes without Leverage: Women in American Electoral Politics, 1920–1970*. Cambridge: Cambridge University Press, 1998.

Hewitt, Linda L. *Women Marines in World War I.* Washington, D.C.: History and Museum Division, Headquarters, U.S. Navy, 1974.
Hickel, K. Walter. "War, Region, and Social Welfare: Federal Aid to Servicemen's Dependents in the South, 1917–1921." *Journal of American History* 87 (2001): 1362–91.
Hickey, Georgina. "Waging War on 'Loose Living Hotels' and 'Cheap Soda Water Joints': The Criminalization of Working-Class Women in Atlanta's Public Space." *Georgia Historical Quarterly* 82 (Winter 1998): 775–800.
Higashi, Sumiko. *Cecil B. DeMille and American Culture: The Silent Era.* Berkeley: University of California Press, 1994.
Higginbotham, Evelyn Brooks. "Clubwomen and Electoral Politics in the 1920s." In *African American Women and the Vote, 1837–1965,* edited by Ann D. Gordon and Bettye Collier-Thomas, 134–55. Amherst: University of Massachusetts Press, 1997.
Higonnet, Margaret R., and Patrice L. R. Higgonet. "The Double Helix." In *Behind the Lines: Gender and the Two World Wars,* edited by Margaret Randolph Higonnet and Jane Jenson, 31–47. New Haven: Yale University Press, 1987.
Higonnet, Margaret Randolph, and Jane Jenson, eds. *Behind the Lines: Gender and the Two World Wars.* New Haven: Yale University Press, 1987.
Hine, Darlene Clark. *Hine Sight: Black Women and the Reconstruction of American History.* Bloomington: University of Indiana Press, 1994.
Hooks, Janet M. *Women's Occupations through Seven Decades.* Women's Bureau Bulletin 218. Washington, D.C., 1947.
Horne, John, ed. *State, Society, and Mobilization in Europe during the First World War.* Cambridge: Cambridge University Press, 1997.
Hunter, Tera W. *To 'Joy My Freedom: Southern Black Women's Lives and Labors after the Civil War.* Cambridge: Harvard University Press, 1997.
———. "'The Women Are Asking for BREAD, Why Give Them STONE?' Women, Work, and Protests in Atlanta and Norfolk during World War I." In *Labor in the Modern South,* edited by Glenn T. Eskew, 67–72. Athens: University of Georgia Press, 2001.
Irwin, Julia F. *Making the World Safe: The American Red Cross and a Nation's Humanitarian Awakening.* New York: Oxford University Press, 2013.
Isenberg, Michael. *War on Film: The American Cinema and World War I, 1914–1941.* London: Associated University Presses, 1981.
James, Pearl. "Images of Femininity in American World War I Posters." In *Picture This: World War I Posters and Visual Culture,* edited by Pearl James, 273–311. Lincoln: University of Nebraska Press, 2009.
———, ed. *Picture This: World War I Posters and Visual Culture.* Lincoln: University of Nebraska Press, 2009.
Jeffreys-Jones, Rhodri. *Changing Differences: Women and the Shaping of American Foreign Policy, 1917–1994.* New Brunswick: Rutgers University Press, 1994.
Jellison, Katherine. *Entitled to Power: Farm Women and Technology, 1913–1962.* Chapel Hill: University of North Carolina Press, 1993.
Jensen, Joan M. *The Price of Vigilance.* New York: Rand-McNally, 1968.
Jensen, Kimberly. *Mobilizing Minerva: American Women in the First World War.* Urbana: University of Illinois Press, 2008.

Jones, Adrienne Lash. "Struggle among Saints: African American Women and the YWCA, 1870–1920." In *Men and Women Adrift: The YMCA and the YWCA in the City*, edited by Nina Mjagkij and Margaret Spratt, 160–87. New York: New York University Press, 1997.

Jones, Jacqueline. *Labor of Love, Labor of Sorrow: Black Women, Work, and the Family from Slavery to the Present*. New York: Basic Books, 1985.

Jones, Marian Moser. *The American Red Cross from Clara Barton to the New Deal*. Baltimore: Johns Hopkins University Press, 2012.

Judson, Sarah Mercer. "'Leisure Is a Foe to Any Man': The Pleasures and Dangers of Leisure in Atlanta during World War I." *Journal of Women's History* 15 (Spring 2003): 92–115.

Keegan, John. *The Face of Battle*. New York: Penguin, 1976.

Keene, Jennifer D. "A Comparative Study of White and Black American Soldiers during the First World War." *Démographie Historique* 1 (2002): 71–90.

———. "Images of Racial Pride: African American Propaganda Posters in the First World War." In *Picture This: World War I Posters and Visual Culture*, edited by Pearl James, 207–40. Lincoln: University of Nebraska Press, 2009.

Keire, Mara. *For Business and Pleasure: Red-Light Districts and the Regulation of Vice in the United States, 1890–1933*. Baltimore: Johns Hopkins University Press, 2010.

Kennedy, David M. *Over Here: The First World War and American Society*. New York: Oxford University Press, 1980.

Kennedy, Kathleen. "Declaring War on War: Gender and the American Socialist Attack on Militarism, 1914–1918." *Journal of Women's History* 7 (1995): 27–51.

———. *Disloyal Mothers and Scurrilous Citizens: Women and Subversion during World War I*. Bloomington: Indiana University Press, 1999.

Kerber, Linda K. *No Constitutional Right to Be Ladies: Women and the Obligation of Citizenship*. New York: Hill and Wang, 1998.

Kernodle, Portia B. *The Red Cross Nurse in Action*. New York: Harper, 1949.

Kessler-Harris, Alice. *Out to Work: A History of Wage-Earning Women in the United States*. New York: Oxford University Press, 2002.

Kilander, Ginny, ed. "'Over There with the YMCA': A Wyoming Educator in French Canteen Service." *Annals of Wyoming: Wyoming History Journal* 82 (Spring 2010): 2–13.

Kingsbury, Celia Malone. *For Home and Country: World War I Propaganda on the Home Front*. Lincoln: University of Nebraska Press, 2010.

Kornweibel, Theodore, Jr. *"Investigate Everything": Federal Efforts to Compel Black Loyalty during World War I*. Bloomington: Indiana University Press, 2001.

Koven, Seth, and Sonya Michel, eds. *Mothers of a New World: Maternalist Politics and the Origins of Welfare States*. New York: Routledge, 1993.

Krieger, Nancy. "Queen of the Bolsheviks: The Hidden History of Dr. Marie Equi." *Radical America* 17 (1983): 55–73.

Kudlick, Catherine. "Fighting the Internal and External Enemies: Alcoholism in World War I France." *Contemporary Drug Problems* 12 (Spring 1985): 129–58.

Kuhlman, Erika. *Reconstructing Patriarchy after the Great War: Women, Gender, and Postwar Reconciliation between Nations*. New York: Palgrave Macmillan, 2008.

Kunzel, Regina G. *Fallen Women, Problem Girls: Unmarried Mothers and the Professionalization of Social Work: 1890–1945*. New Haven: Yale University Press, 1993.
Ladd-Taylor, Molly. *Mother-Work: Women, Child Welfare, and the State, 1890–1903*. Urbana: University of Illinois Press, 1994.
Lahue, Kalton C. *Bound and Gagged: The Story of the Silent Serials*. New York: Castle Books, 1968.
Latham, James. "The Kaiser as the Beast of Berlin: Race and the Animalizing of Germanness in Early Hollywood's Advertising Imagery." *Western Virginia University Philological Papers* 50 (2003): 16–30.
Lau, Peter F. *Democracy Rising: South Carolina and the Fight for Black Equality since 1865*. Louisville: University of Kentucky Press, 2006.
Lehrer, Susan. *Origins of Protective Labor Legislation for Women, 1905–1925*. Albany: State University of New York Press, 1987.
Leiby, James. *A History of Social Welfare and Social Work in the United States*. New York: Columbia University Press, 1978.
Lemons, J. Stanley. *The Woman Citizen: Social Feminism in the 1920s*. Urbana: University of Illinois Press, 1973.
Lentz-Smith, Adriane. *Freedom Struggles: African Americans and World War I*. Cambridge: Harvard University Press, 2009.
Lewenson, Sandra Beth. *Taking Charge: Nursing, Suffrage, and Feminism in America, 1873–1920*. New York: Garland, 1993.
Lindenmeyer, Kriste. *A Right to Childhood: The U.S. Children's Bureau and Child Welfare, 1912–46*. Urbana: University of Illinois Press, 1999.
Lipsitz, George. "Dilemmas of Beset Nationhood: Patriotism, the Family, and Economic Change in the 1970s." In *Bonds of Affection: Americans Define Their Patriotism*, edited by John Bodnar, 251–72. Princeton: Princeton University Press, 1996.
Lubove, Roy. *The Professional Altruist: The Emergence of Social Work as a Career, 1880–1930*. Cambridge: Harvard University Press, 1965.
Lumsden, Linda J. "Beauty and the Beasts: Significance of Press Coverage of the 1913 National Suffrage Parade." *Journalism and Mass Culture Quarterly* 77 (Autumn 2000): 593–611.
Lunardini, Christine A. *From Equal Suffrage to Equal Rights: Alice Paul and the National Woman's Party, 1910–1928*. New York: New York University Press, 1986.
Macdonald, Anne L. *No Idle Hands: The Social History of American Knitting*. New York: Ballantine Books, 1988.
Mahar, Karen Ward. *Women Filmmakers in Early Hollywood*. Baltimore: Johns Hopkins University Press, 2008.
Marchand, Roland. *The American Peace Movement and Social Reform, 1898–1918*. Princeton: Princeton University Press, 1972.
Marks, Carole. *Farewell—We're Good and Gone: The Great Black Migration*. Bloomington: University of Indiana Press, 1989.
May, Elaine Tyler. *Great Expectations: Marriage and Divorce in Post-Victorian America*. Chicago: University of Chicago Press, 1980.
May, Lary. *Screening Out the Past: The Birth of Mass Culture and the Motion Picture Industry*. Chicago: University of Chicago Press, 1980.

McCartin, Joseph A. *Labor's Great War: The Struggle for Industrial Democracy and the Origins of Modern American Labor Relations, 1912–1921*. Chapel Hill: University of North Carolina Press, 1997.

McLoughlin, Virginia. "'Hoeing Smokes': A New Milford, Connecticut, Unit of the Woman's Land Army, World War I." *Connecticut History* 40 (2001): 32–60.

Meyerowitz, Joanne J. *Women Adrift: Independent Wage Earners in Chicago, 1880–1930*. Chicago: University of Chicago Press, 1988.

Mickenberg, Julia L. "Suffragettes and Soviets: American Feminists and the Specter of Revolutionary Russia." *Journal of American History* 100 (2014): 1021–51.

Miller, Richard E. "The Golden Fourteen, Plus: Black Navy Women in World War One." *Minerva* 13 (December 1995): 7–13.

Mintz, Stephen, and Susan Kellogg. *Domestic Revolutions: A Social History of American Family Life*. New York: Free Press, 1988.

More, Ellen S. "'A Certain Restless Ambition': Women Physicians and World War I." *American Quarterly* 41 (December 1989): 636–60.

Morgan, Francesca. *Women and Patriotism in Jim Crow America*. Chapel Hill: University of North Carolina Press, 2005.

Muhammad, Robin Dearmon. "Separate and Unsanitary: African American Women Railroad Car Cleaners and the Women's Service Section, 1918–1920." *Journal of Women's History* 23 (Summer 2011): 87–111.

Mullendore, William Clinton. *History of the United States Food Administration, 1917–1919*. Stanford: Stanford University Press, 1941.

Muncy, Robyn. *Creating a Female Dominion in American Reform, 1890–1935*. New York: Oxford University Press, 1991.

Murphy, Miriam B. "'If Only I Shall Have the Right Stuff': Utah Women in World War I." *Utah Historical Quarterly* 58 (October 1990): 434–50.

Neal, Steve. "Action-Adventure Genre as Hollywood Genre." In *Action and Adventure Cinema*, edited by Yvonne Tasker, 71–83. New York: Routledge, 2004.

Neth, Mary. *Preserving the Family Farm: Women, Community, and the Foundations of Agribusiness in the Midwest, 1900–1940*. Baltimore: Johns Hopkins University Press, 1995.

Neverdon-Morton, Cynthia. *Afro-American Women of the South and the Advancement of the Race*. Knoxville: University of Tennessee Press, 1989.

Nielsen, Kim E. *Un-American Womanhood: Antiradicalism, Antifeminism, and the First Red Scare*. Columbus: Ohio State University, 2001.

Norton, Mary Beth. *Liberty's Daughters: The Revolutionary Experience of American Women, 1750–1800*. Ithaca: Cornell University Press, 1980.

Norwood, Stephen H. *Labor's Flaming Youth: Telephone Operators and Worker Militancy, 1878–1930*. Urbana: University of Illinois Press, 1985.

Odem, Mary. *Delinquent Daughters: Protecting and Policing Adolescent Female Sexuality in the United States, 1885–1920*. Chapel Hill: University of North Carolina Press, 1995.

Patterson, David S. *The Search for a Negotiated Peace: Women's Activism and Citizen Diplomacy in World War I*. New York: Routledge, 2008.

Payne, Elizabeth Anne. *Reform, Labor, and Feminism: Margaret Dreier Robins and the Women's Trade Union League*. Urbana: University of Illinois Press, 1988.

Pegram, Thomas R. *Battling Demon Rum: The Struggle for a Dry America, 1880–1933*. New York: Ivan Dee, 1980.

Peiss, Kathy. *Cheap Amusements: Working Women and Leisure in Turn-of-the-Century New York*. Philadelphia: Temple University Press, 1986.

Peterson, Hazel. *Dorothy S. Ainsworth: Her Life, Professional Career, and Contributions to Physical Education*, 2nd ed. Moscow: University of Idaho Press, 1975.

Pivar, David J. "Cleansing the Nation: The War on Prostitution, 1917–1921." *Prologue* 90 (Spring 1980): 29–40.

Pizzitola, Louis. *Hearst over Hollywood: Power, Passion, and Propaganda in the Movies*. New York: Columbia University Press, 2002.

Plant, Rebecca Jo. *Mom: The Transformation of Motherhood in Modern America*. Chicago: University of Chicago Press, 2010.

Plastas, Melinda Ann. "'A Band of Noble Women': The WLPF and the Politics and Consciousness of Race in the Women's Peace Movement, 1915–1945." Ph.D. diss., State University of New York at Buffalo, 2001.

Proctor, Tammy M. *Civilians in a World at War, 1914–1918*. New York: New York University Press, 2010.

Raftery, Judith. "Los Angeles Clubwomen and Progressive Reform." In *California Progressivism Revisited*, edited by William Deverell and Tom Sitton, 144–74. Berkeley: University of California Press, 1994.

Rawls, Walton. *"Wake Up, America!" World War I and the American Poster*. New York: Abbeville Press, 1988.

Reilly, Kimberley A. "'A Perilous Venture for Democracy': Soldiers, Sexual Purity, and American Citizenship in the First World War." *Journal of the Gilded Age and Progressive Era* 13 (April 2014): 223–55.

Rief, Michelle. "Thinking Locally, Acting Globally: The International Agenda of the African American Clubwomen, 1880–1940." *Journal of African American History* 89 (Summer 2004): 203–22.

Rinehart, Alice Dufy, ed. *One Woman Determined to Make a Difference: The Life of Madeleine Zabriskie Doty*. Bethlehem, Pa.: Lehigh University Press, 2001.

Roberts, Mary Louise. *Civilization without Sexes: Reconstructing Gender in Postwar France, 1917–1927*. Chicago: University of Chicago Press, 1994.

Robertson, Nancy Marie. *Christian Sisterhood, Race Relations, and the YWCA, 1906–46*. Urbana: University of Illinois Press, 2007.

Rodgers, Daniel T. *Atlantic Crossings: Social Politics in a Progressive Age*. Cambridge: Belknap Press of Harvard University Press, 1998.

Romalov, Nancy Tillman. "Modern, Mobile, and Marginal: American Girls' Series Fiction, 1905–1925." Ph.D. diss., University of Iowa, 1994.

Rooks, Noliwe M. *Ladies' Pages: African American Women's Magazines and the Culture That Made Them*. New Brunswick: Rutgers University Press, 2005.

Rosenberg, Emily. *Spreading the American Dream: American Economic and Cultural Expansion, 1890–1945*. Urbana: University of Illinois Press, 1991.

Rosenberg, Jonathan. *How Far the Promised Land? World Affairs and the American Civil Rights Movement from the First World War to Vietnam*. Princeton: Princeton University Press, 2006.

Ross, Ishbel. *Ladies of the Press: The Story of Women in Journalism by an Insider.* New York: Ayer, 1936.

Ross, Sara. "'Good Little Bad Girls': Controversy and the Flapper Comedienne." *Film History* 13 (2001): 409–24.

Ross, Stewart Halsey. *Propaganda for War: How the United States Was Conditioned to Fight the Great War of 1914–1918.* Jefferson, N.C.: McFarland, 1996.

Rudwick, Elliott M. *Race Riot at East St. Louis, July 2, 1917.* Carbondale: University of Illinois Press, 1964.

Ryan, Erica J. *Red War on the Family: Sex, Gender, and Americanism in the First Red Scare.* Philadelphia: Temple University Press, 2015.

Salem, Dorothy. *To Better Our World: Black Women in Organized Reform, 1890–1920.* Brooklyn: Carlson, 1990.

Sannes, Erling. "Queen of the Lecture Platform: Kate Richards O'Hare and North Dakota Politics, 1917–1921." *North Dakota History* 58 (1991): 2–19.

Schaffer, Ronald. *America in the Great War: The Rise of the Welfare State.* New York: Oxford University Press, 1991.

Scharff, Virginia. *Taking the Wheel: Women and the Coming of the Motor Age.* Albuquerque: University of New Mexico Press, 1992.

Schechter, Patricia A. *Ida B. Wells-Barnett and American Reform, 1880–1930.* Chapel Hill: University of North Carolina Press, 2001.

Schneider, Dorothy, and Carl J. Schneider. *Into the Breach: American Women Overseas in World War I.* New York: Viking, 1991.

Schudson, Michael. *Discovering the New: A Social History of American Newspapers.* New York: Basic Books, 1978.

Schwarz, Judith. *Radical Feminists of Heterodoxy: Greenwich Village, 1912–1940.* Norwich: New Victoria Publishers, 1982.

Scott, Anne Firor. *Natural Allies: Women's Associations in American History.* Urbana: University of Illinois Press, 1991.

Scott, Ann Firor, and Andrew McKay Scott. *One Half the People: The Fight for Woman Suffrage.* Urbana: University of Illinois Press, 1982.

Shah, Courtney Q. "'Against Their Own Weakness': Policing Sexuality and Women in San Antonio, Texas, during World War I." *Journal of the History of Sexuality* 19 (September 2010): 458–82.

Shirley, Wayne D. "A Bugle Call to Arms for National Defense! Victor Herbert and His Score for *The Fall of a Nation.*" *Quarterly Journal of the Library of Congress* (Winter 1983): 26–47.

Shover, Michele J. "Roles and Images of Women in World War I Propaganda." *Politics and Society* 5 (1975): 469–86.

Simmons, Christina. *Making Marriage Modern: Women's Sexuality from the Progressive Era to World War II.* New York: Oxford University Press, 2009.

Singer, Ben. "Female Power in the Serial-Queen Melodrama: The Etiology of an Anomaly." In *Silent Film*, edited by Richard Able, 163–93. New Brunswick: Rutgers University Press, 1996.

———. *Melodrama and Modernity: Early Sensational Cinema and Its Contexts.* New York: Columbia University Press, 2001.

Slater, Thomas J. "June Mathis's *The Legion of Death* (1918): Melodrama and the Realities of Women in World War I." *Women's Studies* 37 (October 2008): 833–44.
Smith, Norma. *Jeannette Rankin, America's Conscience*. Helena: Montana Historical Society Press, 2002.
Solomon, Barbara Miller. *In the Company of Educated Women: A History of Women and Higher Education in America*. New Haven: Yale University Press, 1985.
Staiger, Janet. *Bad Women: Regulating Sexuality in Early American Cinema*. Minneapolis: University of Minnesota Press, 1995.
Stamp, Shelley. *Movie-Struck Girls: Women and Motion Picture Culture after the Nickelodeon*. Princeton: Princeton University Press, 2000.
Stansell, Christine. *American Moderns: Bohemian New York and the Creation of a New Century*. New York: Henry Holt, 2000.
Steinson, Barbara J. *American Women's Activism in World War I*. New York: Oxford University Press, 1982.
Stockdale, Melissa K. "My Death for the Motherland Is Happiness": Women, Patriotism, and Soldiering in Russia's Great War, 1914–1917." *American Historical Review* 109 (February 2004): 78–116.
Strom, Sharon Hartman. *Beyond the Typewriter: Gender, Class, and the Origins of Modern American Office Work, 1900–1930*. Urbana: University of Illinois Press, 1992.
Sullivan, Maura. "Social Work's Legacy of Peace: Echoes from the Early 20th Century." *Social Work* 38 (September 1993): 513–20.
Summers, Anne. "Public Functions, Private Premises: Female Professional Identity and the Domestic Service Paradigm in Britain, c. 1850–1903." In *Borderlines: Genders and Identities in War and Peace, 1870–1930*, edited by Billie Melman, 353–76. New York: Routledge, 1998.
Tax, Meredith. *The Rising of the Women: Feminist Solidarity and Class Conflict, 1880–1917*. Urbana: University of Illinois Press, 1980.
Tentler, Leslie Woodcock. *Wage-Earning Women: Industrial Work and Family Life in the United States, 1900–1930*. New York: Oxford University Press, 1979.
Terborg-Penn, Rosalyn. *African American Women in the Struggle for the Vote, 1850–1920*. Bloomington: Indiana University Press, 1998.
Todd, Ellen Wiley. "Photojournalism, Visual Culture, and the Triangle Shirtwaist Fire." *Labor: Studies in Working-Class History of the Americas* 2 (Summer 2005): 9–27.
Triece, Mary E. "Framing Miss-Conduct: The Rhetoric of Paradox in the Struggle of Cleveland Conductorets during World War I." *Women's Studies in Communication* 25 (Fall 2002): 197–222.
Trimberger, Ellen Kay. *Intimate Warriors: Portrait of a Modern Marriage, 1899–1944*. New York: Feminist Press, 1991.
Trout, Steven. *On the Battlefield of Memory: The First World War and American Remembrance, 1919–1941*. Tuscaloosa: University of Alabama Press, 2010.
Tylee, Claire M. *The Great War and Women's Consciousness: Images of Militarism and Womanhood in Women's Writings, 1914–1964*. London: Macmillan, 1990.
Tyler, Helen E. *Where Prayer and Purpose Meet: The WCTU Story, 1874–1949*. Evanston, Ill.: Signal Press, ca. 1949.

Ullman, Sharon R. *Sex Seen: The Emergence of Modern Sexuality in America*. Berkeley: University of California Press, 1997.

Unsel, Juliane. "Woman's Hour: Suffrage and American Citizenship in War and Reconstruction, 1914–1924." Ph.D. diss., University of Wisconsin, 2005.

Usai, Paolo Cherchi, and Lorenzo Codelli, eds. *The DeMille Legacy*. Pordenone: Edizioni Biblioteca dell'Immagine, 1991.

Van Nuys, Frank. *Americanizing the West: Race, Immigrants, and Citizenship, 1890–1930*. Lawrence: University Press of Kansas, 2002.

Van Riper, Paul P. *History of the United States Civil Service*. Evanston, Ill.: Row, Peterson, 1958.

Vaughn, Stephen. *Holding Fast the Inner Lines: Democracy, Nationalism, and the Committee on Public Information*. Chapel Hill: University of North Carolina Press, 1980.

Vining, Margaret, and Barton C. Hacker. "From Camp Follower to Lady in Uniform: Women, Social Class, and Military Institutions before 1920." *Contemporary European History* 10 (August 2001): 353–73.

Wagner, Nancy O'Brien. "Red Cross Women in France during World War I." *Minnesota History* 63 (Spring 2002): 24–35.

Ware, Susan. *Partner and I: Molly Dewson, Feminism, and New Deal Politics*. New Haven: Yale University Press, 1989.

Weiner, Lynn Y. *From Working Girl to Working Mother: The Female Labor Force in the United States, 1820–1980*. Chapel Hill: University of North Carolina Press, 1985.

Weiss, Elaine F. *Fruits of Victory: The Woman's Land Army of America in the Great War*. Washington, D.C.: Potomac Books, 2008.

Westbrook, Robert B. "Fighting for the American Family: Private Interests and Political Obligation in World War II." In *The Power of Culture: Critical Essays in American History*, edited by Richard Wightman Fox and T. J. Jackson Lears, 195–221. Chicago: University of Chicago Press, 1993.

White, Deborah Gray. *Too Heavy a Load: Black Women in Defense of Themselves, 1894–1994*. New York: W. W. Norton, 1999.

Wikander, Ulla, Alice Kessler-Harris, and Jane Lewis, eds. *Protecting Women: Labor Legislation in Europe, the United States, and Australia, 1880–1920*. Urbana: University of Illinois Press, 1995.

Witt, John Fabian. "Crystal Eastman and the Internationalist Beginnings of American Civil Liberties." *Duke Law Journal* 54 (2004): 705–63.

Witz, Danielle. "Reporting on the 'New Woman': Women Journalists and Revolutionary Russia's Female Battalion of Death." Senior honors thesis, Occidental College, 2014.

Woollacott, Angela. *On Her Their Lives Depend: Munitions Workers in the Great War*. Berkeley: University of California Press, 1994.

Yellin, Eric S. *Racism in the Nation's Service: Government Workers and the Color Line in Woodrow Wilson's America*. Chapel Hill: University of North Carolina Press, 2013.

Zeiger, Susan. *In Uncle Sam's Service: Women Workers with the American Expeditionary Force, 1917–1919*. Ithaca: Cornell University Press, 1999.

———. "The Schoolhouse vs. the Armory: U.S. Teachers and the Campaign against Militarism in the Schools, 1914–1918." *Journal of Women's History* 15 (Summer 2003): 150–79.

———. “She Didn’t Raise Her Boy to Be a Slacker: Motherhood, Conscription, and the Culture of the First World War.” *Feminist Studies* 22 (Spring 1996): 6–39.
Zdriluk, Beth. “‘When a Canadian Girl Became America’s Sweetheart’: Mary Pickford and Questions of National Identity during the WWI.” *Kinema* 23 (Spring 2005). http://www.kinema.uwaterloo.ca/article.php?id=62&feature/.
Zieger, Robert H. *America’s Great War: World War I and the American Experience*. New York: Rowman and Littlefield, 2001.
Zipser, Arthur, and Pearly Zipser. *Fire and Grace: The Life of Rose Pastor Stokes*. Athens: University of Georgia Press, 1990.

Index

Page numbers in italics refer to illustrations.